Mafanikio Theology

Learning Prosperity with Tanzanian Women

Tamie Davis

Langham
ACADEMIC

© 2025 Tamie Davis

Published 2025 by Langham Academic
An imprint of Langham Publishing
www.langhampublishing.org

Langham Publishing and its imprints are a ministry of Langham Partnership

Langham Partnership
PO Box 296, Carlisle, Cumbria, CA3 9WZ, UK
www.langham.org

ISBNs:
978-1-78641-045-0 Print
978-1-78641-208-9 ePub
978-1-78641-209-6 PDF
DOI: https://doi.org/10.69811/9781786410450

Tamie Davis has asserted her right under the Copyright, Designs and Patents Act, 1988 to be identified as the Author of this work.

All rights reserved. No part of this publication may be reproduced, stored in a retrieval system or transmitted, in any form or by any means, electronic, mechanical, photocopying, recording or otherwise, without the prior written permission of the publisher or the Copyright Licensing Agency.

Requests to reuse content from Langham Publishing are processed through PLSclear. Please visit www.plsclear.com to complete your request.

Scriptures taken from the Holy Bible, New International Version®, NIV®. Copyright © 1973, 1978, 1984, 2011 by Biblica, Inc.™ Used by permission of Zondervan.

British Library Cataloguing-in-Publication Data
A catalogue record for this book is available from the British Library

ISBN: 978-1-78641-045-0

Cover & Book Design: projectluz.com

Langham Partnership actively supports theological dialogue and an author's right to publish but does not necessarily endorse the views and opinions set forth here or in works referenced within this publication, nor can we guarantee technical and grammatical correctness. Langham Partnership does not accept any responsibility or liability to persons or property as a consequence of the reading, use or interpretation of its published content.

For Stephie
Can't wait to tell you

Contents

Abbreviations xv

Chapter 1 1
Introduction
    1.1 "Just have more faith in God and he will heal you." 1
    1.2 Statement of the Problem and Objectives 2
    1.3 Significance of the Study 3
        1.3.1 Why Prosperity Theology? 3
        1.3.2 Why Tanzania? 4
        1.3.3 Why TAFES Graduates? 6
        1.3.4 Why Women? 7
    1.4 Research Design 8
    1.5 Research Question 8
    1.6 Definition of Terms 9
    1.7 Assumptions and Limitations of the Study 9
    1.8 Conclusion and Outlook 10

Chapter 2 15
Literature Review
    2.1 Origins of the Prosperity Gospel in Africa 16
        2.1.1 Affiliations of the Prosperity Gospel in Africa 16
        2.1.2 History of the Prosperity Gospel in Africa 17
        2.1.3 Relationship between Prosperity Gospel And
             African Traditional Religion 20
    2.2 Defining the Prosperity Gospel in Africa 25
        2.2.1 Definitions of the Prosperity Gospel 26
        2.2.2 Prosperity Teaching in Tanzania 31
    2.3 Effects of Prosperity Theology 33
        2.3.1 Effects on Discipleship 34
        2.3.2 Effects on Development 36
        2.3.3 Effects for Women 42
    2.4 Conclusion 45

Chapter 3 47
Methodology
    3.1 Introduction 47
        3.1.1 Qualitative Research 47
        3.1.2 Critical Realism 48

- 3.1.3 Ethnographic Methods 49
- 3.1.4 Theological Content 50
- 3.1.5 Feminist Scope 51
- 3.2 The Research Process 52
  - 3.2.1 Selection 52
  - 3.2.2 Selection Criteria 53
  - 3.2.3 Research Permissions 53
  - 3.2.4 Access 53
  - 3.2.5 Timeframe 54
  - 3.2.6 Preparation 54
- 3.3 Methods of Data Collection 55
  - 3.3.1 Semi-structured Interviews 55
  - 3.3.2 Focus Groups 57
  - 3.3.3 Participant Observation 58
- 3.4 Ethical Considerations 58
- 3.5 The Researcher 60
  - 3.5.1 The Researcher's Role 60
  - 3.5.2 Relationship between the Researcher and Research Participants 61
- 3.6 Capturing and Analysing Data 63
- 3.7 Theological Method 66
- 3.8 Conclusion 68

Chapter 4 69
Understanding Mafanikio *Theology*

- 4.1 Participant Demographics 69
- 4.2 Translation Notes for *Mafanikio* 72
- 4.3 What Is *Mafanikio*? 73
  - 4.3.1 Reaching Goals 73
  - 4.3.2 Ongoing Process 74
  - 4.3.3 God's Will 75
- 4.4 Scope of *Mafanikio* 76
  - 4.4.1 Areas of *Mafanikio* 77
  - 4.4.2 The Role of God in *Mafanikio* 80
- 4.5 Limits of *Mafanikio* 83
  - 4.5.1 *Mafanikio* without God? 84
  - 4.5.2 *Mafanikio* without Wealth? 85
  - 4.5.3 Case Study: Does the Widow in the Village Have *Mafanikio*? 86
  - 4.5.4 What Is the Opposite of *Mafanikio*? 91
- 4.6 Purpose of *Mafanikio* 95

  4.7 Features of *Mafanikio* 97
    4.7.1 Effort 97
    4.7.2 Perseverance through Hardship 100
    4.7.3 Righteousness..101
    4.7.4 Knowledge..103
    4.7.5 Features: Conclusion..105
  4.8 Conclusion 106

Chapter 5 109
  Locating Mafanikio *Theology*
  5.1 Historically: Charting between Two Trends 110
  5.2 Culturally: The Problem of Passivity..115
    5.2.1 Knowing God Rightly 118
    5.2.2 Identity Change 119
    5.2.3 Environmental Change...121
  5.3 Biblically: The Hermeneutics of *Mafanikio* Theology 123
    5.3.1 Saturation And Immediacy..125
    5.3.2 Use of Biblical Figures..129
    5.3.3 Connections with Wisdom Literature 131
    5.3.4 Presence of Common Prosperity Gospel Passages 133
    5.3.5 Assessing the Women's Hermeneutics...................................137
  5.4 Conclusion 138

Chapter 6 141
  Mafanikio *Theology as Prosperity Theology and Discipleship*
  6.1 *Mafanikio* Theology in the Landscape of Prosperity Theology..141
    6.1.1 *Mafanikio* Theology among Tanzanian Prosperity
      Theologies...142
    6.1.2 *Mafanikio* Theology among African Prosperity
      Theologies...146
    6.1.3 *Mafanikio* Theology among Gifford's Six Registers of
      Prosperity Theology...148
    6.1.4 *Mafanikio* Theology as Prosperity Theology and
      Critique...151
  6.2 *Mafanikio* Theology as Discipleship 153
    6.2.1 The Parable of the Sower 154
    6.2.2 Rocky Ground?: *Mafanikio* Theology and Suffering.........154
    6.2.3 Thorny Ground?: *Mafanikio* Theology And Christ 164
    6.2.4 Conclusion: The Good Soil of *Mafanikio* Theology..........169

Chapter 7 173
    Mafanikio *Theology as an African Theology*
        7.1 Un-African? 175
            7.1.1 Prosperity and Materialism 175
            7.1.2 *Mafanikio* Theology and Materialism 178
        7.2 Too African? 182
            7.2.1 *Mafanikio* Theology and African Traditional Religion 183
            7.2.2 *Mafanikio* Theology in the Landscape of African
                  Theology 189
        7.3 Patronage 193
            7.3.1 Defining Patronage 194
            7.3.2 Theological Implications of Patronage 195
            7.3.3 *Mafanikio* Theology and Patronage 196
        7.4 Conclusion 201

Chapter 8 203
    Mafanikio *Theology's Holism in Global Perspective*
        8.1 Introduction 203
        8.2 Rene Padilla and Integral Mission 206
            8.2.1 A Comparison of Integral Mission And *Mafanikio*
                  Theology 207
        8.3 *Ubuntu*: Holism in Africa 210
            8.3.1 Relationship of *Ubuntu* to Prosperity Theology 211
            8.3.2 Other Influences that Overlap with *Mafanikio*
                  Theology's Holism 212
        8.4 Threats to *Mafanikio* Theology's Claim to Holism 215
            8.4.1 Political Engagement 215
            8.4.2 Creation Care 218
            8.4.3 Rest and Recreation 221
        8.5 *Mafanikio* Theology and the Cross 224
            8.5.1 *Mafanikio* Theology and the Work of Christ 227
            8.5.2 *Mafanikio* Theology and the Way of the Cross 230
        8.6 Conclusion 235

Chapter 9 239
    Conclusion
        9.1 "What Is the TAFES Women's Theology of Prosperity?" 239
        9.2 Original Contributions of this Research 241
        9.3 The Significance of *Mafanikio* Theology 242
        9.4 Recommendations for Further Research 244

Chapter 10 247
    Afterword: Advancing the Mission Conversation in Australia
        10.1 Pleasure, Pain . . . and Prosperity 248
            10.1.1 Swift and Emotional Cosmology 249
            10.1.2 Worldview Paradigms 250
            10.1.3 Pleasure-pain 251
            10.1.4 Prosperity Theology 255
            10.1.5 *Mafanikio* Theology 257
            10.1.6 *Mafanikio* Theology, Pleasure-pain, and Sin 260
            10.1.7 *Mafanikio* Theology, Pleasure-pain, and Suffering 262
            10.1.8 Conclusion 264

Appendix 1 267
    Map of Tanzania's Regions

Appendix 2 269
    List of Interviews

Appendix 3 271
    List of Focus Groups

Appendix 4 273
    List of Participant Observations

Appendix 5 275
    Semi-structured Interview Questions

Appendix 6 277
    Focus Group Questions

Appendix 7 279
    Mind-map of Codes

Appendix 8 281
    Swahili Quotations

Bibliography 291

List of Figures

Figure 1.1 Concentric circles of conversation with *mafanikio* theology 11
Figure 2.1 An impression of types within African prosperity theology 31
Figure 4.1 Participants by tribe 69
Figure 4.2 Participants by denomination 70
Figure 4.3 Participants by age 70
Figure 4.4 Participants by TAFES region 71
Figure 4.5 Participants by undergraduate TAFES region 71
Figure 4.6 Areas of *mafanikio* by interviewee 78
Figure 4.7 Does the widow have *mafanikio*? 87
Figure 4.8 What have we learned about *mafanikio* theology (MT)? (Chapter 4) 108
Figure 5.1 Concentric circles of engagement with *mafanikio* theology (Tanzania) 110
Figure 5.2 Flow chart towards no prosperity 115
Figure 5.3 Common prosperity gospel Bible verses 134
Figure 5.4 What have we learned about *mafanikio* theology (MT)? (Chapters 4–5) 139
Figure 6.1 Concentric circles of engagement with *mafanikio* theology (African prosperity theology) 142
Figure 6.2 Form of lament Psalms 162
Figure 6.3 Rhoda's lament 162
Figure 6.4 References to Jesus 165
Figure 6.5 What have we learned about *mafanikio* theology (MT)? (Chapters 4–6) 171
Figure 7.1 Concentric circles of engagement with *mafanikio* theology (African theology) 174

Figure 7.2 What have we learned about *mafanikio* theology (MT)? (Chapters 4–7) 202

Figure 8.1 Concentric circles of engagement with *mafanikio* theology (Global discussions of holism) 206

Figure 8.4 What have we learned about *mafanikio* theology (MT)? (Chapters 4–8) 237

Abbreviations

AFES	Australian Fellowship of Evangelical Students
AIC	African Inland Church
ASET	Africa Society of Evangelical Theology
CCM	*Chama Cha Mapinduzi*
CICCU	Cambridge Inter-Collegiate Christian Union
COSTECH	Commission of Science and Technology
CMS	Church Missionary Society
EAGT	Evangelical Assemblies of God Tanzania
FGBFC	Full Gospel Bible Fellowship Church
FPCT	Free Pentecostal Church of Tanzania
GCTC	Glory of Christ Tanzania Church
IFES	International Fellowship of Evangelical Students
MT	*Mafanikio* theology
NGO	Non-Governmental Organisation
NPCs	Neo-Pentecostal Churches
PAFES	Pan-African Fellowship of Evangelical Students
PPCs	Progressive Pentecostal Churches
SCM	Student Christian Movement
SDGs	Sustainable Development Goals
SLIM	Single Ladies International Ministries
TAFES	Tanzania Fellowship of Evangelical Students
TAG	Tanzania Assemblies of God
UDSM	University of Dar Es Salaam
UN	United Nations
USA	United States of America
UK	United Kingdom

CHAPTER 1

Introduction

1.1 "Just have more faith in God and he will heal you."

I was speaking to thirty university students from the Tanzania Fellowship of Evangelical Students (TAFES) in the classroom of a boarding school in Dodoma, Tanzania, where we had gathered for TAFES's Discipleship Training Seminar over Easter in 2015. The students had been sitting at wooden desks but now they were suddenly rising out of their chairs, voices raised, and my Swahili could not keep up with their tumbling words. I had just said that when someone is suffering you should not say to them, "Just have more faith in God and he will heal you."

My reasoning was that this phrase guarantees healing to those who have enough faith while blaming those who are not healed for their lack of faith. Criticising teaching like this, Tanzanian Anglican Bishop Mwita Akiri explained that it implies people who have not been healed, "lack faith or they have some form of God's judgement due to sin or sins they have committed but not confessed."[1] He identified such teaching as part of the prosperity gospel, also known as the health and wealth gospel. The seminar I had been asked to teach was on caring for those who are suffering, and I had given this prosperity gospel phrase as an example of something that was unhelpful to say to a suffering person. Yet, the students vehemently disagreed. Every one

---

1. Akiri, "The Prosperity Gospel." Akiri was speaking against the prosperity gospel here, not in favour of it.

of them said that when they were suffering, they wanted someone to say to them, "just have more faith in God and he will heal you."

In my bewilderment, I turned some weeks later to a cultural mentor. She and her husband had been involved in TAFES ministry for many years, and she was also an elder at her Tanzania Assemblies of God (TAG) church. When I described the situation to her, she told me, "if they don't go to God, they will go to the witchdoctor." I saw the phrase "just have more faith in God and he will heal you," as a staple of the prosperity gospel, a movement I understood to be problematic, theologically, and pastorally. My cultural mentor patiently explained to me a different perspective. In Tanzania where the supernatural infuses life, healing is understood to be available and the question is, from whom will you get it: God or another power such as the witchdoctor? A phrase like "just have more faith in God and he will heal you," is an appeal to people to continue in fidelity to God, trusting him for healing, even when it is slow in coming, instead of opting for a witchdoctor.

The students were in uproar because they saw me as removing God as the source of healing, leaving only the witchdoctor. What I had thought was a prosperity gospel mantra that blamed vulnerable people for their predicament was, I saw, an encouragement to perseverance, endurance, and fidelity.

1.2 Statement of the Problem and Objectives

A common definition of the prosperity gospel is: the belief that "God has met all the needs of human beings in the suffering and death of Christ and every Christian should now share the victory of Christ over sin, sickness and poverty."[2] Faith is expressed in complete belief that the believer will receive these blessings and in "positive confession," that is, speaking aloud one's demands of God.[3] The prosperity gospel is associated with flamboyant preachers who encourage congregants to give "seed offerings" to the church, in expectation of having these funds miraculously multiplied back to the congregant at a later date.[4] In this understanding, the prosperity gospel in Africa

---

2. Gifford, "Expecting Miracles," 20–24; See also Mbamalu, "'Prosperity a Part," 8; Mbe, "From Asceticism," 47–66; Quayesi-Amakye, "Prosperity and Prophecy," 291–305; Togarasei, "The Pentecostal Gospel," 336–50.

3. Ageboyin, "A Rethinking of Prosperity," 70–86.

4. Aguwuom, "'Everything Is Permissible," Kindle edition, 276.

sees pastors exhort their congregations with superficial theology, impoverishing congregants for their preacher's gain, with socially disastrous results.[5]

However, through experiences like the one above, and as I listened to Tanzanian preachers and teachers, I came to question this assessment. The people I was interacting with were using language that sounded something like the prosperity gospel, yet their teaching sought fidelity and perseverance in the listeners, and they were not exploiting others for money. I became intrigued by the version of prosperity theology I was encountering, which did not seem to align with the accepted view of the prosperity gospel. Indeed, studies of prosperity theology in Africa have tended to focus on the above outlined version of the prosperity gospel with more moderate versions of prosperity theologies assumed to be diluted forms of the prosperity gospel.[6] Little scholarly attention has therefore been given to these other versions of prosperity theology, or what role they might play in Africa. I had heard the claim that prosperity theology was widespread in Africa, but few were asking the question, "*What kind* of prosperity theology?" and engaging deeply enough to give a robust answer. This thesis is an attempt to supply data about one kind of prosperity theology, that held by TAFES female graduates. My objective is not to defend the Christians I know by making them sound better than they are; it is to give an accurate picture of what is happening—one which Tanzanian Christians themselves can recognise as representative of them—and to analyse, evaluate, and critique it.

1.3 Significance of the Study

1.3.1 Why Prosperity Theology?

It is commonly accepted that prosperity theology in Africa is widespread not only in Pentecostalism but in other Christian denominations as well. Its prevalence among African Christians, who make up a quarter of Christians worldwide, is a reason to understand it in greater detail and nuance.[7]

---

5. For further examples, see Peter Mdebe Oyugi, "Why Prosperity Gospel Preachers."; Biwul, "Preaching Biblically," 121–34.

6. Gifford, "The Development," 81–94.

7. Zurlo, *Global Christianity*, Kindle edition, 3.

Second, because prosperity theology is widespread, any person living in Africa is likely to encounter it at some point. If these engagements are to be fruitful, a more nuanced understanding of prosperity theology in Africa is necessary.

Third, the diversity of prosperity theologies raises the possibility of divergence between prosperity theologies at some level. Understanding the nature and reasons for these divergences can provide local resources for combatting harmful forms of the prosperity gospel.

1.3.2 Why Tanzania?

The United Republic of Tanzania was established in 1964, joining together the Democratic Republic of Tanganyika and the People's Republic of Zanzibar.[8] The "Father of the Nation" President Julius Nyerere sought to build a cohesive Tanzanian identity among Tanzania's more than 100 tribal groups, uniting the country around Swahili as a common language. Following independence, Tanzania embarked on the great socialist experiment of *Ujamaa*, marked by villagization and self-reliance. Economically, *Ujamaa* was a failure and by the mid-1980s Tanzania's economy was decimated.[9] Under President Ali Hassan Mwinyi, Tanzania began the process of market liberalization. In July 2020, following two decades of sustained economic growth, Tanzania graduated to lower-middle income country status in the World Bank global rankings. Tanzanians are immensely proud of this status, in part because the identity as a poor nation is still held strongly. This is true even among those who could be considered elite, like university students and graduates.[10] It is not uncommon in lectures or university fellowships for speakers to make statements like, 'We are a poor country' before going on to discuss how to overcome this. This mix

---

8. Both had been British Protectorates prior to their independence in 1961 and 1963 respectively. Tanganyika had previously also been subjected to German colonialism from 1885–1919 and Zanzibar to Portugese occupation in the fifteenth to seventeenth centuries and Omani rule from 1698.

9. *Ujamaa* was not the only factor that contributed to this. There was also a severe famine, and a war with Uganda as well as various outside economic factors.

10. The most recent data provided by the Tanzania Commission for Universities is from 2018 and records fifty thousand students (0.07 percent of the population) entering university education in 2018 and approximately the same number graduating. Assuming three-to-four year degrees, this means there are about two hundred thousand university students in Tanzania (0.3 percent of the population). College education is more widespread. "Higher Education Students Admission."; "State of University Education."

makes Tanzania a very interesting candidate for a study of prosperity theology, as a country which has both recently experienced increase in prosperity but where there is much more still to do be done with regards to prosperity.

Tanzania is religiously plural. Statistics vary and the government does not collect religious data in the national census, but both Christianity and Islam are strong.[11] Islam tends to be stronger on the coast, along the traditional Arab trading routes and Christianity is stronger inland, though there are exceptions to this.[12] Though there were earlier interactions with Christianity through Portuguese traders, Christianity in Tanzania is thought to date back to 1844 when Anglican missionary Johann Ludwig Krapf of CMS arrived, and Islam to the twelfth century.[13] Traditional religious beliefs and practices persist as well. Tanzania's government is secular with no official policy regarding the political affiliation of leaders, but people have explained to me multiple times over the years that it is generally understood that the ruling party, *Chama Cha Mapinduzi* (CCM), alternates its Presidential Candidate between Muslim and Christian, and that if the President is a Muslim, the Vice President will be a Christian and vice versa. While there are religious tensions in certain areas from time to time, by and large Tanzanians are proud of their country's peace and point to their religious tolerance as a reason for this harmony. At my home in Dar Es Salaam, I am woken by the Muslim Call to Prayer from the three surrounding mosques every morning, and go to sleep to the equally loud Christian singing from nearby churches many evenings. The latter singing includes both Pentecostal praise and worship and Roman Catholic choral music. This plurality does not necessarily result in good understanding between religions and there has been little study of religion within Tanzania. Thus, a study of the theology of a group of Tanzanian university graduates contributes to what is indeed a small field.

Religion permeates all aspects of Tanzanian life. For example, buses and other means of transportation carry Christian messages such as "Jesus is Lord" and Muslim pictures of praying girls in hijabs alongside soccer paraphernalia or imitation fashion designer insignia. On the roadside, one might

---

11. Gina Zurlo's data from 2020 has Christianity at 57 percent and Islam at 31 percent with 10 percent traditional religionists. Pew Research from 2020 estimated 63 percent Christian, 34 percent Muslim. Zurlo, *Global Christianity*, 285. "Pew-Templeton Global."

12. Zurlo, *Global Christianity*, 286.

13. Zurlo, 285; McKinnon, "On Being Charismatic," 71.

see boards advertising a witchdoctor's phone number next to a plumber's, and a hotel adjacent to a rally for healing. Similarly, phrases like "if God wills it" (*Mungu akipenda / Insha'allah*) and "be blessed" (*ubarikiwe*) are common especially at partings, regardless of religious affiliation. Study of theology in Tanzania, including prosperity theology, is not a niche topic; it is lived out on the streets and in the marketplace.

1.3.3 Why TAFES Graduates?

TAFES is the Tanzania Fellowship of Evangelical Students. Its roots are older than the United Republic of Tanzania itself. What is today known as TAFES started as part of the Pan African Fellowship of Evangelical Students (PAFES) which was founded in 1958 and in East Africa adopted the name FOCUS East Africa in 1973.[14] When the East African Community collapsed in 1977, operational issues meant that autonomous national movements were required.[15] During this time, FOCUS Tanzania operated under Scripture Union (Tanzania) before registering with the Tanzanian government under the Societies Ordinance of 1954 as Tanzania Fellowship of Evangelical Students in June 1990.[16] It is affiliated with the International Fellowship of Evangelical Students (IFES).

TAFES is active in eight regions around Tanzania, with fellowships at between five and twenty-five campuses in each region.[17] Fellowships range in size, with the larger ones having hundreds of attendees. As a campus ministry, TAFES's tagline is "Reaching Students, Transforming Lives" as it seeks to equip Christian students on university and college campuses to reach their peers with the gospel of Jesus Christ. A distinctive of TAFES is running Bible studies and its flagship program is called Best-P, which trains students in Bible exposition as the engine room of discipleship.

TAFES Associates are graduates and supporters of TAFES. Their support is not only financial or a ministry of encouragement: they are also the primary teachers at TAFES events and programs. TAFES Associates are thus both

---

14. Tanzania Fellowship of Evangelical Students Financial Statement, 20 September 2019, 1.
15. TAFES Financial Statement 2019, 1.
16. TAFES Financial Statement 2019, 1.
17. For a map of Tanzania, see Appendix 1.

products and shapers of TAFES and are therefore a logical group to study when seeking to understand the theology of TAFES's people.

Today, TAFES is a somewhat minor player on the campus ministry scene in Tanzania. Denominational fellowships, dating back to the proliferation of tertiary institutions in Tanzania starting in the year 2000 are often larger and better funded. However, during my time as an Assistant Chaplain at St John's University of Tanzania (2013–2015) I had the opportunity to get to know many fellowships on campus, both denominational and TAFES. I observed a stronger focus on Bible study and discipleship at TAFES which sets it apart. As a missionary, I would at times mix with bishops from various denominations or be introduced to community or government leaders and I was astonished by how many of those of good repute were TAFES graduates. Anecdotally, TAFES graduates have a reputation as fine Christian leaders and it is worth exploring the theology of such influential people.

However, TAFES's interdenominational nature has been viewed with suspicion by denominational church leaders who would prefer their students to be in a denominational fellowship. Those telling me about TAFES graduates would often do so confidentially because of this suspicion, even while identifying TAFES as key in their own formation. There is therefore a need for some research on TAFES which could take assessment of it beyond anecdote or rumour. This study seeks to supply data on the theology of TAFES graduates which is representative of TAFES and informative for those who view it with suspicion.

1.3.4 Why Women?

Though there are many fine male graduates of TAFES, my own interest is in women's theologies and so I chose to limit my study to TAFES Associate women. Throughout the course of the research, I was often asked why I chose to study women as a group, instead of, for example, pastors. My standard response was that theological teaching is not only done by pastors or from a pulpit. While as Dana Robert observed, "men are typically the formal, ordained, religious leaders and theologians," women nevertheless play a significant teaching role in World Christianity.[18] Women teach in seminars and women's fellowships, at kitchen teas, at events in people's homes, and, of

---

18. Robert, "World Christianity," 180–88.

course, at TAFES events on campus.[19] Women are active theological teachers but they are also somewhat invisible because they do not fit neatly into pre-defined ecclesiological categories. By researching the prosperity theology of TAFES Associate women, this study seeks not the theology of the pulpit but a grassroots theology. In Africa, a grassroots approach is an entirely appropriate approach for theological reflection since, as Kenyan scholar Humphrey Waweru says, in African life there is an "interweaving of the metaphysical or religious realm with the empirical realm."[20] Indeed including a grassroots perspective enriches rather than obscures theology.

1.4 Research Design

This study is qualitative research of a theological nature. It seeks to use ethnographic methods to hear from TAFES women about their theology of prosperity. I lived in Tanzania during the period of research and writing, as I had for a number of years prior. I engaged in interviews with TAFES Associate women representing all eight TAFES regions as well as conducting focus groups and attending TAFES events as a participant-observer.[21] Twenty women were interviewed and a total of thirty-one women participated in the research overall.

1.5 Research Question

The research question in view here is "What is the TAFES women's theology of prosperity?" The goal is first to understand the prosperity theology of TAFES women in their own words. Having established this, viewing their theology from a variety of angles, and bringing it into conversation with other theologies, will shed greater light on it. This information is distilled in a table at the end of each chapter, which provides a cumulative picture of what we have learned about their theology of prosperity. The table serves as a quick reference guide and is not exhaustive.

---

19. See also Mwaura, "Gender and Power," 422.

20. Waweru, *The Bible*, 54.

21. Throughout, I refer to these women as TAFES Associate women, TAFES women, research cohort, etc.,

1.6 Definition of Terms

I give a detailed discussion of terms like prosperity theology and prosperity gospel in chapter 2. In general, in this study, prosperity theology refers to Christian theology in Africa which substantially teaches that prosperity is God's will for his people. Prosperity gospel is one subset of prosperity theology in Africa, taught by the flamboyant preachers and accompanied by other practices such as seed offering. At times, I will also refer to this as profligate prosperity gospel. I will refer to the prosperity theology of the TAFES women as *mafanikio* theology and I give an extensive treatment of it in Chapter 4.

Grassroots theology refers to theology that exists in the Christian church among ordinary believers, who have not undertaken formal theological study. It is not an indicator of demography or social class.

The meaning of "woman" and "man" which have become unstable elsewhere in recent decades are fairly static in Tanzania. When I tell Tanzanians I am researching the prosperity theology of women, no one questions what I mean by woman. In keeping with this, distinctions between "sex" and "gender" are not common. For the purposes of this work, sex is biological, and gender is the social behaviour of that sex. In this study "woman" refers to human beings of female biological sex.

1.7 Assumptions and Limitations of the Study

In his book *Grassroots Asian Theology*, Singaporean Pentecostal Simon Chan argues that taking the grassroots seriously means assuming that people have good reasons for the theology they hold, and greater light can be shed on it by asking, "What is right here?" rather than seeking to critique without sufficient nuance.[22] I therefore take an appreciative posture in my research, not as a way of covering up issues but as a way of unmasking what may have been previously hidden by bias, that it might be better understood and engaged.

This study profiles the theology of TAFES Associate women and brings it into conversation with other theologies. It is not a polemic for or against prosperity theology. It seeks to understand and engage the TAFES women's

---

22. Chan's book 'Grassroots Asian Theology' was influential in my thinking. Chan, *Grassroots Asian Theology*, Kindle edition, 33.

prosperity theology but not attack or defend it. The assessments of *mafankio* theology are in aid of understanding its nature and how it functions.

This study has further limits that are important to note at the outset. First, this study is not representative of all Tanzanians or of Tanzanian prosperity theology. It is limited to the prosperity theology of TAFES Associate women. Second, the focus of this study is on the theology of this group of women in their own right; it is not a comparison with men's theologies, and I do not draw comparisons between "women's theology" and "men's theology." Third, this study is not a systematic theology of TAFES women. It is limited to their prosperity theology. The research asked the women specifically about prosperity, not, for example, Christology, soteriology, or eschatology. While I will comment on some of these topics, it is only insofar as they relate to the TAFES women's prosperity theology and these comments ought not to be taken as exhaustive for those topics.

1.8 Conclusion and Outlook

While prosperity theology in Africa has garnered significant attention, little research has been done in Tanzania, among women or in interdenominational contexts. This study addresses these deficits. Adopting an appreciative posture, I use ethnographic tools for theological means, exploring the prosperity theology of TAFES Associate women. I profile their theology and explore its roots and theological intersections.

In chapter 2, I survey the existing literature related to prosperity theologies in Africa, including Tanzania. I note the growing interest in grassroots theologies of prosperity and identify the need for an inductive, ethnographic, and theological study of prosperity theology in an interdenominational context, which this study meets.

Chapter 3 outlines my research approach and process, and ethical considerations. I detail my ethnographic methods, giving particular attention to the triangulation of data which I see as essential to the integrity of the project. I seek to be transparent about my advantages and limitations as a researcher who is both a foreigner in Tanzania and someone who has lived in country many years.

Chapter 4 is dedicated to reporting the results of my ethnographic fieldwork. It functions as an in-depth profile of the TAFES women's prosperity theology, what I will call *mafanikio* theology.²³ It examines *mafanikio* theology from several different angles, not only defining it but also asking what its scope, limits, purpose, and features are. This chapter gives a robust picture of the prosperity theology held by TAFES women which provides a foundation for the subsequent analysis. At the end of this chapter, a table appears listing some key findings about *mafanikio* theology. This table is then added to in each subsequent chapter to provide an easy, visual reference point for the thesis's key findings about *mafanikio* theology.

Having understood the content of *mafanikio* theology, I then work in a series of broadening concentric circles, first viewing *mafanikio* theology in its immediate context in chapter 5, and then bringing it into conversation with other African prosperity theologies (chapter 6), African theology more broadly (chapter 7), and global models of holism (chapter 8).

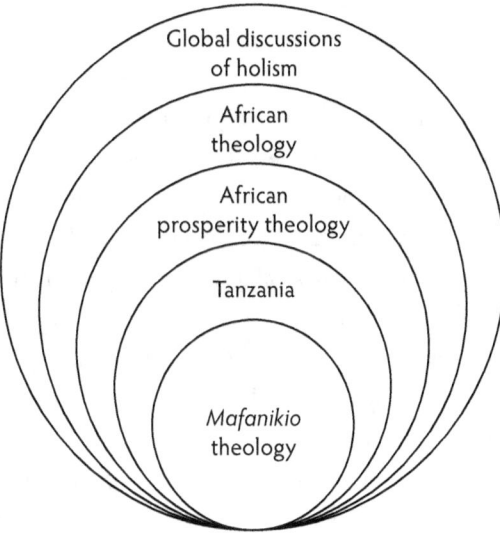

Figure 1.1 Concentric circles of conversation with *mafanikio* theology

Chapter 5 locates *mafanikio* theology in its historical and cultural contexts and its hermeneutical approach. In this chapter, I explore how *mafanikio* theology is a product of both its environment and the Bible.

---

23. *Mafanikio* is pronounced muh-fuh-ni-KEE-oh. For English speakers, the pseudo-rhyme 'Havana Rio' may give a sense of the rhythm of the word and its vowel sounds.

In chapter 6 I identify how *mafanikio* theology operates as both a prosperity theology and a critique of prosperity theology. *Mafanikio* theology's goal is discipleship and I take the Parable of the Sower as a lens to examine this because the parable is about growth towards, and hindrances to maturity. The Parable of the Sower presents two major obstacles to ongoing commitment in the Christian life: suffering, and consumption by worldly pursuits. I therefore examine *mafanikio* theology's capacity to engender endurance and faithfulness instead, concluding that *mafanikio* theology navigates both these admirably.

In chapter 7, I consider *mafanikio* theology as an African theology. Prosperity theologies in Africa are accused of both foreignness and syncretism and so I interrogate *mafanikio* theology on both counts before moving on to consider the worldview behind it and to show how it relates to this worldview theologically. I also highlight patronage as an important and underutilised cultural construct for interpreting *mafanikio* theology, one which could possibly be applied fruitfully to other prosperity theologies.

In chapter 8, the largest concentric circle, I examine *mafanikio* theology's claim to be holistic by comparing it with other models of holism. I discuss *mafanikio* theology's likeness to integral mission and its relationship to *ubuntu*,[24] before going on to consider whether *mafanikio* theology adequately encapsulates both the physical and spiritual dimensions of faith, as it claims to. Regarding the physical dimension I particularly address controversies around rest, creation care and political engagement and in the spiritual section I give my attention to the TAFES women's theology of the cross, highlighting their holistic theology of the atonement and how cruciformity plays out in their lives.

Finally, I conclude with a summary of *mafanikio* theology, a comment on its significance, and give suggestions for further research. I have also included an Afterword, which is a worked example of how I have applied my learning about *mafanikio* theology to missiological issues in my home country of Australia. The subtitle of this book is "Learning prosperity with Tanzanian women." My conviction is that God has taught Tanzanian women something about prosperity which can benefit his global church. It was in

---

24. *Ubuntu* means "I am because we are".

this spirit that I undertook the research and I invite the reader to join me in this learning experience.

CHAPTER 2

Literature Review

There is a significant body of literature about the prosperity gospel in African Christianity, broadly answering three questions: Where has it come from? What is it? and, what are its effects? I will examine the literature pertaining to each of these questions in order.

It may seem counter-intuitive to examine the literature concerning where the prosperity gospel has come from before actually defining it as a term, but I take this approach because this study seeks at all times to view the theology at hand in context. Resisting the inclination to extract a theology from its context, thereby obscuring its meaning, I start here with the question of whose it is, what are its associations and influences, and who lays claim to it?

Having reckoned with what the literature reveals about *whose* this prosperity gospel is, the discussion is able to move forward to considering *what* the prosperity gospel is. While many studies define the prosperity gospel somewhat perfunctorily before moving on to critique it or consider its effects, there is a growing group of scholars who argue that what has been termed prosperity gospel is a much broader set of theologies and any one prosperity theology cannot be assumed to have the same features as others. In line with this emerging paradigm, from this point in the study, I change my language to speaking about prosperity theology, with prosperity gospel as a subset of that. My discussion of the effects of prosperity theology is influenced by this growing diversity in the literature, highlighting that the effects of prosperity theology, like prosperity theology itself, are mixed.

In reviewing the literature, a key learning that emerges is that when engaging any prosperity theology, it is imperative to understand this prosperity theology in its particularity. This is what this study seeks to do in examining the TAFES women's theology, which fills key demographic gaps in the study of prosperity theology in Africa.

2.1 Origins of the Prosperity Gospel in Africa
2.1.1 Affiliations of the Prosperity Gospel in Africa

The prosperity gospel is in common parlance almost synonymous with Pentecostalism.[1] Discussions of Pentecostalism in Africa give attention to it by necessity, and criticisms of it are often conflated with Pentecostalism itself.[2] However, the prosperity gospel is generally regarded as a newer development of Pentecostalism. Scholars are broadly agreed on three waves of heightened global Pentecostal activity and renewal. In the introduction to her edited volume with Amos Yong about the socio-economics of the prosperity gospel, Katherine Attanasi outlines these waves broadly as: classic Pentecostalism of the early twentieth century, the charismatic movement of the 1960s and 70s, and neo-Pentecostalism, on the rise since the 1980s.[3] Neo-Pentecostalism is known for its affinity with prosperity messages. It is distinct from the other two in its posture of being world-affirming. Prior to the 1980s, Pentecostalism had advocated a retreat from worldliness, but neo-Pentecostals are distinguished by their emphasis on the spiritual value of earthly or material blessings.[4]

The neo-Pentecostal movement in Africa, specifically, has also been characterised by a strongly global inclination and trans-denominational spread.[5] Indeed, Pew research in sub-Saharan Africa found that over half of Christians believe in the prosperity gospel and it is a distinctive feature of African diaspora churches as well.[6] Heuser considers it to span the full

---

1. Gbote and Kgatla, "Prosperity Gospel," 1–10.

2. Two excellent introductions to Pentecostalism are Asamoah-Gyadu, *African Charismatics: Current Developments*; Kalu, *African Pentecostalism: An Introduction*.

3. Attanasi, "Introduction: The Plurality," Kindle edition, 1–12.

4. Niemandt, "The Prosperity Gospel," 203–19; Heuser, "Charting African Prosperity Gospel," 1–9.

5. Heuser prefers "glocalized," emphasizing that the global took African shape. Heuser, "Religio-Scapes," 17. See also Meyer, "'Delivered from,'" 236–55.

6. For examples, see Burgess, "Megachurches and 'Reverse Mission,'" 243–68; Kwabena Asamoah-Gyadu, "To the Ends," 23–44; Liesen, "Contextualizing the Prosperity Gospel," 52–73.

range of Christianity in Africa.[7] Ghanaian theologian Johnson Kwabena Asamoah-Gyadu speaks of a "parallel Pentecostalising process" where the historic mission churches, faced with losing swathes of their people to neo-Pentecostal churches, embarked on a strategy of allowing renewal groups to function within their ranks, in an effort to retain members.[8] Naomi Haynes, who has done ethnographic work on the Zambian Copperbelt, concurs that there has been a "Pentecostalisation of the Zambian mainline;"[9] Ghanaian Joseph Quayesi-Amakye, considered this form of Pentecostalism to have become ubiquitous;[10] and Andrew Wildsmith concurs from his context of theological education in Kenya that its influence and presence is far-reaching.[11] Just as Pentecostalism is not limited to the Pentecostal denominations, likewise the prosperity gospel is much broader. As Tanzanian Jean Bosco Kambale says: "the Prosperity Gospel [sic] is spread over the entire continent of Africa, involving different contexts, various ecclesiological traditions, spirituality systems, and a multitude of categories of ministers of the Word."[12] However, research on the prosperity gospel has tended to consider it within a Pentecostal denominational context or neo-Pentecostal church, with little attention given to the phenomenon in mixed or non-Pentecostal contexts.[13] In light of the prosperity gospel's appeal across denominational lines, there is a warrant to study the theology of prosperity in an interdenominational context. My cohort, from TAFES, are one such interdenominational group which could enhance our understanding of prosperity gospel.

2.1.2 History of the Prosperity Gospel in Africa

The prosperity gospel is largely seen as a Pentecostal phenomenon which has spread to other denominational contexts but there is some debate over its genesis, specifically, to what extent it can be thought of as a North American import.

---

7. Heuser, "Religio-Scapes," 23.
8. Asamoah-Gyadu, "Pentecostalism in Africa," 14–39.
9. Haynes, "'Zambia Shall Be Saved,'" 5–24.
10. Quayesi-Amakye, "A Yeast," 71–84.
11. Wildsmith, "The Ideal Life," 147–64.
12. Ngwobia, Kambale, and Ngomo, "Misleading Theologies of Wealth," 204–304.
13. Notably, Martin Lindhardt's research into the New Life movement in Iringa in Tanzania's southern highlands is an exception to this. Lindhardt, "More than Just Money," 41–67.

Since Paul Gifford's influential work on Reinhard Bonnke's "Christ For All Nations" crusade in 1987, it has become common to view the prosperity gospel as a North American import.[14] Indeed, Gifford was a pioneer in the study of the prosperity gospel in Africa, and has become such an authority on it, that many scholars state his theory as its genesis and move on.[15] Because of his publishing over many years and his prominence, he is a voice that must be taken into account, but his version effectively ignores the historic relationship of prosperity gospel to African Pentecostalism. It has little appreciation of the state of play of African Christianity prior to 1987, and so Africans become "mere clones, consumers or imitators of innovations that originated outside their context."[16] While early leaders of the second wave of Pentecostal renewal in Africa, like Nigerian Archbishop Benson Idahosa, and South African Ray McCauly took some college courses in the USA, stressing their North American education or envisioning them as importers of a North American prosperity gospel disregards their conversion and early nurture in African Pentecostal churches, or the fact that they had their own reasons for incorporating North American resources.[17]

This interplay between North American ideas and indigenous African movements is illustrated by Kalu's story of one of the former leaders of the Christian student movement in Kenya who, when he heard Oral Roberts speak in 1968, named his son after him.[18] This leader already had an itinerant ministry in Kenya, Uganda and Tanzania, an indigenous charismatic ministry which was obviously encouraged by its interaction with Roberts, but nevertheless underway prior to Roberts's ministry in Kenya. Neither is the USA the only influence. Prosperity teachers from South East Asia, the West Indies, and the UK also feature in Africa.[19] A stunning example of opting for a teacher from beyond North America is the Zimbabwe Assemblies of God who rejected the teachings of the Reinhard Bonnke's Harare Fire Campaign of 1986 after one of its leaders wrote a criticism of their country upon his return

---

14. Gifford, "'Africa Shall Be Saved,'" 63–92.

15. See, for example, Haynes, "'Zambia Shall Be Saved!'" 8; Niemandt, "The Prosperity Gospel," 205; Young, "Prosperity Teaching," 3–18; Gbote and Kgatla, "Prosperity Gospel," 6.

16. Asamoah-Gyadu, *African Charismatics*, 12.

17. Heuser, "Religio-Scapes of Prosperity Gospel," 17.

18. Kalu, *African Pentecostalism*, 107.

19. Kalu, 259.

to the USA and word of it got back to the Zimbabwean press. They opted instead for the teaching of black, Bahamas-based preacher Myles Munroe, a graduate of Oral Roberts University with a strong emphasis on black pride and self-actualisation.[20]

The language of appropriation of North American ideas is more fitting and more accurate than that of import or export. While Gbote and Kgatla, writing from a South African context, follow American David Platt in describing the prosperity gospel as a dissemination of the American dream, they critically fail to acknowledge that the prosperity gospel may be a fitting response to an *African* dream.[21] In contrast, as Kalu discusses the interaction of African Pentecostals with North American ideas due to the rise of new media, he notes shared symbols, values and moral culture, but sees these as having been taken and applied, with some alteration, to the African context.[22] Similarly, Ruth Marshall, a political scientist whose work has focused on West African religion, recounts her experience in Nigeria of hearing a girl preach in Yoruba with an American accent not as evidence of "Americanisation" but rather of accessing prestige by assuming a register normally reserved for the Nigerian elite.[23] Indeed, Africans assume elements of other Christianities as suits their purposes, and are not limited to North America. Even Gifford acknowledges that:

> Fundamentalist, charismatic, Pentecostal, Evangelical are all labels that have been used, but they are all labels taken from Western divisions of Christianity; it is not evident that the dynamics that gave rise to the labels in their original contexts are the same here.[24]

While there is little argument that North American prosperity theology has influenced prosperity gospel in Africa, to conceive of this as a simple import is to miss the indigenous roots of the Pentecostal movement, its subsequent waves of renewal, and its deployment of foreign resources for its own African purposes. Marshall considers the international ties of the movement

---

20. Maxwell, "'Delivered from the Spirit," 350–73.
21. Gbote and Kgatla, "Prosperity Gospel," 6.
22. Kalu, *African Pentecostalism*, 107.
23. Marshall-Fratani, "Mediating the Global," 278–315.
24. Gifford, "The Development and Political," 81.

to be largely symbolic, as revenues in neo-Pentecostal churches are generated locally.[25] Kenyan Catholic priest Mboya corroborates: while critical of the theology of neo-Pentecostal churches, he nevertheless admires their self-reliance and independence in church management.[26] Thus Asamoah-Gyadu can argue that these charismatic movements reflect "modern African ingenuity" in their appropriation of modern North American techniques as a source of enchantment and inspiration.[27] It is thus vital to interact with prosperity theologies as distinct contextual theologies in their own right. This is what I seek to do in this study of the prosperity theology of TAFES women.

2.1.3 Relationship between Prosperity Gospel And African Traditional Religion

While the prosperity gospel cannot be divorced from its indigenous roots in the African Pentecostal movement, scholars have also reckoned with an African connection which is far older. Prosperity in Africa is not an invention of the prosperity gospel. In Tanzanian Catholic priest Laurenti Magesa's *African Religion*, a detailed study of the cosmology and ethics of African Traditional Religion, the word prosperity is mentioned several times and the concept of prosperity is frequently used, such as when he concludes that the sum of African religious practice is to "promote the abundance of human life and not diminish it," and in the book's subtitle: "the moral traditions of *abundant life* [emphasis mine]."[28] Words such as life-giving, vivification, harmony, well-being, restoration of life, and vital force – arguably aspects of prosperity – all feature.[29] Indeed, Nigerian Catholic scholars Stan Chu Ilo and Joseph Ogbonnaya equate "abundant life" with "peaceful and prosperous societies."[30] Similarly, the concept of prosperity is also present in Nigerian Agbonkhianmeghe Orobator's view that African "religious practice is essentially oriented toward enhancing and strengthening life broadly conceived."[31] Yusufu Turaki, who is less positive about African Traditional Religion,

---

25. Marshall-Fratani, "Mediating the Global" 294.
26. Mboya, "Gift Challenges," 16–42.
27. Asamoah-Gyadu, "Pentecostalism in Africa," 29.
28. Magesa, *African Religion: The Moral*, 263.
29. Magesa, 9, 10, 72, 84, 90, 111, 112, 118–156, 122, 141, 185, 191, 240, 247, 249.
30. Ilo and Ogbonnaya, "Introduction," xv.
31. Orobator, *Religion and Faith*, 46.

nevertheless recognises the "traditional African quest for destiny and well-being."[32] Before embarking on any discussion of a theology of prosperity in Africa, it is essential to note that prosperity has been a long-standing theme in African consciousness and religious life, including prior to Christianity.

Considering the long history of reflection on prosperity in Africa, the question arises as to what extent newer theologising about prosperity, such as the prosperity gospel, relies on African Traditional Religion. There are clear resonances and overlaps between African Traditional Religion and the prosperity gospel. McKinnon argues that "the goal of Pentecostal mission matches the goal of Tanzanian living," and Ilo and Ogbonnaya acknowledge a similarity in goals between African Traditional Religion and Christian faith despite many differences in creed, code, process, and practice.[33] Ghanaian Kwabena Darkwa Amanor notes that many Christians recognise the similarities:

> Many African Christians have had no difficulty readily accommodating the Christian faith into their traditional worldview, seeing in Christianity, elements that make Jesus Christ the One who brings to fulfilment the highest religious and spiritual aspirations of their primal past.[34]

Pentecostalism, with which the prosperity gospel is most often associated, and African Traditional Religion hold in common an enchanted worldview, a holistic outlook, and a concern with the day-to-day.[35] Benno van den Toren summarises it well:

> Neo-Pentecostalism fits with the traditional holistic understanding of salvation. Mission-churches tended to present salvation as mainly or exclusively spiritual. This simply does not make sense in the African traditional worldview. In ATRs spiritual wholeness is always reflected in physical and social well-being,

---

32. Turaki, *Foundations of African Traditional*, 90.
33. McKinnon, "On Being Charismatic Brethren," 279; Ilo and Ogbonnaya, "Introduction," xv.
34. Amanor, "Pentecostal and Charismatic?," 123–40.
35. Worldview refers to basic assumptions about the world. An enchanted worldview is one that includes the spirit world as part of and affecting our world.

and it is the experience of social and physical need or disaster that fuels the desire for spiritual well-being.[36]

While the overlaps are evident to all, scholars differ on whether these similarities are positive or negative.

Scholars such as Allan Anderson, Ogbu Kalu and Asamoah-Gyadu have tended to see African Pentecostalism as a properly African expression of Christianity. Anderson reminds us that missionary Christianity, "often contributed to the feeling in Africa that these churches were 'foreign' and that people first had to become Westerners before becoming Christians."[37] Magesa argues that even those who appear to accept this foreign religion "show their true African religious face particularly in times of crisis," such that "Christianity in Africa today may be said to have two different forms of thought-systems and faith expressions – one official and one popular."[38] It is here, where missions Christianity has failed to be compelling, that Kalu says:

> The born-again people have picked up the gauntlet. The argument here is that Pentecostalism in Africa derived her coloring from the texture of the African soil and from the interior her idiom, nurture, and growth; her fruits serve the challenges and problems of the African ecosystem more adequately than did the earlier missionary fruits.[39]

For these scholars, the resonance of Pentecostalism with African Traditional Religion points to an ownership and Africanisation of Christianity. Anderson argues that any accusation of "syncretism" likely results from "hasty generalisations" since "Christianity everywhere is inherently syncretistic" in that it seeks to be contextual, "expressing God's concerns in a particular human context."[40] Calling neo-Pentecostal churches "thoroughly contextualised" van den Toren concurs, because they take up "central elements of Africa Traditional Religions and worldview."[41]

---

36. van den Toren, "African Neo-Pentecostalism," 103–20.
37. Anderson, "The Gospel," 373–83.
38. Magesa, *African Religion*, 20–21.
39. Kalu, "Preserving a Worldview," 110–37.
40. Anderson, "The Gospel," 375–6.
41. van den Toren, "African Neo-Pentecostalism," 111.

However, several scholars disagree that the prosperity gospel has integrity as an African expression of Christianity.[42] For Orobator the materialism of the prosperity gospel is a distortion of African Traditional Religion, not a feature of it. He describes:

> Cunning, jet-setting preachers and their army of evangelical clones [who] have devised a brand of Christianity that spiritualises Africa's real and deadly challenges. The danger is that [it] trivialises religion and makes it into an instrument for pursuing self-serving interests and achieving personal gains.[43]

In his view, the prosperity gospel extracts African Traditional Religion's "proclivity to explain, predict and control," transforming it into performances that "manipulate, influence and exploit the beliefs of adherents."[44] In light of this, he considers prosperity gospel true neither to African Traditional Religion nor Christianity. However, Orobator also argues that African Traditional Religion is not a religious system one can accept or reject. Instead:

> It is the ground or sub-structure of the religious consciousness of Africans on which the other two religions have been superimposed over the course of time with varying degrees of compatibility ... African Religion is the deep anchor that secures the foundation of either Christianity or Islam to the soul of the African.

While the prosperity gospel may be a distortion of African Traditional Religion then, it cannot be divorced from those roots.

A second objection to the prosperity gospel as an African expression of Christianity is offered by Cameroonian-American scholar David T. Ngong. Unlike Orobator who considers the prosperity gospel to be a distortion of African Traditional Religion, Ngong considers the prosperity gospel's problems to be *born* of African Traditional Religion, reinforcing its worst aspects. In his view, though Pentecostals claim to offer Jesus as an antidote to fear of forces and powers, their preoccupation with victory over such forces and powers reinforces their prominence. For Ngong, this undermines their

---

42. Ngong, "Salvation and Materialism," 1–21.
43. Orobator, *Religion and Faith*, 76.
44. Orobator, 102.

message and the prosperity gospel's focus on appeasing God treats him in line with a pre-Christian worldview.[45] He is critical of Anderson, accusing those who hold his view as ceding an African traditional religious worldview, which has been detrimental to Africans, in order to gain followers.[46] He contrasts this with the work of African philosophers who have critiqued the "unhealthy habits" of African Traditional Religion.[47] The strength of Ngong's argument is this emphasis on agency, which is ironic because he misses that, as Anderson says, transformation between Christianity and African Traditional Religion is bi-directional:

> The Christian message challenges, confronts and changes whatever seems incongruous or inadequate in African religion, and African religion transforms and enriches the Christian message so that it is understandable and relevant within the worldview in which it is submerged.[48]

This debate is best settled from an emic perspective. A term originating in linguistics, *emic* refers to "an understanding of culture from the inside."[49] Many Pentecostals or Pentecostalised-Christians today would be horrified by the notion that they perpetuate rather than challenge fear of forces and power. Jerry Ireland's work in Zambia surveyed Pentecostal church leaders about their views on African Religion. He found:

> Respondents' answers describe a ministerial context in which threats from ng'angas [witchdoctors] and demonic activity are commonplace. Yet, an overwhelming majority of respondents face these seen and unseen spiritual threats *without fear* (Q. 28). Clearly, these leaders understand their calling and their salvation as participation in God's victory over Satan, through His Son Jesus Christ and by the power availed to them through God the Holy Spirit.[50] [emphasis mine]

---

45. Ngong, "Salvation and Materialism," 14.
46. Ngong, 14.
47. Ngong, 14.
48. Anderson, "The Gospel and African," 376–7.
49. Kraft, *Anthropology for Christian Witness*, 103.
50. Ireland, "African Traditional Religion," 260–77.

This evidence at a local level appears to endorse Anderson's more general assertion:

> African Pentecostals confront old views by declaring what they are convinced is a more powerful protection against sorcery and a more effective healing from sickness than either the existing churches or traditional rituals had offered. Healing, guidance, protection from evil, and success and prosperity are some of the practical benefits offered to faithful members of their churches.[51]

Jean Comaroff explains that, "What these movements stress is less an unbroken continuity with indigenous forms of belief than a self-conscious, born-again return to fundamentals."[52] This is how neo-Pentecostals can be both "outspokenly opposed to 'African tradition' per se" and still grant the power of those traditions.[53] Indeed, in her thesis which called for Lutherans to speak to people's Africanness as the neo-Pentecostal churches do, Faith Lugazia noted that deliverance ministries can help people to sever ties with African Traditional Religion.[54]

The worldview of Pentecostalism, and the prosperity gospel within that, overlaps significantly with African Traditional Religion, as it gives Christianity a way to be African. However, Pentecostalism is also distinct from African Traditional Religion, especially by its provision of an alternate solution to the problems African Traditional Religion seeks to address. Whether it manages to do so sufficiently remains contested and it will likely differ from context to context. More research is needed at a local level to clarify this picture, and the current study contributes by examining the prosperity theology of TAFES women, including its Africanness.

2.2 Defining the Prosperity Gospel in Africa

Thus far this survey of the literature has explored the answers of scholars to the question of from whence the prosperity gospel has come. The picture is considerably more complicated than that it is a Pentecostal import from

---

51. Anderson, "The Gospel and African," 376.
52. Comaroff, "Pentecostalism, Populism," 42.
53. Comaroff, 42.
54. Lugazia, "Towards an African Inculturation," 47.

North America. Indeed, the Pentecostalisation of mainline churches means the prosperity gospel is not limited to specifically Pentecostal contexts, and it has deep affinities with African churches and older African religiosity. It is therefore essential to define the prosperity gospel in Africa with reference to its African context.

2.2.1 Definitions of the Prosperity Gospel

As a pioneer in the study of the prosperity gospel, Paul Gifford's definitional work was the standard for much of the past two decades. His oft-quoted definition of the prosperity gospel states: "God has met all the needs of human beings in the suffering and death of Christ."[55] He is joined by Young and Attanasi in locating these blessings in the atonement.[56] However, while Gifford's definition is frequently used, scholars with a more attentive and sympathetic approach, such as Asamoah-Gyadu and Kalu, do not see the atonement figuring heavily; both point to an Old Testament covenant with Abraham as the source of the prosperity promise.[57] Another source of the blessing is put forward by Larbi who sees the incarnation and exaltation of Christ as good news of salvation from fear, disease, economic deprivation, ignorance, and alienation from God.[58] Thus, there is no consensus on what the prosperity gospel teaches regarding the means by which God extends blessing to humankind.

Scholars do agree that the prosperity gospel teaches that God wants to bless Christians, but they are split on the nature of this blessing. Attanasi, along with Young and Asamoah-Gyadu, conceive of the blessing as spiritual, physical and material, while Gbote and Kgatla, and Mboya mention only wealth and good health.[59] Gifford's acknowledgement that prosperity teachers offer holistic blessing is quickly diminished by his insistence that they emphasise the financial, and he is joined by Marshall, Mboya, Nigerian

---

55. Gifford, "Expecting Miracles," 20.

56. Young, "Prosperity Teaching," 6; Attanasi, "Introduction: The Plurality," 5.

57. Kalu, *African Pentecostalism*, 255; Asamoah-Gyadu, *African Charismatics*, 211. Young also includes this covenantal aspect in his analysis. Young, "Prosperity Teaching," 6.

58. Larbi, "The Nature of Continuity," 87–106.

59. Attanasi, "Introduction: The Plurality," 3; Young, "Prosperity Teaching," 4; Eriksen, Blanes, and MacCarthy, *Engaging with Theories*, 144; Asamoah-Gyadu, *African Charismatics*, 211; See also Gbote and Kgatla, "Prosperity Gospel," 2; Mboya, "Gift Challenges," 16.

Obadare and Pentecostal New Testament scholar J.C. Thomas in seeing the prosperity gospel as primarily economically focused.[60] Still others such as Maxwell and anthropologist Harri Englund argue that it is not finances that interest church members, but security.[61] For example, though Lindhardt notes a strong desire to prosper among the members of New Life in Christ in Iringa, and acknowledges this to be partly dependent on the management of spiritual forces, when he asked them about their motivations, "recurring answers by far were protection, security and good health rather than economic prosperity."[62] Nevertheless, scholars are generally agreed that blessings are accessed by faith, which is more than mere belief as it includes positive confession and gifts of money ("seed faith" and tithes).[63] Such a diversity of definitions illustrates Heuser's statement that the prosperity gospel "cannot be reduced to a monolithic canon of ideas, ethics or practices."[64] This does not make classification of the prosperity gospel pointless; there is family resemblance even if it is difficult to specify the exact features held in common.[65]

More recent work has undertaken to understand who the different family members might be in what Norwegian Tomas Drønen calls a "post-Giffordian paradigm."[66] Drønen's experience in Cameroon was that the churches he studied:

> ... had economy and success high on the agenda of themes dwelled upon during sermons—but none of them focused on 'wealth and health' as a direct consequence of having 'the right

---

60. Gifford, "Expecting Miracles," 20; Marshall-Fratani, "Mediating the Global," 282–3; Thomas, "Prosperity Preaching," 163–172. In fact, Obadare understands the prosperity gospel to be inimical to "a state of spiritual, physical, psychic and mental wholeness." Obadare, "'Raising Righteous Billionaires,'" 1–8.

61. Maxwell, "'Delivered from?," 366; Englund cited in Heuser, "Charting African Prosperity," 7.

62. Lindhardt, "More than Just Money," 56–57.

63. Eriksen, Blanes, and MacCarthy, *Engaging with Theories*, 144; Kalu, *African Pentecostalism*, 255; Gifford, "Expecting Miracles," 20; Lindhardt, "More than Just Money," 51; Mboya, "Gift Challenges," 24; Gbote and Kgatla make this the essence of the prosperity gospel, asking, "Does God base his blessings to church members solely on faith?" Gbote and Kgatla, "Prosperity Gospel," 1.

64. Heuser, "Religio-Scapes of Prosperity Gospel," 16.

65. Folarin, "Contemporary State," 69–95.

66. Drønen, "Material Development," 205–18.

faith', as argued by preachers in the famous mega-churches we all are familiar with.[67]

He reflects, "I think that for too long we have been dazzled by the success stories of [Ghanaian megachurch pastor] Mensa Otabil and [founder of Winner's Chapel International] David Oydepo [sic], and have thought that this is what the new Pentecostalism is all about."[68] Similarly, in his study of three African Diaspora churches in Germany, Frank Liesen found at least one "that teaches prosperity yet retains an evangelical call to conversion and transformation" and noted a variety of interpretations of the prosperity gospel.[69] Likewise, Wonsuk Ma refuses to talk about the prosperity gospel, insisting on the language of prosperity gospels (plural) because "similarities in terminology and even sometimes in behaviours of many [prosperity gospel] preachers often conceal radically diverse motivations and theological orientations."[70]

An example of a different kind of prosperity gospel comes from Naomi Haynes's work on the Zambian Copperbelt. She uses the language of "limited prosperity gospel" where, "local definitions of prosperity are characterised not by uniform, individualised wealth, but rather by progress along a gradient of material achievement through relationships that span differences in economic status."[71] Meanwhile Maria Frahm-Arp identified three clusters of prosperity gospel in her work in South Africa:

> *Abilities* prosperity is based on the idea that if Christians live according to biblical principles and work hard, then they will succeed in whatever they choose to do . . . [*Progress* prosperity explains that] people often do not see the prosperity in their lives because their understanding of prosperity is wrong. In this theology "prosperity" means any form of progress in the life of a believer . . . *Miracle* prosperity, on the other hand, is primarily concerned with explaining the way the world is and how prosperity can be achieved through miracles.[72] [emphasis mine]

---

67. Drønen, 207.
68. Drønen, 206.
69. Liesen, "Contextualizing the Prosperity Gospel," 68.
70. Ma, "Blessing in Pentecostal Theology," Kindle edition, 272.
71. Haynes, "Pentecostalism and the Morality," 123–39.
72. Frahm-Arp, "Pentecostalism, Politics," 1–16.

In a similar vein, Joshua Robert Barron observed in Kenya a subset of the prosperity gospel which he calls the Productivity Gospel.[73] Then there are those who affirm the move away from ascetic Christianity to an embrace of prosperity but wish to modify some of the more extreme theologies and practices of the prosperity gospel movement. Nigerian Deji Ageboyin is one such example, asking for a re-think of prosperity theology rather than an outright rejection of it, insisting, "wealth is not evil."[74] Kambale goes even further: "I would like to start affirming that biblically, Prosperity Gospel [sic] should not be considered as a misleading theology, since prosperity is the essence of the Jesus Christ mission."[75] He views prosperity gospels that have no place for suffering, marginalize some church members, or do not lift up whole communities, as a distortion of the true prosperity gospel found in the Bible.[76]

Gifford responded in 2015 to those who see prosperity gospel(s) more positively, arguing that the movement is made up of six "registers:" motivation, entrepreneurship, practical skills, faith gospel, the anointing of the man of God, and defeating spirits blocking one's advance.[77] He sees the more optimistic assessment of the prosperity gospel as focusing on the first three to the exclusion of the last three, which he concludes as more significant because they are more at odds with development.[78] Gifford's work is aimed at building a comprehensive picture of the prosperity gospel movement at the expense of particularity. In doing so, it generalises and therefore misrepresents. Gifford's registers do not work for the above examples of Drønen, Frahm-Arp, Haynes, and Barron because they cannot account for the way the prosperity gospel plays out at a local level. Likewise, because he concentrates on the prominent *man* of God, women are disregarded as contributors to prosperity theology.[79] Gifford's analysis also fails to grapple with more

---

73. Barron, "Is the Prosperity Gospel," 88–103.
74. Ageboyin, "A Rethinking," 70.
75. Ngwobia, Kambale, and Ngomo, "Misleading Theologies of Wealth," 256.
76. Ngwobia, Kambale, and Ngomo, 258–61.
77. Gifford, "The Development," 82–83. "Man of God" is a gendered term; "man" cannot be substituted for "prophet" or "servant."
78. Gifford, 85.
79. Gifford's research into the prosperity gospel has primarily been about the big men; his methodology overlooks women and therefore so do his conclusions. See Gifford, "Ghana's Charismatic Churches," 241–65.

recent innovations of Pentecostalism where development and enchantment are not at odds with one another, such as in what Miller and Yamamori dub the "Progressive Pentecostal Churches" (PPCs).[80] Kyama Mugambi gives two Kenyan case studies of such "progressive Pentecostals" in his study of urban Pentecostalism in Kenya.[81] He argues that they:

> Reimagined Christianity as an active player in the transformation of a society in turmoil. We see a transition beyond a personal Christianity to one in which transformation is mediated by an emerging middle-class Christianity. Theirs was a concrete, holistic spirituality articulated through social transformation without necessarily abandoning the personal, somewhat ethereal enchanted faith appreciated by [earlier Pentecostals].[82]

These simply do not fit Gifford's categories. In the post-Giffordian paradigm, not all teaching of prosperity in Christian circles is prosperity gospel, at least not as it has been described for much of the twenty-first century. I have attempted to represent this diversity visually in Figure 2.1 below. This Venn diagram shows some overlaps between different types of African prosperity theologies. The diagram is not to scale and does not purport to accurately represent these overlaps. Rather, it gives an impression of the variation and relationships. It also leaves space for African prosperity theologies which have not yet been identified. Going forward, I will use the language of prosperity gospel when a scholar refers to it but theology of prosperity or prosperity theology when referring to the broader movement or my own research. This study is not about prosperity gospel per se; it investigates the theology of prosperity as held specifically by TAFES women.

African American scholar Willie James Jennings warns against "possession, mastery, and control of knowledge first" as modes of theological enquiry.[83] In his view, the search for coherence short-circuits "communion, the working and weaving together of fragments in the forming of life together."[84] Indeed, accuracy when understanding and talking about the prosperity gospel

---

80. Miller and Yamamori, *Global Pentecostalism*, Kindle edition, 64.
81. Mugambi, *A Spirit of Revitalization* Kindle edition, 223–285.
82. Mugambi, 19.
83. Jennings, *After Whiteness*, Kindle edition, 33.
84. Jennings, 47.

is found at the local level and that is the level at which this study will operate. The confusion that reigns in trying to understand the prosperity gospel at a macro level is alleviated and perhaps even rendered obsolete if one is willing to explore the micro level.

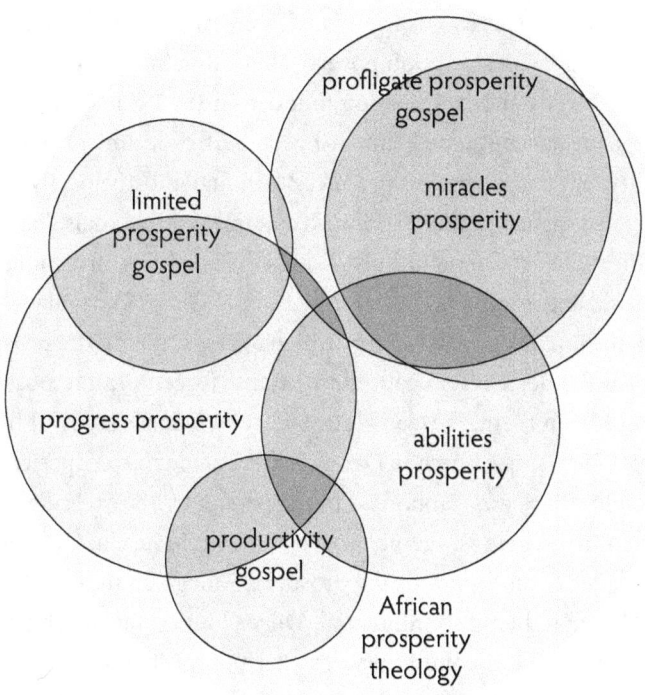

Figure 2.1 An impression of types within African prosperity theology

2.2.2 Prosperity Teaching in Tanzania

In Tanzania, the scholarship about prosperity is not extensive, meaning it is impossible to define or form a comprehensive understanding of prosperity teaching in Tanzania. However, there are "fragments" that form a picture of prosperity teaching in Tanzania and demonstrate both a "family resemblance" and a diversity. Allan Smith McKinnon's doctoral thesis on the Pentecostalisation of Brethren in Tanzania's north does not address theology of prosperity specifically, but the proximity of Pentecostalism to the prosperity gospel makes it an important study for understanding the landscape of prosperity in Tanzania, especially with his study of power and wholeness.[85] Similarly Martin Lindhardt's work, primarily in Iringa and among the interdenominational New Life movement, gives a picture of Tanzanian Pentecostal and charismatic Christians' views on issues such as money, power, community and witchcraft.[86]

Regarding the prosperity gospel in particular, Swiss theologian and ethicist Christine Schliesser's work on poverty alleviation included a case study of Efatha, a Pentecostal denomination founded in 1997. She found that the prosperity gospel strengthened "much-needed 'Afro-optimism' and 'Afro-responsibility,' but it also engages in concrete, though mostly locally limited, projects directed against poverty."[87] Finnish cultural anthropologist Paivi Hasu examined the same denomination, also noting the emphasis on responsibility and hard work, and contrasting this with Glory of Christ Tanzania Church, founded by Bishop Josephat Gwajima, which focuses "not on the prosperity gospel but on the destruction caused by satanic forces and the possibility of deliverance from them."[88] Meanwhile, Hansjorg Dilger's study of the Full Gospel Bible Fellowship Church in Dar Es Salaam found the prosperity gospel (*neno la uzima*) there was "embodied in the person of Bishop Kakobe himself, who went from being a member of the lower middle class to being the successful leader of an economically prospering mega-church."[89] However, despite the big man being so influential, Dilger found that the church also "established a tightly knit community of social and spiritual solidarity that is providing support for church members in times of need and crisis."[90] Similarly, in a study of urban Tanga and rural Arumeru in Tanzania's north, prosperity teaching was accompanied by an emphasis on the community:

---

85. McKinnon, "On Being Charismatic Brethren," 235–8, 264–279.

86. Lindhardt, "More than Just Money"; Martin Lindhardt, "The Ambivalence of Power"; Lindhardt, "'If You Are Saved,'" 240–72; Lindhardt, "Mediating Money," 147–60.

87. Schliesser, "On a Long Neglected," 339–59.

88. Hasu, "Prosperity Gospels," 78.

89. Dilger, "Healing the Wounds," 59–83.

90. Dilger, 61. The term "big man" (sometimes capitalized) spans across academia and the grassroots. It refers to a man of wealth, status, and influence, and can carry connotations of self-interest and exploitation of those below him.

On the question of Christian teachings on wealth accumulation, a majority of respondents felt that the teachings of their churches supported the creation and accumulation of wealth. However, respondents indicated that religious leaders encouraged those with more wealth to provide financial assistance to the poor if they can.[91]

Faith Lugazia also noted the strong emphasis on community in neo-Pentecostal churches, in contrast to her own Lutheran background.[92] Her experience is that neo-Pentecostal churches have caused great upheaval in mainline churches and argues that this is in part because they better understand and appeal to Tanzanians as Africans.[93] Calling on Lutherans to learn from this she concludes:

> Should it happen that a Lutheran decides to join Neo-Pentecostalism, [let it] be due to other personal reasons but not to seek the Holy Spirit who is currently claimed to be absent in the Tanzanian Lutheran church.[94]

When it comes to prosperity teaching in Tanzania, a family resemblance is evident, primarily in a positivity towards wealth creation and a community orientation. This study will add to this growing body of knowledge, seeking to understand how the women of TAFES fit into this theological family.

2.3 Effects of Prosperity Theology

Having seen that prosperity theology orients itself towards wealth creation and community, it is time to consider what the literature reveals about the capacity of prosperity theology to achieve this. Whether this capacity is achieved by prosperity theology is a significant preoccupation of the literature, along with scholarship which assesses the integrity of prosperity theology as a Christian movement. It is therefore to the literature regarding prosperity theology's effects on discipleship, development, and women that I now turn.

---

91. Kipacha, Dugbazah, and Mesaki, "Religious Teachings and Development," 120.
92. Lugazia, "Towards an African Inculturation," 16.
93. Lugazia, 60.
94. Lugazia, 233.

2.3.1 Effects on Discipleship

Theology is a driver for discipleship. What we believe about God and ourselves influences how we live our lives. A number of scholars have seen the prosperity gospel as working against the life of Christian discipleship. For example, pastor-theologian Ken Mbugua calls it a false gospel which has turned Christians into idolators and he is joined by fellow Kenyan Michael Otieno Maura who believes it motivates people to pursue "worldly success, happiness, and fulfilment in this short life."[95] Similarly, Nigerian Seventh-Day Adventist Efe Ehioghae argues that the prosperity gospel leads to "indulgence of the flesh," giving "the impression that no Christian should experience suffering, whether it be material or otherwise."[96] If he is correct, the stakes are high, for "the cross which stands at the centre of Christianity is a symbol of suffering and sacrifice" and prosperity gospel denigrates it.[97]

Indeed, the prosperity gospel has been accused of creating selfish, self-serving Christians. Gbote and Kgatla see the prosperity gospel as the embodiment of greed, and, with Mboya, believe it misses relationship with God in favour of what the believer can get out of him, and is more about receiving than giving.[98] In their view, the prosperity gospel is intemperate, with no emphasis on contentment, abstinence, or self-denial.[99] Nigerian Innocent Aguwuom is more measured, admitting that there is:

> No doubt that Pentecostal-Charismatic Christianity is breeding a good number of saints, good Christian women and men, whose spiritual quests are earnest and honest. These are making some change in the society.[100]

Nevertheless, he sees this difference as far outweighed by corruption, supported by the extravagant wealth of Pentecostal preachers.[101] However, Anderson considers it an "oversimplified and patronising idea that "prosperity" churches in Africa are led by unscrupulous manipulators greedy for

---

95. Maura, Mbewe, and Mbugua, *Prosperity? Seeking the True Gospel*, 36.
96. Ehioghae, "Prosperity Gospel," 31–46.
97. Ehioghae, 39.
98. Gbote and Kgatla, "Prosperity Gospel," 9; Mboya, "Gift Challenges," 38.
99. Soothill, *Gender, Social Change*, 40; Obadare, "'Raising Righteous Billionaires,'" 5.
100. Aguwuom, "'Everything Is Permissible,'" 72.
101. Aguwuom, 70.

wealth and power," arguing that this "doesn't account for the increasing popularity of these [Newer Pentecostal Churches] with educated and responsible people, who continue to give financial support and feel that their needs are met there."[102] Such a comment is pertinent to this study in which participants are university educated and leaders in their communities. This study seeks to shed light on these "educated and responsible people" and their theology of prosperity, including their relationship to the prosperity gospel.

While Ghanaian Ben-Willie Golo sees the prosperity gospel existing hand in hand with individualism, selfishness, and profligate consumption, at a local level there is evidence of wealth being put to different use.[103] Asamoah-Gyadu's study of Ghanaian megachurch pastor Mensa Otabil found that he teaches that money is given to those who are righteous *to be used for good purposes*.[104] According to Zimbabwean Lovemore Togarasei, those who receive are encouraged to be generous givers, though he acknowledges the potential for ulterior motives.[105] The churches Deborah James studied in South Africa and Kenya also taught about providing for the needs of the less well-off, including the poor and those suffering from HIV/AIDS.[106] While Lindhardt's interviewees did believe that God would respond to their tithes by making them prosperous, they did not see these as part of an exchange relationship, since the income already belonged to God. Their self-perception was not of selfishness, but of fulfilment of an obligation and a moral commitment to refrain from robbing God of what is his.[107] They spoke of waiting patiently for God to act in his time, a teaching which is advocated by itinerant Tanzanian preacher Christopher Mwakasege too.[108] While ethicist Douglas Hicks warns against viewing God as "contractually bound," there may be greater nuances that need attention, such as how cultural ideas of patronage play out both in prosperity teaching and in the Bible.[109]

---

102. Anderson, "The Newer Pentecostal?," 167–84.

103. Golo, "Africa's Poverty," 366–84.

104. See Asamoah-Gyadu's discussion of Mensa Otabil in Asamoah-Gyadu, *African Charismatics*, 206.

105. Togarasei, "The Pentecostal Gospel," 347.

106. James, "New Subjectivities," 33–50.

107. Lindhardt, "More than Just Money," 51.

108. Lindhardt, 58, 60; Hasu, "World Bank & Heavenly Bank," 679–92.

109. Hicks, "Prosperity, Theology and Economy," Kindle edition, 224–38.

The prosperity gospel has its well-publicised excesses particularly among its leaders. I shall refer to this form as the profligate prosperity gospel. However, it may not be representative of how adherents at a grassroots level see their own leader or church or experience prosperity teaching. While much attention has been given to a profligate prosperity gospel and its leaders in both scholarship and the media, there has been comparatively little study given to the grassroots and how prosperity is understood by ordinary people. This research seeks to contribute to this paucity.

Pentecostal theologian Frank D. Macchia argues:

> If [a] prosperity message does not reduce the gospel to personal prosperity or make material prosperity the central core of its message, there is potential for viewing it as a legitimate contextualisation of the gospel message rather than as a heretical accommodation of the gospel to the larger cult of personal prosperity.[110]

Macchia allows here for the diversity of prosperity teaching, which I have also been emphasizing in showing the preoccupation of scholars with a generalized "prosperity gospel," often to the detriment of exploring the nuances of prosperity teaching as it is exists in local communities. If indeed the "saints" Aguwuom mentions do exist in prosperity gospel churches, it is worth asking whether prosperity theologies play a part in discipleship, and if so, in what ways.[111]

2.3.2 Effects on Development

Questions as to the efficacy of the prosperity gospel carry weight not only for the integrity of Christian faith but also because of the context of poverty throughout Africa. Writing of a Malawian context, American Seventh-Day Adventist Gorden Doss worried that it is "cruel to committed Christians whose poverty persists, because it implies that they are people of little faith and low spiritual maturity," and can be "arrogant and self-congratulatory

---

110. Macchia, "A Call," Kindle edition, 232.

111. McKinnon suggests that the theological concept of *shalom* may interact with these kinds of prosperity theology; several African scholars also raise the language of *Ubuntu* with regard to prosperity, which is worth investigation. McKinnon, "On Being Charismatic," 268, 292; Mashau and Kgatle, "Prosperity Gospel," 1–8; Ngwobia, Kambale, and Ngomo, "Misleading Theologies of Wealth," 227.

when more prosperous people preach it to less prosperous ones."[112] Meanwhile Nigerians Ehioghae and Ageboyin, together with Kenyan Mbugua, and Paul Gifford contrast the extravagance of the lifestyles of prosperity preachers, exemplified in their use of private jets, with the poverty of those to whom they are preaching.[113] However, accusations of prosperity preachers exploiting the poor lose their resonance at a local level.[114] When it came to the "ordinary pastors," James observed in South Africa and Kenya, and Haynes in Zambia, lifestyles were far more modest even though pastors taught fervently on wealth accumulation as God's will and blessing.[115] Thus Asamoah-Gyadu contends that the flamboyance of some prosperity gospel leaders is "just one side of the story."[116]

The other dimension in the prosperity gospel's role in development is the empowerment it brings, making it what Schliesser calls a long-neglected player in discussions of poverty alleviation.[117] This neglect has been due to a disconnect between the academic and grassroots levels. Heuser's survey from 2016 acknowledges a range of responses to the prosperity gospel at a local level even while seeing academic research as unanimously doubtful about its social capacity.[118] Indeed, Nigerian O. A. Dada casts the prosperity gospel as a delusion on the grounds that adherents' economic status was unchanged.[119] Meyer concurs that it cannot offer efficient remedies against economic misery on a large scale, and South African biblical scholar Ntozakhe Simon Cezula follows her.[120] However, Nigerian scholar Afeosimeme Adogame warns this focus on change at a statistical level may obscure development as experienced

---

112. Doss, "A Malawian Christian Theology," 148–52.
113. Ehioghae, "Prosperity Gospel," 32; Ageboyin, "A Rethinking of Prosperity," 75; Gifford, "The Development and Political," 87; Maura et al., *Prosperity?*, 55.
114. Cezula, "Reading the Bible," 131–53.
115. James, "New Subjectivities," 40; Haynes, "Pentecostalism and the Morality," 123.
116. Asamoah-Gyadu, "'Get up,'" 337–54.
117. Schliesser, "On a Long Neglected," 359.
118. Heuser, "Charting African Prosperity Gospel," 6.
119. Gifford, "Expecting Miracles," 22; Dada cited in Togarasei, "The Pentecostal Gospel," 343.
120. Cezula, "Reading the Bible," 146; Meyer, "Christianity in Africa," 447–74.

by ordinary people.[121] Kalu also suspects that positive grassroots change is not necessarily reflected by statistics.[122]

The economic fate of countries is complex, and Adogame favours a case-by-case basis as more accurate than making generalisations. For his part, Adogame offers several examples of Pentecostal churches that are involved in AIDS education, earthquake relief and drug rehabilitation programs.[123] Similar examples abound. Canadian researcher Elsie Lewison, whose fieldwork took place in East Africa, identifies a substitute education system in Pentecostal churches as ambitious young people who were not able to continue with their education listen to sermons which adopt aspects of a formal university lecture, or use the language and tools of the business world.[124] Indeed, Marshall, Maxwell and Togarasei all include details of employment and education opportunities provided by Pentecostal churches in addition to the promotion of lifestyle choices that support industry.[125] Until the statistical level and the grassroots are able to be integrated, the data will remain inconclusive as to the economic effects of the prosperity gospel.[126] This study does not attempt such a feat; instead, it contributes to the data on the grassroots. It also does not attempt an outside assessment of the effects of the prosperity gospel on development; instead, it asks how TAFES women see prosperity and its implications for development.

As scholarship has tended towards asking if the prosperity gospel "works," with inconclusive results, scholars have theorized the path to modernity in Africa and the potential of the prosperity gospel to bring this about. In the early twentieth century, Max Weber argued that the economic expansion of early industrial society was nurtured by the Protestant Work Ethic and so scholars have debated whether the prosperity gospel is sufficiently modern

---

121. Adogame, "African Christianities," 1–11.

122. Kalu, *African Pentecostalism*, 215, referring to Bernstein, "Flying under South Africa's Public Radar: The Growth and Impact of Pentecostals on a Developing Country." A paper presented at the 'Spirit in the World' Symposium, University of Southern California, October 4–7, 2006.

123. Adogame, "African Christianities," 8–9.

124. Lewison, "Pentecostal Power," 31–54. Maxwell also notes a "business culture" in these churches. Maxwell, "'Delivered from the Spirit?," 362.

125. Marshall, "Power in the Name," 21–37; Maxwell, "'Delivered from the Spirit?," 353; Togarasei, "The Pentecostal Gospel," 347.

126. Chesnut, "Prosperous Prosperity," Kindle edition, 219–220.

in its outlook to similarly midwife economic growth in Africa.[127] Gifford conceives of the prosperity gospel's promotion of determination and perseverance as evidence of modernity in Pentecostalism. Yet, he also notes the emphasis on divine over human agency, and wonders which of these strands may be more determinative.[128] In doing so, he eclipses any attempt at an African modernization with an expectation that any modernization will follow the same process as Western modernization.[129] While Pentecostalism may share modern traits such as individualism and an entrepreneurial spirit with Western modernism, it does not follow that these necessitate abandoning an enchanted worldview. There is a possibility of "individualization 'African style'" as Belgian anthropologist Pierre-Joseph Laurent says, which transforms social ties and can bring an enormous amount of change without requiring the "disenchantment of the world."[130] Thus, Meyer can argue that Pentecostalism entails a kind of conversion to modernity—breaking with individual and collective pasts, and connecting globally—while Marshall-Fratani cautions that this autonomy does not imply a secular subject.[131] It is an alternative modernity and it would be a theological misstep to see this modernity as implying a break from an enchanted worldview.[132]

If an enchanted worldview is part of the prosperity gospel's modernity, a theological dimension is an asset when discussing the prosperity gospel's capacity to contribute to development. In 2012, Asamoah-Gyadu and Hasu both made studies of the Ghanaian prosperity megachurch preacher Mensa Otabil, who emphasises "hard work and the application of business principles to achieve success in life."[133] With his teaching that "underdevelopment is caused by human decisions" he may seem like he is downplaying a theological dimension.[134] However, the opposite is true. Instead, Otabil re-enchants the secular workplace, teaching in Hasu's account, that:

---

127. Comaroff, "Pentecostalism, Populism," 42.
128. Gifford, "Expecting Miracles," 22.
129. Balcomb, "Disenchanting Pentecostalism," 22–38.
130. Laurent, "Transnationalisation and Local Transformations," 272.
131. Marshall-Fratani, "Mediating the Global," 286; Meyer, "Commodities and the Power," 751–76.
132. van den Toren, "African Neo-Pentecostalism," 112–113.
133. Asamoah-Gyadu, "Learning to Prosper," 64–86.
134. Hasu, "Prosperity Gospels," 75.

> God is a working God; his work produces results, he is a producing God, he is a creative God, he is a God who does things. And man has been created in his image, as a working and creating man.[135]

Here, knowing God's activity in the world animates industry. Justice Arthur's 2017 study of Otabil shows that this includes social development projects and a broader vision for the good of society.[136] Far from being what Arthur calls "a pie-in-the-sky model,"[137] this enchantment drives the Christian towards the present day. Asamoah-Gyadu sees in Mensa Otabil's biblical prosperity series an affirmation that God is active in the adherent's life, even though they experience a life of poverty.[138] Similarly, Lindhardt found his interviewees to have what he considered to be "rather realistic expectations concerning their own future economic prosperity,"[139] while in Lewison's study, future economic success gave adherents "assurance and confidence in their personality and agency today."[140] This identity change, wrought in an enchanted world, has implications for development. Dena Freeman comes to what she suggests is a somewhat surprising conclusion: "That Pentecostal churches are often more effective change agents than are development NGOs," for complex reasons, including their ability to bring about "personal transformation and empowerment."[141] In the case of Otabil and those who are influenced by him, such as the Tanzanian *Efatha* church Hasu studied, the path to development may have recognisable elements of Western modernity but it takes on its own shape as well, most notably, including an enduring enchantment of the world. As Kenyan Kyama Mugambi says in his history of African urban Pentecostalism in Nairobi, it is able to be both "enchanted" and pragmatic.[142] This study's intentional theological attention to the theme of prosperity seeks to contribute to understanding this dynamic.

---

135. Hasu, 75
136. Arthur, "Prosperity Theology(ies)," 401–19.
137. Arthur, 418.
138. Asamoah-Gyadu, *African Charismatics*, 224.
139. Lindhardt, "More than Just Money," 42.
140. Lewison, "Pentecostal Power," 51.
141. Freeman, "The Pentecostal Ethic," 3.
142. Mugambi, *A Spirit of Revitalization*, 291.

A danger of prioritizing grassroots change in discussions of development is that global forces like capitalism are backgrounded, even though they also affect the grassroots and arguably disadvantage them disproportionately.[143] Indeed, scholars are generally agreed that the prosperity gospel has a congenial relationship with capitalism.[144] However, Togarasei, despite his focus on the local, is not naïve, recognizing the business orientation of the Western free market as a possible contributor to poverty in Africa.[145] However, his concern is not in overhauling a world system but on empowering Africans:

> Although a lot needs to be done by Pentecostals in terms of actions for poverty alleviation, I am convinced that if Africa is to conquer poverty, we need such a positive mindset. With a history of slavery and colonialism behind us, we need a message that underlines our humanity and our equality with all other races and colours. We need to be made to believe in ourselves and graduate from the donor mentality.[146]

Similarly, South African theological educator Nelus Niemandt acknowledges that the prosperity gospel aligns with consumerist ideology, such that it sanctifies rather than "challeng[es] the colonial power matrix."[147] However, in its local expression, Niemandt sees prosperity gospel as having the capacity to deconstruct coloniality, because, in Kalu's words, it encourages "the individual to fight back, to refuse to accept defeat, want, failure, pessimism, or negativity."[148]

Evidence is starting to emerge regarding this kind of agency at a systemic level in the progressive Pentecostal movement. While the progressive Pentecostal movement has been accused of being "simply a tool of capitalist ideology," because "it helps create sober, hardworking, honest employees," Miller and Yamamori argue that it does seek change in systems though

---

143. Comaroff and Comaroff, "Ethnography on an Awkward Scale," 147–79.
144. Mashau and Kgatle, "Prosperity Gospel," 2; Methula, "Decolonising the Commercialisation," 1–7; Meyer, "Christianity in Africa," 454; Heuser, "Charting African Prosperity Gospel Economies," 4.
145. Togarasei, "The Pentecostal Gospel," 345.
146. Togarasei, 347.
147. Niemandt, "The Prosperity Gospel," 215.
148. Niemandt, 217; Kalu, *African Pentecostalism*, 214.

perhaps not in ways that Westerners immediately recognize.[149] Progressive Pentecostals "seek to build alternative institutions rather than overturn existing ones," preferring a "trickle-up" model of social change.[150] If this seems naïve, Miller and Yamamori respond that while Westerners are more used to thinking of liberation in terms of confrontation, "the imagery of Pentecostals tends to be organic in tone, emphasizing harmony and purity."[151] This imagery overlaps significantly with the values and morality of African Traditional Religion which gives yet another reason to explore the theological landscape in which prosperity theology functions, as this study seeks to do.

2.3.3 Effects for Women

Women are estimated to make up a majority of Christians worldwide and in Africa, such that Dana Robert argues World Christianity can be analysed as a women's movement.[152] They also make up the majority of Christians in Tanzania.[153] Given the rise of neo-Pentecostalism and the presence of strong charismatic expressions of faith across the spectrum of denominations in Tanzania, women must not be overlooked as significant adherents to prosperity theologies.[154] However, scholarship related to women and prosperity has largely centred on examining their place within these churches and wondering at the sociological appeal of the prosperity gospel to them.

Some of the most prominent women in the prosperity gospel movement are pastors' wives. Fatokun gives an impressive list of women leaders in neo-Pentecostal churches in West Africa including Sam Amaga of Foundation Faith Church, Faith Oyedepo of Winners Chapel, Bimbo Odukoya of Foundation of Life Bible Church in Lagos, Funke-Nelson Adetuberu of By Faith Ministry International Churches, and Deola Ojo of Grace Family Church Ibadan. However, his claim that women therefore experience equal footing with men in neo-Pentecostal churches is undermined by his reference to these women as "help-mates to their husbands in co-running churches/

---

149. Miller and Yamamori, *Global Pentecostalism*, 213.
150. Miller and Yamamori, 214.
151. Miller and Yamamori, 215.
152. Robert, "World Christianity," 180.
153. Zurlo, *Global Christianity*, 286.
154. Zurlo, 285.

ministries."[155] British scholar Jane Soothill gives the example of Francisca Duncan-Williams, the wife of pastor Nicholas Duncan-Williams, who enjoyed considerable influence over women's ministries at Christian Action Faith Ministries, describing her as a "big woman."[156] However, Soothill argues that her authority was not sustainable outside of her relationship with Nicholas Duncan-Williams since she was ejected from the church and largely vilified in press coverage and by her own children following her divorce.[157] Similarly, Agadjanian found that wives of congregation leaders were typically identified according to their husband's role. Though this afforded them considerable influence, they were always quick to stress full harmony with their husband, agreement with his decisions and actions, and his headship over them.[158]

There are some examples of women who have founded neo-Pentecostal churches. Tanzanian Nandera Mhando and her colleagues examined two such women in Dar Es Salaam finding that they legitimized their leadership through recognizable Pentecostal practice, offering spiritual power to the congregants, an air of mystery, the use of titles and other displays of pomp, and charity work.[159] More common is for women to create somewhat parallel spaces within the neo-Pentecostal movement. When Kenyans Elizabeth Wahome, Judy Mbugua, and Margaret Wanjiru, and Nigerian Busola Olatu found themselves limited either by leadership structures that preferred males or by a neglect of issues pertinent to women, they started their own ministries.[160] Mwaura and Parsitau argue that the proliferation of groups like these feminizes the landscape of neo-Pentecostalism; even if a church is male-dominated, groups like these influence the women who are in those churches, and speak to them.[161] However, little attention has been given to the theology of these women or indeed the theology of women prosperity teachers more generally. The prosperity movement itself may emphasize the big man, but just as this does not stop women from teaching, it ought not define the limits

---

155. Fatokun, "Women and Leadership," 193–205.
156. Soothill, *Gender, Social Change*, 137–180.
157. Soothill, 119.
158. Agadjanian, "Women's Religious Authority," 982–1008.
159. Mhando, Maseno, Mtata, and Senga, "Modes of Legitimation," 319–33.
160. Deacon and Parsitau, "Empowered to Submit," 1–17; Mwaura and Parsitau, "Gendered Charisma," 123–46; Olademo, "New Dimensions," 62–74.
161. Mwaura and Parsitau, "Gendered Charisma," 14

of theological exploration. Women are teaching prosperity; this study aims to contribute to the dearth of scholarship on this topic by asking, since women are teaching about prosperity, what are TAFES women teaching about it?

Attention given to the sociological appeal of the prosperity gospel to women implies the reality of women as theological agents in their own right, giving credence to such a study as this. In Soothill's study, most women denied that they were attracted by the offer of empowerment, instead citing fervent prayer and the happiness it brings as the factor that drew them to prosperity-teaching churches.[162] However, in general the literature is oriented towards sociological rather than theological agency. British scholar Charlotte Spinks argues that while it may seem logical that the neo-Pentecostal movement would attract women because it gives them a way to escape from the marginalization of patriarchal societies, it is the relevance of the message to their socio-economic aspirations that women find attractive.[163] Professor of religion Rosalind Hackett highlights the entrepreneurial and professional skills extolled in neo-Pentecostal organizations, even as she critiques their emphasis on women as "helpers" rather than a more radical message of equality.[164] Meanwhile Botswanan Musa Dube's argument that women's oppression has been dependent on denying them material wealth, finds an answer in neo-Pentecostalism which gives women a measure of economic independence.[165] The building block of the kind of agency Spinks, Hackett, and Dube note is the dignity afforded to women in meetings. Feeling affirmed and hearing empowering Christian messages gives women the power to confront the socio-cultural ills that threaten their day to day well-being, such that the neo-Pentecostal movement can become a source of liberation.[166] Deacon and Parsitau concur that experience in a neo-Pentecostal church "leads to a valuing of the self in relation to God and others that increases women's autonomy and undermines patriarchal public culture."[167] However, these analyses largely examine agency while ascribing only a minor complementary role to theology.

---

162. Soothill, "The Problem," 82–99.
163. Spinks, "Panacea or Painkiller?," 21–25.
164. Hackett, "Women, Rights Talk," 245–59.
165. Dube, "Between the Spirit," 1–7.
166. Musau, *The African Woman*, 13.
167. Deacon and Parsitau, "Empowered to Submit," 15.

While much of the literature has concentrated on the roles open to women or the functions they perform, much less attention has been given to their own theology. Perhaps this is because it is assumed their theology can be read from their actions, in what Gabaitse terms "the unarticulated Pentecostal hermeneutic."[168] Deacon and Parsitau, and Soothill give some interaction with the topics covered in women's teaching, but this is largely in the service of analysing gender roles and assessing the liberative extent of the teaching. Thus, arguments can be advanced about what the roles of women are, and how the neo-Pentecostal movement contributes to women's empowerment, but a theological study of their teaching has not been undertaken. While there is research about what contributes to women's empowerment, a crucial missing element is how women themselves define prosperity. In the preoccupation with women's empowerment, treating their theology as worthy of study in its own right has been neglected. I submit that this is a way in which even feminists have marginalized the voices of women. Their lens has been interested in the position of women, but less on their words. Nevertheless, the above discussion points to women having their own reasons for pursuing the theology they do, and this expression of agency cannot be ignored. Thus, a different angle is worth considering, moving the discussion away from asking, "does this teaching empower women?" and towards "what are these women teaching about prosperity?"

2.4 Conclusion

Whether in defining prosperity gospel or assessing its effects on Christian discipleship or development, scholarship has tended to describe prosperity gospel with overviews. However, these broad overviews have been critiqued by how prosperity plays out at a local level. There is growing evidence that at the grassroots, prosperity teachings exist that do not resemble the prosperity gospel as it has been known, with its connotations of extravagant wealth and distorted theology. This study contributes to the budding scholarship focusing on the grassroots, picking up on demographic features and methodological approaches that are currently under-researched.

---

168. Gabaitse, "Pentecostal Hermeneutics," 1–12.

First, in terms of demography, this research cohort is interdenominational in contrast to former approaches which have focused on individual churches or denominations. It is also made up entirely of respected, educated people, not the classic poor or undereducated adherents often associated with the prosperity gospel. Additionally, being made up exclusively of women, the cohort of the present study deviates decisively from the demographic of male preachers often thought to define the prosperity movement in Africa.

Second, though there has been much interest in the prosperity gospel, this study is about a theology of prosperity without assuming it to be the prosperity gospel as it has formerly been understood. Using a post-Giffordian paradigm, it seeks to work inductively and at a highly localised level. After forming a localised picture of TAFES women's prosperity theology, this image may be contributed to and located within the broader landscape of prosperity teaching, including the prosperity gospel. The contribution of this study is recognised not as a summary of the full image of prosperity theology, but as a formerly missing fragment of the picture.

Third, this study makes a unique contribution to the current literature in that it is expressly and unapologetically theological. While many studies have sought to explain the prosperity gospel sociologically or practically, this study seeks to understand prosperity teaching in terms of its theological influences and motivations.

CHAPTER 3

Methodology

3.1 Introduction

This study is qualitative in nature, critical realist in epistemology, ethnographic in method, theological in content, and feminist in scope. At the outset it is worth briefly defining each of these aspects. The aim of doing so is to outline the parameters of the research rather than to suggest that these have been exclusively or strictly adhered to. As Bell and Waters point out, researchers have flexibility to move as the research requires.[1]

3.1.1 Qualitative Research

Qualitative research arose out of an understanding that propositional and positivist approaches give little insight into subjective understandings of the world and indeed may marginalise certain perspectives.[2] Though there is a broad spectrum of qualitative research, there is nevertheless a consensus that, "qualitative research is a naturalistic, interpretative approach concerned with understanding the meanings which people attach to phenomena (actions, decisions, beliefs, values etc.) within their social worlds," that is, it is concerned with how people perceive the world.[3] Rather than seeking to prove a

---

1. Bell and Waters, *Doing Your Research Project*, 23.
2. Snape and Spencer, "Foundations of Qualitative Research," 2–23; Bernard, *Research Methods in Anthropology*, Kindle edition, loc.201; Cameron and Duce, *Researching Practice in Ministry*, Kindle edition, loc.834.
3. Snape and Spencer, "Foundations of Qualitative Research," 3; Bell and Waters, *Doing Your Research Project*, 9.

hypothesis, qualitative research sets out to explore a research problem, generating data in the process of research. In qualitative research, this data takes the forms of words, images and observations which can then be analysed.[4]

3.1.2 Critical Realism

Qualitative research can be undertaken from multiple epistemological perspectives including critical realism, which emphasises that "everyone is coming from somewhere."[5] A critical realist epistemology rejects a relativist ontology that suggests that objective reality does not exist. However, critical realism simultaneously holds to epistemic relativism, that is, that we can only know the objective reality that exists from our own perspectives. However, this does not dismiss the need for critical interaction and evaluation.[6] The interaction with Christian theology will be explored more fully below but it must be stated that critical realism is entirely appropriate for a Christian researcher, because it recognizes that as human beings, we only ever know in part. Unlike God, we are limited by our context and our fallibility, and yet we can seek to understand God's world, believing that we can know in truth, however fragmented or limited. The incarnated son Jesus himself was limited by his time and culture yet was able to speak truth; we have his Spirit who enables us to do the same.[7] This same Spirit that seeks truth also teaches us humility and love, guiding epistemological principles of critical realism. Furthermore, the impetus in critical realism to question existing assumptions by being open to other perspectives coheres with New Testament images of the body of Christ and reconciliation of peoples.[8] To build on the imagery of 1 Corinthians 12, a body can experience the world through different senses. For example, a nose smells a flower, and an eye sees it, while hands hold it, and fingers caress its textures. The flower is real and each of these body parts has a different perspective which contributes to the body's overall understanding of the flower. In the same way, different parts of Christ's body, the global

---

4. Creswell, *Educational Research*, 19.
5. Cameron and Duce, *Researching Practice in Ministry*, loc.834.
6. Archer et. al., "What Is Critical Realism?"
7. Kraft, *Anthropology for Christian Witness*, 92.
8. Cameron and Duce, *Researching Practice in Ministry*, loc.834.

church, can contribute their perspectives, and these can be received by other parts of the body as a gift.

3.1.3 Ethnographic Methods

Ethnography literally means "a description of people," and it seeks to do so in their own context.[9] Angrosino argues that it is both a science and an art and emphasises that it "deals with people in a collective sense" rather than individuals.[10] Moschella defines it as, "at its heart, a listening practice" which requires the researcher to cease being the expert and become a learner.[11] This deep listening is augmented by collection methods which triangulate the conclusions, in this case, participant observation, semi-structured interviews, and focus groups.[12] It seeks to suspend judgement in favour of maintaining curiosity in pursuit of deeper understanding.[13] It is field-based, long term and personalised, which makes it embodied and allows it to be multi-factorial.[14] The researcher is literally there in context, both affecting and being affected by the field. She therefore cannot pretend objectivity and is required instead to reflect deeply on herself, both how her own background affects her perceptions and how she is being changed by what she is experiencing.[15]

The grounded theory approach developed by Glaser and Strauss in the 1960s seeks to generate theory from data without preconceptions or agendas.[16] Despite its commitment to data, it can fall into abstractions and Charmaz has innovated it in light of this to bring an emphasis on views, values, beliefs and even language of the participants.[17] Her innovation therefore provides a basis for grounded theory to examine theological views not only practice. I followed a grounded theory approach here insofar as I began with research questions rather than a hypothesis and have sought to be grounded in and

---

9. Angrosino, *Doing Ethnographic and Observational Research*, Kindle edition, loc.208; Bell and Waters, *Doing Your Research Project*, 17.
10. Angrosino, *Doing Ethnographic and Observational Research*, loc.485.
11. Moschella, *Ethnography as Pastoral Practice*, 141–2.
12. Angrosino, *Doing Ethnographic and Observational Research*, loc.498.
13. Moschella, *Ethnography as Pastoral Practice*, 143.
14. Angrosino, *Doing Ethnographic and Observational Research*, loc.498.
15. Bennett, *Your MA in Theology*, 55; Moschella, *Ethnography as Pastoral Practice*, 142.
16. Bell and Waters, *Doing Your Research Project*, 18; Creswell, *Educational Research*, 423.
17. Bell and Waters, *Doing Your Research Project*, 20; Creswell, *Educational Research*, 429.

form my theories from the data. However, having lived in Tanzania and interacted with TAFES for seven years before beginning the research, I did have some ideas about what I would find. In particular, I had a pre-defined purpose to this research: to honour the women I was researching. I believed that this could be achieved by bringing attention to their theology as I had come to believe that it was sophisticated and well suited to their context. On one hand, this kind of agenda does not fit neatly within a grounded theory approach because it has its own bias; on the other hand, it is well suited to Charmaz's constructivist grounded theory approach because of its appreciative view of the participants.

3.1.4 Theological Content

This research is explicitly theological in that it seeks to understand a theology, that of TAFES Associate women. My interest is not primarily sociological or anthropological, but theological and ethnographic methods are a tool to this end. Such an approach is not isolated: as Joel Robbins notes, "the anthropology of Christianity is well established as one of the major trends in the 21st-century discipline."[18] However, Robbins also laments that anthropology of Christianity cannot reckon adequately with its theology because of its unfamiliarity with Christianity tradition and thought.[19] This thesis is one attempt at filling this gap. Indeed, it is pressing to engage theologically because, as Sarita Gallagher points out, "the Church of Latin America, Asia, and Africa has birthed a vibrant theological discussion that is contextual, engaged with current issues of injustice, poverty, and materialism, and is biblically grounded," and thus worthy of more than "a marginal hearing."[20] This thesis seeks to do so, engaging the TAFES women as theological discussion partners. My task is therefore not only to record or observe these women's theology but to engage it as a theology in its own right, that is, as a part of a historical and global Christian movement. The ethnographic data thus becomes theological data; just as one can research a theological aspect of Calvin's Institutes, this is research is about the theology of TAFES women.

---

18. Robbins, "World Christianity," 15–37.
19. Robbins, 24.
20. Gallagher, "The Elephant in the Room," 108–25.

3.1.5 Feminist Scope

Feminist research is a somewhat contested term. As Brooks and Hesse-Biber say, "just as we cannot reduce all women to one group with a uniform experience, race, class, or culture, there is no one single method, methodology, or epistemology that informs feminist research."[21] However, historically, feminist research has illuminated women's experiences and views,[22] often previously invisible, such that feminist researchers have been, in Nicola Slee's words, "cartographers of neglected landscapes, charting maps that have not been made, until now."[23] I am not locating the feminist aspect of this research so much in its methodology as in its scope: this research deliberately privileges the voices of women, seeking to know their experiences and theology.[24] As the literature review made clear, there has been very little research into how women understand prosperity. This feminist scope is therefore justified.

This commitment to researching women supersedes any political or theoretical feminist impulse. Jennifer Randles, Lynne Gerber and Orit Avishai ask the question, "what do you do when your feminist politics clash with your empirical findings?" because this was their experience during their research.[25] Each of them worked in conservative settings which would normally be described as antifeminist, even misogynistic, at odds with a feminist agenda, where women would, in classic feminist conceptions be seen to have made Kandiyoti's "patriarchal bargain" in which there is an "agreed upon set of gendered rules within which women could negotiate for personal advantage, as long as the general system was not challenged."[26] However, "feminism's insistence on privileging the voices and interpretations of those we study encouraged us to be institutionally reflexive about how the existing theories related to our topics did not adequately explain the particularities of our cases."[27] Their feminist methodological training thus provided them with the means to listen carefully to these women's stories even though they did not appear to comply with a Western feminist agenda. In doing so, they

---

21. Brooks and Hesse-Biber, "An Invitation to Feminist Research," 2–24.
22. Brooks and Hesse-Biber, 7.
23. Slee, "Feminist Qualitative Research," 13–24.
24. Slee, 17.
25. Randles, Gerber, and Avishai, "The Feminist Ethnographer's Dilemma," 1–33.
26. Randles, Gerber, and Avishai, 11.
27. Randles, Gerber, and Avishai, 13.

were surprised to find that the situation was far more complex than they could see with "orthodox feminist interpretive frameworks" and that there were progressive elements within these conservative spaces which could not be acknowledged by those frameworks.[28] In Tanzania there has been some research into the shortfall between the United Nations' (UN) Sustainable Development Goals (SDGs) and the situation of women within Tanzanian churches.[29] However, this kind of research, which is deficit focused as it is and has an intense focus on rights-based approaches, can obscure other modes in which women operate.[30] While the UN's SDGs provide empirical data about one aspect of women's lives, they are a limited framework that is not comprehensive of women's lives. The question here is not one of comparison with men or with another standard, but of how women themselves understand and speak about prosperity. It is the focus on the women themselves and their views that make it feminist.

3.2 The Research Process

3.2.1 Selection

A sample size of twenty interviews and two focus groups was chosen for this research. Qualitative data is aimed at depth rather than breadth, so it was not necessary to interview every TAFES woman associate or even to aim for this.[31] However, it was felt that in order for it to be representative of TAFES as a whole, it was necessary for all eight regions of the TAFES national movement to be represented. These regions include Lake Zone (Mwanza and surrounds), Arusha, Kilimanjaro, Dar Es Salaam and Pwani, Morogoro, Dodoma, Iringa and Mbeya.[32] TAFES is interdenominational, and Tanzania has an histori-

---

28. Randles, Gerber, and Avishai, 25.

29. See, for example, Kategile, "The Bible and Gender Equality," 41–54; Lyimo and Tonnessen, *Empowerment and Autonomy*, Kindle edition.

30. Hodgson, *Gender, Justice*, 14.

31. Saturation rather than size is the determining factor in the adequacy of a sample. However, according to Hennink and Kaiser's recent work in medical qualitative research, sample sizes of nine to seventeen interviews or four to eight focus groups are adequate for saturation. This study's point of saturation is addressed in 3.7. Creswell, *Educational Research*, 16, 433; Blaikie and Priest, *Designing Social Research*, Kindle edition, 145; Hennink and Kaiser, "Sample Sizes for Saturation," 1–10.

32. See appendix 1 for a map of Tanzania's regions. Towards the end of the fieldwork phase, TAFES pioneered a new region in Tanga. It is not included in this study.

cally strong national identity. Therefore, no special care was taken to select women from a diversity of denominations or tribes. As expected, this diversity occurred naturally.

3.2.2 Selection Criteria

Participants were professional women who were university graduates with at least a bachelor's degree, who were involved in a TAFES fellowship during their studies and have continued to serve as TAFES Associates.[33] Associates are friends and graduates of TAFES who financially support the ministry and teach at TAFES events including student fellowships and staff trainings.

3.2.3 Research Permissions

Any researcher in Tanzania is required to obtain a research permit from the Commission of Science and Technology (COSTECH). This process requires ethics approval by the researcher's home institution, affiliation with a local institution, and permission from the associated NGO. The research permit gives permission for research to be conducted, but foreign researchers must also undertake a process with the Tanzanian Immigration Department to obtain a residence permit or equivalent as well. Some aspects of the process were opaque to me, and I consequently obtained a COSTECH research permit in January 2021 before applying for affiliation with the University of Dar Es Salaam (UDSM). This was out of order and aroused suspicion when I then needed university affiliation to get my residence permit. However, I obtained affiliation with UDSM in March 2021. My residence permit was approved in April 2021, but an IT issue meant I was unable to pick it up until August 2021. I obtained a special letter from the Immigration Department in lieu of the permit.

3.2.4 Access

In January 2021 I met with then TAFES National Director Mussa Kimaro and TAFES Deputy National Director (Campus Ministry Coordinator) Joan

---

33. It is normal in Tanzania to have multiple sources of income. For example, you may be a university law professor who practices law on the side and also runs a chicken farm. Most Christian professionals also have a ministry involvement as well, from running their own seminars to preaching at their church. They may or may not receive "thanksgiving contributions" from people who attend.

Wanjiru to put together a list of possible participants from the eight TAFES regions. There were over forty women on this list, so I deemed it sufficient to work from this list without engaging in snowballing.[34] However, when I interviewed the women, several recommended others to interview and I added them to the list. When it was time to interview the women, I sent them a Swahili WhatsApp message or SMS introducing myself and my research and asking for permission to call them to invite them to participate. Mussa also gave me a letter endorsing me to the women and asking for their cooperation, but I did not end up using it. All of the women found my explanation that I was a TAFES Associate myself sufficient and were eager to help.

3.2.5 Timeframe

I initially expected that the fieldwork component of the research would take eighteen months to two years. However, early in 2021 my husband ran into some issues with his work permit, and it became possible that we would be required to leave Tanzania by the end of the year or possibly the middle of the following year. These issues were eventually resolved later in 2021 but as we did not know that at the time, I accelerated my timetable in order to finish the interviews by the end of 2021. All interviews, focus groups, and participant observation were completed by 6 January 2022, which was when my research permit expired.

3.2.6 Preparation

Before conducting any interviews, I did a pilot interview with the wife of one of the pastors at my church in Dar Es Salaam. She is not a TAFES graduate and therefore did not meet the recruitment criteria, so I did not use this interview. However, it helped me to hone my interview questions and also gave me confidence that my Swahili was sufficient for a long, in-depth conversation.

---

34. Snowballing is a method of sampling using referrals from participants. "Once contact is made with one member of the network, that person can be asked to identify other members and their relationships." Blaikie and Priest, *Designing Social Research*, 173.

3.3 Methods of Data Collection

3.3.1 Semi-structured Interviews

A semi-structured interview follows an interview guide, with freedom to pursue leads as they come up.[35] As I developed my research guide it settled into about fifteen questions which are listed in appendix 7. Not every question was asked in every interview and the wording varied at points.[36]

I conducted twenty semi-structured interviews and made audio recordings of each. The interviews are listed in appendix 5. Participants came from the following regions: Dar/Pwani (four), Arusha (four), Lake Zone (three), Dodoma (three), Morogoro (two), Kilimanjaro (two), Mbeya (one) and Iringa (one).[37] Participants came from ten denominations and sixteen tribes. I travelled to the regions to conduct these interviews, with the exception of four interviews which were conducted at the TAFES Associates Transformers' Conference in September 2021. Some were in the home of the interviewee; others were at a neutral meeting point such as a café or the TAFES office. Modes of transport used included aeroplane, bus, *bajaji* (three-wheeled taxis), and motorbike taxi.

Interviews took between twenty-five minutes and two hours, but on average about forty-five minutes. Some were interrupted briefly by visitors or domestic responsibilities, but these were minor disruptions. With the exception of one, they were conducted in Swahili though several of the participants mixed in English words or phrases at times. The conversation flowed sufficiently and, since I am a fluent Swahili speaker, I did not need a translator.

I kept a journal of the interviews, reflecting on the responses I received and what I wanted to change. I honed my questions in this process. I found that, contrary to the prevailing wisdom of many books about how to do semi-structured interviews, my participants responded much better to questions grounded in scenarios than abstract questions. For example, better than, "Can you tell me some good prayers about prosperity?" was, "If a TAFES student comes to you and says they're about to go to church and pray for

---

35. Blaikie and Priest, loc.3693.

36. Bell and Waters note that precise wording is not as important in interviews as in other methods such as questionnaires. Bell and Waters, *Doing Your Research Project*, 179.

37. Dar/Pwani encompasses the city of Dar Es Salaam and the surrounding area. Lake Zone refers to the area around the southern shore of Lake Victoria, around Mwanza. See appendix 1 for a map.

their prosperity and they want advice about what to pray, what would you tell them?"[38] This also opened up new lines of inquiry as participants would sometimes refuse the premise of the question and say the student's question to them was misguided. Though I asked open-ended questions like, "Tell me the meaning of prosperity," and "How is a person prospered?" I generally moved away from open-ended questions because the participants responded much more enthusiastically to closed questions. For example, I asked, "Can you say, 'I have attained and now I can rest'?" Though this is a closed question, it arose out of earlier interviews where this idea came up and I found that participants did not see it as a '"yes/no" question but rather an invitation to speak at length about the ongoing process of prosperity.[39] This preference for scenario-based questions, whether narrative based or propositional, coheres deeply with African worldview. Clifton R. Clarke writes that for African peoples, theology is "deeply rooted in their personal identity and worldview. It is experienced and expressed through prayers, folktales, songs, myths, folksongs, proverbs, and riddles."[40] Theology in Africa is most easily and honestly spoken about in concrete terms like experience, scenario, story, and example; even a question about prayer cannot be answered when extracted from context. Similarly, it was not unusual for abstract questions to be answered with a story, scenario, or example.

I also added in some questions which I found myself asking frequently as follow up questions in earlier interviews, including one about contentment and one about what the opposite of prosperity is. At the end of the interview, I asked if the participant had anything else at all she wanted to share about prosperity and most of the time this resulted in a summary statement which effectively answered: "Tell me the meaning of prosperity," but was more succinct than what the participant had said in answer to that at the start of the interview.

---

38. *Mafanikio* is the Swahili word most often used when discussing prosperity. I will discuss it at length in chapter 4.

39. Bernard argues that the concern about closed questions can be overstated and that at times these kinds of directive probes are appropriate, especially in long term research such as this. Bernard, *Research Methods in Anthropology*, loc.3879.

40. Clarke, *Pentecostal Theology in Africa*, Kindle edition, loc.831.

3.3.2 Focus Groups

Two focus groups were conducted in Mwanza and Dar Es Salaam. They were each attended by seven participants; three of these fourteen also participated in an interview. I made video recordings of the focus groups so that I could easily identify who was speaking. The focus groups and participants are listed in appendix 5.

In Mwanza, the chair of the Regional Associates Committee contacted all participants, invited them to participate, followed them up, and forwarded the participant information sheets and consent forms ahead of time. For the Dar group I attained the consent of the Regional Associates Committee but since I am part of the Dar Associates, they felt it appropriate for me to contact the participants myself. I did this by sending an initial WhatsApp invitation and then following up with a phone call. I also created a WhatsApp group for communicating about the logistics and posted the forms there.

The Mwanza focus group was conducted in the upstairs room of a pub which was set aside for our exclusive use. The Dar Es Salaam focus group took place at the TAFES headquarters at Boko. A start time was set but, in both cases, only one participant was present at this time; this is not unusual in Tanzania. Both focus groups got underway about two hours after the advertised start time. Refreshments were provided.

Participants were given copies of a sheet with four statements regarding prosperity which I had heard and recorded here in Dar Es Salaam.[41] These statements were read aloud and then the women were asked to give their opinions on these statements. I planned to do very little facilitating of these groups as there are strong cultural values around hearing from everyone. This worked well in Mwanza and the group ran for about fifty mins, but the Dar group would have benefited from more direction from me. There were some strong personalities who spoke for extended periods of time and the session went for over two hours.[42] Like the interviews, both focus groups were mainly in Swahili with the odd English phrase or word thrown in.

---

41. See Appendix 8.

42. These comments were extended because of verbosity or lengthy illustrations. While these women dominated the airspace to some extent, they made a similar number of points to women who spoke more succinctly and thus are not overrepresented in the data.

The focus groups enriched the data in two ways. First, the group interaction sharpened the women's responses. They challenged each other on their views or nuanced them. Sometimes other participants would heartily agree with what another woman had said though they had not initially said it themselves. Second, the focus groups were more focused on critique. While the interviews were open-ended, and aimed at allowing the women to give their own theological constructions of prosperity, the focus groups asked them to respond to statements that others had given about prosperity. It gave me a chance to see how they exegeted these statements and what aspects of them they found pertinent. The focus groups also gave an opportunity for the women to compare and contrast their own views with statements about prosperity found in wider society.

3.3.3 Participant Observation

Throughout the year I attended seven events where TAFES women Associates were speaking and teaching. These included visits to the bereaved, training events, plenary conference speeches at Transformers' Conference, Bible studies, and seminars. These are listed in appendix 6. With the exception of Transformers' Conference, these were in Dar Es Salaam. Meanwhile I continued to be involved in TAFES Associates social media where Associates freely share their views (such as WhatsApp groups). Because of the COVID-19 pandemic (hereafter Covid), some of the women switched from regular teaching events to online Zoom meetings or used podcasts and YouTube channels to broadcast their teachings. While these did not have the same element of gathered participation, I listened along to these as well.

3.4 Ethical Considerations

Any ethnographic research brings with it an inherent power imbalance: the researcher is perceived to be the one driving the research; she is asking the questions and will be the one reporting on them. As the sole researcher, I am the only one who has seen the data and the fact that it is in Swahili diminishes the capacity for accountability. I have taken this very seriously and striven to uphold the highest levels of integrity in my interactions with the data.

In a context like Tanzania, my relationship with my participants is set against a backdrop of colonial, post-colonial, and neo-colonial factors. The participants of this research are not considered a vulnerable group. They are an elite within Tanzania, educated, relatively wealthy, and powerful within their own networks.[43] However, it was White people like me who were Tanzania's colonial rulers, including, at times, missionaries, and many missionaries continue to occupy positions of authority or teaching roles. Additionally, I am wealthier than some of the women I interviewed and educated to a higher degree than some of them. This is to some extent alleviated by the length of time I have lived in Tanzania, and my language and culture acquisition – I am "*mgeni mwenyeji*," a local foreigner. My status within TAFES is the same as or lower than those I interviewed. Several of them hold leadership positions and I do not. While I hold no official position within TAFES my husband is on the national staff team and wives are often ascribed status on account of their husbands. However, my husband is in a consultant role, existing outside of the organizational structure of TAFES. This is a privilege in its own right but also effectively removes him from having positional power over anyone in TAFES. I tried to position myself as a learner and explicitly said so to my participants. I do not think they modified their responses to align more to what they thought I wanted to hear because what I heard in the interviews aligned with what I heard in focus groups and participant observations. However, it is nevertheless a possibility.

All participants were given a participant information form prior to interviews and focus groups. These were available in English and Swahili, since for many, Swahili is an oral language and they prefer to read in English. All participants signed consent forms with many already familiar with this process from their own university experience.

Participants were not paid for their participation, but they were each given a block of chocolate at the end as a thank you gift. Imported Cadbury Dairy Milk chocolate is readily available in Dar Es Salaam where I live and in most urban centres in Tanzania. These gifts were uniformly received with surprise and great joy! I explained it as something from my culture that I wanted to share, that to thank people we give them chocolate. One woman brought a gift for me as well – a beaded necklace – and I accepted it.

---

43. Liamputtong's extensive discussion of vulnerable groups has guided my thinking here. One definition she gives of the vulnerable is those who are, "impoverished, disenfranchised, and/or subject to discrimination, intolerance, subordination, and stigma." Liamputtong, *Researching the Vulnerable*, 2–3.

3.5 The Researcher

Reflexivity is the capacity of the researcher to be aware of her own background and viewpoint and how these affect her research. It strengthens rather than undercuts the researcher's objectivity because once aware of her perspectives she is able to attempt to account for their distortions.[44] Therefore it is not only worthwhile to spend some time thinking about myself and my role as a researcher, but it is necessary.

3.5.1 The Researcher's Role

Norman Blaikie has identified six possible stances for a researcher: detached observer, empathetic observer, faithful reporter, mediator of languages, reflective partner, dialogic facilitator.[45] The *detached observer* is a pure scientist, making their observations with as little involvement or emotion as possible. The *empathetic observer* considers subjectivity integral to understanding and seeks to place themselves in the position of those being researched while the *faithful reporter* considers this only possible through being immersed in the world in which they are researching and becoming sufficiently a part of it to know it well enough to allow research participants to "speak for themselves." These first three all assume a measure of detachment, that the researcher's own perspective does not come into it. However, in seeking to report faithfully, the researcher may find herself needing to connect everyday language to social-scientific or technical language, in which case she becomes a *mediator of languages*, with the understanding that objectivity is impossible because the researcher's voice will be present somehow. The researcher may then seek to advance this role by adding an emancipatory element through being a *reflective partner*. In this case, there is a dialogic dynamic where researcher and participants conscientize each other and the researcher's own assumptions and perspectives are not only acknowledged but active. Finally, a *dialogic facilitator* returns to the desire to have participants speak for themselves and seeks to reduce their own bias by seeking a variety of local voices that produce a "polyphony" of voices.

While there are incompatibilities between each of these positions, not all of them are mutually exclusive. I reject the role of detached observer as an

---

44. Spickard, "Why Reflexive Ethnography Matters," 180–94.
45. Blaikie, *Designing Social Research*, 45.

impossibility and I am also not seeking to be emancipatory or educative of the women I am researching; though I do hope that this kind of research will bring greater dignity and respect to these women which may in turn have emancipatory results. Like the empathetic observer and faithful reporter, I want very much to see things from the perspective of the women I am researching and to communicate that faithfully. My immersion in TAFES over the past several years and in Tanzania more broadly place me in the faithful reporter category, but I see no way to make sense of this to others without some degree of mediation of language. This role of mediator exists at multiple levels for me: between the grassroots and the academy, and also between Western and majority world theologies.

I was very open with the women about my role. When I asked them to participate in their research, I narrated to each one my experience of coming to Tanzania expecting to find one thing, being surprised by what I found here, and then wanting to communicate that to others in a way they could understand so that they could see the value in what TAFES women are teaching.

3.5.2 Relationship between the Researcher and Research Participants

As a white Western woman in a country that was colonized by white, Western powers, and where neo-colonial factors continue to influence development, entertainment, politics and church life, I was conscious that there could be a perceived power imbalance between me and the research participants. However, this seemed to be of far greater concern to me than to my research participants. I have been known to several of the participants for many years and others who did not know me accepted me as a fellow Associate of TAFES. My involvement in the organization over many years was therefore an asset, allowing familiarity to mitigate other sociological factors such as ethnicity. I also dressed in a local style and conducted the interviews in Swahili which helped to decrease some cultural distance. Both of these are unusual among white people in Tanzania and are generally seen as means of honouring Tanzanians.

Without wanting to downplay any effect that my presence may have had, it is also worth noticing that the concern with power differentials was far more prominent in my estimation than it was in theirs. There are several reasons which could account for this. First is the general culture of openness and sharing in TAFES. For example, in the past it has been normal for all staff at retreats and training camps to be critiqued by their fellows on their performance and character. This has even included critique of the National Director and other senior people in the organization! In focus groups, when younger women spoke openly and boldly about their views even in the presence of their elders, it was little different to TAFES Bible study groups that they had been involved in. Second, as I noted above, these women are not a vulnerable group; treating them as such comes across as condescending. Third, while it is appropriate for me to reflect on where I am coming from and the tensions that come with that, expecting these women to also do that might be a little self-absorbed. I simply do not take up that much space in their heads! Even as we wrestle with our impact on the world, past and present, we from the West need the humility to recognize our own insignificance.

Most of the research participants lead busy lives, engaged in full-time work, caring responsibilities, running businesses and community leadership. I was conscious of taking their time, but this was largely a product of my cultural background. I was frequently invited to stay for a meal after the interview and if I tried to refuse it was insisted that I stay.

A description I often used during the research process when describing it to other people was a sense of standing on holy ground.[46] I knew that very little research of this nature had been done and felt tremendously privileged to be doing it. In addition, the theological content of the research meant that the women were sharing with me deep and guiding principles for their lives and communities. It was about what God is doing in and among them and how he has been revealing himself to them, just as he revealed himself to Moses at the burning bush (Exodus 3:1–17). I felt a great responsibility to handle this material with care and do justice to the women.

I had to contend with bias on two fronts. First, there was the bias of my own theological background that might skew my perceptions of what they were saying. Asking follow-up questions during interviews helped to clarify this as I could bring up common objections from my own theological background and have them answered. The source of my second bias was my desire to provide data that could challenge popular Western perceptions of Africa and prosperity theology. What if in the process of the research, the evidence

---

46. Slee, "Feminist Qualitative Research," 17.

supported that TAFES women's prosperity teaching was indeed superficial or unbiblical? Would I have the eyes to see it, and if I did, would I have the courage to acknowledge it if I thought it would bring them into further disrepute? I decided that I would, because I did not feel I should be the arbiter of whether these women's theologies were worthy of a greater exposure or not. These two biases warred with each other to some extent, and, I believe, guarded against one becoming dominant.

3.6 Capturing and Analysing Data

Data collection is an iterative process, with analysis occurring in the collection of the data and this analysis also affecting the research process.[47] Creswell identifies several stages in this process including collection of data, preparation, reading through, and coding for themes and descriptions.[48]

I used NVivo computer software to assist in data organization and analysis. I uploaded the recordings of the interviews and focus groups into NVivo and worked within there to transcribe, translate, and analyse. When I uploaded the interviews and focus group recordings, I gave each woman a pseudonym. Letters and numbers depersonalize participants and generic Swahili names would overlap with some of the women's names or those of other TAFES associates. Instead, I used women's names from the Bible. I felt that in doing so I was naming my participants as spiritual mothers alongside the women of the Bible, together among the great cloud of biblical witnesses (Hebrews 11). I hoped this would have the effect of both concealing their identities and capturing something of their authority as teachers of God's people.

Transcription and translation services were available through the University of Dar Es Salaam but were expensive and, in the end, unnecessary since I was capable of doing both. However, I did acquire a new skill in the process. Swahili has the same alphabet and keyboard as English but touch typing involves the muscle memory of the order in which you frequently press keys as well. This means that a common sentence starter such as "I think" will require a different succession of keys for the Swahili "*nafikiri.*" Just as in language learning, my tongue learned to construct phrases without having

---

47. Creswell, *Educational Research*, 238.
48. Creswell, 237.

to think about how to do so, and I found my fingers had to learn a new set of automatic movements and frequently used words. While I had typed in Swahili before, the kind of speed required by transcription brought a significant improvement in this area. Doing the transcription and translation myself also gave me more time with the data. Though it is painstaking work, I chose to think of it not only as a research discipline but as a spiritual discipline, cultivating habits of slowing and denying myself the ease of using a service in order to immerse myself more fully in the women's reflections about God.[49]

I encountered some issues with the format NVivo requires for audio files but was quickly able to resolve these. More laborious was NVivo's tendency to freeze during transcription, sometimes every twenty seconds. When this occurred, I took a photo of the computer screen on my phone so that I could quickly re-type the lost data instead of re-transcribing it.

After I transcribed and translated each interview, I wrote brief notes in my learning journal including novel ideas from that interview or ways this interview intersected with the others. I also used my learning journal to engage in what Creswell calls a preliminary exploratory analysis.[50] I recorded the general sense I was getting from the interviews, including ideas and hunches and possible ways of organizing the data.

I had initially planned to give each participant the entire transcript of her interview to check but decided against this as too laborious for her. For several of the women, Swahili is their preferred oral language (in which the interview was conducted) but their preferred written language is English; so reading a Swahili transcript may bring complications but giving them only the translation would not necessarily reflect what they recalled saying. Instead, I decided to send only the quotes I used from each participant's interview, supplying the Swahili and my English translation. I sent this with an offer to modify anything the participant wished.

After transcribing and translating each interview, I then coded it. I transcribed, translated and coded all of the interviews, then circled back around. On this second pass I corrected typos, listened to the interviews again and read back over the translations. In the course of this I also amended the coding and in some cases added in codes. The later interviews generated

---

49. Slee, "Feminist Qualitative Research," 20–21.
50. Creswell, *Educational Research*, 243.

more codes and I needed to see if the earlier interviews also had these ideas in them; they did, so I added in those codes. My ideas were clarified by this iterative process.

Coding is "the process of segmenting and labelling text to form descriptions and broad themes in the data."[51] Codes may apply to chunks of text or even to single words and do not have to contain the code word in them because they are primarily about the presence of a concept.[52] In line with my grounded theory approach, I coded inductively, looking for the themes that emerged from the text rather than seeking to find evidence of a hypothesis.[53] This meant that I acquired more themes as I went along. However, by about halfway through the interviews, few new codes were arising, a sign that a level of saturation had been reached. Saturation is "the subjective determination that new data will not provide any new information or insights for the developing categories."[54] Nevertheless, I continued with the interviews both for the sake of representation across TAFES and in order to further clarify the codes and my understanding. At this point then, my coding approach was somewhere between inductive and deductive.

I did not have a consistent approach to choosing codes: some codes were very specific and were later able to be subsumed as layers under particular themes; however, other codes were more general to start with and needed to be broken down later on.[55] An example of the latter is that I initially coded any Bible reference or allusion to one as "Bible verse" but later on it was helpful to see the breakdown of verses and to be able to pull all references to a particular Bible verse.

I had a working mind-map where I grouped codes to help me organize my thoughts.[56] As I came to writing, there were concepts and phrases that I found I had not coded but which I needed to engage in my discussion. I used word searches in NVivo to guide the investigation at this point. I used both English and Swahili in the coding, especially for key concepts that needed to be retained in Swahili. Word searching was only possible in English so I

---

51. Creswell, 243.
52. Bell and Waters, *Doing Your Research Project*, 239.
53. Bernard, *Research Methods in Anthropology*, loc.9130.
54. Creswell, *Educational Research*, 433.
55. Creswell, 251.
56. A version of this can be found in appendix 7: Mind-map of codes.

would use it to find the English paragraph to give me a general idea of which interview or part of an interview would be good to examine in Swahili.

These codes, generated from the empirical data and organized in a mind-map, became the structure upon which I built my chapters. For example, chapter 4 primarily deals with the "Definition" arm, including areas and features of prosperity, while chapter 5 discusses the various sources. The prominence of discipleship and holism generated chapters 6 (Discipleship) and 8 (Holism) respectively while the significance of African Traditional Religion on the "Other theologies" arm warranted chapter 7. Thus, the data collected through interviews and analysed through NVivo and Grounded Theory, generated the themes and concepts that have shaped this study.

3.7 Theological Method

This study uses ethnographic methods in pursuit of theological understanding. Significant questions have been raised about whether ethnographic methods are sufficient for theological inquiry, since, as Kate Lassiter admits, these methods rely "on the interpretation of theological doctrinal discourse by practitioners, who may confuse their own desires for revealed, true, and sacred doctrine."[57] Such concerns betray a somewhat static understanding of theology, supposing that doctrine is set and unable to be critiqued or innovated by its practitioners, but they point to fundamental differences in approach: where the ethnographer might seek to describe a theology, the theologian constructs one. It was the mother of African theology, Mercy Amba Oduyoye who famously said, "theology is something you struggle to do – not something you receive."[58]

However, Lassiter nevertheless maintains that ethnographic methods can be useful tools in the construction of theology because they teach "theology to name concretely and specifically a problem or subject of study that is grounded," and teach the value of suspending judgement in order to understand more deeply.[59] As Charles Kraft points out, the latter is a deeply

---

57. Lassiter, "Seeking Wisdom, Naming Puzzles," 1–5.

58. Oduyoye, Interview of Christina Landman with Oduyoye at World Council of Churches Meeting in Harare on 11 December 1998; cited in Landman, "Mercy Amba Ewudziwa Oduyoye," 187–204.

59. Lassiter, "Seeking Wisdom, Naming Puzzles," 4.

Christian practice and resistance to it is "indicative of our enslavement to monocultural ethnocentrism," for "God Himself has shown us that the way of patience and love is His way in such matters."[60] Esther Meek's work on epistemology characterises this hesitancy as love: "Love accords space and true otherness to the other rather than seeking to absorb it. It involves a pledge to accord space and dignity to the other."[61]

While ethnographic methods do not threaten theological integrity, Joel Robbins argues that "theological humility does not go as far as suspending judgement altogether," and that this is what sets ethnographic theology apart from pure anthropology.[62] He identifies two common approaches among theologians: those who take a theology and check it against the Bible or traditional Christian teaching, and those who ask if the theology has successfully rendered the Christian message meaningful in its context.[63] I resist the first because of its de-contextualized nature. Theology is not revelation and can only ever be understood as a human construction which takes place in a particular context.[64] I therefore favour the second but I am cautious about the language of "rendering a Christian message" because the heart of Christianity is not a message but a person: Jesus Christ of Nazareth. While Christians are certainly bearers of good news (a message), we are followers of Jesus, not subscribers to a set of propositions. I therefore subordinate doctrinal issues to discipleship taking the latter as a lens for my theological analysis and, ultimately, judgement.

In my theological discussion, I will take British practical theologian Stephen Pattison's critical conversation as a starting point:

> The basic idea here is that the student should imagine herself as being involved in a three-way conversation between (a) her own ideas, beliefs, feelings, perceptions and assumptions, (b) the beliefs, assumptions and perceptions provided by the Christian

---

60. Kraft, *Anthropology for Christian Witness*, 103.
61. Meek, *A Little Manual for Knowing*, Kindle edition, loc.268-9.
62. Robbins, "World Christianity," 29.
63. Robbins, 29–30.
64. Gallagher, "The Elephant in the Room," 110.

tradition (including the Bible) and (c) the contemporary situation being examined.[65]

Pattison's model is not constructed with ethnographic methods in mind, and it is therefore the idea of conversation rather than his distinct categories that I will adopt here. My conversation is more like a four-way conversation between (a) my own ideas, beliefs, feelings, perceptions and assumptions (reflexivity), (b) the theology held by the TAFES women, (c) their context, and (d) other Christian traditions (including the Bible). This thesis broadly follows that pattern as I devote chapter 4 to understanding the women's theology on their terms and, where possible in their own words, chapter 5 to their context (biblically, historically, culturally), and then the following concentric circles of chapters 6–8 to bringing the women's contextualized theology into conversation with other theologies and Christian traditions. The conversation I will construct is somewhat open-ended in that I resist providing what Pattison calls "eternally valid answers."[66] As Pattison points out, conversation does not imply agreement and indeed conversation may be short-circuited by a lack of honesty about this.[67] It is in the conversational tensions where our view – including our judgements – of the other has space to become more complex and sophisticated and this is my goal for the theological conversation I undertake in this study.

3.8 Conclusion

This chapter has given attention to the theoretical background of the study, the practicalities of conducting it, cross-cultural issues and reflexivity, and methods of data collection and analysis. Having formed an understanding that the study can be described as qualitative, critical realist, ethnographic, theological, and feminist, and seen how these perspectives have initially played out in the fieldwork, it is now appropriate to move on to examining the data in detail, asking, what TAFES Associate women's theology of prosperity is.

---

65. Pattison, "Some Straw for the Bricks," 135–45.
66. Pattison, 142.
67. Pattison, 140.

CHAPTER 4

Understanding *Mafanikio* Theology

4.1 Participant Demographics

Thirty-one women participated in the study in either an interview or a focus group. Seventeen did an interview only, eleven did a focus group only and three did both. They came from sixteen Tanzanian tribes and ten denominations.[1] Lutheran and Pentecostals are the two largest Protestant groups in Tanzania, and this is reflected in the participants.[2]

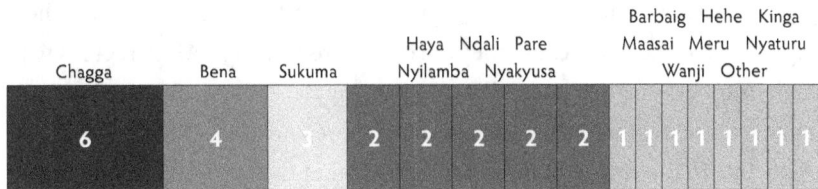

Figure 4.1 Participants by tribe[3]

---

1. Tribal breakdown was: Chagga six, Bena four, Sukuma three, Haya two, Nyakyusa two, Ndali two, Nyilamba two, Pare two, and one each from Barbaig, Hehe, Kinga, Maasai, Meru, Nyaturu, Wanji. These numbers reflect the size and mobility of the tribes in Tanzania. One participant was born into a Kenyan tribe. Denominational breakdown was Lutheran twelve, Tanzania Assemblies of God (TAG) nine, African Inland Church (AIC) two, Free Pentecostal Church of Tanzania (FPCT) two, and one each from Anglican, Catholic, Evangelical Assemblies of God Tanzania (EAGT), Moravian, Vineyard, and Pentecostal Bible Fellowship (PBF).

2. Zurlo, *Global Christianity*, 286.

3. Colour here and following illustrations indicates the number of participants, not any other grouping.

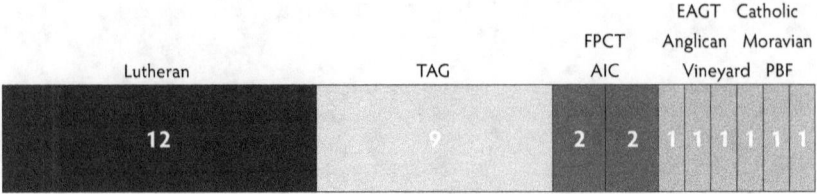

Figure 4.2 Participants by denomination

The majority of women were in the 40–49 age group (nineteen) with nine in 30–39, and two in 50–59. This reflects their status as university graduates, as many students do not finish university or establish themselves until they are at least thirty years old.[4]

Figure 4.3 Participants by age

All TAFES regions were represented in the research.[5] The overrepresentation of Dar/Pwani and Lake Zone (see chart 4.4) is because the focus groups were conducted in those regions, thus inflating the numbers. These regions were chosen because they are considered strong TAFES regions with high numbers of Associates willing to participate. Participants were taken to represent the region if they currently live there and are involved as a TAFES Associate in the region; it does not indicate that they grew up in that region or that they studied in it. Chart 4.5 indicates their undergraduate university, but several participants had studied at multiple universities: fourteen held masters degrees and two had PhDs. It is not surprising to see that over a third of participants studied their undergraduate degree in Dar/Pwani region as, prior to the proliferation of educational institutions in the early 2000s, it was

---

4. The older age of university graduates in Tanzania is due to a variety of factors including availability of funds for university study (whether from family or student loans) and bureaucratic issues which delay enrolment and graduation.

5. See Appendix 1 for a map of Tanzania's regions. Some interviews were conducted outside of the TAFES region they represented. At Transformers' Conference in Dodoma, I interviewed representatives from Mbeya, Iringa and two from Arusha.

Tanzania's educational hub and because of their age demographic many of the participants were undergraduates prior to 2000.

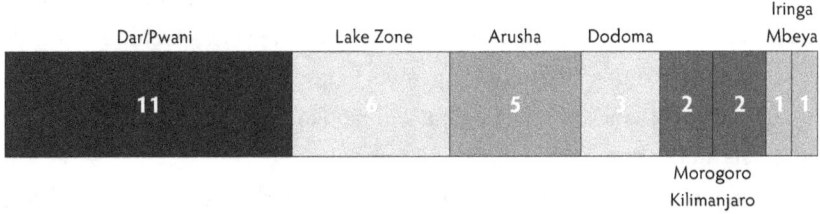

Figure 4.4 Participants by TAFES region

Figure 4.5 Participants by undergraduate TAFES region

Occupation was less straightforward. The industries represented included education (five), development (five), business (five), tertiary education (four), health or public health (four), organizational management (three), accountancy (two) and caring (two). However, these categories are loose and overlapping. Some women did not identify according to their profession. For example, I met with Ruth at her workplace, a hospital where she is on the management team, but when I asked for her occupation, she told me she was an entrepreneur as she runs multiple small businesses, as well as working in the NGO sector. Similarly, Joanna listed herself as a carer for her small children even though she works part-time at a university and runs a side-business making handicrafts. On the other hand, Priscilla came to the focus group straight from the farm but did not list herself as a farmer or even a businesswoman, preferring to identify by her career which was in development. A feature of this demographic of women is that they are juggling multiple roles. They have the agency to choose how they identify but they also feel stretched by their many roles.

4.2 Translation Notes for *Mafanikio*

In Swahili, *mafanikio* (muh-fuh-ni-KEE-oh) is the noun and *-fanikiwa* is the verb.[6] *Kufanikiwa* is the gerund and can be used in place of *mafanikio*.[7] In the standard Swahili-English dictionary, the translation for *mafanikio* is "achievement, accomplishments, success."[8] However, the verbal form *-fanikiwa* has the meaning "to succeed, prosper, to flourish." These give some sense of the semantic range of the term but a great deal more is needed in order to understand the complex usage of this term.

While "to prosper" appears as one of the possible definitions for *-fanikiwa*, it is neither the first listed nor even present in the definition for *mafanikio*. Indeed, when you ask for a straight translation of *mafanikio*, most often people say success. For example, Junia told me, "*Mafanikio* is just a different word in Swahili for success."[9] However, when you ask for the Swahili for prosperity, most often people will answer with *mafanikio*. I asked about *ustawi* (welfare, prosperity) as an alternate translation for prosperity, but this term was met with confusion or disagreement; it is a less common term, used in development or government documents but not part of common parlance in the way that *mafanikio* is. Thus, while *mafanikio* may not be a precise translation for prosperity, it is the best word available. Priscilla explained, "With regard to prosperity if you look at the translation of prosperity in Swahili, I suppose there aren't many words apart from *kufanikiwa*."[10] When people want to talk about prosperity then, they use some form of *-fanikiwa* / *kufanikiwa* / *mafanikio*. In participant observation where people often threw in English words or switched between the two languages, prosperity was the substitute for *mafanikio*. It is therefore not the translation of the word, but its usage and nuances brought through context and explanation which bring clarity to its meaning, and it is to this that I now turn.

---

6. For English speakers, the pseudo-rhyme 'Havana Rio' may give a sense of the rhythm of the word and its vowel sounds.

7. In Swahili, verbs ending in -wa are passive forms. However, -fanikiwa is a passive form of the verb; there is no active form either (presumably -faniki). Nevertheless, the word carries this grammatically passive sense of prosperity being something that happens to a person.

8. Taasisi ya Taaluma za Kiswahili, *Kamusi Ya Kiswahili-Kiingereza Swahili-English Dictionary*, 280.

9. Interview 5 (Junia), 17 April 2021, Mwanza. Where a reference for the Swahili quotation is not supplied, the interviewee spoke in English.

10. Focus Group 2, 6 November 2021, Dar Es Salaam, Swahili quotation 1.

Later on, I will talk about theology of prosperity but for now as we acquaint ourselves with the thought world of these women, I will continue using the noun *mafanikio* instead of prosperity. However, the verb *-fanikiwa* is more difficult to use in English because of the grammatical constructions so will be rendered using "to prosper." My aim is to explore what the women mean when they use this idea, and I hope that by using the Swahili for now, at least in the noun form, when I later come to discussing prosperity, we will be able to import a Swahili understanding of *mafanikio* rather than an idea of prosperity from somewhere else. In these next sections I will discuss how the women defined *mafanikio* at its most basic level and then go on to examine its scope, limits, purpose, and features. Thus, many of the ideas briefly introduced in the "What Is *Mafanikio*?" section will be subsequently expanded and explored in further depth.

4.3 What Is *Mafanikio*?

4.3.1 Reaching Goals

When asked "what is *mafanikio*?" many of the women appeared to give answers that align with the dictionary definition in terms of success or achievement. Secondary teacher Abigail spoke of it as reaching your goals.[11] University lecturer Lois used the language of taking steps and moving from one stage to another.[12] Public health official Huldah clarified that these stages need to be discernible enough that you can assess them, and for businesswoman Rhoda you know that it's *mafanikio* if that change has been advantageous.[13] Leah, who is not in formal employment as she cares for her four children, runs multiple small businesses out of their home, and is heavily involved in TAFES ministry on campus, fleshed this out:

> A situation in which I or any person is able to see that the situation is different, going from a low situation to a higher situation,

---

11. Interview 2 (Abigail), 14 February 2021, Arusha; Jochebed and Ruth also used this language. Interview 19 (Jochebed), 29 October 2021, Dar Es Salaam; Interview 20 (Ruth), 3 November 2021, Dar Es Salaam.

12. Interview 10 (Lois), 14 May 2021, Dodoma; See also Interview 11 (Lydia), 14 May 2021, Dodoma, and Interview 17 (Leah), 9 October 2021, Moshi.

13. Focus Group 2; Interview 15 (Rhoda), 4 August 2021, Dodoma.

or from a place of not having to a place of having, or a situation of not being able to a situation of being able.[14]

This change is not something that simply happens to a person. Public Relations Officer and minister's wife Puah points out that there is a relationship between a person's situation and a change in the person themselves:

> *Mafanikio* is that situation where a person grows in positive outlook... A person who comes from a certain place where their situation has been poor and then climbs up. OK I am able to say changes – *mafanikio* is a situation of positive changes in a person's life.[15]

Mafanikio, then is concrete, intentional, positive change in a person's life.

4.3.2 Ongoing Process

This idea of personal growth and positive changes in one's life is reflected in another way the women spoke about *mafanikio*: as an ongoing process. The language of reaching goals does not imply completion but something more like a milestone in a continuing journey. Bilhah, who has recently given up paid employment to start her own business training housegirls and nannies, put it this way: "*Mafanikio* is an ongoing thing. You can't say, I've reached it and that is it."[16] Puah and Rhoda both gave the example of studies: you can reach your goal at university by completing your studies and this is *mafanikio*.[17] However while gaining a university degree is a goal in its own right, it is also something that prepares you for the next stage. Rhoda said, "One step produces another."[18] Therefore, Zipporah, who works for a development NGO, agreed: "You can't say, 'I've finished, I've arrived,' because for us as Christians, there is always something more God calls us to do."[19]

This sense of forward momentum is so much a part of *mafanikio* that if you stop striving, you endanger your prosperity. Damaris, who owns multiple small businesses on top of managing her husband's publishing business, said,

---

14. Interview 17 (Leah), Swahili quotation 2.
15. Interview 7 (Puah), 18 April 2021, Mwanza, Swahili quotation 3.
16. Interview 14 (Bilhah), 3 August 2021, Dodoma, Swahili quotation 4.
17. Interview 7 (Puah); Interview 15 (Rhoda).
18. Interview 15 (Rhoda), Swahili quotation 5.
19. Interview 16 (Zipporah), 4 August 2021, Dodoma, Swahili quotation 6.

"Everything on which a person depends can collapse. That person returns down to zero . . . But *mafanikio* is about continued development and it needs effort."[20] Momentum is tied to productivity and arrested motion to passivity.

The women viewed this perpetual motion as an encouragement to those who have little. Eunice's husband holds a high position in the Tanzanian government and yet she went on to explain to me that her husband and his driver both pursue *mafanikio*, as appropriate to their level.[21] Junia said that even children are included in this: as they grow and move to the next level of development, they can be considered to be succeeding.[22] *Mafanikio* is therefore about moving on to the next level, not where you are starting from. It is thus not the purview of the elite. It is available at all levels of society.

Effort and continued striving are thus vital to *mafanikio*. Though language of success, achievement and meeting goals may sound (in English) like something that is over once complete, *mafanikio* is about continuing in a state of effort. When you achieve, it is not an endpoint but the next marker on the continuing journey. It is also not the purview of only the wealthy or the advantaged; all people are to pursue *mafanikio* and those who start thinking they don't need to may be in the greatest danger of losing it. Thus far, a working definition of *mafanikio* could be: a process of taking steps to move to the next level. However, for the women interviewed this is insufficient without the caveat that it is the will of God for his people.

4.3.3 God's Will

All of the women who participated in the study shared a strong conviction that *mafanikio* was the will of God. In focus groups, the women were asked to respond to the following statement (given in English):

> God wants us to prosper in all areas of our lives here on Earth! It is not God's desire to see his children suffering spiritually, intellectually and physically on Earth where they are supposed to be ambassadors of the almighty God.

---

20. Interview 3 (Damaris), 24 February 2021, Dar Es Salaam, Swahili quotation 7.
21. Interview 1 (Eunice), 13 February 2021, Arusha. Abigail made a similar point, using those who dig the roads as her example, saying that even in a menial job, there are opportunities to grow things like leadership skills. Interview 2 (Abigail).
22. Interview 5 (Junia).

Not one woman disagreed with this statement, especially the first part. (There was some contention about the part about being ambassadors.) Though in general, focus groups provided the opportunity for the women to sharpen each other's statements, they considered this statement uncontroversial. Deborah, Jael, Susanna and Puah stated their agreement, emphasizing that this prosperity applies to all areas of life.[23] Susanna saw a binary: either God makes human beings to prosper or to be troubled.[24] However, the latter was not considered a viable option. Medical doctor Dorcas envisioned this scenario, "You finish life in poverty, you die and you have not done anything here on earth, [as if] there is no difference from when you were here or not here."[25] Such a life would be pointless, she felt, and this kind of futility is not the will of God. When the women spoke of reaching goals in an ongoing process of taking steps, they believe themselves to be playing out the will of God in their lives.

The women were in agreement that *mafanikio* is the will of God. This is where *mafanikio* stops merely being a word used to refer to a life process and starts to carry theological significance as it speaks to who God is and what his purposes are in the world. The women had a great deal to say about how it is manifested in the world, and it is to these issues that we now turn.

4.4 Scope of *Mafanikio*

My working definition of *mafanikio* – a process of taking steps to move to the next level; it is the will of God for his people – does not specify the parts of life to which *mafanikio* pertains. The women commonly described *mafanikio* as broad (*kitu kipana*). Anna, Eunice, Fibi, Leah, Mariamu, Puah, Shiphrah and Zipporah[26] and all used this language and Eunice, Fibi, Lydia

---

23. Focus Group 1, 17 April 2021, Mwanza. Focus Group 2.
24. Focus Group 1.
25. Focus Group 2, Swahili quotation 8.
26. Interview 13 (Anna), 2 August 2021, Dodoma; Interview 1 (Eunice); Interview 4 (Fibi), 6 March 2021, Dar Es Salaam; Interview 17 (Leah); Interview 12 (Mariamu), 14 May 2021, Dodoma; Interview 7 (Puah); Interview 9 (Shiphrah), 13 May 2021, Morogoro; Interview 16 (Zipporah).

and Jochebed contrasted this with how many people understand *mafanikio* to mean only wealth.[27]

4.4.1 Areas of *Mafanikio*

During interviews, the women spoke about the various areas in which one can experience *mafanikio*. These included: spiritually, economically, relationally, in terms of health, intellectually, and experiencing inner peace.[28] In Figure 4.6 these areas are tabled according to which interviewees mentioned them.

These results do not include the focus groups where participants were given statements and asked to respond. They come from the women who participated in semi-structured interviews. Participants were asked to talk about what *mafanikio* is and in the process of answering they spontaneously referred to these areas. Some women offered them confidently as if they had thought about them before; others seemed to be making up categories as they went along, adding or modifying. However, there was a remarkable amount of overlap and agreement. Two areas were unanimously identified (spiritual and economic) and the remaining four (relational, health, inner peace, intellectual) were mentioned by over half of the women.

---

27. Interview 1 (Eunice); Interview 4 (Fibi); Interview 11 (Lydia); Interview 19 (Jochebed).

28. They also used a shorthand of "spiritual" and "physical," with the latter then broken down into the categories of economic, relational, health, etc. Spiritual *mafanikio* always referred to one's relationship with God. Some categories could be broken down further. For example, the relational category includes both societal and personal relationships and health includes both mental and physical health. The latter was distinguishable from inner peace which referred to settled-ness of mind or conscience though there was also some reference to anxieties to do with not being able to meet daily needs. There is also some overlap in the terms. For example, references to being able to get educated were sometimes counted as intellectual and sometimes counted as economic depending on the context of the comment. Similarly, one's health is also dependent on one's ability to access medical care and is therefore related to one's economic situation.

Figure 4.6 Areas of *mafanikio* by interviewee

	Spiritual	Economic	Relationships	Health	Inner peace	Intellectual
Abigail	X	X	X	X		X
Anna	X	X	X	X	X	
Bilhah	X	X	X		X	X
Damaris	X	X	X	X	X	X
Eunice	X	X	X	X	X	X
Fibi	X	X	X	X	X	
Jochebed	X	X	X		X	X
Junia	X	X		X		X
Leah	X	X	X	X	X	
Lois	X	X	X	X		
Lydia	X	X		X		
Mariamu	X	X	X	X	X	
Martha	X	X	X			X
Puah	X	X	X	X	X	X
Rhoda	X	X	X	X		X
Ruth	X	X			X	X
Salome	X	X		X		
Shiphrah	X	X			X	
Susanna	X	X			X	X
Zipporah	X	X	X	X	X	
Total	20	20	14	14	13	10

The breakdown of areas reflects the breadth of *mafanikio* as the women understand it, covering every aspect of life. However, the robustness of that breadth may be called into question by two notable absences: there was no mention of politics or ecology. The women did not speak of political activity when referring to the relationships (societal) area of *mafanikio*. This area was primarily about how people relate within communities and at a communal level; it was not about organized or official activity. Meanwhile, when the women spoke of their environment and a prosperous environment, they referred to having supportive peers and opportunities for employment, not about the prospering of the natural world. In the highly relational context

Understanding *Mafanikio* Theology

of Tanzania, the human world looms large and *mafanikio* is about human prosperity. I chose not to ask the women about ecology or politics as I wanted to preserve their understanding of the breadth they referred to. In chapter 8, I will interrogate whether this absence calls into question their claim that *mafanikio* is holistic, covering every area of life.

The absence of ecology and politics may have been exacerbated by the demographic. None of the women were politicians or scientists so when they considered *mafanikio* these dimensions may not have been prescient in their thinking. This is not to say that this cohort has no awareness of either the political or the ecological. Priscilla, a focus group participant, founded and is now on the board of a small climate change NGO directed at climate change advocacy as well as helping people to adapt to the changing climate. Likewise, during my participant observation at TAFES Transformers' Conference where I interviewed four of the women, one of the seminars was about Christian influence in politics.[29] (I did not attend this; it was an elective and I was in a different one.) Additionally, because *mafanikio* can be thought of as meeting goals, if you made it your goal to become a politician or to cultivate a forest and succeeded in this, the women would agree that this was *mafanikio*. However, these were not areas of life with which they were deeply engaged and so they did not feature in their extemporaneous answers.[30] The absence of these areas does not undercut the women's assertion that *mafanikio* is broad. *Mafanikio* pertains to life as a person experiences it and their areas of life experience are thus reflected in the answers.

This breakdown of areas is somewhat artificial because each area affects the others. For example, greater economic prosperity affords a person more opportunities for intellectual growth such as education or travel. Similarly, both societal stability and good health provide the conditions for economic prosperity. The women were at pains to show me that these areas were interconnected. Eunice shared about how this works out at an individual level:

---

29. TAFES Transformers' Conference, 2–5 August 2021, Dodoma.

30. In chapter 8, I will reflect on how the understanding of *mafanikio* theology gained from other areas of life may be applied in areas like ecology and politics.

> *Mafanikio* depends on prospering in all parts . . . if you don't eat food and if there are challenges you are passing through, so you have a lack of food you also have a lack of peace.[31]

Meanwhile Fibi, a human rights lawyer, insisted that economic prosperity could not be sustained on its own without relational prosperity, giving the example of a friend who built a great mansion with its own electricity but did not contribute to the development of the surrounding roads or his neighbours, who were still living in mud houses.

> You'll be on a bad road in the dark and your car will break down and others will be happy because you only prospered yourself. You have cut them off from yourself and they are isolated. Being isolated is not *mafanikio*. Because . . . you will have problems when you need people. People will not come to the mansion. They will leave you on your own. Because you have many ways where money cannot help you. You need people. There are possessions and money, but they do not help.[32]

Mariamu, a secondary school teacher, referred to the different areas of *mafanikio* as linked and said *mafanikio* only becomes complete when they cohere together. The women were in agreement that *mafanikio* can and ought to manifest in every area of life. Furthermore, when *mafanikio* is present in these areas, the whole is greater than the sum of the parts.

4.4.2 The Role of God in *Mafanikio*

There was one area that women in both interviews and focus groups considered more foundational to *mafanikio* than the others and that was the spiritual area. This referred most often to one's relationship with God. At one level, spirituality is one area in which one can pursue *mafanikio*. This is how university lecturer Junia is using it when she says, "As a Christian, prosperity is all about our relationship with God and when it comes to prospering that particular area it is about knowing God and being deep with God."[33]

---

31. Interview 1 (Eunice), Swahili quotation 9.
32. Interview 4 (Fibi), Swahili quotation 10.
33. Interview 5 (Junia).

However, the women also spoke about spiritual *mafanikio* as the source of other areas of *mafanikio*. Shiphrah, a researcher in development, said:

> *Mafanikio* comes from God himself because God has purposed every person for where they will arrive. When he created me, he knew that, Shiphrah, I want you to reach here. So, it teaches us that if we live in the plan of God, we will arrive at the *mafanikio* which God has purposed for us.[34]

Spiritual *mafanikio* is therefore the fuel of other types of *mafanikio*. Businesswoman Lydia said, "Our *mafanikio* starts spiritually,"[35] and Damaris argued similarly, quoting 1 John 3:2 to say that "if your spirit prospers then *mafanikio* will follow from above. So the Bible wants first for our spirits to prosper so we have a relationship with God."[36]

However, this does not mean that it is permissible for a person to follow God merely to access blessings. Susanna, who works for a development NGO, rebuked:

> Many times, we do not want God, we want his things, that is, the things we want. Currently this is a big problem in Christianity. So me, when I talk with [students], I will tell them . . . the law of God says you must know him first and then the other things will come.[37]

God is not a means to prosperity, but prosperity flows from relationship with him. This is an important distinction: ten of the women insisted that the Christian must seek God first, not wealth or the blessings he gives.[38] The women described preachers who centre on wealth and how to extract it from God as manipulators (Ruth), self-interested (Damaris), careless (Leah), unable to make true disciples (Eunice), and untrue (Anna).[39] To use relationship with God for the sake of prosperity is pointless anyway. A person who is doing

---

34. Interview 9 (Shiphrah), Swahili quotation 11.
35. Interview 11 (Lydia), Swahili quotation 12.
36. Interview 3 (Damaris), Swahili quotation 13.
37. Interview 6 (Susanna), 17 April 2021, Mwanza, Swahili quotation 14.
38. Interview 6 (Susanna); Interview 16 (Zipporah); Interview 1 (Eunice); Interview 3 (Damaris); Interview 12 (Mariamu); Interview 18 (Martha), 9 October 2021, Moshi; Interview 7 (Puah); Focus Group 2; Interview 20 (Ruth); Focus Group 1 (Dorcas and Joanna).
39. Interview 20 (Ruth); Interview 17 (Leah); Interview 1 (Eunice); Interview 13 (Anna).

this is not genuinely pursuing relationship with God and therefore does not have spiritual *mafanikio* and cannot experience the benefit of that in other areas of *mafanikio*. Not only do we now have *mafanikio* as God's will for his people, but we begin to see that the spiritual is behind everything, such that every area of *mafanikio* is imbued with theological meaning because it flows out of the spiritual area.

However, when the women spoke of other areas of prosperity flowing from spiritual prosperity, they did not envision this as other-worldly or merely supernatural. While they saw eternal security as an ultimate form of spiritual prosperity, but they explicitly rejected the idea that prayer is sufficient to access the benefits of relationship with God. Businesswoman Chloe mentioned the immaturity of people who think they "can sit still and pray and ask for things and they come, or if they go [to church], they'll just drop down," and this language of dropping down was repeated by Fibi, Jochebed and Zilpah.[40] Relationship with God is something that is practised. Priscilla explained, "The meaning of loving God is that we live in the foundations of all his principles, not as law, but we have this relationship with God."[41] Therefore, spiritual *mafanikio* manifests in knowing God and knowing his good ways for navigating his world.

Some of these good ways ("principles") included working hard, pursuing knowledge, living uprightly, working in small steps, and keeping relationships in good order.[42] At one level, these principles may seem like common sense: one would expect a person to see fruit from working hard and smart. However, the women did not understand these principles apart from God. Everything comes from him; any wisdom a person has is from him. Lois, who holds a PhD in development, said, "The Bible teaches us that God is the source of *mafanikio*. God gives a person intelligence. God gives a person understanding, strategy."[43] The more a person knows God and the deeper they go into his word, the wiser they become, so they will be better workers,

---

40. Focus Group 1, Swahili quotation 15; Interview 4 (Fibi); Interview 19 (Jochebed); Focus Group 2.

41. Focus Group 2, Swahili quotation 16.

42. Interview 13 (Anna); Interview 1 (Eunice); Interview 4 (Fibi); Interview 19 (Jochebed); Interview 7 (Puah); Interview 15 (Rhoda); Interview 10 (Lois); Interview 11 (Lydia); Interview 6 (Susanna); Interview 14 (Bilhah); Interview 20 (Ruth); Interview 5 (Junia).

43. Interview 10 (Lois), Swahili quotation 17.

friends, and family members; they will care for their bodies and tend to the life of the mind; their knowledge of God's character brings them peace whatever the circumstances. Prosperity in other areas flows out of a person's relationship with God because that relationship with God changes both the person and their view of the world. The spiritual shapes and animates every other area of *mafanikio*.

We have seen that *mafanikio* – a process of taking steps to move to the next level, which is the will of God for his people – is applicable in all aspects of human life. It is robust, encompassing more than just one area, recognising that each area of human life has an effect on the others. However, spiritual *mafanikio* is the foundation for all the others because in knowing God well and seeking to live in his ways, a person gains greater wisdom, understands the world more clearly, and is equipped to navigate it. *Mafanikio* is therefore unmistakably theological, shaped by God and his purposes in the world. Further understanding of these dynamics can be gained by asking if there are exceptions to this, and it is to this issue that I now turn.

4.5 Limits of *Mafanikio*

We have thus far seen how all-encompassing *mafanikio* is, applicable to every part of life, and also creating an integrated whole. We have seen that it is fuelled by spiritual *mafanikio*, not in a magical sense, but from personal growth in wisdom that comes from knowing God. The robustness of this holism can be interrogated by asking what happens if one element of *mafanikio* is not present. For example, since all the women identified spiritual and economic as areas of *mafanikio*, can *mafanikio* still be present if one of those is removed? Up to this point, the definition of *mafanikio* has been largely theoretical. Though the women's examples are practical, and they see *mafanikio* encompassing the whole of life, their statements about how God has set up the world are without reference to actual situations. I asked a series of questions designed to test whether this was sustainable in the real world. If one area of *mafanikio* is lost, is *mafanikio* overall lost? What does this tell us about the nature of *mafanikio*?

4.5.1 *Mafanikio* without God?

We saw above that other types of *mafanikio* and overall *mafanikio* flow out of spiritual *mafanikio*. It is therefore unsurprising to hear Huldah state, "there is no *mafanikio* outside of Christ."[44] However, the women did point to four other ways in which people seek *mafanikio*: consulting witchdoctors, immorality, being in league with Satan, and concentrating on other types of *mafanikio* to the exclusion of one's spiritual life. Whichever example a woman gave, she concluded it could not be *mafanikio* because it neglects the spiritual dimension of *mafanikio* which is intrinsic to its meaning in their views. Eunice and Damaris both explained that even if a person looks like they are wealthy, educated and have good relationships with others, without the spiritual dimension they miss the kind of wisdom which leads to *mafanikio*.[45] These so-called prosperities can therefore only ever be temporary and Ruth and Damaris both saw their fall as inevitable.[46] For Martha, who works in Allied Health, this is all part of Satan's plan. Unlike God who brings prosperity, "Satan opposes *mafanikio*,"[47] so he tries to trick people into pursuing false paths to prosperity, paths that will ultimately lead to their destruction.

Not only is their present *mafanikio* not all it appears, but they endanger their eternal future as well. Fibi said of her friend with the mansion, when "he died money was not able to help him."[48] Anna, Dorcas, Eunice and Puah all referred to Matthew 16:26 / Mark 8:36 like Bilhah who spoke of the importance of tending to one's soul, with eternity in mind:

> What will it benefit a person to have the whole world and lose his soul? That means that in the Bible it is not prospering at all if you only have money, possessions, children, etc. and have lost your soul . . . I think *mafanikio* is that your soul is at peace with your God and after you finish here on the earth and sleep, you go to be with God.[49]

---

44. Focus Group 2, Swahili quotation 18.
45. Interview 1 (Eunice); Interview 3 (Damaris).
46. Interview 20 (Ruth); Interview 3 (Damaris).
47. Interview 18 (Martha), Swahili quotation 19.
48. Interview 4 (Fibi), Swahili quotation 20.
49. Interview 14 (Bilhah), Swahili quotation 21.

Therefore, *mafanikio* must be pursued in a way that does not compromise one's eternal salvation. Abigail said, "[If] I bend a rule in my office in order to build my multi-storey building . . . I do not have *mafanikio* . . . you are outside the aim of God."[50] As soon as one strays from the will of God, then, they also stray from true *mafanikio*, both spiritually and physically. While others in their society may see *mafanikio* differently, the women were unanimous in believing that promises of *mafanikio* outside of relationship with God cannot provide the necessary foundation for *mafanikio* and that these alternatives cannot deliver *mafanikio* either in this life or the next.

4.5.2 *Mafanikio* without Wealth?

If overall *mafanikio* is impossible without spiritual *mafanikio*, what of economic *mafanikio*? Can overall *mafanikio* be said to be present when wealth is missing? This greatly depends on your definition of wealth. While these urban educated women did not see wealth in traditional terms such as having cows (a type of wealth identified by Zipporah, who is from the Maasai tribe[51]) neither did they see it in terms of extravagance. Martha said:

> Because when you say wealth and poverty, wealth is not that I have five or six houses. I see wealth as having a place to sleep, being able to eat – this is wealth.[52]

For these women, wealth was defined as meeting basic needs. These included food, shelter, medical care, and providing for your family including the ability to educate your children. They were unanimous that if there is no wealth at least at this basic level, there is no *mafanikio*. To ascribe *mafanikio* where there are not at least basic needs is to play down the physical in a way that does not cohere with the holism of *mafanikio*. Wealth at some level is therefore an indispensable part of *mafanikio*.

However indispensable wealth may be, it cannot be allowed to become the overarching framework for *mafanikio*. Susanna and Leah both described wealth as a subcategory ("inside") of *mafanikio*.[53] Meanwhile Anna, the Director of a school in Tanzania's southern highlands, said, "Many people

---

50. Interview 2 (Abigail), Swahili quotation 22.
51. Interview 16 (Zipporah).
52. Interview 18 (Martha), Swahili quotation 23.
53. Interview 6 (Susanna); Interview 17 (Leah).

interpret *mafanikio* to be wealth. *Mafanikio* is not wealth, so the teaching is not correct."[54] Nevertheless, they emphasised that great wealth, the kind of having multiple houses, does not endanger a person's *mafanikio* if stewarded correctly. Thus, Ruth said that great wealth, "is no problem if it is in the right perspective, a godly perspective."[55] She cited the biblical examples of Joseph of Arimathea, Lydia and Dorcas who were, "able to have money and be a person who has fear of God."[56] Likewise Bilhah cited the examples of Abraham, Job and Solomon as wealthy individuals in the Bible, concluding: "The Bible agrees totally that [a Christian] is able to be a wealthy person."[57] Continuing to strive for greater wealth is an important part of *mafanikio*. Otherwise, you have stopped growing, which, we have already seen above, is a threat to *mafanikio*. The women's answer to whether you can have *mafanikio* without wealth is a qualified no, depending on how wealth is defined and provided it is kept in proper balance with the other areas of *mafanikio*.

4.5.3 Case Study: Does the Widow in the Village Have *Mafanikio*?

To further explore this question of the interaction of physical and spiritual in *mafanikio*, in interviews I gave the following case study:

> Suppose there is a widowed grandmother in a village. She is very faithful Christian. She goes to church every day for prayers, she works hard in the fields, she looks after the grandchildren but still she is poor. Does she have prosperity?

Many of the women found this a very difficult question to answer. Their responses fell into the following categories, which I will expand below:

- Possibly, because she might be happy that way.
- Yes (A) because she still has God.
- Yes (B) because she has something to build on.
- Yes (C) because she is succeeding at her level.

---

54. Interview 13 (Anna), Swahili quotation 24.
55. Interview 20 (Ruth), Swahili quotation 25.
56. Interview 20 (Ruth), Swahili quotation 26.
57. Interview 14 (Bilhah), Swahili quotation 27.

Understanding *Mafanikio* Theology

- No (A) because she needs at least some kind of wealth in order to qualify for *mafanikio*.
- No (B) because she is caught in negative thinking.
- No (C) community has failed her.

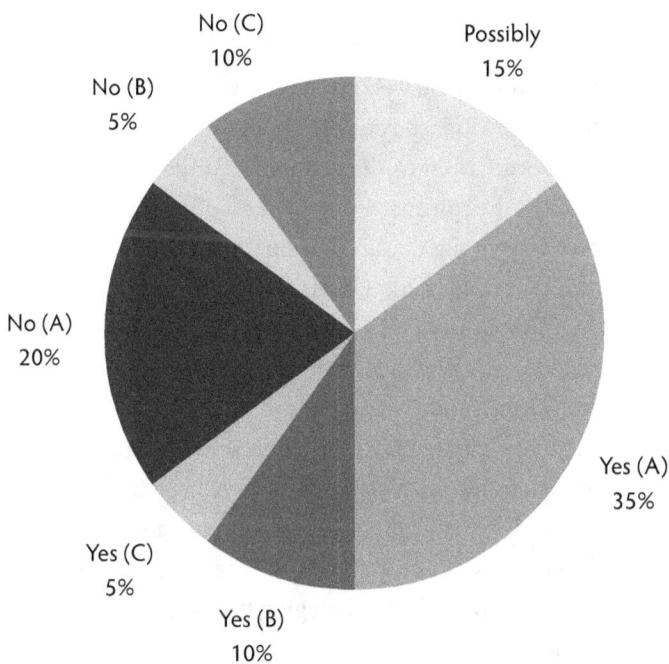

Figure 4.7 Does the widow have *mafanikio*?

4.5.3.1 *Possibly, because she might be happy that way.*

Anna, Jochebed and Eunice shared a concern that people of lower socio-economic status should not be judged to be inferior by those whose standard of living is higher.[58] For example, Eunice, who works with a poverty alleviating NGO, said:

> Many times we think that people in the village have problems but if you go to the village you'll see they have peace and they are happy even though . . . the life they are living is hard. We

---

58. Interview 13 (Anna); Interview 19 (Jochebed); Interview 1 (Eunice).

think 'Why do they not have this or that?' or 'How come they live in this bad house?' but actually . . . their environment it is really fine for them."[59]

Anna's own grandmother is in this situation: While it is not a state Anna has chosen for herself, she was reluctant to judge it.[60]

4.5.3.2 Yes (A) because she still has God

This was the most popular answer, given by seven women, that because the widow continued with God, she could be said to have *mafanikio*. However, this was not a subordination of the economic to the spiritual because the women believed that the spiritual would make a difference to the economic. Ruth said, "You can't say she doesn't have *mafanikio* because she has Christ who owns all things."[61] Leah said, "God is able to take her from that situation and do anything."[62] Lois saw that God had already provided and so would continue to provide: "*Mafanikio* is there because she has good health, God is giving her protection, food, even a place to lie down . . . God gives her life. One day God will bring to fruition the thing she is asking for."[63] Puah had her own testimony of such an experience: "I have been in that situation and God fed me. So the issue is whether I trust God to care for me. A valuable thing is that she continues to be with God."[64] These women saw the widow's continued relationship with God as bringing the potential for change in her other circumstances.

4.5.3.3 Yes (B) because she has something to build on

While the women in Yes (A) saw potential for change in relationship with God, the two women in this category pointed to the potential of what was already available to her. They reframed wealth to be about resources rather than money. For example, Martha said, "She doesn't have *mafanikio* in terms

---

59. Interview 1 (Eunice), Swahili quotation 28.
60. Interview 13 (Anna).
61. Interview 20 (Ruth), Swahili quotation 29.
62. Interview 17 (Leah), Swahili quotation 30.
63. Interview 10 (Lois), Swahili quotation 31.
64. Interview 7 (Puah), Swahili quotation 32.

of possessions but she does have *mafanikio* in her grandchildren."[65] Bilhah suggested she make some *maandazi* (savoury donuts) and put her grandchildren to work selling them![66] They also pointed out that she has some land which she could farm, though she may need help learning better techniques for doing so.[67]

4.5.3.4 Yes (C) because she is succeeding at her level

The final 'Yes' response came from Junia, who said that the widow could be understood to have *mafanikio* if she was making some progress "according to her exposure . . . worldview . . . the resources within her."[68] Here *mafanikio* is about direction rather than accomplishment. In this view, lack or struggle is part of her environment with which she is contending and *mafanikio* is being able to eke something out of that, in contrast to the next answer which felt a certain standard needed to be achieved.

4.5.3.5 No (A) because she needs at least some kind of wealth

Four women felt that this widow's basic needs had not been met and therefore that *mafanikio* could not be said to be present. Rhoda's summary is representative of their view: "We cannot say she has prospered because still there are things with which she struggles, especially having daily food."[69]

4.5.3.6 No (B) because she is caught in negative thinking

When Susanna spoke about the widow, she saw a cycle of poverty that would perpetuate itself: "I see there is a weakness here. That this person knows God, but what about the grandchildren who were born and came to be directed here? Why should they be pacified? This is a way to continue to do things which continue to make the widow poor."[70] For her, this situation is particularly difficult because of the low potential for change, not because of a lack of effort, but because of a deficiency in mindset or even theology. She wondered

---

65. Interview 18 (Martha), Swahili quotation 33.
66. Interview 14 (Bilhah).
67. Interview 18 (Martha); Interview 14 (Bilhah).
68. Interview 5 (Junia).
69. Interview 15 (Rhoda), Swahili quotation 34.
70. Interview 6 (Susanna), Swahili quotation 35.

whether the widow subscribed to the false belief that the spiritual is all that matters but insisted that the will of God was not to continue a cycle of poverty.

4.5.3.7 No (C) because her community has failed her

While the other answers focus on the widow's situation and her capacity to change it together with God, Salome and Zipporah drew in a societal aspect, asking where the people are who could support her and in particular, whether her church was playing its role to lift her out of poverty.[71] Zipporah said that while a person is normally prospered by, "good morals, fear of God, working hard with effort," prior to this unjust systems must be removed in order to allow this to happen, as a matter of biblical social justice.[72]

Though there are significant variations in these answers, with the exception of "Possibly," none of the answers thought the widow's situation in life ought to stay as it was. The Yes answers (A–C) looked for a foundation to build on and the No answers (A–C) attempted to address what was lacking. For both the Yes and the No answers, the assumption was forward motion. Where does answer "Possibly" fit in then? Eunice gave her reasoning:

> So you are able to see a person lives in a hard environment like this but in their heart they have peace and great peace which *even is more than a person who is in town and has work and wages* but it is not enough to fulfil their needs.[73] [emphasis mine]

Her concern here is to avoid excluding the rural poor from the process of *mafanikio*. Eunice's attempts to show the potential of the village too, in contrast to urban environments. She therefore leaves the possibility open for good things to come even out of the village rather than assuming that only one particular echelon of society experiences *mafanikio*. *Mafanikio* is always about going to the next level and, in so doing, it is dignifying: it consigns no one to their fate. I wrote in my learning journal:

> [The interviewees] have all got edgy when I asked them about poverty – not because they don't want to acknowledge it exists

---

71. Interview 8 (Salome), 13 May 2021, Morogoro; Interview 16 (Zipporah).
72. Interview 16 (Zipporah), Swahili quotation 36.
73. Interview 1 (Eunice), Swahili quotation 37.

but because they seem to be very cautious of anything that could be construed as encouraging passivity.[74]

Their hesitancy ought not to be a surprise considering what we now know about the continual striving of *mafanikio*. Even when assessing whether a person has *mafanikio*, the emphasis is on where she could get to rather than where she currently is, since, *mafanikio* is always about the next step, not the current situation.

As we have examined what happens when an element of *mafanikio* is removed, we have looked at various scenarios and asked whether *mafanikio* is present there. We have moved inductively here, looking at a situation and assessing it. Can the limits of *mafanikio* also be assessed deductively, that is, is there something that can be universally said to not be *mafanikio* or to be its opposite?

4.5.4 What Is the Opposite of *Mafanikio*?

When I asked about the opposite of *mafanikio* (*kinyume cha mafanikio*), Fibi commented that even the word for opposite (*kinyume*) is quite technical[75] and Anna said it was difficult to express opposites in Swahili.[76] In Swahili you can express the idea of *not* doing something with the infix *-to-* and this was how Fibi, Leah, Lydia, Ruth, Jochebed, Mariamu, Bilhah, Rhoda, Salome and Puah answered my question about the opposite of *mafanikio*, simply saying, "The opposite of *mafanikio* is not prospering!"[77]

They added more, however, and their answers were often impressionistic. Fibi's response was typical:

> The opposite of *mafanikio*. I could say 'to not prosper' but the opposite of *mafanikio* is to be defeated, to not prosper, to not continue. I can't say the opposite of *mafanikio* is poverty, but it is to fail to meet your goals. Because I can't – I said the opposite of *mafanikio* is poverty – hmm this is hard in Swahili – but there

---

74. Excerpt from Learning Journal Entry, 26 February 2021.
75. Interview 4 (Fibi).
76. Interview 13 (Anna).
77. Interview 4 (Fibi); Interview 17 (Leah); Interview 11 (Lydia); Interview 20 (Ruth); Interview 19 (Jochebed); Interview 12 (Mariamu); Interview 14 (Bilhah); Interview 15 (Rhoda); Interview 8 (Salome); Interview 7 (Puah).

is poverty of spirit and there is poverty of the body and there are many different types of poverty. The opposite of *mafanikio* is to fail, to be defeated in reaching the things which you expected. It is being behind on development. When you have goals that you need to reach and when you desire to do various things you fail to reach there.[78]

By now reaching goals is a familiar aspect of *mafanikio* to us and it makes sense that the opposite of *mafanikio* would be failure to reach them. However, it is not so much the endpoint that is on view as the capacity to reach them. While Martha thought that the opposite of *mafanikio* was poverty, and Susanna suggested it was about lack, they both also defined those terms as being about mindset and potential, not only possessions, or, as Jochebed said, closedmindedness.[79] For Junia, it was about a failure to make progress rather than a particular station in life.[80] Like the definition of *mafanikio* itself, the opposite is dynamic and holistic. It is about whether progress can be made and whether the conditions exist for it.

4.5.4.1 *The relationship between* mafanikio *and contentment*

With this emphasis on constant progress, one might wonder whether discontent is a necessary part of *mafanikio*, in order to propel the forward motion, and whether contentment is therefore *mafanikio*'s opposite. However, the women did not see *mafanikio* and contentment as at odds with one another. For them, contentment did not imply satisfaction with current circumstances. Ruth said, "Contentment is not the same as saying I'll stay still . . . People confuse contentment with staying in your comfort zone."[81] Instead, contentment is about choosing to work within the means that God has given you as you pursue *mafanikio*. Martha explained, "Contentment has the meaning that you got your *mafanikio* from the right path."[82] Zipporah said a person who is not content falls into "traps" (*mitego*) like attaining *mafanikio* by stealing or forgery. She said the thinking goes, "'I don't have this, I want this . . . if I

---

78. Interview 4 (Fibi), Swahili quotation 38.
79. Interview 18 (Martha); Interview 6 (Susanna); Interview 19 (Jochebed).
80. Interview 5 (Junia).
81. Interview 20 (Ruth), Swahili quotation 39.
82. Interview 18 (Martha), Swahili quotation 40.

don't have it I will use any means [to get it].'"[83] Rhoda spoke about coveting another's phone instead of valuing the phone you have and using it to progress to the next level.[84] On the other hand, the content person, according to Mariamu, is able to look at what they have and be thankful, and, in Leah's words, to press "straight ahead with joy."[85] Contentment is a key component in keeping a person within the will of God as they pursue *mafanikio*, working within their means without falling into temptation. Contentment therefore enhances *mafanikio* because it ensures spiritual *mafanikio* (from which other areas of *mafanikio* flow.)

A person's relationship with God is the model for how contentment and *mafanikio* work. A person must be committed to God, not looking for another god or being tempted away from the true God (contentment), but they are also never to stop growing in God (progress). Salome argued that just as we should always be growing in our relationship with God, the same goes for *mafanikio* more generally:

> But from the spiritual perspective you cannot say that you've already prospered, I already know God fully, I will stop praying and reading the Bible. We say it's an ongoing process. So in my view *mafanikio* is you can't be saying, 'I've already arrived', because God has given each of us a thing inside ourselves which will not be satisfied and so you continue to desire something better.[86]

Increase is therefore entirely appropriate for the Christian, and Bilhah, Jochebed and Rhoda saw no conflict between increase and contentment.[87] These three quoted 1 Timothy 6:6, that godliness with contentment is of great benefit and it is as we come to understand their theologies of creation and eschatology that we see how they harmonise increase and contentment both as aspects of godliness.

---

83. Interview 16 (Zipporah), Swahili quotation 41.
84. Interview 15 (Rhoda).
85. Interview 12 (Mariamu); Interview 17 (Leah), Swahili quotation 42.
86. Interview 8 (Salome), Swahili quotation 43.
87. Interview 14 (Bilhah); Interview 19 (Jochebed); Interview 15 (Rhoda).

4.5.4.2 The relationship between mafanikio, creation and eschatology

As we have seen, a Christian must keep within God's ways when pursuing *mafanikio*: this is the meaning of contentment. Yet, one of those ways is to pursue increase. Leah, Damaris, Puah, and Zipporah all referred to the creation mandate in Gen 1:28 as setting the pattern for human life.[88] As Leah said, God "gave them the work of producing and increasing."[89]

The women saw a continuity between their work and the creation mandate given to Adam and Eve in the garden of Eden.[90] Humankind's task is still to carry out this work; that has not changed. As Susanna explained, we exist in the same eschatological epoch as Adam and Eve, one where work is required: "The Bible tells us when reaching heaven, there we will be comfortable and without problems."[91] Eschatology is conceived here not in terms of future fulfilment or consummation but to give a mandate for how to live in the present age. Though there are other tasks given to human beings as well, for example evangelism, which is discussed below, these do not override to replace the obligation to constant growth; the creation mandate endures. Production therefore continues to be not just appropriate but necessary for the human being in God's world. Just as fidelity to God requires you to keep within the resources God has given you (contentment), so it also requires you to increase in order to fulfil God's purposes for you in this eschatological epoch.

The creational and eschatological requirements of *mafanikio* also play out at a societal level. Lois said, "We live in a community, we are not isolated . . . The demand is there every day – there are people in need, orphans, sick people."[92] For Dorcas, having prosperity is a God-given way to meet these needs.[93] Indeed, for Salome it cannot be counted *mafanikio*, "If I see my life going well but the society surrounding me has troubles still, and I stay that way. If I stay this way, it means I do not love others."[94] This is the reality of daily life for these women. Eunice and her husband adopted three distant

---

88. Interview 17 (Leah); Interview 7 (Puah); Interview 16 (Zipporah).
89. Interview 17 (Leah), Swahili quotation 44.
90. Interview 13 (Anna); Interview 15 (Rhoda).
91. Interview 6 (Susanna), Swahili quotation 45.
92. Interview 10 (Lois), Swahili quotation 46.
93. Focus Group 2.
94. Interview 8 (Salome), Swahili quotation 47.

relatives, small children whose father had died and whose mother had abandoned them. (They first attempted to set the mother up in business so that she could care for the children, but she was experiencing mental illness and this failed.) For Eunice, this adoption was not only about fulfilling familial obligations; it was about practising her Christian faith and extending her own *mafanikio* to others in need. When my family stayed with hers in Arusha, it was a joy to see these disadvantaged children being nourished by both food and love. According to Bilhah, a person who enjoys the fruit of their labours while others continue to struggle is both unchristian, in that they are not fulfilling God's plan for them, and un-African.[95] *Mafanikio* and the pursuit of it is both intrinsic to being human and to being a Christian in today's world.

4.6 Purpose of *Mafanikio*

Having seen how important *mafanikio* is to being human at both a personal and societal level, one might think this is its purpose: to bring wholeness and healing to the individual and society. There is certainly an element of this in *mafanikio*, but such an aim is subordinated to a much greater purpose. According to Ruth, it is to extend the kingdom of God.[96] Again, this flows out of relationship with God. Susanna explained that as you love God more, you will want to do things which build his kingdom, and Shiphrah spoke of living "for his sake not our own sakes."[97]

There is a very practical level to this building of God's kingdom in that ministry requires funds and resources. In the scenario of a mission to a village, Abigail, Rhoda and Zilpah all pointed out that transport there is costly, and Rhoda added that when you reach a village you need a sound system which costs money.[98] Building God's kingdom may also be about providing for others. Damaris and her husband have used their wealth to build a large house, with multiple wings, with several set aside to house local missionaries and Christian workers, some long term. At one level then, prosperity is required in order that the practical needs of a ministry be met. Contributing

---

95. Interview 14 (Bilhah).

96. Interview 20 (Ruth). The women did not use 'kingdom of God' in a technical sense but rather as a catch-all term for bringing about God's purposes on the earth.

97. Interview 6 (Susanna); Interview 9 (Shiphrah), Swahili quotation 48.

98. Interview 2 (Abigail); Interview 15 (Rhoda); Focus Group 2.

to this is a right and proper end of prosperity but this is not the only way that prosperity builds the kingdom of God.

In focus groups, the women discussed Christians as ambassadors and therefore the role their life plays in evangelism. As education specialist Deborah said, "People are watching you . . . your neighbours are watching you to see proof of your Christianity."[99] Junia felt that a person's life must reflect God and for Susanna that included seeing God's abundance: "In order that we build the kingdom we are in need of good knowledge, a good state of spirit and even physically, so you can convince a person when they see that you are in a better situation than them."[100] If this sounds a little like using wealth as bait, accountant Zilpah reminds us that in addition to preaching, Jesus also healed and touched people who were hungry.[101] This is not a trick of evangelism or a lure but a genuine offer to life with God, which is better by far. She explained:

> When Jesus was crucified on the cross, he lay like this [stretches out arms] and the meaning is that one side touched on spiritually and the other on ordinary life, meaning social services like education, health and all the needs involved in normal life of humans here on earth.[102]

To her mind, the extension of the kingdom of God is not only manifest in evangelism but in God's broader creational purposes for the world. God's purposes extend into our vocations and societies as well, and when one lives within those purposes, they are bringing about God's kingdom.

Interviewees also saw that one's professional work can expand the kingdom of God. For Anna, this meant recognising one's professional skills as a gift from God and the work as a task from God.[103] Eunice identified that this task must be carried out in ways that please God: without corruption, underperformance, poor time management, or dishonesty.[104] After all, as we have seen, if one's *mafanikio* endangers the kingdom of God, then, it is

---

99. Focus Group 2.
100. Focus Group 1; Swahili quotation 49.
101. Focus Group 2.
102. Focus Group 2, Swahili quotation 50.
103. Interview 13 (Anna).
104. Interview 1 (Eunice).

not true *mafanikio*. Abigail gave the example of walking past a poor person but not stopping because you are in your expensive clothes or because you are busy. Her assessment of this was, "It damages the name of God. Let us share the things we have so that when we do, the name of God is helped."[105] Prosperity is there for God's purposes in the world, for creating and building as well as for witness, and the former two feed the latter.

4.7 Features of *Mafanikio*

Thus far in this exploration of *mafanikio*, I have given a working definition of *mafanikio*: a process of taking steps to move to the next level; it is the will of God for his people. I have discussed in detail what aspects of life *mafanikio* touches and the relationship between God, wealth and *mafanikio*. While we have seen how holistic *mafanikio* is, it still remains to give some more descriptive detail of *mafanikio* in terms of its features and how these relate to the Christian life. What is the nature of this process of taking steps? That is what this section addresses. The features that will be discussed are: effort, perseverance, righteousness, and wisdom.

4.7.1 Effort

We saw earlier that the women strongly opposed the idea that one can expect prosperity through prayers alone, and that they believed this faulty method to come from an ignorance of God's ways. It is not that prayers are fruitless. Zipporah and Puah pointed out that God is the owner of all wealth and Fibi and Mariamu quoted Haggai 2:8: "'The silver is mine, and the gold is mine,' declares the Lord Almighty."[106] It makes sense to ask the one who has everything for prosperity. However, Jochebed explained that prayers and effort have often been taken as an either/or, discouraging people away from effort.[107] Leah also mentioned "miracle money" as something that takes away priority on working and Zilpah asked where people could find the time to work if they are constantly in church praying.[108] Damaris likened simply praying to

---

105. Interview 2 (Abigail), Swahili quotation 51.
106. Interview 16 (Zipporah); Interview 7 (Puah); Interview 4 (Fibi); Interview 12 (Mariamu).
107. Interview 19 (Jochebed).
108. Interview 17 (Leah); Focus Group 2.

sitting in a dark room refusing to turn on the light switch, because you expect it to happen miraculously!¹⁰⁹ Therefore she, together with Lois, Jochebed and Mariamu spoke of having a part to play in bringing about *mafanikio*.¹¹⁰ A Christian will pray because they know apart from God there is no *mafanikio*, but such prayers will not lead them to passivity but to action.

Playing one's part applied not only to the economic area of *mafanikio* but was also relevant to health. A person must pray and go to the doctor Damaris insisted, because if you are healed by a doctor, this is the work of God. She acknowledged that some people have no money for such medical care and believed that Jesus alone would heal them but did not see this as a reason for a person who has the means to refuse to seek medical treatment.¹¹¹ Both focus groups discussed the role of faith in healing and Chloe and Priscilla mentioned people they knew who had felt convicted to refuse medical treatment in favour of allowing God alone to heal them and found these examples inspiring. However, they did not consider them normative.¹¹²

The women emphasized our own part because they felt that people who teach that prayers are enough set people up to fail in their faith. Zilpah argued:

> You find a person in a poor area, a poor person who doesn't have enough for their daily needs and at the end of the day, a person come to despair even in their faith in God. But as you teach them this issue of working hard, the Bible says the one who does not work will not eat.¹¹³

This verse, from 2 Thessalonians 3:10 was a recurring theme, mentioned by Shiphrah, Puah, Anna, Rhoda and Leah as well.¹¹⁴ Puah argued that those who do not work hard do not know God or his word, and Rhoda contrasted this with the example of Jesus who, "was able to fly around to preach the gospel but [instead] he walked or he used a boat and since he did, he is our

---

109. Interview 3 (Damaris).
110. Interview 3 (Damaris); Interview 10 (Lois); Interview 19 (Jochebed); Interview 12 (Mariamu).
111. Interview 3 (Damaris).
112. Focus Group 1; Focus Group 2.
113. Focus Group 2, Swahili quotation 52.
114. Interview 9 (Shiphrah); Interview 7 (Puah); Interview 13 (Anna); Interview 15 (Rhoda); Interview 17 (Leah).

role model."[115] Bilhah and Leah found inspiration in the Proverbs 31 woman's industry arguing that, far from suggesting she was not reliant on God, her efforts were an outworking of God's will.[116] Martha saw it as a way to partner with God.[117] God is at work in his world and so his people are to be workers in it as well.

The emphasis on effort did not imply individualism, however. Salome and Shiphrah both pointed to family, peers, and a supportive environment as contributing factors to a person's ability to work hard, and Anna saw that none of us prosper without help from others at some point.[118] In a focus group, Huldah told a story of when she was at boarding school. Her parents had not provided adequately for her, and she was down to her final one thousand shillings, so she prayed for God to transform it into ten thousand shillings:

> I stretched out my money, held it high, that 1000 shillings and I closed my eyes and I believed that God is able to change it from 1000 shillings into 10,000 shillings. I ask you, is God able or is he not able? He is able! . . . I stretched up, I prayed to God, I opened my eyes and it was still 1000 shillings.[119]

The women in the focus group found this story hugely entertaining. In the end, a father of a school friend provided for Huldah, which she saw as an outworking of his *mafanikio*. Prospering by one's effort does not preclude receiving help from others, especially since that person's *mafanikio* requires them to help others lest they lose it. However, reliance on such to the exclusion of working shows, according to Mariamu, that a person has not understood that "God has said we are blessed by the work of our hands."[120] It is work, not passivity, that is to characterize the Christian, and which is necessary for *mafanikio*.

---

115. Interview 7 (Puah); Interview 15 (Rhoda), Swahili quotation 53.
116. Interview 14 (Bilhah); Interview 17 (Leah).
117. Interview 18 (Martha).
118. Interview 8 (Salome); Interview 9 (Shiphrah); Interview 13 (Anna).
119. Focus Group 2, Swahili quotation 54.
120. Interview 12 (Mariamu), Swahili quotation 55.

4.7.2 Perseverance through Hardship

Mafanikio might sound like it's all about success or an easy life, for example, when Rhoda said, "Jesus suffered so that we could have eternal life and not so that we would live with problems."[121] However, it is more accurate to say that it's about persevering through trials. We have seen that effort is a key feature of *mafanikio* and this led Anna to be suspicious of "get rich quick" schemes and Lois to urge that we "not become tired or give up."[122] Challenges in life were not seen as an aberration in the Christian life but as part of it. Puah said, "Having God does not mean that you will not go through hardship or that having God helps everything to go smoothly but having God helps you to carry the hard thing without returning to sin."[123] Eunice insisted that struggles do "not mean *mafanikio* has been removed."[124] Neither do they imply, according to Naomi, that "our faith has made this happen, that it's a poor faith—no."[125] The reverse is true as well: wealth does not necessarily indicate great faith. After all, Joanna pointed out, "People are able to have a good situation and still their faith is not good."[126] Instead, as Jael, Joanna and Naomi said, God remains God.[127] Anna and Abigail concurred, adding that God has a right to act how he wants in his world, and, Susanna added, in his time.[128] This was not to say that all trials are God given. Shiphrah said that sometimes our life circumstances are due to the "will of the enemy" and Martha spoke of Satan opposing prosperity.[129] However, Abigail was confident that God can "glorify himself even in a person who is down."[130] This emphasis on God's sovereignty did not imply that God is unconcerned with the welfare of human beings: Puah's comment about God helping a person to carry their suffering indicates his closeness and involvement.

---

121. Interview 15 (Rhoda), Swahili quotation 56.
122. Interview 13 (Anna); Interview 10 (Lois), Swahili quotation 57.
123. Interview 7 (Puah), Swahili quotation 58.
124. Interview 1 (Eunice), Swahili quotation 59.
125. Focus Group 1, Swahili quotation 60.
126. Focus Group 1, Swahili quotation 61.
127. Focus Group 2; Focus Group 1.
128. Interview 13 (Anna); Interview 2 (Abigail); Interview 6 (Susanna).
129. Interview 9 (Shiphrah), Swahili quotation 62; Interview 18 (Martha).
130. Interview 2 (Abigail), Swahili quotation 63.

Understanding *Mafanikio* Theology

In all this, the women did not explicitly speak of the Fall. We know that they expect suffering in this life, but they shied away from explanations which suggested that suffering does not have a purpose or is unproductive. Similar to what we saw in the case study of the widow in the village, they were concerned to see forward momentum somehow, because staying still or being passive makes *mafanikio* an impossibility. While suffering in this world is normal, one must not become resigned to it or content with it. Perseverance is not about sitting back and waiting for trouble to pass but about continuing to contend with challenges by remaining faithful to God and looking for what he might be doing in any given situation. In this way, *mafanikio* can also be present in suffering, to the extent that a person contends rightly with it and grows because of it. Challenges are a reality in our world and require perseverance not resignation or passivity. Persevering through them is a feature of *mafanikio*.

4.7.3 Righteousness

Effort and perseverance are insufficient in *mafanikio* if they are not married to righteousness. Leah pointed out that it's possible you can put a great deal of effort in the wrong places, like promiscuity or theft.[131] However, simply veering away from sinful paths is not enough either. Lydia and Fibi both said that it mattered why you were doing something as well, and that the reason to pursue one path over another, for example in business, was because it was in line with God's purposes for you.[132] At all times in the process of *mafanikio*, it is imperative to operate in right ways; if one fails to do so, it is no longer *mafanikio* and that process is disrupted. As Fibi said, that *mafanikio* is, "to do something true with true people and in a true season for a true time."[133] This righteousness plays out in both pure motivation and pure action.

4.7.3.1 *In motivation*

Pure motivation is to focus on seeking God. The women emphasised that they would teach TAFES students to make this the focus of their prayers when seeking *mafanikio*. Puah said "The first thing is, 'God, mould me, make me

---

131. Interview 17 (Leah).
132. Interview 11 (Lydia); Interview 4 (Fibi).
133. Interview 4 (Fibi), Swahili quotation 64.

pleasing to you. Let me be a person who is able to please God.'"[134] She gave an example of this "tough prayer" about *mafanikio*: "God, bless me where you want me to be. No matter the environment, no matter the wages, no matter what, bless me in the place where I am within your purpose."[135] This is not merely theory for Puah. She and her husband are part of a church community in an informal settlement ("slum"). When she introduced me to the senior pastor, he explained that the church was planted by wealthy educated people, like himself and Puah, who felt a strong call from God to live among them despite the knowledge that this poor community would not be able to provide for their needs.

A failure of pure motivation will disrupt the process of *mafanikio* according to Ruth, but Susanna insisted that a delay in plans coming to fruition did not necessarily indicate a problem with motivation.[136] In fact, it could indicate the opposite, that a person is seeking God's plans before their own. Susanna said, maybe "having everything which I ask for is not the plan of God at this time."[137] If you are in the plan of God, on the other hand, "he will give it to you," so the most important thing was for a person to conform their desires to God's.[138]

4.7.3.2 In action

This pure motivation of desiring to please God must be married to right action, that is, in obedience to him according to Abigail who referenced Psalm 128:1: "Blessed are all who fear the Lord who walk in his ways."[139] Such obedience can be complex with the many competing factors of life but Lydia warned that for it to be *mafanikio*, they must all be kept in balance: "*Mafanikio* is something which will not destroy relationships with people, *mafanikio* will not hurt our children . . . or our churches. So, we need wisdom and the leading of God as we attain *mafanikio*."[140] Priscilla highlighted this as a particular concern for women. When she spoke in the Dar Es Salaam focus group of

---

134. Interview 7 (Puah), Swahili quotation 65.
135. Interview 7 (Puah), Swahili quotation 66.
136. Interview 20 (Ruth); Interview 6 (Susanna).
137. Interview 6 (Susanna).
138. Interview 6 (Susanna).
139. Interview 2 (Abigail).
140. Interview 11 (Lydia), Swahili quotation 67.

women being "caught in the middle" of the various obligations of *mafanikio*, she was met with an outpouring of sympathy and agreement from the other women.[141] She herself has had an international career and held "very high positions" yet lamented, "We are failing to prosper because we are not doing the things which God originally created us for. We have less time with our kids, we have less time to make our homes . . . We women, we are overused."[142] Priscilla is not advocating for women to be only in the home but reflecting on the complexity of trying to obey what appear to be competing demands. *Mafanikio* can be said to be present when a person is marked by righteousness in both motivation and action. The complexity of carrying this out requires the final feature of *mafanikio*: knowledge.

4.7.4 Knowledge

Several Swahili words converge for this feature of *mafanikio* which I have called knowledge but could equally be called wisdom. They have overlapping meanings that change depending on usage and context. They include:

- Hekima (wisdom, prudence)
- Akili (intelligence, reason, brain)
- Elimu (education, knowledge)
- Maarifa (strategy, technique)
- Busara (good judgement, know-how)
- -fahamu (to know, understand, discern)
- -jua (to know)

These words are often grouped together when talking about *mafanikio*, for example, when Rhoda said, "A person is prospered by strategy, skills, teaching, direction," or when Lydia said, "Pray that God would give them wisdom, strategy, good judgement."[143]

Knowledge as a concept undergirds all three of the previous features. Eunice equated a failure to work with a lack of knowledge about what effort produces.[144] On the issue of perseverance Anna felt that knowledge of God

---

141. Focus Group 2.
142. Focus Group 2, Swahili quotation 68.
143. Interview 15 (Rhoda), Swahili quotation 69; Interview 11 (Lydia), Swahili quotation 70.
144. Interview 1 (Eunice).

equipped the Christian to interpret their circumstances rightly so they can press forward.[145] Third, on the issue of righteousness, Chloe insisted that it was only in knowing the principles of God that a Christian can live in line with God's ways.[146] This feature is about the life of the mind and its role in the process of *mafanikio*.

We have already seen that the intellectual realm is one area in which one can experience *mafanikio*. However, knowledge is also a means of pursuing *mafanikio*. For Jochebed, openness to knowledge is key to *mafanikio*: "Closedmindedness affects *mafanikio* . . . If you are closedminded, you will not reach your goal because you will be just staying with one perspective [like] this is what I did and I got it, or this is what the pastor says."[147] Needing more knowledge was a key theme for the women. Fibi exhorted, "Grasp knowledge. Study well."[148] Even if one is already wealthy, such as those who have inherited from their parents, Damaris argues that the pursuit of knowledge is vital for them to steward that well.[149]

A key area of knowledge that preoccupied the women was strategy. This included goal setting, prioritising, planning of concrete steps, and creating conditions for success.[150] They saw this as a way of bringing order instead of accepting chaos as something that just springs up as Abigail said many people are inclined to do.[151] Such ordering of the world comes from God. Lois, Lydia and Susanna saw God as the source of knowledge, which can be attained first by knowing God.[152] Leah and Abigail quoted the refrain from Proverbs, that fear of the Lord is the beginning of wisdom.[153]

God provides this wisdom in multiple ways. First, it is available in the Bible. Bilhah said:

---

145. Interview 13 (Anna).
146. Focus Group 1.
147. Interview 19 (Jochebed), Swahili quotation 71.
148. Interview 4 (Fibi), Swahili quotation 72.
149. Interview 3 (Damaris).
150. Interview 13 (Anna); Interview 19 (Jochebed); Interview 3 (Damaris); Interview 15 (Rhoda); Interview 4 (Fibi), Interview 10 (Lois); Interview 17 (Leah); Interview 2 (Abigail); Interview 14 (Bilhah); Interview 8 (Salome); Interview 11 (Lydia); Interview 16 (Zipporah).
151. Interview 2 (Abigail).
152. Interview 10 (Lois); Interview 11 (Lydia); Interview 6 (Susanna).
153. Interview 17 (Leah); Interview 2 (Abigail).

> If a person asks me [about *mafanikio*], saying, "I like to farm," then I will take them in the Bible, so they can read well and understand the normative principles of God for doing business and doing this. The person must apply the principles together with working hard with effort, and seeking God.[154]

Rhoda agreed that these biblical principles can be applied to everything from business to academics.[155] The women are not expecting to find a farming manual or a business plan in the Bible, but are convinced that biblical principles such as effort, perseverance and righteousness are applicable and useful for pursuing *mafanikio* in any area.

However, knowledge is also available in God's world. Leah said, "God has left for me knowledge and I am able to do everything using this knowledge which I received to be able to prosper."[156] Likewise, Damaris saw that the scientific knowledge a doctor has acquired in medical school comes from God, himself the great scientist.[157] Susanna similarly saw knowledge gained in law school and agricultural school as God's equipping for *mafanikio*.[158] Even practical knowledge forming a habit of saving was conceived by Mariamu as from God himself.[159]

4.7.5 Features: Conclusion

The four features of *mafanikio* explored here – effort, perseverance, righteousness, and knowledge – provide an ethical framework for *mafanikio*, both eschewing passivity and directing purity. Lest a person be tempted to passivity, the women's teaching about *mafanikio* encourages effort and perseverance. Yet, such activity needs direction as well, and so *mafanikio* must find itself within the limits of righteousness, as growing knowledge brings each of the preceding three features into greater clarity. Avoidance of passivity and the embrace of purity keep one on the path of *mafanikio*.

---

154. Interview 14 (Bilhah), Swahili quotation 73.
155. Interview 15 (Rhoda).
156. Interview 17 (Leah), Swahili quotation 74.
157. Interview 3 (Damaris).
158. Interview 6 (Susanna).
159. Interview 12 (Mariamu).

4.8 Conclusion

Mafanikio is a common word in Tanzania and has a variety of meanings. To some, it is synonymous with wealth; to others it is about attaining success. However, for these women, *mafanikio* had a broader meaning. Wealth is one area in which one can attain success, but there are many others too. While one can speak about attaining *mafanikio* in each of these areas, *mafanikio* can also be thought of as when there is a holism that encompasses all of these areas and when this happens the sum is greater than the parts. Even in this all-encompassing sense, it can exist at all levels of society because it is not about achieving a certain level but about growing from wherever you are.

I asked the women if there was another word to use instead of *mafanikio* which would more precisely capture their meaning or avoid confusion with other less holistic interpretations. *Ustawi* (welfare) had been suggested to me by another missionary as an alternative. However, this was largely met with confusion by the women. It is used in technical or official documentation but is uncommon in everyday life. They preferred to take *mafanikio* and imbue it with their own meaning. This is not an uncommon approach in Swahili where words are often elastic and determined by context. For example, if you say that you will '*-piga*' someone, you could be calling them on the phone or hitting them. *Mafanikio*, like many words in Swahili, is a tool for discussing broader concepts rather than having a rigid, pre-determined meaning.

For these women the meaning of *mafanikio* was broad and holistic. I have used the working definition: a process of taking steps to move to the next level, which can be applied in the economic, spiritual, relational, physical, and intellectual spheres as well as to the experience of inner peace. However, the women did not simply interact with *mafanikio* as a word but as a theology. For them, *mafanikio* comes from God and it is only in God that *mafanikio* can be both understood and attained. Not only is it the will of God but it tells us what God is like, what his purposes are and how to live in these purposes as human beings.

In this theology, which I will call *mafanikio* theology, God is a wealthy God, owning all creation and equipping his people to live abundantly in it. He does not simply drop this down from heaven but invites human beings into partnership with him, using their effort to increase the abundance of creation and expand his kingdom. He cares for his people and their relationship with him, using suffering to increase their reliance on him, vindicate their faith in him, teach them important lessons, and build them into people whose *mafanikio* will last.

Meanwhile, human beings are created to know God and out of that relationship, to experience prosperity. While there appears to be other sources of prosperity, these are false, and they do not provide the holistic or enduring prosperity that God does. It is therefore imperative for the human being to seek prosperity God's way and any deviation from this endangers that person's *mafanikio* and the Christian must only pursue *mafanikio* with the resources God has given them. This can be a complex task, but God gives wisdom and closeness with him which enhances a person's ability to discern the right path. The key is to not stagnate in seeking *mafanikio* because this would halt something that is by definition a process. To do so would also misunderstand our eschatological location. When things appear confusing or one feels their *mafanikio* is endangered despite their own fidelity to God, they must remember that they are but a human and God is sovereign. However, knowing who God is, they can be confident of better days ahead and work towards those. After all, *mafanikio* is the will of God for his people.

Figure 4.8 What have we learned about *mafanikio* theology (MT)? (Chapter 4)

Chapter 4	Chapter 5	Chapter 6	Chapter 7	Chapter 8
In MT, prosperity is a process of taking steps to move to the next level. This process manifests across all areas of life and when all areas are affected, the result is greater than the sum of the parts. In MT, God is the source of prosperity. In MT, prosperity is characterised by effort, perseverance, righteousness and knowledge.				

CHAPTER 5

Locating *Mafanikio* Theology

We have seen that the TAFES women believe prosperity to be an ongoing process of taking steps to move to the next level. We have seen that it is the will of God for the extension of his purposes in the world and that if either the spiritual or the physical is diminished, prosperity is threatened. The robustness and integrity of prosperity is upheld by effort, perseverance, righteousness, and knowledge. *Mafanikio* theology teaches, expounds, and applies this understanding of prosperity.

The foregoing discussion has provided us with an understanding of the women's theological system of *mafanikio*. As our understanding of *mafanikio* has been expanded, it remains to understand the world in which this theology operates. A robust theology of *mafanikio* also requires understanding the biblical, historical, and cultural factors that influence it and the women spoke to these as well, though in less detail. While in chapter 4 we were understanding *mafanikio* on its own terms, here we are answering why it exists and how it came to be. This is the first of our concentric circles of engagement moving out from *mafanikio* theology.

In this first concentric circle, we seek to see *mafanikio* theology in conversation with the world immediately around it, before moving on to consider it more broadly in the context of African prosperity theology, African theology, and holistic theology.

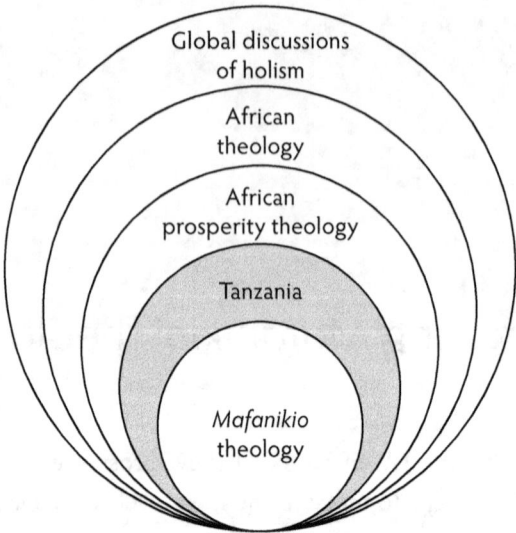

Figure 5.1 Concentric circles of engagement
with *mafanikio* theology (Tanzania)

First, I will engage the historical and cultural reasons for *mafanikio* theology. However, the women were generally less interested in my questions about this. For them, *mafanikio* theology is a product of their Bible reading and the Bible is the immediate context that has produced it. In light of this, I will give considerable attention to their relationship to the Bible and its role as the source of *mafanikio* theology.

5.1 Historically: Charting between Two Trends

Several scholars argue that prosperity theologies arose as a response to the context of poverty in Africa with several pointing to the World Bank's Structural Adjustment Programs (SAPs) of the 1980s and 90s as the catalyst. Broadly speaking, according to Matthews Ojo, they created, "political instability, economic recession, social tension . . . uncertainties and deteriorating living conditions."[1] His analysis is echoed by Nigerians Ebenezer Obadare and David Ogungbile as well as Kenyan Kyama Mugambi, and Dena Freeman

---

1. Ojo, "Pentecostalism, Public Accountability," 110–33.

notes that this experience was common to many African countries.² Tanzania was one of these countries.³ Obadare sees the African person as traumatised by these events and the privatisation of the SAPs as setting the stage for a shift towards a self-empowering individualist message as championed by prosperity messages.⁴ Meanwhile Golo sees that in the wake of a devastated and receding state, people looked for metaphysical solutions to their woes.⁵ Sarai located the advent of prosperity in Tanzania at approximately thirty years ago, which coincides with the period described by the scholars above.⁶

However, the TAFES women did not conceive of prosperity theology as primarily a response to increasing poverty. They saw it as a response to an entrenched theology that failed to provide Christians viable routes to holiness, a poverty theology rather than poverty itself. Previous Christian teachings had insisted that wealth was inappropriate for Christians. Martha explained: "In the past there were people who said that it is not appropriate to have a lot of money, that . . . it means that you match with those who don't love God."⁷ Sarai heard people in her childhood church say that possessions are a sin.⁸ Anna and Ruth both pointed to Jesus's teaching that it is harder for a camel to pass through the eye of a needle than for a rich person to enter the kingdom of God as a frequent teaching at this time, used to argue that a Christian cannot be wealthy and also be holy. In this way, Leah said Africans were taught to be content with their poverty because they were taught that, "the Bible opposes prosperity."⁹ Thus the Christian was faced with a choice: either be a poor Christian or a wealthy unbeliever. As poverty continued to beset their context, the Christian faith offered no way out and faced irrelevance. Moreover, those who did want wealth were forced to abandon their faith and seek prosperity elsewhere. The women therefore saw this theology as leading

---

2. Obadare, "'Raising Righteous Billionaires,'" 2; Ogungbile, "African Pentecostalism," Kindle edition, loc.3434–3884; Mugambi, *A Spirit of Revitalization*, 143; Freeman, "The Pentecostal Ethic," 3–4.

3. Ngowi, "Economic Development and Change," 259–67; Hasu, "Prosperity Gospels and Enchanted," 68.

4. Obadare, "'Raising Righteous Billionaires,'" 4.

5. Golo, "Africa's Poverty," 370.

6. Focus Group 2.

7. Interview 18 (Martha), Swahili quotation 75.

8. Focus Group 2.

9. Interview 17 (Leah), Swahili quotation 76.

to twin enemies of prosperity: hopelessness on one hand and immorality on the other. Additionally, it robbed the Christian church of wealthy patrons who could support kingdom work. Prosperity theology was a response to this milieu, presenting a Christian way to be wealthy, one that called Christians to optimism and righteousness. As the women see it, prosperity theology entered the African scene as a discipleship tool. It provided Africans in their context of poverty with a viable way to be a Christian. Prosperity theology was not only aimed at reducing poverty: it was also aimed at increasing Christian discipleship by countering theologies which had forced people into ungodly ways of life.

This discipleship dimension in the history of prosperity theology is not often brought to the fore in the scholarship. While Schliesser's work on Efatha acknowledges the "emphasis on hard work, diligence and individual responsibility" and teaching on sharing, she examines these for their poverty alleviating effects, not the effect on discipleship. Meanwhile Drønen's work in Cameroon highlights Iya Moussa's teaching that, "True discipleship is about working hard and giving priority to spiritual matters," but this is not in contrast to a theology that condones poverty but to formulaic methods of manipulating God in order to gain wealth.[10] Scholars such as Anderson, Kalu and Asamoah-Gyadu do engage the theme of discipleship in their treatments of Pentecostalism, from the perspective of exploring Pentecostalism's ability to be truly African and to speak to African concerns.[11] For them, the paucity of responses to poverty in Africa is one legacy of missionary Christianity. Anderson argues that teaching on prosperity is one means by which "the needs of people have been addressed more fundamentally than the rather spiritualised and intellectualised legacy of European and North American theology."[12] Addressing these needs – in contrast to missionary Christianity – provides a way for Christianity to be truly African and thus for Africans to be Christian disciples. However, the women did not cite a missionary legacy when referring to the prosperity-negative message. On the contrary, Zilpah spoke of missionaries as sources of prosperity in the past for their patronage

---

10. Drønen, "Weber, Prosperity," 321–35.

11. See, for example, Asamoah-Gyadu, "'Get up . . . Take the Child . . .,'" 350; Anderson, "The Gospel and African Religion," 374–77; Kalu, "Preserving a Worldview," 130–136.

12. Anderson, "The Gospel and African Religion," 375.

and donations.[13] That said, they did not attribute the prosperity-negative teaching to anyone; they merely noted it was present and needed to be dealt with. It is reasonable to assume that there is considerable overlap between the teaching they referred to and the missionary legacy critiqued by Anderson, Kalu and Asamoah-Gyadu. The women do not conceive of this discipleship in terms of contextualisation to Africa; they see it as providing an alternative to ungodly forms of behaviour. However, because these ungodly forms of behaviour are caused by a failure of theology to reckon with Africans' felt needs, it is legitimate to view their words as adding further evidence to the link between contextualisation and discipleship which Anderson, Kalu and Asamoah-Gyadu draw.

However, scholars are far more likely to conceive of prosperity teachings as undermining discipleship. Nigerian Gwamna Dogara Je'Adayibe worries that the "search for wealth accumulation . . . [causes] people [to] lose the sense of care, love, sympathy and mercy for their fellow human beings, attributes that make up true Christian character."[14] The women shared this concern. Lydia spoke of people focusing too much on money and Anna was concerned about people becoming materialistic.[15] Meanwhile, one of the first steps in Ruth's financial education business is correcting the mindset that, "it's all about myself, they come believing prosperity is all about me and me."[16] If prosperity becomes all-consuming like this, then people are just as likely to resort to ungodly means to obtain it as they are when prosperity is not spoken about at all. One of those ungodly means is praying and expecting to "get something in a blink" in Jochebed's words.[17] The women opposed those who teach such things because they neglect Christian virtues such as care for others and hard work, but also because they point people to themselves rather than to God. Eunice gave the example of men who come to a church saying that if you touch their suit it will "prosper you at work or to get a car or increase your wages," and Damaris spoke of people who belittle others because they are wealthy and make further demands of the poor.[18] Ruth called

---

13. Focus Group 2.
14. Je'adayibe, "'Where Your Treasure Is,'" 29–45.
15. Interview 11 (Lydia); Interview 13 (Anna).
16. Interview 20 (Ruth), Swahili quotation 77.
17. Interview 19 (Jochebed).
18. Interview 1 (Eunice), Swahili quotation 78; Interview 3 (Damaris).

them parasites and robbers who manipulate people for their own gain.[19] I will refer to the prosperity gospel taught by these preachers as the profligate prosperity gospel. The women's concern with the profligate prosperity gospel was less about the flamboyance or great wealth of these people or desire for wealth, and more about how they treated people and spoke about God and relationship with him. Because these profligate preachers claim to be from God, Susanna and Zilpah worried that those who are left without their every need fulfilled will despair of their faith in God when their investment appears to be unfulfilled or they do not become wildly wealthy.[20] We saw in chapter 4 that in focus groups, the women affirmed that the Christian life involves suffering and that God is close to those who are suffering. They therefore opposed a prosperity teaching that had no place for suffering, generosity, or the development of Christian character.

Several scholars offer that the antidote to a profligate prosperity teaching is to emphasise suffering in the Christian life and to downplay prosperity.[21] However, for the women, this approach does not lead to discipleship. They see both teaching which upholds poverty and a profligate prosperity gospel as looking to sources other than God for wealth. One provides no way for Christians to access wealth; the other provides a phoney way. Old ways of thinking are therefore just as futile as the profligate prosperity gospel. This is depicted in the flow chart Figure 5.2 where both the profligate prosperity gospel and what I have called the poverty gospel end in a lack of prosperity. The former provides faulty means to prosperity, the latter no means. Because neither offers a viable path to prosperity, they both lead either to hopelessness or immorality. Neither of these options leads to prosperity.

---

19. Interview 20 (Ruth).
20. Focus Group 1; Focus Group 2.
21. See, for example, Mboya, "Gift Challenges and Transforms," 35; Mbugua, "Suffering," in *Prosperity?*, 65–78; Boamah, *The Cross or Prosperity Gospel*, Kindle edition.

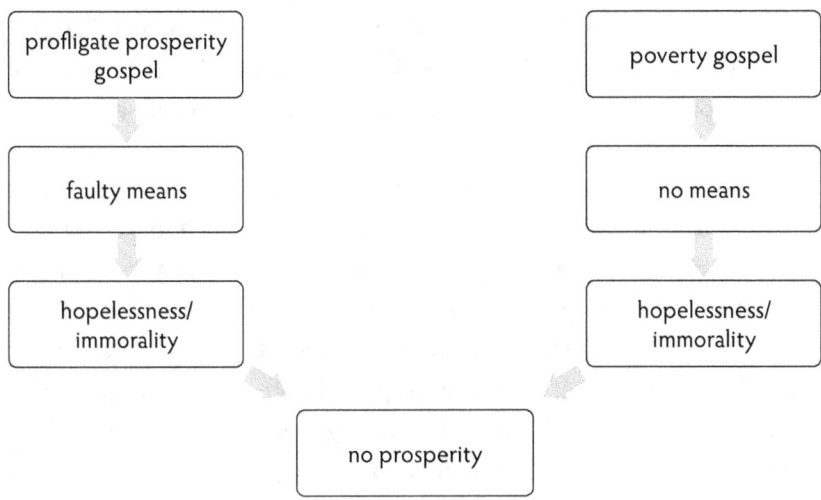

Figure 5.2 Flow chart towards no prosperity

This is where a teaching is needed which sees wealth as positive, yet is able to marry that with faith in God, and teach ways of obtaining it which align with God's ways. *Mafanikio* theology meets this need, not captive to the poverty theology of years gone by, yet also standing against the profligate prosperity gospel that exploits people. The women thus respond to two different historical trends here, avoiding both and charting a different course. Instead, they say, learn how God has set up the world. God's plan is to prosper human beings, so look to him to learn his good ways for attaining prosperity.

5.2 Culturally: The Problem of Passivity

We have seen that *mafanikio* theology charts its course between two historical theologies: one which downplays physical prosperity and teaches that wealth is inappropriate for the Christian, and the other which focuses on wealth accumulation but in ways that are inappropriate for a Christian even though it may come in Christian garb. Understanding God's purposes for prosperity – and the means he provides for obtaining it – is a tool the women use to respond to a major flaw they perceive in their culture: a tendency towards passivity.

A participant observation session I attended was Joy's training for the TAFES staff on managing change. We started with a *pambio* "Natamani *kuenda mbinguni*" ("I desire to go to heaven").[22] The song is about keeping on the straight path so that one will reach heaven. After an introduction about herself and her background, Joy proceeded with the session. Much of it was sharing her professional expertise from her work in Human Resources, but she began with a game in which we were asked to swap seats with each other and then to reflect on how we felt after each change. She then spoke of change as a norm in life and something that God effects in our lives and requires of us. This was a lengthy point, emphasising that growth is only possible with change, and she returned to it several times during the seminar. For Joy, the normal attitude to life of Tanzanians is passivity. This is often coupled with sympathy but culturally Tanzanians are change-averse and resistant to taking action.[23] Thus she argued at length for change being a part of God's world and a part of faithful Christian life. I recount this session at length here because it is indicative of the cultural situation in which Tanzanians find themselves, and which the women respond to in their theology.

Sometimes this passivity is expressed in a kind of fatalism which results in inaction; for Christians this can mean fervent prayer, expecting God to do everything while they remain otherwise inactive. It is for this reason that Gifford argues the prosperity gospel subverts any effort "to promote self-help, self-reliance, self-esteem, self-determination, responsibility, and autonomy" because it instead encourages Christians to trust God supernaturally to provide for all their needs.[24] Similarly for Obadare, an enchanted view of the world is problematic: "wealth or success in the Pentecostal world is consistently advertised as something that happens 'accidentally' or miraculously, and not necessarily issuing from prior investment in terms of individual preparation."[25] Reliance on this kind of miraculous intervention is completely at odds with *mafanikio* theology which, as we saw in chapter 4, encourages effort not only as a means of pursuing prosperity but a *God-given* means. Several of the women spoke strongly against the idea of praying and expecting

---

22. A *pambio* is a Tanzanian chorus of just a few lines. Often sung without music, the leader starts and each line is repeated by the congregation. Various modifications are made to the lyrics as the repetition continues.

23. See, for example, Tanzanian Laurenti Magesa's plea for hope and action over cynicism and despair. Magesa, "Christian Discipleship In Africa," 283–99.

24. Gifford, "Christian Fundamentalism and Development," 9–20.

25. Obadare, "'Raising Righteous Billionaires,'" 6.

that to make a difference unless you play your part. They are not alone in this. For many in the prosperity gospel movement, prayer and passivity are not a natural pair. From the Zambian context, Naomi Haynes admits that in the past, seed offerings were seen to be sufficient to bring about prosperity, but highlights a turning of the tide, towards the "excellence model" which stresses the importance of human efforts.[26] She quotes one of her interlocutors, Pastor Mwanza: "We cannot ask God to bless the work of our hands if our hands are not doing any work!"[27] As he recalled Deuteronomy 28:12 here, so did Mariamu, Chloe and Puah, with Eunice even arguing that a person who has "fiery prayers" but does not work with their hands obstructs God's blessing.[28] Gordon Doss's Malawian interlocutors felt that God gives opportunity which a human can then choose to take up.[29] Similarly, in Asamoah-Gyadu's analysis of Mensa Otabil, deliverance from "poverty, disease, oppression and hatred ... will not happen by prayer alone, but by hard work and resourcefulness."[30] While Anthony Balcomb's respondents from five different African countries gave prayer as their top factor in making one successful in business or work, hard work was a close second, followed by a number of aspects of good character.[31] Similarly, the churches Deborah James studied in South Africa lay a strong emphasis on self-help.[32] Quayesi-Amakye's call for critics of the prosperity gospel to do "due diligence on the ground" is therefore warranted.[33] Similarly for the women in this study, though they identified passivity as a major problem in Tanzania, they did not see their *mafanikio* teaching as upholding passivity but challenging it.

As Joy did in her seminar on change management, the women grounded their responses to this passivity theologically. They identified a cultural problem (passivity), and the answer that they gave was a Christian one. They

---

26. Haynes, "'Zambia Shall Be Saved!,'" 18.
27. Haynes, 18.
28. "The Lord will open the heavens, the storehouse of his bounty, to send rain on your land in season and to bless all the work of your hands. You will lend to many nations but will borrow from none." (Deut 28:12) Interview 12 (Mariamu); Focus Group 1; Interview 7 (Puah); Interview 1 (Eunice), Swahili quotation 79.
29. Doss, "A Malawian Christian Theology," 150.
30. Asamoah-Gyadu, *African Charismatics*, 224.
31. Balcomb, "Disenchanting Pentecostalism," 28.
32. James, "New Subjectivities," 36
33. Quayesi-Amakye, "A Yeast in the Flour," 79.

therefore present Christianity as culture-transforming. They identified three contributing factors to passivity: false beliefs about God, negative self-identity, and an environment which is not conducive to change. They seek to change these by helping people to know God rightly; by forming a new identity in them, and by changing the tone of the environment in which people find themselves respectively.

5.2.1 Knowing God Rightly

We have already seen some of the false theologies that necessitate *mafanikio* theology, specifically that wealth and Christianity are incompatible. On this issue Bilhah insists that though the Bible says, "It is difficult for wealthy people to enter into the kingdom of God, it does not say it is impossible. So, when [Jesus] says it is hard for wealthy people to enter into the kingdom of God, he means that *it is possible* to enter into it but it is hard" [emphasis mine.][34] She is asking people to change their view of God and his kingdom here, that God is not anti-prosperity or pro-poverty. One need not make a choice between being wealthy – or even having daily needs met – and being a Christian. As one comes to know God more through his word, they can discover that his will is to prosper his people. This changing view of God helps to dismantle the idea that Christianity and wealth are at odds with each other.

The second obstacle they hope to remove is that of hopelessness, or a belief that nothing will change. Rhoda said many people see how far the road ahead is and become despondent:

> Many young people when they are told they must start at the bottom refuse . . . If you tell them, I started at the bottom, they say, 'No it's not possible,' but guess what! It is possible! Even I started at the bottom, and I had a little money and a little money and then challenges like being robbed but if we don't despair and we continue, at the end of the day, it is possible.[35]

Behind a tendency towards passivity and a resistance to change lies cosmology and theological beliefs about how the world is set up and what is possible in it. This means that hopelessness is a fundamentally theological

---

34. Interview 14 (Bilhah), Swahili quotation 80.
35. Interview 15 (Rhoda), Swahili quotation 81.

problem, even if that is unacknowledged. Underlying beliefs about God support and uphold passivity. This is why Joy taught about God being a God who brings change. A Bible study seminar I went to for participant observation opened with the *pambio*, *Wewe ni Mungu wetu, Mungu anayeweza* which translates to "You are our God, the God who is able." Because God is able, hopelessness need not be the order of the day. In order to change their culture, the women insist on knowing who God is. This progress is powered by God: "And God is there so continue to pray to God. You will go far."[36] As Nigerian George Folarin argues, knowing "that God is interested in all the affairs of Africans" checks a belief in God's ambivalence to human affairs and "gives hope to the hopeless."[37]

5.2.2 Identity Change

Second, the women work for culture change by transforming people's identity. We have seen the emphasis that humans are created to work, and that they are made to produce. An additional aspect of self-identity was of having the strength to carry out the task that God has given a person. Fibi said, "I have strength unlimited. I am unlimited. I am strong. I believe . . . that I am able to do anything as long as God is with me."[38] For her, this self-perception was necessarily gendered. In Tanzania, femininity is already associated with strength, but Fibi saw her femininity as fused with God's indwelling of her:

> Because I am a woman of TAFES I carry God inside me but I [also] carry motherliness inside me. A woman of TAFES because she knows God, she has the grace of God, the Bible, inside her, she carries God inside herself. For every thing which she increases she carries femininity.[39]

Fibi explained that this Christian self-identity contributes to what you become: "There are others who do not prosper. This is because they say, "I am poor I have not prospered, I have no money," and that speaks poverty . . .

---

36. Interview 15 (Rhoda).
37. Folarin, "Contemporary State," 89.
38. Interview 4 (Fibi), Swahili quotation 82.
39. Interview 4 (Fibi), Swahili quotation 83.

[it is] a poverty of spirit."⁴⁰ What you believe about yourself matters because it results in what you say about yourself, and words have power.

The practice of speaking either poverty or prosperity is also called positive confession and is a hallmark of prosperity teaching. It is a practice advocated by famous American preachers of the "Word of Faith" movement such as Kenneth Hagin, E. W. Kenyon and Kenneth Copeland.⁴¹ American historian Kate Bowler has argued convincingly that these preachers drew on the mystical New Thought movement of the nineteenth century as they developed the American "Word of Faith" movement in the twentieth century.⁴² If the African prosperity gospel is a simple import from America, then one could read Fibi's words as also advocating this same practice from the "Word of Faith" movement, but the relationship between the American and African prosperity gospels is much more nuanced than that. Tanzania has its own beliefs about the effect of words. Danish anthropologist Martin Lindhardt found in his study in Iringa that like many Bantu peoples, "the Wahehe and the Wabena conceive of words as an extension of a person's life force and believe that their existence continues after being uttered."⁴³ To the extent that "Word of Faith" teachings have influenced the African prosperity gospel, it is justified to assume that their appeal was a coherence with beliefs about the power of words which were already present in Tanzania.

However, even if words have no mystical power, how one talks about certain things still has an impact on self-identity. Paivi Hasu argues that faith-based development organisations, with their ultimate goal of "conversion, salvation and the creation of new persons, attitudes and personal morality by way of character building . . . may have intended and unintended short-term and long-term consequences."⁴⁴ She lists among these, "personal empowerment, social responsibility and possibilities of development in general."⁴⁵ A similar progression can be seen in Ruth's argument that once you understand that you are strong in the power of God, you are able to see yourself

---

40. Interview 4 (Fibi), Swahili quotation 84.
41. Adeleye, *The Preachers of a Different*, 64–65.
42. Bowler, *Blessed: A History*, Kindle edition, 13–14.
43. Lindhardt, "'If You Are Saved,'" 244.
44. Hasu, "Prosperity Gospels and Enchanted," 68.
45. Hasu, 68.

as a contributor to others, "a channel of blessing."[46] This is her experience in her financial literacy classes. She spoke of people who are "transformed to transform"[47] by what they learn there, concluding that, having changed their self-identity, a person "blesses others as God told Abraham, I bless you to be a blessing.[48] These contributions are part and parcel of how God has designed human beings, that is, to be workers. With their frequent references to the creation narratives in Genesis, the women were at pains to show that an identity as a worker is not only permitted for a Christian but indeed required. Declarations like "I was faithful in my work," as Eunice said, uphold this identity.[49]

5.2.3 Environmental Change

The women challenge the theological obstacle to prosperity that Christianity and wealth are incompatible, and they provide a theological mandate for prosperity by arguing that God is able to bring change. They also want to change people's self-identity, so they see themselves as people who are powerful in God's strength and able to bless others. Finally, they believe that as these two things happen, the environment in which people find themselves is changed, which creates a cycle whereby positive people create a positive environment which empowers others to be positive, which has further ripple effects. Leah identified peers and general ways of being as obstacles to prosperity, and Damaris noted the empowering flow-on effects of employing someone and giving them an identity as a worker.[50] This kind of entrepreneurship is for Togarasei a direct result of a belief that because God is provider "no one should experience poverty."[51] Once a group of people believe and begin to act differently, it changes the environment in which everyone operates, engendering what Schliesser calls an Afro-optimism not only at the individual level but also in society more generally.[52] Thus, Hasu notes that though many prosperity teaching churches run few social projects, "their theological

---

46. Interview 20 (Ruth).
47. Interview 20 (Ruth).
48. Interview 20 (Ruth), Swahili quotation 85.
49. Interview 1 (Eunice), Swahili quotation 92.
50. Interview 17 (Leah); Interview 3 (Damaris).
51. Togarasei, "The Pentecostal Gospel," 344.
52. Schliesser, "On a Long Neglected Player," 342.

discourse has broad development-related implications" and this is the case for the TAFES women.[53]

The women spoke at a community level without reference to global market forces which arguably disproportionately disadvantage Africans and thus have a great effect on the environment in which they find themselves. In this way they differ from Kyama Mugambi's Kenyan "progressive Pentecostals" who are "engaged with economic and political aspects of society,"[54] and they do not work for the kind of "meaningful transformations that make the economic system increasingly more humane, especially for those currently facing economic deprivation" that Christian economic ethicist Douglas Hicks calls for.[55] However, this need not mean that their work to change their environment be viewed as futile or that the situation is ultimately hopeless. We still do not know the overall economic effects on the development of prosperity teachings. However, we do know that the women see passivity as a key factor in hindering Tanzanians' economic production and that they believe their theology addresses this; therefore removing some obstacles to economic involvement and creating an environment where prosperity is possible. Scholars who remain pessimistic about economic development might need to revisit the women's conviction that God is for prosperity and at work in his world to bring it about. This is not to diminish the importance of that structural work; those who are involved in such work can see it as service to God and a possible means by which God will bring prosperity to Africa.

TAFES women are working to create a positive environment for prosperity in Tanzania, by removing the theological obstacles that stop people from pursuing prosperity, and by imbuing a new identity as a worker and producer in God's kingdom and in his service. They therefore see themselves as people who raise up, unlike those who tear down, whether by keeping people in poverty or by promising wealth through foolish, false, or ungodly means.

While we can see *mafanikio* theology from a historical perspective, as correcting theological errors of the past, and from a cultural perspective of seeking to combat passivity, when the women speak of where it comes from, their

---

53. Hasu, "Prosperity Gospels and Enchanted," 70.
54. Mugambi, *A Spirit of Revitalization*, 147.
55. Hicks, "Prosperity, Theology and Economy," 250.

answer is that it comes from the Bible. It is therefore worth giving significant space to understanding how they conceive of this and their hermeneutics.

5.3 Biblically: The Hermeneutics of *Mafanikio* Theology

The women all held a high view of Scripture. Ruth said, "I am a believer and I believe in the Bible when I read the word of God."[56] However, reading or belief are incomplete without action. Jochebed urged people to "live the Bible" and Fibi simply said, "The Bible shapes us."[57] Mbugua's conception of prosperity gospel hermeneutics as being "twisted . . . [into] a deceptive man-made message" is at odds here with how the women describe their own relationship to the Bible.[58] For them, the Bible is the authority and they come to it expecting to be shaped by it, not the other way around.

However, the women did share Mbugua's concern that the Bible be interpreted rightly. Jochebed and Anna gave examples of pastors who do not interpret the Bible rightly and Damaris gave an example of one who does.[59] There was a consensus that it was important to interpret the Bible rightly. This is unsurprising given the wider context of TAFES. Bible study is a feature of TAFES fellowships with many students experiencing it for the first time at TAFES. Hermeneutics and Homiletics are taught as part of the TAFES year both to students and staff. This reflects TAFES's evangelical nature. While evangelicalism is a notoriously slippery term, biblicism is an well-established feature of it.[60] The Doctrinal Statement of the IFES, of which TAFES is a part, affirms, "The divine inspiration and entire trustworthiness of Holy Scripture, as originally given, and its supreme authority in all matters of faith and conduct."[61] Here trustworthiness is a more pietistic category where the Bible cannot be known outside of personal relationship with God, in contrast

---

56. Interview 20 (Ruth), Swahili quotation 87.
57. Interview 4 (Fibi), Swahili quotation 88.
58. Maura et al., *Prosperity?*, 15.
59. Interview 19 (Jochebed); Interview 13 (Anna); Interview 3 (Damaris).
60. Bebbington, *The Evangelical Quadrilateral*, 37.
61. International Fellowship of Evangelical Students, "What We Believe."

to scientific-rationalist approaches to the text.[62] The women's approach to Scripture reflects these evangelical values.

In focus groups, there was also a spirited discussion about who is responsible for biblical interpretation. The women were asked to respond to the following statement:

> All people who listen and believe the preachers who promise that they will get a house, car, millions, billions and success in business, all of them together – these preachers and these listeners – have abandoned the faith and are not following Jesus Christ.[63]

Huldah wanted to place blame with the teachers, which was how the Mwanza focus group responded as well.[64] She felt it was not fair to ask especially new believers or those with little education to know how to interpret the Bible well. However, Priscilla and Sarai argued that the Bible is for all and is not mediated by an authority figure.[65] Priscilla said, "Ignorance is not an excuse—that curtain has been torn in two, all of us face God direct ... Truth and life are in the word of God. So whatever the preacher says, I believe a person must stand and use their mind."[66] Even those who were unable to immediately interpret the Bible well thus had a personal responsibility for learning it.

Holding the Bible as their authority and taking care to interpret it correctly, the women therefore believe their theology to be biblical, including their theology of *mafanikio*. Indeed Abigail, Anna, Bilhah, Ruth, and Susanna referred to their theology of prosperity as biblical.[67] This is not simply a matter of checking their theology with the Bible but of their theology having flowed out of biblical teaching. As Jochebed said, "The Bible directs us towards

---

62. Joset, "The Priesthood of All Students?," 230.
63. See Appendix 5 Focus Group Questions.
64. Focus Group 2; Focus Group 1.
65. Focus Group 2.
66. Focus Group 2, Swahili quotation 89.
67. Interview 2 (Abigail); Interview 13 (Anna); Interview 14 (Bilhah); Interview 20 (Ruth); Interview 6 (Susanna).

prosperity."⁶⁸ For Lois, the Bible speaks about its own function in terms of prosperity:

> 2 Timothy 3:16 says that every Scripture is suitable for teaching which warns, rebukes and teaches us. So every word in the Bible has a teaching which is able to prosper us.⁶⁹

While the women believe that their prosperity teaching is biblical, thereby upholding the Bible's authority, we can understand more about how *mafanikio* theology functions as a biblical theology by examining their hermeneutics in more depth.

5.3.1 Saturation And Immediacy

The women's Bible knowledge and ease with referencing the Bible was evident. In the course of interviews and focus groups, they cited over forty different Bible passages as well as speaking about over twenty Bible characters in addition to the members of the Trinity. They saw prosperity as a strong biblical theme saturating the Bible. Abigail, Bilhah, Damaris, Rhoda, and Ruth argued it was there from the first page to the last.⁷⁰

However, their interaction with the theme of prosperity in the Bible was somewhat abstracted from salvation history, that is the progressive narrative of the Bible, from creation through the fall to the people of God in Israel in its various stages (seeking the Promised Land, monarchy, exile and return), culminating in Jesus and the ushering in of the kingdom of God, to be consummated on the final day. This approach is championed in my own background. In Australian Fellowship of Evangelical Students (AFES) where my faith was nurtured as a university student, seminars are regularly taught on this way of understanding the Bible and *According to Plan* by Graeme Goldsworthy has been recommended reading.⁷¹ Goldsworthy was a lecturer at Moore College in Sydney, where many AFES staff train. In this hermeneutic, each passage must be located in its salvation history in order to ascertain what

---

68. Interview 19 (Jochebed), Swahili quotation 90.

69. Interview 10 (Lois), Swahili quotation 91.

70. Interview 2 (Abigail); Interview 14 (Bilhah); Interview 3 (Damaris); Interview 15 (Rhoda); Interview 20 (Ruth).

71. In Australia, this theology is sometimes just referred to as "biblical theology" not because it is the only way to read the Bible but as a technical term to refer to this way of approaching the Bible.

it meant first to its original hearers and then how it might be applied today. UK pastor-theologian Vaughn Roberts has argued in *God's Big Picture: Tracing the Story-line of the Bible* that this approach safeguards against "dipping into [the Bible] at random and extracting individual verses without any regard for their context. I am almost bound to misunderstand the Bible if I read it that way."[72] It is thus a tool to be used for evangelical means of upholding the authority of the Bible rather than shaping it to one's own agenda. However, locating a particular passage or character within this narrative scope was not an approach shared by the TAFES women. For example, Bilhah referred to Abraham as a Christian even though he lived two millennia before Christ.[73] Additionally, the promises of Deuteronomy were referred to without consideration of whether or how they apply to Christians today. Their approach assumed that what applied to the Old Testament people of God easily applies to God's New Testament people, that is, all Christians. While they had a sense that God's people in the Old Testament are different from God's people in the New Testament, they nevertheless thought that Scriptures pertaining to God's Old Testament people apply to his New Testament people, including Christians today. For example, Zipporah said, "God talks a lot in this book of Deuteronomy, that if you follow God, these blessings will stick with you."[74]

The promises of Deuteronomy were frequently mentioned and therefore provide a good case study for how the women interact with the Old Testament. They saw an immediacy between themselves and the promises of the Old Testament, collapsing the hermeneutical distance. However, these promises were spoken of by Chloe, Eunice, Rhoda, Puah, Susanna, Bilhah, Anna, and Priscilla as principles.[75] Warning against using them as a formula for instant success, Junia explained:

> Because if you teach people the word of God, they will automatically prosper, because they will know the word of God, they will work according to what God wants. If you teach them that this is the word 1, 2, 3, 4, this is the principles of the word of God,

---

72. Roberts, *God's Big Picture*, 18.
73. Interview 14 (Bilhah).
74. Interview 16 (Zipporah), Swahili quotation 92.
75. Focus Group 1; Interview 1 (Eunice); Interview 15 (Rhoda); Interview 7 (Puah); Interview 6 (Susanna); Interview 14 (Bilhah); Interview 13 (Anna); Focus Group 2.

then they will prosper because they will know this is what is supposed to be done . . . But if you just tell them that when you do this you get this, then they go astray to the principles of God.[76]

These Old Testament promises functioned to show how God has set up his world and how people can live well in it. The women read the promises as endorsing a predictability in the world and explaining its order. Thus, when it comes to economic prosperity, Zilpah said, "Everything has an order, there are principles or order of how to get this money."[77] Thus though the women saw an immediacy in their application of Deuteronomy, they did not treat Deuteronomy as a formula, an accusation levelled at prosperity preachers.[78]

How do the women avoid a formula when reading Deuteronomy? Their emphasis on principles provided some boundaries for how to interact with any one text. Take the following example from Ruth, speaking about how to interpret Deuteronomy 11:

God told the people of Israel, he will look after your fields . . . but it is not an excuse to be lazy because there are challenges of people who do not succeed at all because they say, "Lord, you are able to do for us as you do for the bird," so they just sit there. Now, that's very wrong. Because God says . . . "The one who does not work will not eat." So we must live a balanced life.[79]

Here Ruth takes a promise from Deuteronomy and argues that it must not be allowed to grow out of proportion because that would contradict other biblical principles, here from Matthew 6 and 2 Thessalonians 3. This was typical of how the women interacted with the Bible. Bilhah said verses cannot be taken in isolation because, "The verses depend on each other" and Anna scoffed at a preacher who used "only one verse for a sermon of one hour."[80] A comprehensive reading of Scripture guards against one or a few verses growing out of proportion or dominating theology, and therefore prevents an extreme or lopsided theology. Reading in the context of the surrounded

---

76. Interview 5 (Junia).
77. Focus Group 2, Swahili quotation 93.
78. Ageboyin, "A Rethinking of Prosperity," 82.
79. Interview 20 (Ruth), Swahili quotation 94.
80. Interview 14 (Bilhah), Swahili quotation 100; Interview 13 (Anna).

pericope was mentioned by Ruth, but in general it was the broader context of other Bible passages and Bible themes that provided the framework for interpreting a particular passage. Other examples of these, which I explored at length in chapter 4, included the importance of relationship with God and the sovereignty of God ("God is still God"). Thus, though salvation history did not factor strongly in their women's hermeneutics, principles they found elsewhere in the Bible acted as a guardrail, preventing promises from becoming guarantees and instead orienting the Christian towards fidelity to God and learning his ways.

This is in line with African storytelling conventions, where stories function in a "cyclical linear" rather than pure linear fashion where "the story does progress forward but not in a straight line."[81] In contrast, a salvation history hermeneutic tends to function in a more linear way, arguably an approach more in line with Western ways of thinking. Indeed, as Timothy Gabrielson has pointed out, at times this approach seems to diverge even from how biblical authors themselves interpret the Old Testament.[82] This is not the place to interrogate the extent to which a salvation history hermeneutic is beholden to Western cultural ways of thinking; suffice to say, we each have our cultural ways of reading the Bible. Meanwhile, in Africa, there is a validity to harking back, as well as to past events having an immediacy in the present. Gabrielson calls this a "contemporizing hermeneutic" where other parts of the Bible bring "an older passage up to date, accounting for God's actions in the world." While the women do not tend to use salvation history as the framework for interpreting Old Testament passages, they do certainly look to New Testament passages to inform how they understand the Old Testament. Thus, Damaris gave the example of Abraham's near sacrifice of Isaac as a type of Christ, insisting that, "There are many many many things in the Old Testament. We cannot say, 'Ok but it's gone,' because this is not true. They also apply to us."[83] As Zipporah urged that one book of the Bible not be read in isolation from others, she was arguing for taking the witness of the whole of Scripture.[84] Thus the women emphasized knowing the whole

---

81. Mburu, *African Hermeneutics*, Kindle edition, 20.
82. Gabrielson, "Along the Grain of Salvation," 71–90.
83. Interview 3 (Damaris), Swahili quotation 96.
84. Interview 16 (Zipporah).

Bible and bringing each verse into conversation with the others. The way they did so can be seen to be in line with African ways of reading the Bible.

5.3.2 Use of Biblical Figures

A preoccupation with biblical figures was reflected in the women's *mafanikio* theology as well. This is a common hermeneutical feature of TAFES more broadly. When Associates are asked to teach on a topic, they are often given a short outline or suggestion to guide them. When I have been asked to teach, I have been frequently directed to give examples of biblical figures as part of the teaching.

Use of archetype and story are common modes of teaching in Africa and, as Kenyan theologian Elizabeth Mburu reminds us, most of the Bible is written in story.[85] It is therefore not surprising that biblical figures would feature in the women's theology, as they do in many African theologies, according to Asamoah-Gyadu.[86] Two archetypes are worth highlighting in particular because they were used similarly: Abraham and Job. Damaris, Bilhah, Susanna, Ruth and Dorcas all saw Abraham as archetypal for prosperity because he was wealthy.[87] Salome and Shiphrah added that Abraham is an example to us because of his commitment to walking with God through hard times or when he did not understand the situation.[88] Likewise, when speaking of Job, the women commonly cited his riches as an example of prosperity, while his faithfulness was also on view.[89] Indeed, the second was heightened by the loss of the first, that having lost so much, according to Salome, "Job still did not abandon God."[90] Though both Abraham and Job were cited as wealthy people, this was not a mandate for all Christians but an apologetic for wealth being a blessing from God. They were also not cited as patterns to follow in order to live a life of blessing, in contrast to how scholars have cited

---

85. Mburu, *African Hermeneutics*, 120.
86. Asamoah-Gyadu, "Learning to Prosper," 70.
87. Interview 3 (Damaris); Interview 14 (Bilhah); Interview 6 (Susanna); Interview 20 (Ruth); Focus Group 2.
88. Interview 8 (Salome); Interview 9 (Shiphrah).
89. Interview 6 (Susanna); Interview 8 (Salome); Interview 10 (Lois); Interview 7 (Puah); Focus Group 2 (Huldah, Priscilla, Dorcas).
90. Interview 8 (Salome), Swahili quotation 97.

the role of the Abrahamic covenant in the prosperity gospel.[91] The women acknowledged that both men went through periods of suffering and trial and that their faith was vindicated, such as when Isaac was replaced by the ram and when Job's wealth was returned to him.[92] However, the women gave far more of their attention to the faithfulness of Abraham in walking closely with God and the perseverance of Job.

In the case of Job, it was not the case that his life was seen as two periods of prosperity bookending a period of difficulty. Instead, prosperity is found in continuing to walk with God in all circumstances. This faithfulness is for its own sake, not in order to precipitate blessing. In focus groups, the women were asked about the principle of sowing and reaping and whether a person who was suffering had not sown adequately. The biblical figure they used to refute this was Job, because in Susanna's words, "Job was a person of great faith and even he had sickness."[93] Job's suffering was not a direct result of some failure on his part, but neither was his vindication caused by his endurance. The women saw the return of his prosperity as a blessing from God that came at the end of this endurance but not as a result of his endurance. Priscilla and Bilhah spoke of enduring *until* God heals rather than enduring *so that* God will heal.[94] The ethical framework we saw in the features of *mafanikio* is therefore determinative in how the women approached the story of Job. They used it to exhort listeners to perseverance and righteousness in particular. The same theological commitments we saw when exploring perseverance as a feature of *mafanikio* (section 4.7.2) guide the reading of the story of Job, such that he becomes an archetype of prosperity because of his fidelity and endurance. Without such theological commitments underpinning *mafanikio*, Job could easily become a case study of how God always bestows great wealth on those who endure. While the vindication of God is not absent from the women's treatment of the story of Job, for them this is not the point of the story because this is not where their theological emphasis lies. The

---

91. Asamoah-Gyadu, *African Charismatics*, 207; Ngwobia, Kambale and Ngomo, "Misleading Theologies of Wealth and Poverty in the Context of Faith," 293–4; Golo, "Africa's Poverty and Its Neo-Pentecostal 'Liberators,'" 368; Young, "Prosperity Teaching in an African Context," 6.

92. Interview 9 (Shiphrah); Focus Group 2; Interview 14 (Bilhah).

93. Focus Group 1, Swahili quotation 98.

94. Focus Group 2; Interview 14 (Bilhah).

interpretation of the story of Job is therefore guided by the theological principles of *mafanikio*, ensuring that focus remains on encouraging faithfulness rather than making demands of God.

5.3.3 Connections with Wisdom Literature

Both principles and archetypal figures are common features of the Bible's wisdom literature, so it is fruitful to consider connections between the women's hermeneutical approach and the Bible's wisdom literature.

The Old Testament wisdom literature is generally thought to comprise of Proverbs, Ecclesiastes, Job, and Song of Songs. While Proverbs lays down normative patterns for how the world works, Ecclesiastes and Job interrogate exceptions to these. We have already seen that the women's conception of prosperity in Job is continued faithfulness despite circumstances rather than eventual vindication. In this sense, they read Job not as a pattern for how to attain future prosperity but as an example of how to live life well – that is, prosper – in a present that includes suffering. Job therefore speaks to the everyday in the women's understanding, in concert with the rest of the wisdom literature, such as Proverbs which Lindsay Wilson says, "focuses on everyday life: what works, what brings success and so on."[95] However, for the women in this research, the relevance to everyday life applies not only to the wisdom literature but to the whole Bible. As Anna said, the Bible "is a road map for everything, directing us in everything."[96] Thus, if one needs to know how to live life well in God's world (a major wisdom theme), the whole Bible is relevant.

While above I argued that the immediacy of the women's application of Deuteronomy may be attributed to African approaches to storytelling, such that past events and periods are seen as relevant to today, here we have another reason for why the women's interactions with the Bible appear to be abstracted from salvation history: because they interact with much of the Bible as though it is wisdom literature. Scholars have long puzzled over where the wisdom literature fits in the unfolding narrative of the Bible. E. C. Lucas says theological writers have found it difficult to assimilate the wisdom literature because of the "lack of reference to Israel's historic traditions, including the fundamental

---

95. Wilson, *Proverbs: An Introduction*, 25.
96. Interview 13 (Anna), Swahili quotation 99.

ones of exodus from Egypt and the establishment of the covenant and Sinai."[97] If the women interact with Deuteronomy and much of the rest of the Bible as if it is wisdom literature, then the same dynamic may be at play, where the narrative of salvation history can fade into the background as it does when reading the wisdom literature.

Whether this is an appropriate reading of Deuteronomy or indeed other parts of the Bible is another question. Wisdom elements are not limited to the Bible's wisdom literature. Though Deuteronomy's opening words situate it in a particular time (the fortieth year of Israel's wandering in the desert, Deut 1:3), place (East of the Jordan in the territory of Moab, Deut 1:6), and point in Israel's history (preparing to fulfil the covenant with Abraham by entering the promised land, Deut 1:6–8), it is not wholly separate from wisdom connotations. Discussions around the compilation of Deuteronomy in the latter half of the twentieth century included the affinities between Deuteronomy and wisdom literature.[98] This does not mean that Deuteronomy ought to be read as a wisdom text; to do so is to make a mistake of genre and to diminish salvation history as a biblical theme. From this perspective, reading Deuteronomy as if it is wisdom literature is invalid.

However, Deuteronomy shares at least one thing with wisdom literature: that the same God speaks through it. A hallmark of biblical wisdom literature is its Yahwism, most famously expressed in the refrain from Proverbs that the fear of Yahweh is the beginning of wisdom, a concept referred to by Abigail, Damaris, Ruth and Zipporah.[99] D. J. Estes therefore argues that the God who speaks in wisdom literature is the same one "revealed in the Law, the Prophets and the Psalms".[100] The reverse is also true: the God of covenant relationship is the same one who teaches his people how to live well in his world. While Deuteronomy ought not be read as wisdom literature, it does not only teach about salvation history; it also teaches about who God is. We saw in the previous chapter that prosperity flows from wisdom which comes from knowing God. Any exercise in knowing God can therefore be thought of as an exercise in wisdom that can lead to prosperity. It is on this grounds

---

97. Lucas, "Wisdom Theology," 901–12.

98. Longman III and Dillard, *An Introduction*, 108.

99. Interview 2 (Abigail); Interview 3 (Damaris); Interview 20 (Ruth); Interview 16 (Zipporah).

100. Estes, "Wisdom and Biblical Theology," 853–58.

that the women approach Deuteronomy expecting to gain "principles" by which to live. While their understanding could perhaps be enriched by a salvation history element, it must be acknowledged that it is motivated by desire to know God and his ways more deeply through his word in order to live for him more fully.

The women's personal and direct reading of the Bible also has a democratizing effect: if knowledge about God's world is found in the Bible then, as Zipporah said, "The directions are open," and there is no need for special revelations from pastors, prophets or other mediators.[101] This openness was the basis for the women to exhort others to know the Bible better and deeper. Not only does their wisdom approach give them a personal and direct experience of Scripture, it also encourages them to know Scripture better and in more richness.

5.3.4 Presence of Common Prosperity Gospel Passages

Thus far we have seen that the women use passages and biblical figures abstracted from salvation history but in both cases, other theological commitments rein in interpretations of the passages which might lead them to become formulaic or lopsided. Because it is framed around wisdom and knowing God better through his word, even when they misread genre, their theology remains recognizably biblical. I have worked inductively here, seeking to understand how the women view and treat the Bible on their own terms. However, several scholars give lists of Bible passages commonly used by people in the prosperity gospel movement and it is worth surveying the data the women provided to ascertain how frequently and in what ways these passages were mentioned. Such a deductive approach will be helpful in ascertaining to what extent the women's hermeneutics resembles those of the wider prosperity gospel movement and whether their exegetical deficits continue to be minor when viewed in light of the theology they produce.

The table below gives an indication of the verses mentioned by several scholars who addressed hermeneutics:[102] Three verses are consistent across

---

101. Interview 16 (Zipporah).
102. Maura et al., *Prosperity?*; Ehioghae and Olanrewaju, "A Theological Evaluation," 69–75; Ngwobia, Kambale, and Ngomo, "Misleading Theologies of Wealth"; Adeleye, *The Preachers of a Different Gospel*; Young, "Prosperity Teaching." I have omitted from this list reference to

three of these five scholars: Isaiah 53:4–5, 2 Corinthians 8:9, 3 John 2. These verses are also frequently listed by scholars discussing or describing the prosperity gospel but who do not necessarily give great attention to hermeneutics.[103] For this reason, I will take them as three paradigmatic verses of the prosperity gospel as represented in the literature and compare them with the women's treatment of the verses.

Figure 5.3 Common prosperity gospel Bible verses

	Maura et al.	E&O	Ngomo	Adeleye	Young
Prov. 11:25				*	
Jer. 29:11			*		
Isa. 45:11				*	
Isa. 53:4–5	*		*		*
Mal. 3:10					
Matt. 6:33				*	
Matt. 7			*		
Mark 8:16–17					*
Mark 10:29, 30		*			
John 10:10			*		
John 15	*				
2 Cor. 8:9	*		*		*
Phil. 4:19			*		
Heb. 11				*	
3 John 2		*		*	*

2 Corinthians 8:9 and Isaiah 53:4–5 have similar themes and were mentioned by the same three scholars (Mbugua, Ngomo and Young) so I shall take them together.

---

sowing and reaping and to Deuteronomy. Though these arise frequently in these discussions, I have addressed the women's treatment of them above.

103. See for example Golo, "Africa's Poverty," 368; Gbote and Kgatla, "Prosperity Gospel: A Missiological Assessment," 10; Gifford, "Christian Fundamentalism and Development," 13.

For you know the grace of our Lord Jesus Christ, that though he was rich, yet for your sake he became poor, so that you through his poverty might become rich. (2 Corinthians 8:9)[104]

> Surely he took up our pain
>   and bore our suffering,
> yet we considered him punished by God,
>   stricken by him, and afflicted.
> But he was pierced for our transgressions,
>   he was crushed for our iniquities;
> the punishment that brought us peace was on him,
>   and by his wounds we are healed. (Isaiah 53:4–5)

Mbugua, Ngomo and Young give examples of prosperity preachers who locate an end to both poverty and suffering in the current age in these verses. Mbugua argues that this interpretation of 2 Corinthians 8 fails to take into account the immediate context of the passage, which is about sacrificial giving, with Christ the example of such which Christians are to follow. The interpretation of Isaiah 53:4–5 meanwhile, overlooks that these promises were inaugurated at the cross but will only be consummated at the Parousia. Therefore, taking these verses to suggest that Christians ought to be rich and never suffer is incorrect. However, the women in my research cohort did not reference these verses at any point whether in interviews, focus groups or participant observation. There is nothing to say about whether the women's interpretation coheres with either Mbugua's or with the prosperity preachers he criticises, because they simply do not include these passages in their theology of prosperity. While this does not mean the women have not heard these verses or used these verses, when discussing prosperity, in the course of this research these passages were not at the foreground of their theological reckoning. Considering the breadth of verses they did refer to, if these verses were significant in any way, it is surprising that they did not appear. Two out of three of the paradigmatic verses of the prosperity gospel simply did not feature in the women's theology.

---

104. All Scripture quotations are from The Holy Bible: New International Version. Grand Rapids: Zondervan, 2011.

However, the women frequently referenced 3 John 2 when speaking about prosperity:

> Dear friend, I pray that you may enjoy good health and that all may go well with you, even as your soul is getting along well.

Nigerian Seventh-Day Adventists Ehioghae and Olanrewaju argue that any application of this to financial prosperity is a misunderstanding because the verse is simply a customary greeting and not making a theological statement.[105] Adeleye quotes Jim Bakker, a repentant prosperity preacher, to argue the same.[106] Neither engage whether both could be true, that is, that a customary greeting could contain theological truth. This is because they conceive of teaching around this verse to be about prosperity which is only about financial gain. The women, on the other hand, do see the verse as making a theological statement that God wills prosperity for his people but, as we have seen, relegate financial prosperity to one necessary component of a holistic prosperity. For them, to wish a person's life may go well includes and implies financial prosperity because the different areas of prosperity all depend on each other. To remove one area of prosperity from that definition, is to endanger overall prosperity. Thus, it appears that Ehioghae and Olanrewaju, and Adeleye / Bakker's interpretation, with its omission of financial prosperity, is in fact wishing a person a lack of prosperity, since prosperity is only prosperity when it is holistic. In contrast, the women do not need to reject this verse as teaching theological truth because their definition of prosperity is sufficiently robust. For the women, 3 John 2 is indeed paradigmatic in the sense that, as we saw in the previous chapter, prosperity with all its component parts is only available in a holistic sense, flowing from relationship with God.

In interviews and focus groups, the women thus only used one of the three paradigmatic verses of the prosperity gospel movement as advanced by scholars who discuss its hermeneutics, and their treatment of that verse is quite different from the treatment of that verse in the prosperity gospel movement, as represented by those scholars. In this sense, the women's hermeneutics do not resemble that of the wider prosperity gospel movement; on the contrary, the conclusions they come to mirror Adeleye's. Adeleye is a particularly

---

105. Ehioghae and Olanrewaju, "A Theological Evaluation," 73.
106. Adeleye, *The Preachers of a Different Gospel*, 54–55.

important voice because he is prominent in the International Fellowship of Evangelical Students (IFES) of which TAFES is a part. Let me illustrate the coherence of the women's theology with his, by discussing two more verses which could be thought to form the paradigmatic triad for these women.

In addition to 3 John 2, there are two other foundational verses upon which the TAFES women build their prosperity theology. These were the creation mandate of Genesis 1:28, and Matthew 6:33. Both of these are already familiar to us from chapter 4 and are mentioned by Adeleye in his discussion of the prosperity gospel's misreading of Scripture. He argues that prosperity preachers' use of Matthew 6:33 frequently omits the reference to pursuing God's righteousness yet we have already seen the emphasis the women place on righteousness and their insistence that seeking God not be displaced by desire for other things. On Genesis 1, Adeleye argues that prosperity preachers elevate Adam and Eve to the status of "little gods," thereby contravening the first commandment "You shall have no other gods but me."[107] We have seen, however, that the women use Genesis 1 not to argue for a deification of humanity, but for our responsibility to work in God's world on this side of the Parousia. Thus, while the verses that make up the women's triad of paradigmatic verses are also present in the prosperity gospel more broadly, we see again that their use of them is very different. Indeed, their conclusions are fairly similar to Adeleye's own, such that there is a closer comparison between their theology and an evangelical leader than with theology commonly attributed to the prosperity gospel.

When it comes to frequently cited verses in the prosperity gospel movement, the women have some overlap but have some striking omissions. They also supply their own paradigmatic verses which in general move away from the alleged extremes of the prosperity gospel, instead emphasizing hard work and relationship with God. Their triad thus complements the breadth of Bible knowledge that is a hallmark of the women's hermeneutics overall.

5.3.5 Assessing the Women's Hermeneutics

Whatever the issues of exegesis or method in the women's hermeneutics, the fruit is evident. The women's theology avoids many pitfalls commonly attributed to the prosperity gospel even as their hermeneutic appears undisciplined,

---

107. Adeleye, 51, 56.

from a Western cultural perspective. However, when viewed in the light of African storytelling conventions, it becomes evident that they do in fact have boundaries on their treatment of the Bible. Furthermore, these boundaries function to produce a balanced theology where Bible verses hold one another in check. There is a challenge here for those who insist upon "correct" methods for scriptural interpretation. Gabrielson points out that many of the Bible's own authors fail to meet modern standards of biblical interpretation and that many Christians are low on confidence when it comes to reading the Bible, worried that their interpretation will fail without further study. He concludes: "Academic study is beneficial, but we who have had the privilege of it must not deprecate how the Spirit speaks to all Christians through his holy Word. There is sacredness to all thoughtful, earnest reading of Scripture."[108] This is exactly what we find in the women's reading of Scripture. The key thing for them is to know and love God and to know and love the Bible. Thus, they come to the Bible and are transformed by it. They are indeed taught, rebuked, and trained in righteousness as they read the Bible. The means of their transformation is the Bible, even if, when viewed from a Western cultural perspective, there are some hermeneutical deficiencies. Indeed, God's word is living and active in these Tanzanian women with their cultural ways of reading it. Furthermore, because they are engaged deeply in seeking to know the Bible better and interpret it well, we can expect that the more they continue in this endeavour, the more the Holy Spirit will, if necessary, refine their hermeneutic.

5.4 Conclusion

This chapter has sought to understand why the women hold their *mafanikio* theology, taking into account historical, cultural and biblical perspectives. There are at least three reasons why they hold it: because they believe it to be biblically true, because it corrects historical errors, and because it speaks to current needs in their culture. What does it do, then? *Mafanikio* theology nourishes the women as African Christians in ways that make sense to them, from the word of God, equipping them to live well for God in his world, avoiding the errors of the past and the follies of the present.

---

108. Timothy A. Gabrielson, "Along the Grain of Salvation History: A Suggestion for Evangelical Hermeneutics," *Trinity Journal* 36, no. 1 (2015): 71–90,.

Figure 5.4 What have we learned about *mafanikio* theology (MT)? (Chapters 4–5)

Chapter 4	Chapter 5	Chapter 6	Chapter 7	Chapter 8
In MT, prosperity is a process of taking steps to move to the next level. This process manifests across all areas of life and when all areas are affected, the result is greater than the sum of the parts. In MT, God is the source of prosperity. In MT, prosperity is characterised by effort, perseverance, righteousness, and knowledge.	MT responds to a poverty gospel on one hand and profligate prosperity gospel on the other. MT combats passivity through knowing God rightly, identity change, and environmental change. MT locates itself in the Bible, with hermeneutics that emphasise a comprehensive knowledge of Scripture to provide a balanced theology.			

CHAPTER 6

Mafanikio Theology as Prosperity Theology and Discipleship

6.1 *Mafanikio* Theology in the Landscape of Prosperity Theology

We have come to understand *mafanikio* theology as a process of taking steps to move to the next level which is the will of God for his people. We have seen it as a product of its historical and cultural location and as an African way of reading the Bible. Having examined what it is and where it comes from, we are now in a place to begin bringing it into conversation with other theologies, the first of a movement of broadening concentric circles. This first concentric circle brings *mafanikio* theology into conversation with prosperities very close to home, that is, prosperity theologies within Africa. Where does *mafanikio* theology fit and what contribution does it make?

My argument has worked within Drønen's post-Giffordian paradigm, seeking to know the women's theology at its local level. I have resisted making broader statements about the prosperity gospel specifically or prosperity theologies more generally in favour of examining this particular prosperity theology. While it may only be a fragment of the broader movement, the specificity leads to greater accuracy than generalisations. We have "met" this family member in depth. It is now time to see the extent to which she resembles her other family members. I will compare *mafanikio* theology with other individual family members, starting from other Tanzanian prosperity theologies then expanding to other local African prosperity theologies before re-visiting how this modifies our understanding of prosperity theology in Africa more broadly. I will consider its contribution as a critique of other African prosperity theologies and then turn my attention to interrogating the extent to which *mafanikio* theology can sustain commitment to Christ and nourish a life of discipleship.

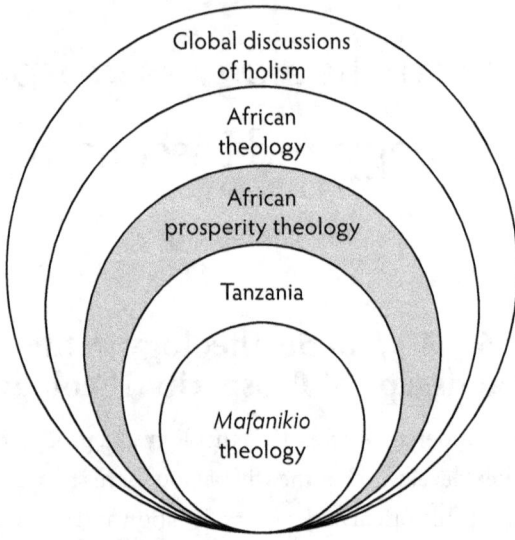

Figure 6.1 Concentric circles of engagement with *mafanikio* theology (African prosperity theology)

6.1.1 *Mafanikio* Theology among Tanzanian Prosperity Theologies

Drawing on over a decade with the charismatic Brethren in Tanzania, Allan Smith McKinnon, identifies the *goal* of Tanzanian living as wholeness, the *means* of achieving it as spiritual power, and its *outlook* as pragmatic ability, that is, deliverance now and in the age to come.[1] He locates the appeal of Pentecostalism among the Brethren in the extent to which it aligns with these preoccupations.[2] These preoccupations are also shared by *mafanikio* theology.

---

1. McKinnon, "On Being Charismatic Brethren," 298.
2. McKinnon, 279–284.

Mafanikio theology also shares a great deal in common with the prosperity theology espoused in the Tanzanian independent neo-Pentecostal denomination Efatha as presented by Hasu.[3] Theologically, they both teach that poverty is not a Christian virtue, and that God wants Africans to be wealthy. Rather than placing their emphasis on miraculous means to achieve prosperity, they emphasize attitude, hard work, and responsibility. They both expect that individual prosperity is to be shared with others, especially the poor. Efatha and the women in this research come from the same demographic (the educated middle class) so it is perhaps not surprising to find such similar theologies at play here.[4] Some form of what I have called *mafanikio* theology is not unique to TAFES; it is present in middle class churches as well. Does it go beyond the middle class, though?

Hasu draws a comparison with the Glory of Christ Tanzania Church (GCTC) headed by Bishop Josephat Mathias Gwajima whose church, with its lower socio-economic demographic, focuses on "delivering people from the powers of darkness," rather than teaching about prosperity.[5] This is not to say that prosperity is irrelevant at GCTC or that there are no parallels with *mafanikio* theology. After all, in *mafanikio* theology, prosperity is opposed by Satan and his forces and therefore spiritual warfare can be a logical precursor to pursuing prosperity. However, TAFES women tended to emphasise God's order for the world over the disorder created by Satan.

The middle class is also extremely broad and somewhat porous. Dilger notes that attendees of the Full Gospel Bible Fellowship Church (FGBFC) of Bishop Kakobe are those who have been "affected by urbanisation and globalisation processes," having migrated to Dar Es Salaam in search of employment, or engaging in small business entrepreneurship.[6] They are not the rural poor and their aspirations set them apart from the urban poor, although their actual income may not differ greatly from the latter. Dilger argues that at FGBFC they find peace as the church deals with "feelings of powerlessness and frustration [by] its gospel of wealth and health" and "morally acceptable responses to the manifold tensions and ruptures . . . of globalisation and

---

3. Hasu, "Prosperity Gospels and Enchanted Worldviews," 67–87.

4. One Focus Group participant was raised in an Efatha church though after her marriage she became a member of the African Inland Church.

5. Hasu, "Prosperity Gospels and Enchanted Worldviews," 78.

6. Dilger, "Healing the Wounds," 66.

modernity."[7] These twin preoccupations of dealing with hopelessness and providing righteous ways of living align with *mafanikio* theology. However, even in less prosperous areas such as Tanga and rural Arumeru in Tanzania's north, there is evidence of Christian emphases on spiritual progress, changed values and beliefs as well as material progress – though in those areas such values also align with tribal characteristics.[8] While *mafanikio* theology most clearly operates in the affluent middle class, elements of it can be observed in lower socio-economic demographics as well.

While we have seen some overlap between *mafanikio* theology and the theology of prosperity in the FGBFC, their theology addresses different periods in the Christian life. In FGBFC, the contemporary world is understood to be "tightly in the grip of Satan who is spreading immorality, corruption and suffering."[9] Dilger argues that FGBFC's solution to this is the "Gospel of Prosperity," but he is not referring to teaching about *mafanikio* here but about *neno la uzima* (word of life, word of wholeness), available through salvation. He explains:

> The Gospel of Prosperity and the ideology of salvation are based on the claim that while, everyone is born into a state of sin and is exposed to the immoralities of the world from early childhood, a person can be "saved" from perdition by becoming aware of the ways Satan exerts control over a person's life.[10]

This awakening is a prerequisite to forgiveness and entry into the people of God, "entering the state of salvation and escaping the control of Satan by dedicating one's life to God by accepting and spreading the teachings of the Bible."[11] Here, prosperity is intimately tied to the conversion experience: one crosses from a life controlled by Satan to a new life centred on God. In *mafanikio* theology, however, the conversion experience is insufficient. Many Christians are converted and yet continue to experience a lack of progress or victory in their life. Their problem is not that they are unconverted but that they lack sufficient knowledge of God and how God has set up his world

---

7. Dilger, 62, 64.
8. Kipacha, Dugbazah, and Mesaki, "Religious Teachings and Development," 107–128.
9. Dilger, "Healing the Wounds," 65.
10. Dilger, 65.
11. Dilger, 65.

in order to flourish in it. It is not as simple as "accepting and spreading the teachings of the Bible" unless those teachings include the kind of wisdom that equips people to live well in God's world.[12] While the FGBFC's prosperity gospel, at least as Dilger presents it, is about moving from one kingdom (of captivity) to another kingdom (of prosperity), *mafanikio* theology asks how life in the second kingdom works once you have entered it. McKinnon makes a useful distinction here in his discussion of Tanzanian Brethren and their quest for wholeness by explaining the nuances of two Swahili words for "life," *uzima* and *maisha*. *Uzima* is "is more idealistic and tends to be oriented toward the life to come."[13] *Maisha*, on the other hand "describes the earthly experience of living from day to day."[14] FGBFC's prosperity theology operates at the *uzima* level, a theology of conversion; *mafanikio* theology operates at the *maisha* level as a theology of discipleship. Conversion and discipleship are part of one continuum, and it is not wise to draw too clear a line between the two. After all, the FGBFC does provide guidance for Christians after conversion; likewise, the TAFES women perceive a role for *mafanikio* theology in evangelism, for example when unbelievers see a Christian's prosperity and are attracted to find out more. However, their emphases differ in terms of where they locate prosperity. For FGBFC, prosperity is yours at the moment of conversion, leading Dilger to suspect that it is "often only imaginary," whereas for the TAFES women, prosperity is a result of a process of going deeper with God each day over time.[15] Their emphases and their timelines differ. While the FGBFC offers the unbeliever an "escape from socio-economic hardships," *mafanikio* theology offers an invitation to know God, with all the benefits that brings – an invitation that extends beyond conversion.[16] Prosperity in *mafanikio* theology is not an offer that you claim; it is a process that you undertake.

---

12. Dilger, 65.
13. McKinnon, "On Being Charismatic Brethren," 271.
14. McKinnon, 271.
15. Dilger, 62.
16. Dilger, 62.

6.1.2 *Mafanikio* Theology among African Prosperity Theologies

As we broaden out the scope to the rest of Africa, Maria Frahm-Arp has built on Drønen's observation of churches that "talked much about success and faith, but always connected this to hard work, studies, and the spirit of entrepreneurship," and thus did not fit the picture provided by scholars who concentrated on the prosperity gospel of mega-churches as representative.[17] Her taxonomy of the prosperity movement in South Africa (see section 2.2.2.) serves as a starting point for asking what type of prosperity theology is at play. *Mafanikio* theology has more in common with progress prosperity than abilities or miracles prosperity. Like abilities prosperity, *mafanikio* theology holds, that "if Christians live according to biblical principles and work hard, then they will succeed in whatever they choose to do," it does not ascribe to abilities prosperity's belief that unrepentant sin as the cause of a person's lack of progress.[18] It also does not fit the miracles cluster where wealth "is achieved not through hard work or a strict moral code. . . . but rather through God's desire to bless people with miraculous wealth."[19]

Progress prosperity, on the other hand, "holds that any small blessing or step of progress is a form of prosperity" much as *mafanikio* theology envisions prosperity as a process of taking steps to move to the next level.[20] Naomi Haynes's work from the Zambian Copperbelt adds another local theology to this category. In her "limited prosperity gospel," Christians also do not expect uniform wealth or extravagance but rather some measure of economic progress.[21] Likewise, progress prosperity frowns on aiming for a dramatic change in material circumstances, since those who desire this often do not recognize that "these only come through a relationship with God," a relationship which will in turn teach a person to "see all the ways in which God is blessing them."[22] Progress prosperity also stresses changing your thinking in Jesus, whether that be "incorrect thoughts, which in turn are often connected to unhealthy

---

17. Drønen, "Material Development and Spiritual Empowerment?" 209.
18. Frahm-Arp, "Pentecostalism, Politics, and Prosperity," 7.
19. Frahm-Arp, 7, 8.
20. Frahm-Arp, 8.
21. Haynes, "Pentecostalism and the Morality," 127.
22. Frahm-Arp, "Pentecostalism, Politics, and Prosperity," 9.

influences, human and otherwise" or bad influences in one's environment.[23] This emphasis on changing one's thinking is prominent in African diaspora churches as well "that challenge the broken and marginalised to do something about their lives."[24] Such change is familiar to us from the role the women see *mafanikio* theology playing in correcting false theologies and changing the environment in which people find themselves.

Writing from Kenya, Joshua Barron has identified three "streams" of prosperity gospel: one which is primarily orthodox but requires some correction, a second which is heretical and deceitful (akin to what I am calling the profligate prosperity gospel), and a third which he dubs Productivity Gospel, a combination of "the empowerment theology of the Prosperity Gospel combined with personal accountability and the Protestant work ethic."[25] Barron does not trace the relationship between the Protestant work ethic and this Productivity Gospel so it is unclear whether he is using Protestant work ethic merely to describe the Productivity Gospel or instead to imply a causal link, but this form of prosperity gospel also moderates desire for wealth alone by including spiritual prosperity and directing prosperity in the service of God and others.[26]

Whether there is any historical or geographical link between the churches Frahm-Arp studied, the ones Haynes saw on the Zambian Copperbelt, the phenomenon Barron has observed, and the *mafanikio* theology of TAFES women, it is nevertheless true that the family resemblance between these siblings is strong. *Mafanikio* theology thus contributes to the growing evidence of prosperity theologies which are different from the popular perception of prosperity gospel as advanced by Gifford and those who follow him. These theologies do not dispute the evidence of the kind of prosperity gospel Gifford describes; however, they illustrate that prosperity theology in Africa is broader and more nuanced.

---

23. Frahm-Arp, 9.
24. Asamoah-Gyadu, "'To the Ends of the Earth,'" 27.
25. Barron, "Is the Prosperity Gospel, Gospel?," 98.
26. Barron, 98.

6.1.3 *Mafanikio* Theology among Gifford's Six Registers of Prosperity Theology

Gifford rejects the idea that something different may be happening at the grassroots from the big megachurches, seeing smaller churches as imitations of the larger. While he stops short of considering mega-churches "strictly representative" he maintains the same elements "are present in virtually all African Pentecostal churches" to some degree.[27] In chapter 2, I noted several examples which do not fit Gifford's categories, arguing that they are part of a family of prosperity theologies in Africa but nevertheless distinct from the kind of megachurch prosperity gospel Gifford has advanced. However, as I now seek to locate *mafanikio* theology within that broader prosperity theology movement, Gifford's six registers – and his claim that they are present in all African prosperity theologies – warrant a closer look.

Gifford's first register of motivation is "to get on, to succeed, to prosper, to be important, to take control. Moreover, these things are your right and inheritance as a Christian, which you should expect and can demand."[28] While *mafanikio* theology is certainly aimed at success and prosperity, the TAFES women's motivation did not align with Gifford here. They did not use language of rights and inheritance as a Christian, instead preferring to speak of the responsibilities entrusted to them as human beings in the creation mandate. Furthermore, they shied away from language of demanding from God, instead recognizing his sovereignty and our place as human beings. The roles the women play in their lives may have influenced this orientation. Junia explained to me that women's caring responsibilities direct them towards nurture rather than control or status.[29] Achievement is therefore measured in terms of the well-being of others rather than the accumulation of status symbols such as cars. This study does not have data from men with which to compare, but during my time in Tanzania I have heard men preach similarly so I am hesitant to claim it as an exclusively female emphasis. Barron's Productivity Gospel also directs Christians towards a responsibility to care for others, providing evidence of such an orientation beyond *mafanikio* theology.

---

27. Gifford, "The Development and Political Role," 93.
28. Gifford, 82.
29. Interview 5 (Junia).

The second and third registers of entrepreneurship and practical skills are present in the women's exhortations to take initiative and to work hard. At TAFES, they also share their knowledge and skills for personal living and personal success. However, when asked for how to pursue *mafanikio*, the women did not speak of starting businesses; instead, they spoke of knowing God as a foundation for all success. This element of knowledge of God is present in none of Gifford's six registers. While these first three registers are concrete and practical and the latter three are "enchanted," none of them feature relationship with God. Yet, for the TAFES women, relationship with God is a critical theme. In speaking of Asian grassroots Christians, Simon Chan posits that elites often miss the importance of personal encounter with Jesus Christ in their models of socio-political liberation; this a major oversight of Gifford's registers as well.[30]

The fourth register, faith gospel, is "the belief that faith is all you need to share the victory Christ has already won for us over sin, sickness and poverty."[31] While the TAFES women saw faith in God as an essential part of prosperity, they rejected ideas of "seed-faith" (paying money to pastors in expectation of miraculous recompense) and acknowledged that suffering is a part of the Christian life. Their faith does not match with Gifford's faith gospel.

Gifford's fifth register is the "anointing of the man of God" with pastors' "prophetic words" seen as indispensable and increase in blessings attributed to him rather than to God.[32] However, we have seen that TAFES women place a great emphasis on the Bible as a direct word of God and oppose pastors and preachers who place themselves as intermediaries.

Defeating spirits from blocking one's advance is the final register as "churches counter the negative forces trying to undermine the success that should characterise a Christian."[33] Of all six registers this is perhaps the one least at odds with *mafanikio* theology. The women did acknowledge Satan's opposition to prosperity. However, it was not a major preoccupation. While

---

30. Chan, *Grassroots Asian Theology*, 103.
31. Gifford, "The Development and Political Role," 83.
32. Gifford., 83.
33. Gifford, 83.

Hasu argues that this is a relatively new development in Tanzania, it was nevertheless true of the women's theology.[34]

Having surveyed Gifford's six registers and their overlaps with *mafanikio* theology, we find issues at all six levels. Some registers can only be accepted as cohering with *mafanikio* theology with serious modification; others are simply not present in the way Gifford conceives. This is cause to question Gifford's six registers as descriptive of prosperity theology in Tanzania, if not also in Africa more widely. While they may describe the large mega-churches and even some smaller churches, they are not reflected in *mafanikio* theology. I posit that Gifford is too narrow in his understanding of prosperity theology in Africa and his assertion that the grassroots is always to some degree aping the megachurch needs serious modification. Perhaps he needs to offer a seventh register – that of relationship with God as both motivation, blueprint, and power for prosperity – and modify his argument that all registers need be present in order to allow for diversity of the movement.

There are serious implications for how we define prosperity theology in Africa. Under Gifford's assessment, since *mafanikio* theology does not align with his registers, perhaps it does not count as part of prosperity theology in Africa. However, this line of reasoning would have to overlook *mafanikio* theology's preoccupation with prosperity and how to attain it. It is far more reasonable to look for a spectrum of prosperity theologies across Africa, seeing Gifford's megachurch version as one part, perhaps even a large and influential part of the broader movement, but not paradigmatic. Differences between *mafanikio* theology and Gifford's six registers open up several possibilities, for example, that the grassroots level is ambivalent towards the megachurch, or that it provides an alternative to it, or that it perhaps even critiques megachurch prosperity gospel. This last possibility has significant implications for how we see the prosperity theology in Africa: is it possible to think of it as self-critiquing? In *mafanikio* theology we find a theology preoccupied with attaining prosperity, and yet it opposes many of the ways in which prosperity theology has been understood to play out in Africa. It is to the question of the role of *mafanikio* theology in the broader African prosperity theology movement that I now turn.

---

34. Hasu, "Prosperity Gospels and Enchanted Worldviews," 75.

6.1.4 *Mafanikio* Theology as Prosperity Theology and Critique

If Gifford's description of the prosperity gospel in Africa cannot be taken to apply in some way to all prosperity theologies in Africa, how might one define prosperity theology in Africa? What is the common thread that makes up this "family?" Katharine Attanasi begins her discussion of the prosperity gospel simply by saying that it teaches that "God wants to bless Christians spiritually, physically, materially."[35] This definition places emphasis on a theological principle without codifying the practices that exist in any one prosperity theology. These theologies are therefore united by a conviction that God wants to bless Christians spiritually, physically, materially without prescribing how they may do that: some practices may be efficacious, others nefarious. An advantage of such a definition is that it does not automatically assume that the idea that God wants to bless Christians spiritually, physically, and materially is bad or unchristian, as long as it is able to be held in tension with other Christian practices and disciplines. (I will explore *mafanikio* theology's capacity to do so below in the section on discipleship.) Indeed, even as Jean Bosco Kambale argues against a prosperity gospel which has no place for suffering and upholds the big man, he says:

> Prosperity is the essence of the Jesus Christ mission. Jesus says that he has come to provide an abundant life to his people (John 10:10); to proclaim the good news to the poor; to offer health to the sick, forgiveness to the sinners, freedom to the oppressed, etc. (Luke 4:18–19).[36]

One wonders on what basis one would object to the idea that God wants to bless Christians spiritually, physically, and materially. Surely God's plan is not to curse them! For Africans, such a definition is especially appropriate given the prominent place given in African worldview to prosperity. If Christianity has no place for prosperity theology, what place has it for the African? It is therefore preferable to assume prosperity theology as a whole in Africa to be made of many prosperity theologies which, in their particularity, have strengths and weaknesses.

---

35. Attanasi, "Introduction: The Plurality of Prosperity," 3.
36. Ngwobia, Kambale, and Ngomo, "Misleading Theologies of Wealth," 257.

The TAFES women did understand themselves as part of African prosperity theology. They spoke of the coming of prosperity theology as something that they embraced for its capacity to address the failings of the theology being taught at that time. They continue to affirm that God desires prosperity in all areas for his people. They are part of the prosperity theology movement in Africa, and we have seen in this chapter that *mafanikio* theology bears a resemblance to some other prosperity theologies in Africa. However, we have also seen that this does not mean that they resemble megachurch prosperity gospel as understood by Gifford, nor are they a diluted version of that same prosperity gospel. On the contrary, they teach against more profligate versions of prosperity gospel, such as those that exploit others, discourage hard work, or focus on the big man. In its place, they offer a theology which is still a prosperity theology, but one which they consider to be true and biblical. They therefore offer an alternative to other kinds of prosperity gospel and an indirect critique of them. Indeed, they see *mafanikio* theology as vital precisely because of the need to counter the profligate prosperity gospel (in addition to countering theologies that disparage prosperity theology.) From within Africa and from within the prosperity movement itself, there are critiques and modifications which are arising to the profligate or megachurch prosperity gospel. When encountering a prosperity theology, it is therefore essential to ask what kind of prosperity theology it represents. If all prosperity theology is to be dismissed wholesale, prosperity theology which critiques the profligate prosperity gospel will be rejected along with the profligate prosperity gospel itself. The danger of seeing all prosperity theology as inherently flawed or like Gifford's version of prosperity theology is that it overlooks and disparages a potential ally in opposing the profligate prosperity gospel: *mafanikio* theology and her sisters. They are not part of the problem of profligate prosperity gospel; they are its alternative, its critics and, perhaps, even its antidote.

Those who are concerned about the profligate prosperity gospel would do well to recognise and learn from *mafanikio* theology and on what basis it critiques the prosperity gospel. Critiques of the profligate prosperity gospel that disparage the idea of prosperity theology at all run the risk of returning the church to its state of passivity and irrelevance in the face of Africa's manifold challenges. However, *mafanikio* theology does not object to the profligate prosperity gospel on account of its assertion that God wants his people to prosper in all areas of life. On this count they agree. Instead, *mafanikio* theology critiques the profligate prosperity gospel's exploitation of people, its lack of emphasis on relationship with God, the significance it gives to big men over knowing the word of God, and the dangers it poses to Christian disciplines such as hard work, righteous living, and perseverance. None of these things are inherent in the statement that God wants prosperity for his people and the TAFES women insisted that prosperity is only prosperity when it is found in God. Opposition to the profligate prosperity gospel does not necessitate a rejection of prosperity. In *mafanikio* theology we find an African critique of the profligate prosperity gospel, one which takes seriously African concern for prosperity and seeks God in Africa.[37]

6.2 *Mafanikio* Theology as Discipleship

We have seen that *mafanikio* theology critiques a profligate prosperity gospel on multiple counts while sharing the conviction that God wants prosperity for his people. The TAFES women offer their theology as an alternative and so it is appropriate to scrutinise it: is it any better? Femi Adeleye warns that a "preoccupation with the pursuit of earthly wealth and conveniences has shipwrecked the faith of many."[38] Considering *mafanikio* theology's insistence on pursuit of prosperity in various forms and its conviction that this is the desire of God for his people, the question must be asked whether *mafanikio* theology can in fact sustain a life of discipleship or whether it is just as superficial or corrupt as that which it critiques. I propose taking the Parable of the Sower in Mark 4:1–20 as a way of assessing this.[39] A parable about the reception of the word of God, it casts its reader beyond initial reactions to the word of God, instead looking for long term responses and fruit.[40] In this sense, it can provide a useful lens for discipleship.

---

37. I will investigate further the Africanness of it in the next chapter. Here I simply mean is it concerned about issues in and pertaining to Africa.

38. Adeleye, *The Preachers of a Different Gospel*, 21.

39. The parable also appears in Matthew 13:1–23 and Luke 8:4–15.

40. Snodgrass, *Stories with Intent*, 199.

6.2.1 The Parable of the Sower

> 'Listen! A farmer went out to sow his seed. As he was scattering the seed, some fell along the path, and the birds came and ate it up. Some fell on rocky places, where it did not have much soil. It sprang up quickly, because the soil was shallow. But when the sun came up, the plants were scorched, and they withered because they had no root. Other seed fell among thorns, which grew up and choked the plants, so that they did not bear grain. Still other seed fell on good soil. It came up, grew and produced a crop, some multiplying thirty, some sixty, some a hundred times.' Then Jesus said, 'Whoever has ears to hear, let them hear.' (Mark 4:3–9)

Jesus goes on to explain this parable in Mark 4:14–20. The seed on the path pertains to those who do not respond, and the seed sown in good soil is about those who "hear the word and accept it and bear fruit" (Mark 4:20). The rocky soil is about those who receive the message with joy but because of their shallow roots fall away when trouble or persecution comes on account of the word.[41] Meanwhile, the thorny soil describes those who hear the word but do not yield a harvest because their desire for wealth and the things of this world distracts and consumes them. These two soils align with two deficits Adeleye identifies in prosperity gospel's capacity to sustain a life of discipleship. An impoverished theology of suffering is like rocky ground; an inadequate desire for Christ compared to the lure for wealth is like thorny soil.[42] What then does *mafanikio* theology have to say about suffering? What role does desire for Christ play alongside desire for wealth? I will examine each in depth, first looking at *mafanikio* theology and suffering, and then turning to consider *mafanikio* theology's relationship to Jesus.

6.2.2 Rocky Ground?: *Mafanikio* Theology and Suffering

The rocky soil in the parable refers to a person who falls away when trouble or persecution arises on account of the word. The immediate context in Mark

---

41. The kind of trouble or persecution referred to in the parable is that which arises on account of the word. It therefore likely does not refer to general suffering or the hardships of life.

42. Adeleye, *The Preachers of a Different Gospel*, 21–23.

is of the growing opposition to Jesus.[43] The rocky ground would therefore refer to those who cannot withstand human persecution which comes as a direct result of their faith in Christ. However, in an African or charismatic context, where the lines between human and spiritual activity overlap, persecution is not only human. Suffering is often thought to be a sign of persecution by Satan or by other powers.[44] This was reflected in Martha's comment that Satan opposes prosperity and works against it.[45] Therefore, any suffering becomes part of the picture when discussing how to endure in the face of persecution.[46] I am not attempting to alter the specificity of the original passage by saying this but to consider how it might be understood and applied in an African context. Indeed many prosperity theologies teach that faith is protective against hardship and it is on this basis that the Christian ought to expect that "nothing bad will ever befall them."[47] If something bad does befall them, it is a sign that their relationship with God has been broken by their disobedience or lack of faith, or that they are under demonic oppression.[48] Thus there is no room for brokenness and suffering.[49] As we consider whether or not *mafanikio* theology is rocky ground, we must consider if *mafanikio* theology has anything to offer to those who suffer or experience hardship.

In chapter 4, we saw that the TAFES women viewed suffering as a normal part of life, including for the Christian. For them, heaven is the place where there are no problems, and it is an over-realised eschatology that imports such an expectation into life now. The Christian ought to expect to contend with various issues in this life; the "not yet" of the Christian life is why perseverance is a feature of *mafanikio*. Meanwhile as they set about, in the words of Nigerian Anglican bishop Cyril Okorocha, participating "fully in the redemptive work of God in Christ in the world and appropriate its full benefits," the TAFES women are able to insist that the presence of suffering or hardship is not an

---

43. Schnabel, *Mark: An Introduction*, 98–99.
44. Lindhardt, "Mediating Money."
45. Interview 18 (Martha).
46. This is not necessarily exegetically inventive. For example, Mark Strauss and Walter Wessell acknowledge the immediate context of growing opposition to Jesus but also suggest a broader application to the fickle crowds, those who "follow Jesus for the miracles and the free meals but who want no part in self-sacrificial discipleship." Strauss and Wessell, *Mark*, 758.
47. Biwul, "Preaching Biblically," 127.
48. Biwul, 129.
49. Biwul, "Preaching Biblically," 126; Boamah, *The Cross or Prosperity Gospel*, 17.

indicator that God has abandoned that person.[50] They did not give a complete list of the reasons why a person experiences hardship. However, a prominent theme was that God is close to his people, even when they suffer, growing them in four ways: fostering reliance on him, giving them a chance to prove their faith, teaching them something, or ensuring long-lasting *mafanikio*. I shall look at each of these in turn.

6.2.2.1 Learning to rely on God

Lydia felt that when we have problems, it reminds us that we cannot attain *mafanikio* in our own strength. If we could, she thought, we would not need God.[51] So, as Puah said, "God allows other things so that we recognise the place of our father."[52] Difficult periods remind us that apart from God, we can do nothing: he is either providing for us by sustaining us through difficulty (Ruth) or by lavishing his favour on us (Deborah, Sarai).[53] Either way, we are reliant on him; during difficult periods this is at the forefront of our minds, and the memory of those periods is a lesson for the good times as well.

6.2.2.2 A chance to prove your faith

Eunice, Lois, Fibi and Bilhah all used the language of being tested.[54] Puah distinguished this from a temptation, which is designed to see someone fail; the point of a test is to vindicate a person's faith.[55] Lois said, "He wants to see that you hope in him more than everything else."[56] A person passes the test, according to Eunice, by going to God with their problems rather than to another source of power.[57] It is important to notice here that victory is not about a change in circumstance, but about turning to God. By continuing in fidelity to God, the source of *mafanikio* remains intact and therefore *mafanikio* is present in suffering.

---

50. Okorocha, "Religious Conversion in Africa," 168–81.
51. Interview 11 (Lydia).
52. Interview 7 (Puah), Swahili quotation 100.
53. Interview 20 (Ruth); Focus Group 2.
54. Interview 1 (Eunice); Interview 10 (Lois); Interview 4 (Fibi); Interview 14 (Bilhah).
55. Focus Group 1.
56. Interview 10 (Lois), Swahili quotation 101.
57. Interview 1 (Eunice).

6.2.2.3 A teaching moment

Continuing in fidelity to God grows, according to Fibi, "muscles to endure and get through trials and problems."[58] However, in times of suffering God is not only teaching us to endure in suffering. According to Huldah and Susanna, he may also have a specific lesson he wants us to learn.[59] For example, Rhoda spoke of God teaching her through her business being robbed. Though this was a great hardship for her, she learned how to increase her security and store her goods in a safer way, and she credited God as her teacher.[60]

While suffering may purpose to teach you something, it may also be for someone else's benefit; it does not necessarily suggest that there is a problem with you. Huldah mentioned that people like John the Baptist whose head was cut off were not learning something.[61] However, others may have benefited from seeing that. Anna agreed that one person's hardship can be instructive for others: "They might be warned or they might get more faith, to see this person has this thing but still they continue to believe and serve God."[62] She said as God's servant, she is willing to play this part in bringing about his will in the lives of others. Therefore, suffering is not always because of disobedience or broken relationship with God.

6.2.2.4 Building a foundation for long-lasting *mafanikio*

The women saw slow progress towards *mafanikio* as much more sustainable than quick success, with trials as part of the process of going slowly. Susanna said, "God is able to choose to give you the thing straight away. But many times he does it by steps as he continues to teach you in order that you are able to stand with him."[63] Lois and Bilhah both worried that if God gave too much too fast, he would lose that person.[64] Similarly, Puah asked in a focus group, "If I am a billionaire, is my spirit ready to carry this prosperity and to continue to stay with God?"[65] Eve, an accountant in the same focus group, used simi-

---

58. Interview 4 (Fibi), Swahili quotation 102.
59. Focus Group 2; Interview 6 (Susanna).
60. Interview 15 (Rhoda).
61. Focus Group 2.
62. Interview 13 (Anna), Swahili quotation 103.
63. Interview 6 (Susanna), Swahili quotation 104.
64. Interview 10 (Lois); Interview 14 (Bilhah).
65. Focus Group 1, Swahili quotation 105.

lar language of having the capacity to nurture *mafanikio*.⁶⁶ When God gives trials that appear to slow progress, he is therefore not obstructing *mafanikio* but ensuring that a person has the capacity to nurture it without losing their faith (and therefore losing their *mafanikio* altogether.) What may seem like suffering, therefore, may in fact be God's preservation of your *mafanikio*, as he only gives you the amount of prosperity that you can handle.

In presenting four ways that God grows his people through suffering, the TAFES women provide a picture of suffering as part of God's care for them rather than a sign of his abandonment. Thus, suffering itself can be part of the productive process of prosperity. When suffering or hardship comes, they are directed to look for what God is doing, either in their life or in the lives of others through that suffering. They can know that God is with them, even here in their suffering.

There is another layer to the women's theology of suffering: an operant theology. Helen Cameron and Catherine Duce present four voices of theology, highlighting that theology can be carried in what someone does as much as what someone says.⁶⁷ Above I have given the women's espoused theology of suffering, but I also had the opportunity to participate in some events which gave further context to these. As part of the research process, I participated in two sympathy visits to the homes of people who had lost a loved one.

6.2.2.5 Pole visits⁶⁸

Sympathy visits, or *pole* visits as they are called in Tanzania, occur in the weeks and months after the initial funeral and burial arrangements. This is a cultural Tanzanian practice so not limited to TAFES women; however, the ones I went to were for and attended by TAFES Associates. Both were after the loss of a parent or parents. These events provide a context for teaching which is given about suffering and so it is worth seeing in detail how they proceed.

A time was pre-arranged with the family of the bereaved and prior to the day in a WhatsApp group. TAFES Associates were invited to visit and/or to

---

66. Focus Group 1.

67. Cameron and Duce, *Researching Practice in Ministry*, loc.337-351. The four voices are: operant, espoused, normal, and formal or academic.

68. *Pole* is pronounced POH-lay. It is translated 'sorry' in English but has nothing to do with culpability. The nearest rendering in English is something like "I'm sorry this happened to you," or "My sympathies / condolences."

contribute to a collection of money which would be given to the bereaved at the visit. This money is understood to go towards the hospital and funeral costs of the departed as well as the costs of the bereaved hosting visitors. Carpools were organised and we arrived a couple of hours after the pre-arranged time and were invited to sit down. At the first one I went to there were thirty of us in attendance; in the second there were nineteen. As people continued to arrive there was juice and snacks and informal chatting time.

These events are most often described as going to sit with the bereaved but there is also a formal part to proceedings. This includes:

- Opening prayer
- A *pambio* or hymn
- Each member present introduces themselves by name and says their association with TAFES and/or the bereaved
- A short word or sermon encouraging the bereaved to continue to persevere in faith despite this great loss, prepared and given by a pre-arranged person.
- Open sharing where each person has an opportunity to give an encouraging word, Bible verse or song. If they do not wish to say much, they just verbally give their '*pole*' (sympathy). The content of this sharing included:
    - Warnings to evaluate one's own life and attend to one's own relationship with God.
    - Affirmations that this kind of loss is very difficult, but God is able to be our comfort if we look to him.
    - Encouragements to rely on others and their support.
    - Reminders that God always has a purpose.
    - Comments about how beautiful it is that God has given us to each other.
- The bereaved introduces themselves and their family and gives a biography of the person who died including a narration of how they died. They thank those present for their encouraging words.
- The giving of the pre-collected money.
- Closing prayer and song.
- Meal, provided by the family of the bereaved. From here people can leave as they need to.

These visits can go for several hours. A ministry of presence is important. I attended both events even though I knew the bereaved only a little because the group leader felt that the more people we had in attendance, the greater an encouragement that would be to the bereaved. The tone is one of solemnity, sympathy, and unity. It is in this context that encouragements, warnings, and exhortations are given, by people who have made it a priority to identify with the bereaved and sit with them in their loss.

Understanding *pole* visits has several implications for how we understand the espoused theology of suffering given by TAFES women. First, a belief that God brings or allows suffering for a purpose does not translate into a cavalier attitude towards suffering, a dismissal of what the person is going through, or an implication that the suffering has been brought to meet some deficit in them. Suffering may have some greater redemptive purpose but that does not diminish the fact that it is terrible. While Kenneth Mbugua exhorts Africans to embrace suffering because it is "fundamental to Paul's understanding of serving God," the TAFES women's practice is more aligned with Asamoah-Gyadu who maintains that suffering itself is not a virtue.[69] Second, these women's theology allows significant space for bringing attention to suffering and sharing in it together. While the bereaved is encouraged to persevere and not lose hope, they are also given time to speak about their loved one, how they died and what this meant to them. I am not suggesting that the person's most authentic grief is evident at this time: there is an element of formality and performance to it. Additionally, in her PhD thesis on lament in Tanzania, Anastasia Boniface-Malle recounts that cultural practices prior to missionary influence included loud wailing.[70] While I have seen this done in Tanzania, including at Christian events, this did not occur during my participant observation *pole* visits. It may be that there is a reining in of emotion in order to give this speech. However, there is nevertheless time to speak of and acknowledge the loved one and what they meant to the person. Writing about childlessness, Mercy Oduyoye chose to name that pain, and Nyambura Njoroge affirmed, "Silence and passivity are not options," if fruitfulness is to follow at some point.[71] Njoroge went on to apply this practice of naming pain

---

69. Mbugua, "The Gospel Life," 49–64; Asamoah-Gyadu, *African Charismatics*, 469.
70. Boniface-Malle, "Interpreting the Lament Psalms," 3.
71. Njoroge, "Let's Celebrate the Power," 59–74.

to the death of family members as well. This is what happens at *pole* visits too. To do so is not seen as a threat to perseverance but an important part of exercising compassion and allowing the bereaved the chance to grieve. This space for acknowledging hardship is further evident in an operant theology of lament provided by Rhoda.

6.2.2.6 Lament

Above I mentioned that Rhoda's business was robbed. In line with the espoused theology we have seen, she saw God teaching her through that experience. However, as she narrated the story to me, there were significant elements of lament in her account. I have reproduced it as she told it below:

> I opened a business, a shop. Then thieves came in the night and they broke in and they took some of the things, but they left some things. My heart was downcast, 'Oh God, what is this?' It was a very hard time. What could I do? God told us, work hard and I'd done that. When I had money, I'd given offerings and helped others and helped my family but still these thieves came . . . In this challenge, there were things which you learn as well. So I learned also that I should put more security on the doors, and that I should not put all my goods in my shop, but put a few on display so if people come this doesn't happen again. One day they came again and attacked my shop, but they found that I had improved the doors and they weren't able to, and I continued to thank God that he helps me to know, and that I had the security, but surely God is my guard.[72]

This story is told in the past tense after the problem has been resolved. It is therefore not a full account of the prayer she uttered in the moment of distress. However, Rhoda's story nevertheless offers several elements of a lament prayer. Ugandan Catholic scholar Emmanuel Katongole gives an outline of a generally accepted form of lament Psalm:[73]

---

72. Interview 15 (Rhoda), Swahili quotation 106.
73. Katongole, *Born from Lament*, Kindle edition, 158.

Figure 6.2 Form of lament Psalms

Address	Directing the prayer to God
Complaint	Description of the problem
Request	An exploration of the situation including our emotions and responses to it
Motivation	Confession of sin or assertion of innocence, articulates why God should help
Confidence/praise	Confession of trust in God and confidence in his assistance

Rhoda's story includes several elements of these, as shown below:

Figure 6.3 Rhoda's lament

Address	Oh God, what is this?
Complaint	The thieves came in the night and they broke in and they took some of the things.
Request	-
Motivation	God told us, work hard and I'd done that. When I had money I'd given offerings and helped others and helped my family but still these thieves came.
Confidence/Praise	I continued to thank God that he helps me to know and that I had the security but surely God is my guard.

In Rhoda's story, the request is missing although the address could double as she cries out to God for an explanation. She also immediately points out how God helped her and taught her through the situation, the implication being this was why she turned to him. This is consistent with the timing of her story: she is not in the middle of the distress but telling it afterwards. However, the story gives us a picture of how she responded to it.

First, she turns to God in her distress. For Rhoda, either in the moment or now looking back on it, the robbery does not represent an abandonment by God. She is therefore able to seek God as her deliverer. Second, in her re-telling she acknowledges the psychological load of the event and that it was a difficult time. To those who say that the Christian life should always be happy and victorious or who wish to silence those who speak about their problems, this is a stark contrast. Third, Rhoda points out the dissonance between what should happen according to God's principles and what has happened. That is, she has worked hard, been generous and tithed. Rhoda earlier affirmed these very principles as normative for bringing prosperity in the Christian life and yet here she points out that this was not the case for her. Rhoda is honest about this apparent contradiction. C. C. Broyles points out that such lament prayers show that "the promises of God should be taken seriously and affirm that they should become evident," in contrast to "a passive faith that simply accepts circumstances as God's will."[74] Rhoda's willingness to acknowledge this quandary is evidence of a mature faith and a robust response to suffering.

Told after the fact, this is a story which ultimately has a positive outcome. It therefore could be conceived of as a story of victory. Certainly, the tension resolves and prosperity is the implication at the end. However, this story also contains a narration of a time when this was not the case, and it does not shy away from that. In fact, it narrates it and points out the disconnect with the normative principles of prosperity. It is not a story which dismisses or diminishes adversity or claims it does not have place in the Christian life. It might be better conceived of as what Katongole calls "a narrated hope."[75] Differing from optimism, narrated hope tells "how Christians have concretely experienced . . . death and resurrection at work in the world."[76] It is a story of experiencing adversity, facing the feelings that it brings, struggling through it, and ultimately seeing God's provision in it. Without the element of adversity and how much it affected Rhoda, her story becomes one of victory without effort or perseverance. However, with this element, her story becomes one in which a process of effort and perseverance is a way in which God brings new life. Speaking about these problems and giving space to them is therefore a vital part of *mafanikio* theology, giving assurances that these are not indications that one has strayed from the path of prosperity but rather, under God, one step on the way of prosperity and part of the continuing process of prosperity.

In *mafanikio* theology, suffering is an expected part of anyone's life, including the Christian. It maintains that suffering is not a sign of God's abandonment, but a means God uses to bring about our prosperity. However, this is

---

74. Broyles, "Lament, Psalms Of," 384–99.
75. Katongole, *Born from Lament*, 30.
76. Katongole, 30.

not a case of the ends justifying the means. *Mafanikio* theology gives space to acknowledge suffering, to name it as difficult, and to share in grief together. Thus, *mafanikio* theology equips the Christian to expect suffering and to persevere through it, trusting God. This is not a rocky ground theology of giving up because of hardship. Prosperity and suffering are not at odds with one another in *mafanikio* theology, and the Christian is thereby equipped to both withstand suffering and pursue prosperity.

6.2.3 Thorny Ground?: *Mafanikio* Theology And Christ

The relationship of prosperity theologies to thorny ground appears quite straightforward. The parable explicitly mentions the worries of this life, the deceitfulness of wealth and desires for other things that choke the word. This language aligns easily with Ehioghae and Olanrewaju's accusation that prosperity gospel is "a selfish and materialistic faith with a thin Christian veneer" making people, according to Ageboyin, "conceited and egocentric."[77] The deceit in prosperity theology is that it speaks about Jesus while centering the self. Thus, according to Adeleye, "people are no longer attracted to Jesus for who he is . . . rather they are lured to Jesus for the blessings or benefits they can claim from him."[78]

The TAFES women spoke frequently of Jesus. All interview questions referred to God rather than any one member of the Trinity, so no questions were specifically asked about Jesus.[79] However, in interviews and focus groups, there were nevertheless 154 references to Jesus, omitting interjections such as "Jesus be praised."[80] For comparison, the next most frequently mentioned Bible figures were Abraham and Job at nineteen references each. Clearly, Jesus features strongly in the women's theology. However, the issue at stake in thorny ground is not how frequently Jesus was referred to, but his centrality in their theology. I will consider whether the women were coming to

---

77. Ehioghae and Olanrewaju, "A Theological Evaluation," 73; Ageboyin, "A Rethinking of Prosperity," 82.

78. Adeleye, *The Preachers of a Different Gospel*, 2.

79. One Focus Group question referred to refusing Jesus.

80. References to Jesus, Christ or Jesus Christ. References to Lord were omitted unless they said Lord Jesus as the Swahili term "*Bwana*" has a broad meaning and can refer either to Christ or to God more generally. There were seventy-nine mentions of the Holy Spirit and six references to the Father.

Christ for himself or for his benefits before going on to examine how they see themselves in relationship to Christ.

6.2.3.1 Coming to Christ or coming for his benefits?

Jesus can be mentioned frequently but in ways that lead people to seek gold, not God.[81] To understand this further, I coded the 154 references to Jesus and came up with eighty-seven codes in five categories.[82] These are represented in Figure 6.1. Thirty-four references to Jesus pertained to ways humans ought to relate to Jesus, twenty-seven were about things Jesus said (eleven) or did (sixteen), thirteen were about who Christians are or what we have in Jesus, and two references were to the presence of Jesus. There were also eleven references to either the blood or the name of Jesus, but these all came from one interviewee.[83]

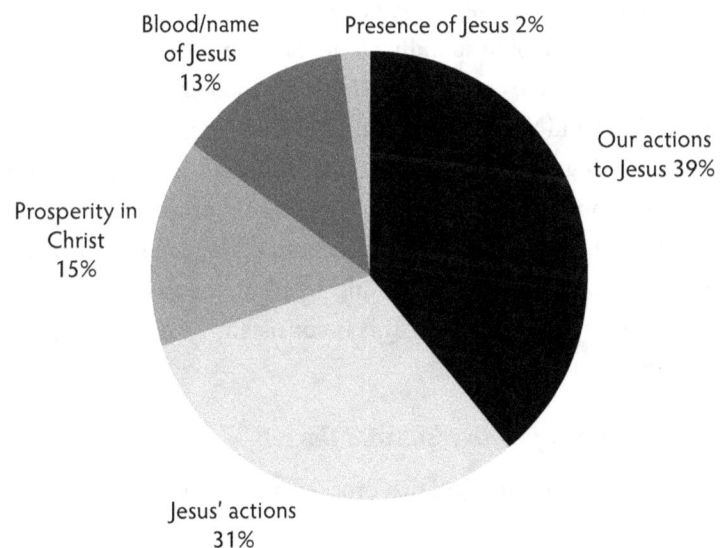

Figure 6.4 References to Jesus

---

81. Maura et al., *Prosperity?*, 4.

82. The reason this number is different from the original mentions is because sometimes the same thing was said about Jesus in the one paragraph or interview and I only counted this as one code.

83. Interview 3 (Damaris).

A surprising factor here is how few of these references pertain to things that Jesus does for us. When the women spoke of things Jesus does for us, it was indeed to give us prosperity (13 percent of references to Jesus.) However, there were many more references to Jesus's actions which had no direct relationship to us. These were almost exclusively from the gospels and included: healed people (four), provided for people (three), did miracles (two), was crucified/died (two), was led by the Spirit (one), prayed to the Father (one), suffered poverty (one).[84] Each of these was used in the context of knowing Jesus's character and priorities through his actions, and knowing his teachings. While these have relevance to us today, Jesus here is known in his own right, not only for what he offers to people.

Our actions towards Jesus reference both conversion and discipleship. Of the thirty-four references to our actions to Jesus, fourteen used language pertaining to initial conversion (e.g. believe in, come to, know, receive Jesus, etc.) and twenty used language of ongoing discipleship (e.g. follow, love, be a servant, stay, wear, etc.). Responding to Jesus therefore continues to shape a person after their initial conversion. *Mafanikio* theology seeks both to draw people to Christ and to see them continue to live for him afterward. It does not envision using Christ for the benefits he brings and then abandoning him when it is no longer convenient. This is not thorny ground that draws the Christian's heart to wealth while using the language of Christ. These women did not see themselves as calling people to the things of Christ or to prosperity but to Christ himself. This is consistent with their emphasis on relationship with God.

6.2.3.2 Relationship with Jesus and the self

It is from relationship with God that prosperity flows. Therefore, the emphasis on relationship with God here does not necessitate a diminishing of the self. On the contrary, commitment to God often translates to an increase in the self. For TAFES women, relationship with God means a new identity as one who is capable and prosperous. A TAFES woman is not passive, weak, or foolish; she is active, strong, and wise. All this flows from her relationship

---

84. The two references not from the gospels were one to Jesus redeeming people and one to Jesus coming into our hearts.

with God. This relationship with God nourishes and forms her self-identity so she is able to be an active participant in his kingdom.

In the gospels, when women encounter Jesus, they frequently experience greater dignity and confidence as a result. For example, the bent woman of Luke 13:10–13 is not only physically healed but lifts her head and praises God. Likewise, the previously shunned woman of John 4:1–31 becomes the first messenger of Jesus's identity. Such a change in their bodies and minds also leads to greater participation in their communities and the kingdom of God. Another example is Mary Magdalene, who, set free from demonic oppression, becomes one of the women supporting Jesus's ministry from her own means (Luke 8:2–3). Similarly, Peter's mother-in-law immediately begins to serve after Jesus heals her (Luke 4:38–39). In her study of Kenyan women's ministry SLIM, Damaris Parsitau notes a similar dynamic: "SLIM changed the way [women] perceive themselves in relation to God. Several pointed out that their participation in SLIM's meetings had enhanced their self-esteem and confidence, while others insisted that it had led to a total transformation of their lives."[85] She calls this a transforming subjectivity, that is, a change from the inside out as women see and experience themselves in new ways.[86] Personal salvation is radical here and includes encouraging women "to rise above stigmatisation and victimhood."[87] Far from being thorns that choke a person's commitment to Christ, this right view of oneself can be the fertiliser that results in their fruitfulness.

The TAFES women are less marginalised than Parsitau's research cohort. TAFES women are educated, comparatively wealthy and in marriages which, while not egalitarian in a Western sense, emphasize sharing and going forward together. Within their own communities, they are reasonably privileged. However, that may not be the metric Tanzanians are using when they consider their position in the world. For many Tanzanians, the cultural memory of being assigned to the "low-income country" bracket by the World Bank during the structural adjustment period of the 1980s continues as a source of shame.[88] As Kenyan missionary priest Gerard Nnamunga writes, the process

---

85. Parsitau, "Agents of Gendered Change," Kindle edition, 203–20.
86. Parsitau, 220.
87. Parsitau, 220.
88. There was great rejoicing in 2020 when it was announced that Tanzania had moved up a bracket into "lower-middle income country".

of colonization has had far reaching effects on the African mind in terms of self-perception.[89] This is true even for university-educated Tanzanians. While Paul urges members of the body of Christ not to think of themselves more highly than they ought (Romans 12:3), the problem in Tanzania is more often that people think of themselves as more lowly than they ought and thus do not contribute to fulfilling God's purposes in the world, either in providing for others or bringing about his kingdom. So, Fibi's affirmation that one who knows God will understand that they are able, does not reflect a status quo, but a rhetorical thrust towards who Tanzanians should be in Christ.[90] A relationship with God does not diminish a person; it unleashes them in his power. Thus, speaking of herself as one who has received Christ, Fibi said, "I have strength unlimited. I am unlimited. I am strong . . . as long as God is with me."[91] In doing so, she does not make herself more important than she ought. She is righting a wrong in self-perception here, encouraging women to take their place as daughters of Abraham (Luke 13:16). This is only possible in Christ: he is woven through every aspect of a TAFES woman's life.

In seeking to counteract a theology which centres on the self, Ken Mbugua argues that the goal of salvation is knowing and being reconciled to God.[92] In the same volume, Michael Otieno Maura argues that the blessings of the gospel are peace with God, access to God, joy from the hope of God's glory, and joy in suffering.[93] *Mafanikio* theology affirms all of these but considers them inadequate because they all sound remarkably passive. Neither Mbugua nor Maura, for example, mention service of God or mission with God. In *mafanikio* theology, it is not enough to merely accept these benefits of salvation; *mafanikio* theology also seeks to give a role for Christians in the world today and to encourage them to take it up. This necessitates some reflection on oneself and who God has made one to be, not as a distraction away from God or a way of being egocentric but in order to better serve God.

---

89. Nnamunga, "Decolonising African Theology," 121–28.
90. Interview 4 (Fibi).
91. Interview 4 (Fibi), Swahili quotation 82.
92. Mbugua, "A False Gospel," 1–14.
93. Maura, "The Blessings," 91–106.

6.2.4 Conclusion: The Good Soil of *Mafanikio* Theology

In our lens of the Parable of the Sower, we have seen that unlike the rocky soil, *mafanikio* theology provides a theology of suffering which equips the Christian to expect suffering and persevere through it. *Mafanikio* theology is also not thorny ground where wealth and selfishness choke commitment to God because its teachings about wealth and the self are deployed in the service of God. *Mafaniko* theology thus avoids these pitfalls to discipleship. By way of conclusion, let me explore whether *mafanikio* theology can be considered good soil, the kind that is fruitful.

Adeleye considers the fruit of the Spirit in Galatians 5:22–23 to be one of "the essential marks of a Christian," along with honesty, integrity, and character.[94] Indeed, the fruit of the Spirit is present in those who belong to Christ Jesus and are keeping in step with the Spirit (Gal 5:24). It therefore presents a reasonable measure of a disciple of Jesus as does the good and fruitful soil of the parable. The language of fruit and fruitfulness is coincidental. The common thread is continuation in Christ.

> But the fruit of the Spirit is love, joy, peace, forbearance, kindness, goodness, faithfulness, gentleness and self-control. Against such things there is no law. Galatians 5:22–23

Scholars agree that the fruit in verse 22 is singular, meaning the virtues given here are not separate fruits of the Spirit but "various aspects of the generative power of the Spirit."[95] For this reason, it is unwise to treat any of these virtues separately from the others and indeed they overlap. I will therefore offer here a short impression of this fruit in *mafanikio* theology rather than a detailed breakdown of each virtue.

Love, joy, and peace were frequently mentioned in the women's interviews and focus groups. Peace was most common with ninety-one references. This mostly referred to inner peace which had ripple effects into being calm in other situations and thus being able to treat others well. Love was next most common with fifty references, an even split between loving God and loving others. The forty-three references to joy were about joy despite one's circumstances. Meanwhile, forbearance, kindness, generosity, faithfulness,

---

94. Adeleye, *The Preachers of a Different Gospel*, 8.
95. Jervis, *Galatians*, 169; See also Soards and Pursiful, *Galatians*, 288.

gentleness, and self-control came up less often as discrete concepts but were present in the emphases on righteousness, perseverance, good relationships, reliability, compassion for the suffering, and being disciplined in one's work. Certainly, the fruit of the Spirit is present in *mafanikio* theology!

Ngwobia offers his own vice list of prosperity theology: that it sanctions selfishness and greed, promotes the idolatry of money, laziness, and lack of compassion for the poor.[96] None of these are present in *mafanikio* theology. Rather, *mafanikio* theology aims to produce disciples who are committed to Jesus and, as they pursue prosperity under him, are characterised by love for God and fellow humans, by joy whatever the circumstances, and by inner peace because they trust God; it aims to form Christians who persevere, who continue in righteousness, and who are faithful, humble, and self-controlled. They are good and fruitful soil. As we saw in the first half of this chapter, *mafanikio* theology affirms the orientation towards prosperity of African prosperity theology, participating in this. However, *mafanikio* theology also critiques some versions of African prosperity theology such as the profligate prosperity gospel. As *mafanikio* theology offers a path of fruitfulness and discipleship then, it does so as a participant in prosperity theology. *Mafanikio* theology is where prosperity theology meets and marries discipleship.

---

96. Ngwobia, Kambale, and Ngomo, "Misleading Theologies of Wealth," 293–4.

Figure 6.5 What have we learned about *mafanikio* theology (MT)? (Chapters 4–6)

Chapter 4	Chapter 5	Chapter 6	Chapter 7	Chapter 8
In MT, prosperity is a process of taking steps to move to the next level. This process manifests across all areas of life and when all areas are affected, the result is greater than the sum of the parts. In MT, God is the source of prosperity. In MT, prosperity is characterised by effort, perseverance, righteousness and knowledge.	MT responds to a poverty gospel on one hand and profligate prosperity gospel on the other. MT combats passivity through knowing God rightly, identity change, and environmental change. MT locates itself in the Bible, with hermeneutics that emphasise a comprehensive knowledge of Scripture to provide a balanced theology.	MT has a strong family resemblance to other prosperity theologies from Zambia, South Africa, Malawi, Cameroon, and Kenya. These are different to how "prosperity gospel" is often described. They are an alternative to it and implicit critique of it. MT promotes perseverance, sympathy, and lament in suffering. MT calls people to Christ himself not just his things. MT embodies the fruit of the Spirit.		

CHAPTER 7

Mafanikio Theology as an African Theology

Thus far we have understood that in *mafanikio* theology, prosperity is a process of taking steps to move to the next level, which can be applied in the economic, spiritual, relational, physical, and intellectual spheres as well as to the experience of inner peace. In *mafanikio* theology, this prosperity both comes from God and is understood and attained best in relationship with God. In the first concentric circle, as I brought it into conversation with other African prosperity theologies, it became clear that a distinctive of *mafanikio* theology is its orientation of the self around serving God and others and that it is well placed to equip Christians for a life of discipleship. But what of African theology more broadly? The task here is to understand *mafanikio* theology in terms of its Africanness.

At one level, *mafanikio* theology is an African theology because it is espoused by a group of African women and taught by them. I have given considerable attention in chapter 5 to the Tanzanian *context* which has given birth to *mafanikio* theology and the Tanzanian issues which it seeks to address. I have also explored how the women's interactions with the Bible reflect African *cultural mores* in terms of orality and storytelling, hermeneutics which have produced *mafanikio* theology. Thus, in terms of its context and methods, we have already understood *mafanikio* theology in African terms and seen it as a product of and for its African context. My aim in this chapter is now to explore in what ways it draws on and interacts with African theological resources.

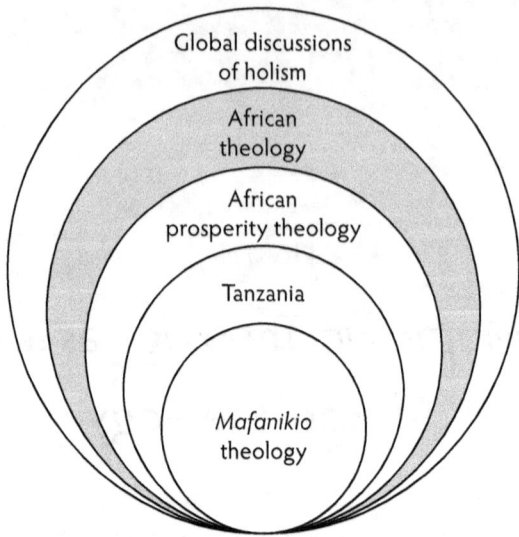

Figure 7.1 Concentric circles of engagement with *mafanikio* **theology (African theology)**

The extent to which prosperity theologies are African has been discussed on two different levels. First, scholars debate the relationship of prosperity theology in Africa to a spirit of materialism, often associated with individualism and capitalism. Thought to be a Western import, this spirit of materialism is seen to threaten the African nature of prosperity theologies. The second level examines an almost inverse issue: the relationship of prosperity theology in Africa to African Traditional Religion and worldview. In this case, the prosperity theology is understood to be African but its integrity as a Christian theology is questioned.[1] I will take each of these in turn, engaging these debates and assessing the relationship of *mafanikio* theology to them. Having done this, I will also turn to an aspect of African culture which has

---

1. Several terms are used for this including African Traditional Religion/s, Primal Religion, African Religion/s, African worldview, African religiosity, African religiousness, etc. Though each of these have slightly different nuances they overlap significantly so this is primarily an issue of nomenclature. See Balcomb, "Primal or Indigenous?," 1–19. At times, they are also used interchangeably. Where possible I have retained the language used by scholars. As a general rule I have used African Traditional Religion to refer to religious or cultic practice or belief that was present prior to Christianity or Islam. This is not to imply that these religions are of yesteryear or no longer innovating but to reference their long history on the continent. When referencing underlying beliefs or assumptions that span across religions on the continent, I use African worldview or African religiosity.

been under-examined in theological debates, namely patronage. I will argue that African patronage thinking is present in *mafanikio* theology and that a patronage lens is useful in understanding prosperity theologies more broadly as well.

7.1 Un-African?
7.1.1 Prosperity and Materialism

There is little disagreement among scholars that in prosperity theologies, "materialist desires are explicit and acknowledged, and are not only sanctioned but promoted."[2] This is true of *mafanikio* theology as well. Though *mafanikio* theology insists on a broad understanding of prosperity and emphasizes the importance of relationship with God regardless of the economic prosperity of the moment, nevertheless, it stands in contrast to former theologies which downplayed daily needs and cast wealth accumulation as a liability to Christian faith. While the TAFES women claim the Bible – not their world – as the source of *mafanikio* theology, several scholars argue that prosperity theologies in Africa are beholden to a materialistic worldview.

Ehioghae and Olanrewaju assert that "preachers have imbibed the materialistic philosophy of this age, the belief that material prosperity is gain. It is a gospel shaped by the materialism of our contemporary culture."[3] Reflecting on the this-worldly focus of the prosperity gospel, economic ethicist Nimi Wariboko unpacks the process by which this materialistic worldview is internalised by believers: As "social and aesthetic values of the society" with their "incessant quests for material accoutrements" become buried within believers' unconscious, their religious visions are shaped by them to the extent that God becomes aligned with these same desires.[4] This is problematic because such a materialistic spirit is contrary to the Bible's teaching about wealth and inhibits Christian discipleship according to Ehioghae and Olanrewaju, who argue that this emphasis "negates clear Biblical teaching on the issue" and is done "at the expense of spiritual prosperity which leaves the believer more

---

2. Freeman, "The Pentecostal Ethic," 19.
3. Ehioghae and Olanrewaju, "A Theological Evaluation," 73.
4. Wariboko, "Pentecostal Paradigms," Kindle edition, 25–60.

impoverished in faith."[5] Nigerian Gwamna Je'Adayibe says, "wealth tends to trap us into self-absorption, materialism and insensitivity to others."[6] Writing from South Africa, Gbote and Kgatla similarly believe that, "the concept of preaching the gospel from the economic perspective of needs and wants makes the human race focus on the greedy perception of consumerism."[7] For them, such a focus is idolatry.[8]

This materialistic spirit of the age is often thought to be an import from the West. Nigerian evangelical Yusufu Turaki accuses: "Western media has enlarged the African appetites and consumerism has inflamed African passions and pleasures into inordinate greed and lust."[9] He sees such conditioning, shaping, and molding of the modern African mind as a kind of neo-colonialism.[10] Indeed, Kenyans Reuben Kigame, Anne Njoroge and Eunice Kamaara also view such "individualism, materialism, and consumerism" as un-African.[11] Such a shift is part of global tides as well. Nigerian Ebenezer Obadare argues that it is not a coincidence that Pentecostalism's themes of "self-actualisation, personal enrichment and prosperity" share a great deal with neoliberalism.[12] He argues that, "so far as prosperity is the *raison d'etre* of neoliberalism, Pentecostalism may rightly be seen as its religious mode or extension."[13] Mashau and Kgatle also see the prosperity gospel as part of "a global phenomenon . . . riding on the wave of capitalism which is sweeping the global economy."[14] According to Wariboko, in this system, desire for God is co-opted into "the capitalist system's production of desires (demand)."[15]

---

5. Ehioghae and Olanrewaju, "A Theological Evaluation," 73.

6. Je'adayibe, "'Where Your Treasure Is,'" 37.

7. Gbote and Kgatla, "Prosperity Gospel," 9.

8. Gbote and Kgatla, 9.

9. Yusufu Turaki, *Engaging Religions and Worldviews* Kindle edition, 96.

10. He explains neo-colonialism this way: "The colonial empires and nation states that ruled the world have been replaced by the corporations, such as the International Monetary Fund (IMF), the World Bank, multi-national corporations, the United Nations and other major power blocks and economic clubs. These institutions spread the new gospel of globalization through the civilizing forces of democracy, advanced science and technology, and market economy or capitalism." Turaki, *Engaging Religions and Worldviews*, 96.

11. Kigame, Njoroge, and Kamaara, "From Knowledge to Wisdom," 85–109.

12. Obadare, "'Raising Righteous Billionaires,'" 3.

13. Obadare, 3.

14. Mashau and Kgatle, "Prosperity Gospel," 2.

15. Wariboko, "Pentecostal Paradigms," 40.

In Marius Nel's words then, the consumerist society "reduces the gospel to the application of the values of this society" and God to "a wealthy capitalist magnate."[16]

Thus, prosperity theology is criticised as having imbibed from Western or global forces a materialistic spirit which distracts from and pollutes the Christian message, absorbing Christians into consumeristic ways of life and directing them to serve capitalism instead of God, all under the guise of teaching God's will.[17] In this understanding, adherents of prosperity theology are victims not only of exploitative preachers and teachers but of a capitalist global system. While both hold out the promise of "redemption from poverty and mediocrity" according to Ghanaian Ben-Willie Golo, they are so focused on individual prosperity, they neglect the vulnerable, future generations and the earth itself.[18] Thus if they are not ineffective in the immediate future, they are certainly short-sighted and cannot be the solution to Africa's problems.

However, not all scholars are as pessimistic. Asamoah-Gyadu concedes that criticism of Pentecostalism "for its promotion of materialism in the name of Christianity" may be warranted if the only consideration was "the backdrop of the flamboyant and materialistic lifestyles of some of its leaders" but he sees this as "just one side of the story," instead highlighting the "very important empowerment and motivational dimension that often gets lost in the discussion."[19] Even while being critical of prosperity theology, American ethicist Douglas Hicks also acknowledges that only "some aspects of this message of prosperity theology derive from the consumer culture."[20] For example, political anthropologist Dena Freeman argues "wasteful consumption" is discouraged and there is "a reorientation towards investment."[21] Naomi Haynes's picture of Pentecostal Christians on the Zambian Copperbelt supports this. She says, "it is a mistake to read consumption – even that of the individualised, capitalist variety that Pentecostalism is so often seen to promote – as automatically socially corrosive."[22] Indeed Zimbabwean Lovemore Togarasei

---

16. Marius Nel, *The Prosperity Gospel in Africa*, Kindle edition, loc.2001.
17. Lauterbach, "Fakery and Wealth in African," 111–32.
18. Golo, "Africa's Poverty," 368.
19. Asamoah-Gyadu, "'Get up . . .,'" 250.
20. Hicks, "Prosperity, Theology and Economy," 241.
21. Freeman, "The Pentecostal Ethic," 20.
22. Haynes, "Pentecostalism and the Morality," 134.

writes from Botswana that Pentecostals are not always consumers. Sometimes they are abstainers because, "prosperity gospel discourages consumption of beer, cigarettes, adultery and all other practices that many African men in particular spend money on."[23] According to Canadian political scientist Ruth Marshall, Pentecostal husbands are also encouraged to be more present in the home, "helping to take responsibility for child rearing, even domestic chores."[24] Thus Korean Pentecostal scholar Wonsuk Ma can conclude, "the simple understanding of the [prosperity gospel] as the combination of Pentecostal Christianity and Western consumerist capitalism no longer holds to diverse socio-economic contexts."[25] With this breadth of stances towards materialism, the task at hand is to ascertain where *mafanikio* theology fits.

7.1.2 *Mafanikio* Theology and Materialism

The TAFES women did not comment on the relationship of their theology to capitalism, but they did comment on materialism, making a distinction between the goodness and importance of material things and being captive to a spirit of materialism. They understood the former to be a good, right, and African thing. University lecturer Junia said, "to own a lot in terms of material, comfortable house . . . [is] part of prosperity in an African context."[26] For entrepreneur Bilhah, to turn your back on this pursuit would be un-African.[27] However, working mother Joanna warned against the pursuit of material things becoming too prominent in a person's life and Junia mentioned this as a danger for churches as well.[28] Thus development worker Zipporah made a distinction between taking the opportunities God gives you for wealth and being driven by material things.[29] They did not associate this kind of materialism with the West as Turaki does but rather with a general worldliness; they saw a right emphasis on material things as consistent with both the Bible and their African background and an over-emphasis as a distortion of both.

---

23. Togarasei, "The Pentecostal Gospel," 348.
24. Marshall, "Power in the Name," 31.
25. Ma, "Blessing in Pentecostal Theology," 272.
26. Interview 5 (Junia).
27. Interview 14 (Bilhah). The reason she gave for it being un-African was because a lack of prosperity limits your capacity to contribute to others.
28. Focus Group 1.
29. Interview 16 (Zipporah).

For the TAFES women, two things guard against materialism. The first is recognizing that prosperity relies on intangible things as well as tangible. These include good relationships with other people (Fibi, Eunice, Lydia, Beatrice), education (Susanna, Martha, Fibi, Salome), mental health (Huldah, Dorcas, Mariamu), encouragement, and wisdom from others (Susanna, Zipporah).[30] While promoting material prosperity, the women thus also relativized it because it cannot be attained by the individual alone. Second, they insisted that wealth is to be used for the benefit of others, from your children to others in the community. Ruth said that if "you are only thinking of me and my family" a person is selfish and has failed to "look at the greater challenges which are here on earth" including contributing to the expansion of the kingdom of God, especially in evangelistic work.[31] For them, the person accumulating the wealth must not be the sole beneficiary of it. Both the acquiring of prosperity and the deploying of it were thus understood in terms broader than the individual. I will reflect further on the concept of *Ubuntu* in the next chapter but for now, it must be noted that "I am because we are" applies to both the acquisition and use of material goods in *mafanikio* theology. In part this is because of the connected nature of life: nurturing good relationships with others is essential and this applies to God as well.

Ehioghae is suspicious of taking the quality of one's relationship with God into account when pursuing prosperity. For him, if giving has benefits for the giver, it is "veiled materialism, with little or no room for altruistic liberality."[32] He makes this comment with regard to the idea of faith being key to abundance through sowing and reaping. However, in Focus Groups where the women were explicitly asked about this practice, they categorically rejected it as too formulaic and diminishing the sovereignty of God.[33] There are models of connecting relationship with God and prosperity other than sowing and reaping. In the case of *mafanikio* theology, the mechanism of sowing and reaping is rejected in favour of nurturing one's relationship with God which has ripple effects for prosperity. However, Ehioghae assumes that

---

30. Interview 4 (Fibi); Interview 1 (Eunice); Interview 11 (Lydia); Interview 2 (Abigail); Interview 6 (Susanna); Interview 18 (Martha); Interview 8 (Salome); Interview 12 (Mariamu); Interview 16 (Zipporah).

31. Interview 20 (Ruth).

32. Ehioghae, "Prosperity Gospel," 39.

33. Focus Group 1; Focus Group 2.

altruism is a biblical principle and essential to a Christian theology of giving, effectively ruling out any kind of patronage system. This is a simplistic model which neither accounts for the Bible's own language nor engages effectively with African cultures, as I will argue in the section on patronage. At any rate, his suspicion is unwarranted. For the TAFES women, giving is not a means – veiled or otherwise – to manipulate God into providing prosperity; it is the right use of the wealth which has been entrusted to them. The women strongly affirmed the goodness of material things and wealth production while resisting making them ultimate. Frequently referring to Jesus's teaching about gaining the world but losing one's soul (Mark 8:36, Matt 15:26),[34] they warned against the idolatry of material things. While Anna did not comment on the source of materialism, she was clear that it is "not biblical."[35] The TAFES women were concerned about materialism, but they saw themselves as an alternative to it, not perpetuators of it.

It is possible to be co-opted into broader systems without being conscious of it, so it is worth asking whether *mafanikio* theology inadvertently propagates capitalistic tendencies, particularly with its emphasis on industriousness and production which overlaps with capitalism's emphasis on continued growth. Indeed, *mafanikio* theology's emphasis on work leaves very little room for rest. Rest was associated with heaven (Zipporah, Susanna) in contrast to our time on earth where our purpose is to work (Rhoda).[36] Despite this, the women did not conceive of human beings only as workers and certainly not as a workforce to be exploited. Human rights lawyer Fibi spoke negatively about the situation of the woman in the village who is so poor she does not have time to rest.[37] Meanwhile, Zipporah and Anna spoke against being driven by anxiety, and climate change advocate Priscilla lamented the case where overwork translates to neglecting one's family or relationships.[38] While *mafanikio* theology emphasises work in its efforts to combat a mindset of passivity, it cannot extend to the kind of working hours that dehumanise people. For the TAFES women, work is humanising because it is part of God's

---

34. Interview 13 (Anna); Interview 2 (Abigail); Interview 14 (Bilhah); Interview 1 (Eunice); Focus Group 2.
35. Interview 13 (Anna).
36. Interview 16 (Zipporah); Interview 6 (Susanna); Interview 15 (Rhoda).
37. Interview 4 (Fibi).
38. Interview 16 (Zipporah); Interview 13 (Anna); Focus Group 2.

design for human beings and God's care for us. Work gives agency and self-esteem, freeing those who were formerly captive to hopelessness or passivity. Nevertheless, these women are all very busy and spoke of feeling the burden of that; there was still a sense in which there were other forces at work on them and they were hampered in living out the ideal of rest.

The women only engaged with forces beyond their control at a personal level. In Africa, personal responsibility does not translate to individualism, and this is the case in *mafanikio* theology as well. It is focused on building healthy families and communities, seeing these as the building blocks of healthy nations. However, in *mafanikio* theology, the focus is on change from the grassroots rather than from structural adjustment. Unlike the progressive Pentecostals identified by Miller and Yamamori, *mafanikio* theology does not engage market forces or register much objection to capitalistic systems more broadly.[39] Mika Vähäkangas raises the issue of whether "playing according to capitalist rules [which] means reinforcing and promoting the capitalist world order" is morally justifiable.[40] He concludes that "the upwardly mobile poor . . . have good reason not to join the crusade against global capitalism," since they are unlikely to change the system, yet by playing by its rules, can benefit "family, clan and faith community."[41] This is the horizon of *mafanikio* theology as well: the women do not see themselves as powerful players in the world system but they do advocate empowerment at the local level; whatever the world system is, *mafanikio* theology seeks to equip Christians to thrive in it. In their view, hard work is not an invention of an oppressive global system but a God-given means of prosperity and one which is culturally familiar to them: the archetypal Tanzanian woman is pictured with a hoe in her hand, a baby on her back and a water bucket on her head. The hard work and industry of women are well entrenched in Tanzanian society and cannot be seen to be a new or uniquely Western or capitalistic contribution.

Thus far I have argued that *mafanikio* theology's affirmation of the goodness of material things and promotion of production differs from a Western spirit of materialism in that it relativises material things as one contributor to prosperity, not the whole. The TAFES women also teach that wealth is to

---

39. Miller and Yamamori, *Global Pentecostalism*, 2–4.
40. Vähäkangas, "The Prosperity Gospel?," 353–80.
41. Vähäkangas, 376.

be used for the good of others and to contribute to God's work in the world, thereby guarding against individualism. To do so, they draw on African ideas of communal life, understanding the maintenance of these as a way of guarding against self-absorption or the hoarding of personal wealth. They thus offer an alternative to a materialistic spirit. While *mafanikio* theology could be co-opted into a capitalistic system of exploitation or extraction, it would at that point betray its own ideals and cease to be *mafanikio* theology. Furthermore, it would cease to be African, since *mafanikio* theology is built on African values. However, capitalism is not the terms on which *mafanikio* theology operates; it is not an economic system but a vision for life which is able to be prosperous, African, and Christian.

Mafanikio theology upholds the importance of production and personal industry, but it is too simple to read these in pure capitalistic terms or as signs of neo-colonialism. *Mafanikio* theology's emphasis on work is a response to its own context of historical and current patterns of passivity in Tanzania. It is not the pollution of the Christian mind with superficial or damaging theology; it is a biblical mandate for the kind of industriousness which benefits whole communities as God intended human beings to do. If idolatry can be identified by what one desires or what one loves then *mafanikio* theology cannot be accused of it, for *mafanikio* theology relativises material things while promoting faithful use of them according to God's design. African communality is thus allied with being a good steward in God's world such that when a Christian serves their community with their prosperity, they are acting both as an African and as a Christian.

7.2 Too African?

While the TAFES women saw communality as an aspect of their Africanness and one that coheres with the Bible, some scholars are less positive about the nature of African worldviews. Cameroonian-American Professor of religion and theology David T. Ngong identifies the salvific discourse of African Traditional Religions – that of power for living – as fundamentally different in telos from the Christian gospel. In his view, prosperity teaching churches have made prosperity the goal of the Christian life, "thus collapsing Christianity into African Traditional Religions."⁴² I have argued above that the material, while prominent, is relativised within *mafanikio* theology but this does not negate the need to examine the relationship between *mafanikio* theology and African Traditional Religions. Ngong is right to raise the issue of the extent to which African Traditional Religions influence modern African religious movements, even though his assessment does not fit *mafanikio* theology. After all, as Ghanaian Darkwar Amanor argues, "Pentecostal and Charismatic churches in Ghana and in Africa have actually ridden on the back of the African religious worldview,"⁴³ and the late Nigerian theologian Ogbu Kalu similarly acknowledged that there is an "element of continuity in the religious lives of Africans."⁴⁴ Thus it is necessary to ask, what is the nature of this continuity? After reviewing the relationship of *mafanikio* theology and African Traditional Religion, I will then evaluate where this approach fits within the spectrum of approaches to African Christian theology.

7.2.1 *Mafanikio* Theology and African Traditional Religion

In 1992 Nigerian Anglican bishop Cyril Okorocha characterised African religiousness by "holism, pragmatism or utilitarianism, communalism and especially dynamism."⁴⁵ Okorocha's examples are primarily from the Igbo people, but they cohere with Tanzanian Laurenti Magesa's 2014 account of African Traditional Religion. For example, for Okorocha, holism refers to the way religion or religiousness permeates all aspects of life, which Magesa calls an interconnectedness.⁴⁶ Similarly, Magesa references communalism when he says, "One cannot ensure the full enhancement of life by oneself. One's life force depends on the life forces of other persons and other beings, including those of the ancestors and, ultimately, God."⁴⁷ On pragmatism or utilitarianism, for Okorocha, African religiousness is pragmatic because religion must serve a practical purpose, with gods who do not deliver being abandoned for a superior alternative. Magesa uses similar terms, describing African Religion

---

42. Ngong, "Salvation and Materialism," 1.
43. Amanor, "Pentecostal and Charismatic Churches," 135.
44. Kalu, *African Pentecostalism*, 174.
45. Okorocha, "Religious Conversion in Africa,"168.
46. Magesa, *African Religion*, 161.
47. Magesa, 58.

as concrete and pragmatic.[48] Finally, dynamism is the term Okorocha uses for this search for power, saying, "the African believes a religion to be useful and worthy of profession only if it embodies and imparts power . . . for enhancement of life."[49] This last phrase – enhancement of life – is frequently used by Magesa as well and he concurs that it is from God or gods that people expect to attain the power for this enhancement, in contrast to those powers which destroy life.[50] Though three decades apart and hailing from opposite sides of the continent, these two authorities on African Traditional Religion show remarkable agreement. Thus, these four characteristics – holism, communalism, pragmatism, and dynamism – form a good template for comparison of African Traditional Religion with *mafanikio* theology.

In chapter 4, the features of *mafanikio* theology were identified as effort, perseverance, righteousness, and knowledge. Because of their emphasis on human action, at first these may appear to have little to do with holism, communalism, pragmatism, and dynamism. A prosperity theology that focuses more on prayer may seem to have more in common with African religiosity than *mafanikio* theology. However, a closer examination of *mafanikio* theology reveals that these four characteristics of African religiousness are indeed present.

7.2.1.1 Holism

First, *mafanikio* theology understands prosperity in holistic terms. Not only does prosperity apply to all spheres of life, but there is also a greater prosperity which is present when this is the case because everything is interconnected.[51] Additionally, *mafanikio* theology understands God to be the source of prosperity even when the mechanics of human action are visible. Prosperity starts spiritually in *mafanikio* theology, flowing out of relationship with God. As university lecturer Lois said, "The Bible teaches us that God is the source of *mafanikio*. God gives a person intelligence. God gives a person understanding,

---

48. Magesa, 157.

49. Okorocha, "Religious Conversion in Africa," 171.

50. Magesa, *African Religion*, 47, 52, 171.

51. See Figure 4.6. The areas of prosperity identified by the interviewees were spiritual, economic, relationships, health, inner peace and intellectual.

strategy."⁵² To separate out the human action of effort from God's provision and work in a person's life is foreign to *mafanikio* theology's holism.

7.2.1.2 Communalism

As in African Traditional Religion where a holistic understanding of the world naturally results in communalism (see above), so too in *mafanikio* theology. Fibi's story from chapter 4 of the person who builds a great mansion in a poor suburb without contributing to the development of the area illustrates that "isolating yourself is not prosperity" and prosperity can only be understood in communal terms.⁵³ Thus, *mafanikio* theology affirms both holism and communalism, sharing these characteristics with African religion. This overlap is not merely coincidental. Though Bilhah rooted her insistence on hard work in the Bible's teaching about the purpose for which God designed human beings, in the same breath she said that not to work would be to fail to contribute to others and therefore not be African.⁵⁴ She appeals to both the Bible and African values in developing her theology of prosperity. She is shaped by both, finding a way to be both biblical and African.

The Africanness of the TAFES women's *mafanikio* theology functioned at the level of worldview, not religious practice or belief. The women were very clear about which God they were referring to – the Christian God – so they did not see themselves as participating in African Traditional Religion itself. However, they shared with African Traditional Religion the assumption that power for the enhancement of life comes from the deity. The difference for the women was their location of prosperity in the Christian God rather than any other(s) and their insistence that even when other sources seemed to be more powerful and therefore appealing, this was not correct. They believed those prosperities would eventually be shown as false because true prosperity flows from one source, God himself. The women's relationship to pragmatism and dynamism was thus more complex than their appropriation of holism and communalism.

---

52. Interview 10 (Lois), Swahili quotation 17.
53. Interview 4 (Fibi), Swahili quotation 10.
54. Interview 14 (Bilhah).

7.2.1.3 Pragmatism

Mafanikio theology is a pragmatic theology in the sense that it equips Christians to live well in the here and now. It rejects theologies which place the Christian's focus solely on the things to come or do not equip Christians with the knowledge they need to pursue prosperity. Instead, it offers a source of power for the enhancement of life and claims that this power works. African worldview is at play here. Okorocha notes that in African Traditional Religion, the enhancement of life must be a constant.[55] Similarly, in *mafanikio* theology, prosperity is a constant process, one where if momentum is lost, prosperity is threatened. *Mafanikio* theology's prosperity is not one which could have evolved anywhere in the world: it is an African prosperity, understood in African terms. Part of the reason it is viable is because it addresses this African need for constant progress. However, in *mafanikio* theology, unlike in African Traditional Religion, there are not multiple sources one can turn to for the constant enhancement of life. Its pragmatism does not allow for an abandonment of God to seek another power.

7.2.1.4 Dynamism

The fourth characteristic of African religiousness, dynamism, is the search for power. *Mafanikio* theology affirms such a search only if it culminates in finding Christ and then ultimately refrains not from seeking power (which continues to be available in Christ), but from switching between power sources. In *mafanikio* theology, it is good and right to search for power for the enhancement of life, but it is not acceptable to seek power elsewhere if God does not appear to be fulfilling one's desires. The women did not see hardship as a sign of God's impotence or unwillingness, instead upholding a theology of God's sovereignty and encouraging fidelity and perseverance through hardship. However, their objection was not based on a fear that people may find a superior power to God, but that their search for power elsewhere would be ultimately futile because all other sources of power are inferior to God. This included those that temporarily appear more powerful, and the women believed these to offer a false prosperity, one without true or lasting power. Dynamism is connected to pragmatism for them: part of the reason to maintain fidelity to the Christian God is simply that this is

---

55. Okorocha, "Religious Conversion in Africa," 171.

the most reliable way of attaining prosperity, a truer means than any other power source. However, *mafanikio* theology's cosmology also offers a reason to maintain fidelity to God and trust his power for the enhancement of life.

African Traditional Religion's dynamism is powered by the remoteness of God. The late Cameroonian Dominican priest Eloi Messi-Matoga noted that while most traditional African Religions have a supreme God, there are "many myths that affirm that he has distanced himself from human beings."[56] He recounted an anecdote from north Cameroon where an old man told a missionary, "Once upon a time, God talked to people but now he has fallen silent, and has left us prey to hunger, sickness and death."[57] Kenyan Anglican Joseph Galgalo explains that this vacuum is filled by "traditional experts such as the medicine men, diviners, and soothsayers or fortune tellers."[58] Without access to the supreme being, humans are left to seek power among these lesser powers, whichever seems to be most effective at the time. However, in *mafanikio* theology, humans are not left attempting to find prosperity among the lesser powers. They have no need of them because they have access to the supreme being himself! Indeed, that very supreme being has come close to human beings, in the incarnation of Christ, that he might bring prosperity, according to businesswoman Rhoda.[59] This closeness is personal, according to development researcher Shiphrah who believes that God created her with a purpose specific to her.[60] So, when Priscilla spoke of the Temple curtain being torn in two, this unprecedented access represents both nearness to God and God's willingness to hear from his children and respond to them.[61] Thus in *mafanikio* theology, God is close, involved and accessible, all of which means his people experience the kind of prosperity which "can convince a person that you are in a better situation than them" in development worker Susanna's words.[62] Okorocha says that this kind of curiosity is common as "others want to learn the secret of such success – the source of the person's

---

56. Messi-Metogo, "Religious Indifference and Critique," Kindle edition, 30–49.
57. Messi-Metogo, "Religious Indifference and Critique," 43.
58. Galgalo, "Syncretism in African Christianity?," Kindle edition, loc.1888.
59. Interview 15 (Rhoda).
60. Interview 9 (Shiphrah).
61. Focus Group 2.
62. Focus Group 1, Swahili quotation 49.

mana [life enhancing force]."[63] Yet in *mafanikio* theology, this is no secret but power that is offered to all. God's ways are not hidden or for a select few in *mafanikio* theology; as Anna said, the Bible lays out the road map for this prosperity, in a format available to all.[64] The availability here is crucial because it effectively does away with the need for a prophet or a big man claiming to have a special revelation from God. *Mafanikio* theology does not contradict the desire for power in one's life, but it directs the human towards God as the source of power, both superior to other powers and more easily available.

However, in *mafanikio* theology it is not enough to simply treat the Bible as if it were an instruction book unless one is also spiritually connected to God. The goal is not for unbelievers to ape Christian lifestyle but to come into relationship with God. In *mafanikio* theology, like in African Traditional Religion, the human being is "God's steward under whom responsible management of the rest of the created order directly lies."[65] However, in *mafanikio* theology, the human's role as God's steward over creation differs from African Traditional Religion as it takes on an additional relational dimension where human and God are relationally connected. Indeed, the human finds their greatest prosperity when their focus is on God. The women affirmed this time and again as they quoted Matthew 6:33: Seek first the kingdom of God and all these things will be added to you. The tension is that God cannot be a mere means to a prosperous end. Once he becomes remote or un-relational, he is like the supreme deity of African Traditional Religion, and his power is no longer available. Thus, the women consistently emphasise the importance of relationship with God as first priority.

Mafanikio theology can be thought of as an African theology in that it draws on and operates within aspects of African worldview such as holism, communality, and pragmatism. However, it heavily nuances the pragmatism such that it cannot end up in a kind of dynamism (search for power) which features abandonment of God when things do not seem to be working out. It does this by presenting God as a superior alternative because he is the supreme being above all the lesser powers but, unlike the supreme being of African Traditional Religion, he is close and involved in his world. The God

---

63. Okorocha, "Religious Conversion in Africa," 170.
64. Interview 13 (Anna).
65. Kigame, Njoroge, and Kamaara, "From Knowledge to Wisdom," 93.

of *mafanikio* theology desires prosperity for his people and has made his good and powerful ways known, available to all who read the Bible in the context of relationship with him. Thus, African religious worldview both permeates *mafanikio* theology and is challenged by it, such that *mafanikio* theology both reflects the way Africans generally see and understand the world, and also creates a new religious expression, one which is both Christian and African. Various models have been offered for theology which is both Christian and African, and I now turn to examine these in order to see the relationship of *mafanikio* theology to them.

7.2.2 *Mafanikio* Theology in the Landscape of African Theology

Historically, African Christian theological approaches have included indigenization, contextualization, reconstruction, and liberation.[66] Each of these seeks to lay down a blueprint for how Africans should theologize. In indigenization, Western theology is more or less retained, but it is clothed in more recognizably African culture so that it appears less foreign, and church leaders should be African.[67] Contextualization wrestles with making theology itself African. Catholic theologians have tended towards inculturation, where those carrying the gospel acculturate to the receiving cultures and the Christian Scriptures are made understandable within them.[68] Thus, in Ghanaian Anglican John Pobee's thinking, the word comes to live in a culture.[69] Kenyan philosopher John Mbiti understood inculturation as a way "to deepen Christianity at the point of African religiosity" as African Christianity drew on its pre-Christian religious roots which had been a preparation for the gospel.[70] For Nigerian Byang Kato, Mbiti's approach did not offer enough guidance on what to do when African Traditional Religion conflicts with Christianity: it runs the risk of being African but not Christian. Both these contextualization approaches view the gospel as distinct from African culture and attempt various levels of engagement between the two. Another step

---

66. Turaki, *Engaging Religions and Worldviews*, 80–89.
67. Turaki, 80.
68. Vincent Donovan's record of his time among the Maasai is an example of this approach. Vincent Donovan, *Christianity Rediscovered*, Kindle edition.
69. Turaki, *Engaging Religions and Worldviews*, 82.
70. Cited in Sakupapa, "The Decolonising Content," 406–24.

on from these contextualization approaches is the reconstruction approach championed by Kenyan scholar Jesse Mugambi and also evidenced in the work of Kwame Bediako. The approach here was to conceive of Christianity within an African thought world not for the sake of synthesizing with an African religious past, but of making new myths for Africa's present situation which includes its history as well as its current crises.[71] Here Africa – not historic creeds or Western theology – is the womb from which African Christian Theology is birthed and grows. The work of Mercy Oduyoye and the Circle of Concerned African Women Theologians arguably does some of this re-mythologising work, taking seriously both African religious symbols and the experiences of women. However, their use of liberative strategies and hermeneutics of suspicion suggests at least some reliance on Western thought.[72]

Contextualisation, reconstruction, and liberation offer different models of a self-conscious African Christian theology, but another must be acknowledged. Pentecostalised Christian theology, including theology of the Pentecostalised mainstream, parallels these models in that it rarely references them and works at the grassroots level. Yet, it has been developing a "unique contemporary Christian expression of Christianity due to its ability to adapt to the African context," according to Ghanaian Presbyterian Cephas Omenyo.[73] He attributes this to its "strands of continuity between African religion and culture and Christianity" and "ability to adapt to the African context . . . [including] African primal world-view."[74] It is at this level of worldview that African charismatics and their prosperity theologies operate, including *mafanikio* theology. Most strongly reject the religious practices of African traditional religions and even speak of feeling called to liberate African culture from its demonic infection.[75] However, the idioms they adopt for speaking of salvation draw on African worldview. For example, while they may oppose the practice of visiting a witchdoctor for success, they may still feel that success has a spiritual component. Pentecostalised Christians may

---

71. Turaki, *Engaging Religions and Worldviews*, 89; Sakupapa, "The Decolonising Content," 412–13.

72. Sakupapa, "The Decolonising Content," 414.

73. Omenyo, "Charismatic Churches in Ghana," 252–77.

74. Omenyo, 252.

75. Omenyo, 277; See also Meyer, "Pentecostalism and Neo-Liberal Capitalism," 5–28.

not recognize this as an assumption which stems from an African worldview but even if it is implicit, it is not accidental.[76] *Mafanikio* theology has done just this kind of work making use of African worldview and idiom and transforming traditional African categories to emphasize fidelity to Christ. While this is not the self-conscious construction of African theology like Mbiti, Pobee, Kato, Mugambi, and Oduyoye, the task of this grassroots theology displays similar inclinations and orientations, finding "in Christianity, elements that make Jesus Christ the One who brings to fulfilment the highest religious and spiritual aspirations of their primal past."[77]

A new and emerging category for African theology that has potential to be applied to *mafanikio* theology is that of decolonization. Where post-colonial studies wrestled with theology in the wake of the withdrawal of colonializing forces and the establishment of African states, decolonization considers the colonial effects not of states but of forces such as neo-liberalism and globalism.[78] According to Nnamunga then, decolonized African theology, "is a rejection of the dominant Western theological paradigms and an acceptance of African reality and world view in theological hermeneutics."[79] This may involve drawing on categories such as inculturation, contextualization, and re-mythologizing. For example, Nnamunga analyses inculturation as having decolonizing inclination because it was aimed at helping Africans "realise the beauty and sanctity of their culture and understand that God speaks to them through their cultures."[80] However, decolonization's context is different to that in which the inculturation approach was developed. Nnamunga explains that inculturation "has been conceived by young people to be irrelevant to the contextual realities which confront Africans. The young generation has perceived inculturation to be a relic of the past."[81] While decolonized African theology undoubtedly stands on the shoulders of the theological approaches

---

76. Anderson, "The Gospel and African Religion," 375.

77. Amanor, "Pentecostal and Charismatic Churches," 124.

78. This does not exclude the ongoing effects of the state-based colonial era. Sakupapa, "The Decolonising Content," 410.

79. Nnamunga, "Decolonising African Theology," 122.

80. Nnamunga, 122.

81. Nnamunga, 125.

of the post-colonial era, decoloniality is responding to a different context.[82] For example, many young Africans may never have interacted with ancestor worship and would thus find Kwame Bediako's "Jesus as Ancestor" paradigm antiquated. However, this does not mean that they do not think and interact in ways influenced by an awareness of the spiritual world or connectedness with others both living and dead. Thus, there is a need for "knowledge construction that is rooted in African experience and relevant to the African situation."[83] *Mafanikio* theology is one such theology that operates at this level of worldview, finding African ways to do theology in a modern world. In this sense, one could think of *mafanikio* theology as a decolonized theology. This is not to say that *mafanikio* theology has a decolonizing agenda. Because colonizing forces are global, decolonization requires not only the resistance of them but also the disruption of them. *Mafanikio* theology is highly local and thus far has not sought to have international influence. However, in drawing attention to *mafanikio* theology, this study seeks to operate as a decolonizing contribution. In contrast to what Sarita Gallagher calls "exclusively Western education standards and ideals," this study prioritizes the promotion of a grassroots theology as a means of resisting monolithic understandings of Christianity and highlighting African epistemologies.[84]

Decolonization brings Omenyo's challenge, "can Christians in the West and African Christian leaders, trained in the classical Western theological paradigm, accept the fact that forms of African expression of Christianity will certainly be, in many respects, radically different from that in the West?"[85] Returning to Ngong's original assessment – that charismatic Christianity's telos of power for living is the telos of African traditional religion – in a decolonized framework, this is not necessarily a threat and does not indicate an uncritical acceptance of African traditional religion. On the contrary, it

---

82. These contributions include foregrounding of African theological agency, resistance of Western theological hegemony, inclusion of African Traditional Religion in theological construction and critical attitude towards mission Christianity. Sakupapa, "The Decolonising Content," 415.

83. Sakupapa, "The Decolonising Content," 420. Turaki lists some of these forces as: (1) the rising power and influence of advanced science and technology; (2) the powerful influence of democratic systems of government; (3) the impact of capitalism and market economy; and (4) the revolutionary influence of communication and transport systems. Turaki, *Engaging Religions and Worldviews*, 46.

84. Gallagher, "The Elephant in the Room," 116.

85. Omenyo, "Charismatic Churches in Ghana," 262.

may suggest a freed mind as Africans have found a way to ask their questions of their culture and find their answers in Jesus.

7.3 Patronage

One dimension of African culture which seldom receives theological attention is patronage.[86] This may be because patronage is more commonly associated with honour-shame cultural paradigms than the fear-power paradigm associated with the dynamism of African religiosity.[87] However as S. E. Freeman and Richard Calenberg point out, in Sub-Saharan Africa, a person gets power for living according to who their patron is: "Being known by others as having a certain big-man patron can elevate social status, and a person can raise his status by gaining the means and status to become a big man himself."[88] Ngong also refers to this dynamic when he says that in African Traditional Religion a human aims, "to gain the favours of spiritual beings such as ancestors, divinities, and ultimately, God, so that material well-being might be attained."[89] Thus in African patronage, an honour-shame paradigm dovetails with a fear-power one. Here a human is a client, looking for a patron (provider) for their material well-being. While patronage is not limited to African societies, it is part of being African.

As American missiologist Jayson Georges notes, patronage cultures are rarely explicit about this social system.[90] Meanwhile, Briton Jim Harries argues that when Western missionaries come into African societies, patronage is the assumed dynamic of the relationship though the missionary may be unaware of it since nothing is ever explicitly mentioned.[91] The meaning of patronage

---

86. Karen Lauterbach argues for the legitimacy of analysing the economic modalities of the prosperity gospel but does not interrogate a hierarchical form such as patronage. Lauterbach, "Fakery and Wealth," 111–132.

87. Paul Hiebert offered three cultural paradigms in 1986: guilt-innocence, honour-shame and fear-power. Guilt/innocence is often associated with Western cultures, honour-shame with Asian ones and fear-power with Africa and animistic cultures. They overlap and interact with each other and therefore are helpful lenses to understand cultures better, not an excuse to essentialise. Hiebert, *Anthropological Insights for Missionaries*.

88. Freeman and Calenberg, "Understanding Honor-Shame Dynamics," 425–38.

89. Ngong, "Salvation and Materialism," 3.

90. Georges, *Ministering in Patronage Cultures*, Kindle edition. I draw heavily from Georges's book in this discussion.

91. Harries, "Re-Strategising Mission," 359–72.

is most accurately found not in statements but in describing relationships. In this section, I will introduce patronage relationships, and consider how they might play out in *mafanikio* theology.

7.3.1 Defining Patronage

When Georges describes patronage as a "reciprocal, asymmetrical relationship" between patron and client, he insists that each word in that definition is crucial.[92]

First, patronage is asymmetrical, occurring between people of unequal status: a wealthy patron and a needy client. Patronage is a system which allows them "to interact without jeopardising their social distinction."[93] In this system, the client's needs are met, and the patron is rewarded with honour. In patronage culture, this is not as simple as a person of low status approaching a person of very high status. That gap can appear too great and so the system is often multi-tiered. Brokers are people who act as intermediaries between patron and client. Higher in status than the client, to them they appear as a patron, yet when they come before the patron, this broker is inferior and acts as a client.[94]

Second, patronage is predicated on reciprocity. Both parties contribute something according to their roles. For the patron, this is likely to be material, such as protection or money; for the client it is social, like praise or loyalty.[95] Accepting the other's offering is part of the relationship including allowing oneself to be praised (in the case of the patron) and accepting blessing or favour (in the case of the client). In patronage relationships, as the late Australian ethnographer Moyra Dale explained, "exchanging gifts does not constitute a 'paying off' of indebtedness. Rather, accepting a gift implies the commitment to return a gift, in what is a further 'investing into' the relationship. The aim of the exchange is not independence, but rather interdependence."[96] The aim of reciprocity is therefore not symmetry but a cycle, as obligation between the two goes back and forth, reinforcing their

---

92. Georges, *Ministering in Patronage Cultures*, 9.

93. Georges, 10. Clients may also give monetary or tangible offerings such as a foodstuff or handicraft. Even if this is meagre or of little value, it is a symbol of desire to build the relationship.

94. Georges, 13.

95. Georges, 10.

96. Dale, *Islam and Women*, Kindle edition, 170.

need for each other. Unlike charity or altruism which is one-sided, patronage is inherently two-sided. Expecting something from your patron is not demanding, it reinforces your commitment to them. If there is no expectation of the other, the relationship is over.

Finally then, patronage is fundamentally relational. It is not a contract or a deal; it cannot be viewed with a legal framework.[97] It is a relationship, somewhat like that between a parent and a child in that it is ongoing and committed, with expectations and obligations that cannot be calcified into rules.

7.3.2 Theological Implications of Patronage

Patronage has at least two implications for the discussion of prosperity theologies. First, money and relationships can go together. Georges says: "I've heard Westerners say, 'They just want money, not a relationship.' This comment reveals a deep-seated cultural assumption: money and relationships should not mingle. The expectations of patronage seem morally wrong to Westerners."[98] However, if one views God as patron, it is natural to think that relationship with him would involve a material element; driving a wedge between who God is and the gifts he gives is unnatural in an African worldview where patronage forms expectations for relationships between unequals.[99] As Anderson says, "When Africans say 'God is good,' 'God is love,' etcetera, they do not separate God's moral attributes from God's provision."[100] God as patron is one who blesses; divorcing God from blessing is nonsensical. It also short-circuits relationship, because without reciprocity and exchange of resources, the relationship cannot be deepened. When African Christians come to God, expecting him to provide, they may in fact be expressing their desire for deeper relationship with him rather than simply using him for what they can get out of him.

The second theological implication of patronage is that obligation is mutual. Neither patron nor client is free to treat the other as they wish. In more democratized societies, it is often assumed that a superior person in a hierarchy has fewer constraints on their behaviour. However, in patronage

---

97. Richards and O'Brien, *Misreading Scripture with Western Eyes*, 162.
98. Georges, *Ministering in Patronage Cultures*, 29.
99. Carter suggests a distinction between hope in God and hope in God's good gifts in his study of Christians in Equatorial Guinea. Carter, *Inside the Whirlwind*, Kindle edition, 216.
100. Anderson, "African Pentecostalism and Prosperity," Kindle edition, 258.

societies, a patron must also act in moral ways, not exploiting their clients and instead fulfilling their obligations to them. Similarly, the client has obligations. They cannot exploit their patron by constantly asking unless they also fulfil their obligations such as obedience, loyalty, and praise. This is all held in check by a system of honour and shame. Georges says, "communities use shame to pressure the patrons into sharing resources. The failure of a rich person to share resources is a cardinal disgrace in collectivistic cultures."[101] This is the case in Tanzania. At times I have felt embarrassed by my comparative wealth, but a cultural mentor explained to me, "The problem is not being wealthy, the problem is if you do not share with others." When God and his relationship with humans is viewed through a patronage lens then, there are constraints on how they relate to one another. A person who takes material blessing from God and does not reciprocate with praise is not a good client; they can expect consequences for this immorality. If God does not provide, his honour is at stake. Though the women resisted the idea of demanding from God in view of his sovereignty as we saw in chapter 6, they were also confident that he would provide in accordance with his promises. Furthermore, when God does provide, these blessings must not remain a secret. It is important to acknowledge them publicly. This is not boasting. It is ensuring that God receives the honour which is due to him.

Having understood patronage relationships and their theological implications, I turn to examining what elements of patronage are present in *mafanikio* theology.

7.3.3 *Mafanikio* Theology and Patronage

Mafanikio theology places God in the role of patron in that he provides materially and spiritually, and people can expect him to do so. Lois said, "God gives prosperity to us. So the Bible tells us that God is the provider of every thing. And we are told that if you are a medical doctor, it's not because of your intelligence. It's God."[102] This prosperity is available only in a reciprocal relationship with God where God blesses, and the human obeys. For example, Zipporah said, a person must be "saved by God and God will bless you so continue to stay in your salvation, continue to follow and learn what God

---

101. Georges, *Ministering in Patronage Cultures*, 14.
102. Interview 10 (Lois), Swahili quotation 107.

says in his word regarding those things which you do as your responsibility."[103] Each one has a part, according to Junia.[104]

In their role as clients, God's people benefit from his provision and respond appropriately to him in a variety of ways. They tithe (Lois, Junia) as a way of maintaining their relationship with him.[105] They also work on his behalf in his world, and God blesses that work (Eunice, Anna).[106] They are obedient (Eunice, Abigail, Damaris).[107] There is a possibility that Christians also do the work of brokers. Fibi spoke of herself as "a bridge of blessing," flowing from God through her to other people.[108] Ruth used the language of being a "channel of blessing."[109]

While patronage terms are clearly present in *mafanikio* theology, prosperity theologies are often thought to employ a distorted version of patronage. For example, patronage is thought to play out in damaging ways as pastors present themselves as big men, acting as patrons or perhaps as God's brokers. Ehioghae sees this as a location of prosperity in a man; Jane Soothill records instances of women assuming this big man role by making others small.[110] In relation to God, Georges says, "the prosperity gospel portrays God as the type of patron who automatically gives material blessings when we perform a certain way. Unchecked assumptions about patronage can warp our theology and cause a purely transactional exchange with God."[111] Meanwhile, Mboya sees that "the prosperity Gospel is overly concerned with 'receiving' more than giving." For Mboya, this cannot be good client behaviour because it portrays God as "a mere source of fulfilment for human desires but not a recipient of our love and gratitude. It depicts God as a non-relational provider."[112] Meanwhile Hicks criticises what he sees as a contractualising of relationship, a

---

103. Interview 16 (Zipporah), Swahili quotation 108.

104. Interview 5 (Junia). This idea was repeated by Leah, Lois, Lydia, Mariamu, Damaris, Ruth, and Zipporah. Interview 17 (Leah); Interview 10 (Lois); Interview 11 (Lydia); Interview 12 (Mariamu); Interview 3 (Damaris); Interview 20 (Ruth); Interview 16 (Zipporah).

105. Interview 10 (Lois); Interview 5 (Junia).

106. Interview 1 (Eunice); Interview 13 (Anna).

107. Interview 1 (Eunice); Interview 2 (Abigail); Interview 3 (Damaris).

108. Interview 4 (Fibi).

109. Interview 20 (Ruth).

110. Ehioghae, "Prosperity Gospel," 37; Soothill, *Gender, Social Change*, 93.

111. Georges, *Ministering in Patronage Cultures*, 86.

112. Mboya, "Gift Challenges and Transforms," 29.

placing of "God and humans on the same level—as signatories on a contract, as parties who can bind one another to their promises."[113]

These are by and large concerns with distortions of patronage rather than patronage itself. Georges notes that patronage in our sinful world is always distorted in some way. He argues that while the Bible affirms God as patron, it also offers four theological correctives. The first two are differences between human patronage and divine patronage; the second two are correctives to distorted divine patronage. First, in Georges's view, while human patronage is a voluntary arrangement, "God foreordained his patronage before the foundations of the world" and "divinely elected . . . the recipients of his favours."[114] Second, while human patronage has a limited time frame, lasting as long as it is beneficial, divine patronage is for eternity. God's generosity will not run out and we do not have the option to move away from him if things do not go as we had hoped. Thus, divine patronage is different from human patronage in terms of its source and its timeframe. Regarding distortions of divine patronage, Georges offers a third and fourth biblical corrective. Third, while clients in patronage cultures alternate between multiple patrons, God demands exclusive spiritual allegiance. Fourth, where people may be tempted to "manipulate the system to squeeze as much benefit out of the other person" (as either the patron or the client), it is relationship that is prioritised in the divine patron-client dyad.[115]

Much of what we have already seen about *mafanikio* theology addresses these concerns. We have already seen in this chapter that *mafanikio* theology directs people away from trust in the big man and towards relationship with God. In *mafanikio* theology, relationship with God is prioritised and it is only in the context of relationship with God that prosperity is possible. If relationship with God is neglected, prosperity is endangered. Fidelity to him is thus essential. God's sovereignty and mystery are also upheld such that calcification or formularisation of the relationship are not permitted. In addition, God is able to bring blessing at whatever stage a person happens to be, meaning a person is driven towards thanksgiving rather than making

---

113. Hicks, "Prosperity, Theology and Economy," 243. It is unclear whether Hicks is aware of patronage dynamics where parties are bound to one another in means other than by contract.

114. Georges, *Ministering in Patronage Cultures*, 84–85.

115. Georges, 85.

demands of God. Since these themes are already well familiar to us from this chapter and the previous ones, I will not dwell on them here. Suffice to say, *mafanikio* theology has no provision for humans treating God as a non-relational benefactor. It emphasizes the maintenance of good relationships and, in keeping with patronage thought, this good relationship is found in coming to God for prosperity, with an expectation that he will provide it. Such provision deepens the relationship rather than endangering it.

In interviews, the language of patronage came out particularly strongly with regard to thanksgiving. The women saw this as a critical and indispensable part of their relationship with God and prosperity. Not only did they think thanksgiving was important, but they also saw it functioning in a variety of ways in the patron-client relationship. In Tanzania, as in other parts of Africa, thanksgiving is tangible, expressed not only in words but also in an offering of some kind.[116]

First, thankfulness points a person towards the patron's role in their life. In a context of poverty, this becomes a reassurance that their patron-client relationship is nevertheless intact. For example, in the scenario of the impoverished widow in the village, Jochebed felt some measure of blessing from God was evident in the fact that the widow had grandchildren.[117] Thus even in her poverty, the woman could approach God with thanksgiving, as a good client would. For a wealthy person, thankfulness directs them to see the role of the patron in their achievements. Eunice said, "In your heart you thank God. But to say, "Yes I have prospered!" is like claiming you did it yourself—it's pride."[118] Thus, whether in riches or poverty, as the Christian recognizes the role of the patron and gives thanks, they are directed away from their own capacity and towards recognizing their dependence on God.

Second, thankfulness is part of maintaining a positive relationship with God, thus ensuring his continued patronage. For Mariamu, prayers start with thanksgiving and end with presenting requests.[119] For Rhoda, it was in thanking God that she felt confident he would be her guard after her shop

---

116. Harries, "Overcoming Invented Ogres," 171–84.
117. Interview 19 (Jochebed).
118. Interview 1 (Eunice), Swahili quotation 109.
119. Interview 12 (Mariamu).

was broken into.[120] Junia felt that any opportunity in business is not only provided by God, but requires his ongoing intervention to proceed, necessitating a right attitude of thankfulness before God.[121] Shiphrah warned that those who did not thank God, such as the rich fool in Luke 12:13–21 would lose the benefits of God's patronage and even their life.[122]

Third, thankfulness increases trust in God, empowering the Christian to continue to pursue prosperity in obedience to God. Eunice said that the appropriate response to receiving blessings from God was to thank God, "trust God and we live a Christian life."[123] Puah said, having seen that God works all things together for good, "So then, let me thank God. I thank God for this. Thank you. I ask you to give me another opportunity to be increased."[124] Thankfulness not only highlights God's role as patron in a person's life and functions to maintain a positive relationship with him; it also provides the grounds on which to move forward together.

Mafanikio theology both points the Christian towards recognising that God is a good patron, and exhorts them to be a good client, fulfilling their obligations towards God. Thankfulness functions to maintain a good relationship with patron God. *Mafanikio* theology thus functions in an African way, by employing patronage themes and concepts. However, it avoids the pitfalls of distorted patronage, reorienting it around God's goodness and relationship with him, expressed in fidelity to him. With God as patron, the Christian finds themselves in a position where they can prosper, but there is no space to treat God as a mere resource, because of the reciprocity of the relationship. This has implications for the questions we asked earlier about capitalism: God cannot be co-opted into a capitalist system or conceived of as merely a resource because he is a relational patron. To treat him otherwise would be to shed one's Africanness.

---

120. Interview 15 (Rhoda).
121. Interview 5 (Junia).
122. Interview 9 (Shiphrah).
123. Interview 1 (Eunice).
124. Interview 7 (Puah).

7.4 Conclusion

In this chapter I have considered the Africanness of *mafanikio* theology in theological terms. We have seen *mafanikio* theology's emphasis on materiality not as a vehicle for a materialistic spirit of the age but as a resistance to it. The women taught the goodness of material things while not making them ultimate. They affirmed both production and industriousness, and taught against the hoarding of personal wealth and in favour of sharing with others. These values cohere with African values derived from African Traditional Religion including holism and communalism. However, the women were more critical when it came to two other aspects of African Traditional Religion, pragmatism, and dynamism. They affirmed pragmatism in their insistence that prosperity is available to Christians now and believed that switching to other gods was an unpragmatic choice, because ultimately these gods could not deliver. To those who may be tempted, they offer the closeness of God and his clear instructions about how to live well in the world as evidence of this better way. Like many in charismatic circles, the women were not consciously drawing on post-colonial theological models as they formulated this African theology, but their theology can be seen as functionally decolonized or at least decolonizing as it operates within an African worldview to find ways of being Christian in the modern world. One such African way of operating is in patron-client relationships. The women draw on these relationships in describing their relationship with God, presenting God as a good patron and themselves as faithful clients. *Mafanikio* theology does not present as a self-conscious African theology. However, it draws on African ways of seeing the world and being in it. These both influence how the women read the Bible and are critiqued by their reading of the Bible.

Figure 7.2 What have we learned about *mafanikio* theology (MT)? (Chapters 4–7)

Chapter 4	Chapter 5	Chapter 6	Chapter 7	Chapter 8
In MT, prosperity is a process of taking steps to move to the next level. This process manifests across all areas of life and when all areas are affected, the result is greater than the sum of the parts. In MT, God is the source of prosperity. In MT, prosperity is characterised by effort, perseverance, righteousness and knowledge.	MT responds to a poverty gospel on one hand and profligate prosperity gospel on the other. MT combats passivity through knowing God rightly, identity change and environmental change. MT locates itself in the Bible, with hermeneutics that emphasise a comprehensive knowledge of Scripture to provide a balanced theology.	MT has a strong family resemblance to other prosperity theologies from Zambia, South Africa, Malawi, Cameroon and Kenya. These are different to how "prosperity gospel" is often described. They are an alternative to it and implicit critique of it. MT promotes perseverance, sympathy, and lament in suffering. MT calls people to Christ himself not just his things. MT embodies the fruit of the Spirit.	MT offers an alternative to a materialistic spirit by drawing on African communal values and Christian ideas of stewarding God's world well. MT draws on holism and communalism as aspects of African worldviews. It modifies pragmatism and dynamism to locate power in God and advocate fidelity to him. Because MT operates in African terms, it can be considered to have decolonising potential. MT operates in African patronage terms, including mutual obligation of God and humans.	

CHAPTER 8

Mafanikio Theology's Holism in Global Perspective

8.1 Introduction

Thus far we have seen *mafanikio* theology as a process of taking steps to move to the next level, which can be applied in the economic, spiritual, relational, physical, and intellectual realms as well as to the experience of inner peace. This all-encompassing prosperity both comes from God and is understood and attained best in relationship with God. We have understood that in its Tanzanian context, *mafanikio* theology seeks a middle way between overzealous denial of earthly provisions and unhealthy love of worldly things, responding to the problem of passivity with a conviction that the Bible shows a better way. In the landscape of prosperity theologies in Tanzania and in Africa, *mafanikio* theology operates both as a prosperity theology and a critique of other prosperity theologies. It fosters discipleship, and it does so in a thoroughly African way, rooted in its context and yet operating in a distinctively Christian manner. Part of its Africanness is holism and at various points throughout this thesis I have referred to *mafanikio* theology as holistic because it applies to all areas of life and sees them as interconnected. In this chapter, I give more attention to this claim to holism in *mafanikio* theology.

Various overlapping and, at times, synonymous terms are used by theologians and practitioners to refer to holism. These include a theology of *shalom*, a Hebrew word denoting peace, completeness and well-being, as well as integral mission and "Mission as Transformation" which I discuss below.[1] Meanwhile, Nelus Niemandt, reflecting on the work of Jürgen Moltmann uses the language of "flourishing life" and connects this to the language of "abundant life," a term which is familiar to us from Laurenti Magesa's work on African Traditional Religion.[2] Theologising around holism has often taken place in missiological spaces, because theology on its own is seen as inadequate without practice. In his edited volume about holistic mission together with Wonsuk Ma, Brian Woolnough defines holistic mission as, "mission which addresses the body, mind and spirit in human beings. It is not exclusively addressed to the spirit, aimed at conversion and personal discipleship, nor is it exclusively concerned with the social gospel, tending to care merely for people's physical welfare."[3] However, it is also inimical to any holistic enterprise to separate out theology from practice. The two are connected in a myriad of ways: theology drives and shapes practice, and reflection on practice orients and modifies theology. Thus, holistic mission's task is inherently theological, weaving together theological threads of spiritual and material and seeking ways of being, doing, and reflecting that integrate them.

Indeed, several scholars acknowledge the connection between prosperity theologies and holism. Katherine Attanasi notes that some "prosperity teachings often equate prosperity with God's *shalom* . . . [which connotes] psychological, social, spiritual and physical wholeness; peace with the natural world, ancestors, God and fellow human beings; and inner satisfaction, contentment and peace."[4] Similarly Joshua Barron argues that "both Prosperity Gospel and Productivity Gospel [his modified version of prosperity gospel] address the holistic concerns which are an intimate part of African worldviews" though he considers the former corrupt and the second biblical.[5] An example of a prosperity teaching that addresses these holistic concerns biblically can be found in Wanjiru Gitau's work on *Mavuno* Church in Nairobi.[6] She con-

---

1. See also Woolnough, "Good News," Kindle edition, 3–14.
2. Niemandt, "Rediscovering Joy in Costly," 1–7; Magesa, *African Religion*.
3. Woolnough, "Good News for the Poor," 4. Woolnough suggests that these alternatives may have been adopted in the West to distinguish them from the rise of alternative health therapies which also used the word 'holistic'.
4. Attanasi, "Introduction: The Plurality of Prosperity," 4.
5. Barron, "Is the Prosperity Gospel?," 100.
6. Gitau, *Megachurch Christianity Reconsidered*, Kindle edition.

trasts "a simplistic way of giving and sending hope that has become the main currency of a lot of churches in Africa" with *Mavuno* Church's ability to "speak substantively to what people are going through . . . so they are not simply passionate about faith and not simply optimistic that God would bless them; they're also knowing how to use the gifts and education that God has given them in an integrated way that brings a holistic way of living."[7] Similar could be said of *mafanikio* theology with its emphasis on effort and enabling from God in all areas of life for the service of others.

Nevertheless, while the women in this study viewed themselves and their theology as holistic, I mentioned briefly in section 4.4.1. that there are areas of life which they do not directly engage in their *mafanikio* theology, such as ecology and politics. There I noted that this may have been a result of their current life experiences. However, I also noted practices in the lives of a few that do pertain to these areas, such as Priscilla's founding of a climate change organisation and others' interest in politics. This could be a case of their operant theology being unaligned with their espoused theology, but it could also be that *mafanikio* has more subtle holistic elements than are first apparent. Indeed, here I shall argue that *mafanikio* theology can be an ally for those who desire greater engagement in these areas. An exploration of *mafanikio* theology's holism is therefore warranted. I shall do this by comparing *mafanikio* theology with two other models of holism – one African, one not – and considering its relationship to them. This brings us to the final concentric circle in this exploration of *mafanikio* theology. It is the largest concentric circle: having moved out from Tanzania and Africa, here *mafanikio* theology is situated as part of a global discussion. Having understood a little more of the nature of *mafanikio* theology's holism, I will then examine how less prominent holistic themes play out in *mafanikio* theology, first on the physical side of things, namely rest, creation care and political engagement, and second from a spiritual perspective, addressing the issue of the role the atonement plays in *mafanikio* theology.

---

7. Gitau, SATS Symposium: meet the African scholar, YouTube, November 12, 2021,.

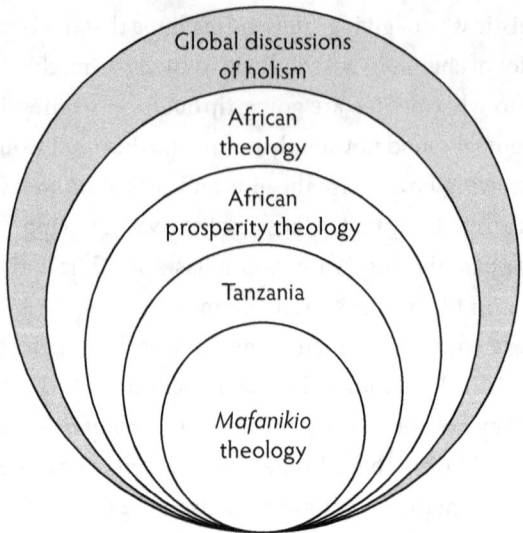

Figure 8.1 Concentric circles of engagement with *mafanikio* theology (Global discussions of holism)

8.2 Rene Padilla and Integral Mission

Ecuadorian Rene Padilla's concept of integral mission came onto the global evangelical scene at a time when the role of evangelism and social action in the church's witness was contested. In 1974, over two thousand Protestant evangelical leaders from one hundred and fifty nations gathered in Lausanne for the International Congress on World Evangelisation.[8] Funded from Western sources and under the leadership of North American Southern Baptist Billy Graham and English Anglican John Stott, it was originally conceived as an alternative to the World Council of Churches' emphasis on social action. However, Padilla argued that dichotomies between evangelism and social action are an export from Western theological methodologies.[9] It was in this context that he introduced and advocated for what became known as *misión integral*, or integral mission. Padilla reflects that at Lausanne in 1974 there was a clear commitment that, "social action and evangelism are essential

---

8. Thomas, *Classic Texts in Mission*, 144.
9. Kirkpatrick, "C. René Padilla," 351–71.

aspects of the church's mission; that proclaiming the Gospel cannot be separated from expressing God's love in concrete ways."[10] Padilla used the image of two wings of a plane to illustrate the necessity of both, though later this came to be widely associated with Stott who became an advocate of Padilla.[11]

However, Padilla needed to continually defend this integration from American leaders whom he saw as "reducing the Church's mission to multiplying Christians and churches through evangelism."[12] He was joined by Mexican Gonzalo Báez-Camargo and Peruvian Samuel Escobar in this task and it was also taken up by Vinay Samuel with his work on Mission as Transformation in the 1980s and 90s. Joset notes that Padilla and Escobar were both senior staff at IFES and that in IFES there was a recognition that a more integrated approach was necessary in order to engage in a world of student revolts and changing geopolitics.[13] There is therefore a sense in which integral mission rose to prominence on a global level out of a need to respond to the Greek dualism that underlies Western thought, seeking to reintegrate what was torn asunder.[14]

8.2.1 A Comparison of Integral Mission And *Mafanikio* Theology

In *mafanikio* theology, the tension between Greek dualism and the need to integrate exists as well.[15] The women spoke of different areas of *mafanikio*, which they broadly conceived of as belonging to either physical or spiritual realms. When Zilpah argued that Jesus's two arms on the cross touch on both spiritual and physical, she was not arguing for an integration of the two but rather that Jesus's work on the cross is relevant to both.[16] I will deal below with how the women conceive of Christ's work on the cross; the relevance of her comments here is to illustrate that *mafanikio* theology has a responsive

---

10. Padilla, *What Is Integral Mission?*, Kindle edition, 38.
11. Kirkpatrick, "C. René Padilla," 354.
12. Padilla, *What is Integral Mission?*, 28.
13. Joset, "The Priesthood of All Students?," 17, 38.
14. Woolnough, "Good News for the Poor," 4–5.
15. The poverty gospel is an example of Greek dualism in Tanzania, possibly brought through Western missionary activity and influence. See the discussion in section 5.1.
16. Focus Group 2.

dimension to it. To those who may seek to diminish either the spiritual or the physical, Zilpah insists that Christ's work encompasses both.

However, the TAFES women also acknowledged the limitations of speaking about different areas of *mafanikio*, insisting that greater prosperity comes when all areas of *mafanikio* are in sync with each other, that this is prosperity in its fullest form (see section 4.4.1.). While they could see how things have been torn asunder, they saw an indissoluble relationship between the spiritual and the physical, because relationship with God (spiritual) is the source of other kinds of *mafanikio*, including physical. However, this relationship does not elevate the spiritual over the physical. Such a theological emphasis is what created the need for prosperity theologies in Africa: the TAFES women consider elevating spiritual over physical to be fruitless. Thus, they insisted that it is not enough to have one kind of *mafanikio* without the other. They struggled to envision a situation in which one could say they had prosperity if only one kind of *mafanikio* was present, as in the case of the widow in the village (section 4.5.3.). Padilla's language of *misión integral* uses the Spanish word for wholemeal flour, an image which suggests an impossibility of sifting one part from another. Likewise, the TAFES women reflect Woolnough's comment that, a "majority world thought pattern starts with a holistic approach to life."[17]

There are some differences between integral mission and *mafanikio* theology. For example, while Padilla was responding to controversies over the importance of evangelism or social action in the global church, the TAFES women's context is more personal. They are not official church leaders or speakers at a Lausanne conference, making statements about what the agenda of the church should be. They are women teaching others about who God is and how that should affect their lives. They therefore tend to be more relationally oriented in their framing of the issue, drawing a direct line between who God is and what he cares about, and how they understand the world and their activity in it. Holism flows out of one's relationship with a God who cares about every aspect of life. While the TAFES women operate at this personal level and Padilla's work spoke to a more overarching agenda, they share a conviction that all Christians can be involved in the work of God wherever they are.[18] This empowers every Christian to be about God's work in the

---

17. Woolnough, "Good News for the Poor," 5.
18. Padilla, *What Is Integral Mission?*, 20–23.

world. Like Padilla's integral mission, *mafanikio* theology's holism observes Christians who are passive in God's world and seeks to give theological reason for them to be active in God's world. The holism has a practical purpose: to empower the church for its witness.

Padilla and the TAFES women disagree on the role of wealth in this witness. Padilla argues that when a church is committed to integral mission:

> It understands that its goal is not to become numerically large; or *materially rich*; or politically powerful. Its purpose is to incarnate the values of the kingdom of God and bear witness to the love and the justice revealed in Jesus Christ, by the power of the Spirit, for the transformation of human life in all its dimensions, on a personal and community level.[19] [emphasis mine]

While the TAFES women agree that being materially rich is not an end in itself, they see the proper use of wealth as an asset in the kingdom of God, an expression of love, and a means of providing for others, including the transformation of human life in all its dimensions. Padilla points to economic inequalities in Latin America as, "an inescapable challenge to our lifestyle," imploring Christians to wholeheartedly search "for coherence between how we use our material possessions and the values of the kingdom of God," including "asking ourselves if [our] luxuries should be postponed to free up resources to satisfy more pressing needs – and not just ours, but those of others."[20] Inequality is an issue in Tanzania as well. Global Finance Magazine reports that 10 percent of Tanzania's population own a little over 50 percent of the wealth, and the poorest 50 percent own just 13 percent of national income.[21] This ought to be a startling statistic for university graduates such as the TAFES women who are an elite. Indeed, the TAFES women share a concern with using material possessions in the service of the kingdom of God and of providing for others. For Dorcas, Abigail, and Ruth one can only fulfil the Bible's instructions to provide for others if one has a measure of prosperity.[22] As I have noted in Puah's example of living in informal housing and Eunice's

---

19. Padilla, 23
20. Padilla, 73.
21. 'World Inequality Ranking By Country 2022' *Global Finance Magazine*. Tanzania ranks at 64th on the world inequality index while Padilla's home country of Ecuador is 106th.
22. Focus Group 1; Interview 2 (Abigail); Interview 20 (Ruth).

of fostering children, for the TAFES women this compassionate action is not postponed in favour of greater acquisition. However, the language of postponing wealth or acquisition does not sit easily with *mafanikio* theology because it sounds disruptive to the progress that it is inherent in *mafanikio*. Pause or postponement in the pursuit of prosperity puts one in danger of going backwards. Continual acquisition which supports continual generosity better describes the TAFES women's approach to providing for the poor.

Mafanikio theology and integral mission both respond to the Greek dualism that underpins Western thought, attempting to reintegrate what has been separated. However, there are differences in terms of audience and attitude to wealth. This is to be expected: Padilla drew on his own context and experiences in Latin America while, as we have seen, *mafanikio* theology is shaped by its African context. While they share common concerns, they draw on different resources. I noted in section 7.1.2. that *Ubuntu*, as an African philosophy, entails the interconnectedness of life and so, in dealing with *mafanikio* theology's claim to holism, examining its relationship to *Ubuntu* will provide greater understanding of what underlies it.

8.3 *Ubuntu*: Holism in Africa

Ubuntu is a Zulu word (in Swahili, *utu*). Expressed initially in the 1970s in Kenyan John Mbiti's theological writing, it was popularised by Anglican Archbishop Desmond Tutu during South Africa's apartheid struggle with the axiom *umuntu ngumuntu ngabantu* (a person is a person because of others) or "I am because we are."[23] It is the philosophy that underpins the holism of African life. Cameroonian-American theologian Elias Bongmba notes that it "upholds individuality and community together," such that South African lay Catholic theologian Nontando Hadebe sees it as active both at grassroots and academic levels.[24] Though *Ubuntu* is sometimes known as African humanism, Hadebe argues that when humans live in line with *Ubuntu*'s defining characteristics "such as interdependence of individual and community, shared

---

23. Ras, "Broken Bodies and Present Ghosts,": 1–7; Masango, "African Spirituality That Shapes," 930–43.

24. Bongmba, "Reflections on Thabo Mbeki's," 291–316; Hadebe, "'Listening to the Elders,'" 26–38.

values and the common good," they reflect the life of the Trinitarian God who is "communitarian, relational and connected."[25]

Ubuntu has been criticized for uncritical applications of African culture, particularly those that marginalize or oppress women.[26] However, the women pushing back against this tendency do not seek to undermine or get rid of *Ubuntu*. Instead, they claim it for themselves, arguing for their inclusion in it and seeking to deploy it in the service of seeing women prosper as well.[27] Thus, though applications of *Ubuntu* have been flawed, in its fullest form it exemplifies a holism that includes all.

8.3.1 Relationship of *Ubuntu* to Prosperity Theology

The relationship of *Ubuntu* to theologies of prosperity depends on one's assessment of prosperity theologies. Mashau and Kgatle, for example, cast *Ubuntu*'s mutual concern as the antidote to the prosperity gospel's greed.[28] However, another group of scholars have seen a less antagonistic relationship between *Ubuntu* and African prosperity theologies. During the 2022 conference of the African Society of Evangelical Theology (ASET), I attended five different sessions that intersected with theologies of prosperity.[29] Though critical of some of the extreme versions of prosperity theology, none of these were aimed at opposing prosperity theology. Instead, they understood prosperity theologies to be attempts at unifying the Western dualism that is a legacy of missionary theology. They drew on *Ubuntu* as a local resource for doing this repair work. Thus, *Ubuntu* and prosperity theologies have a common goal. To the extent that an African prosperity theology engenders an integrated life where individual prosperity contributes to and is part of a greater whole, it can be thought of as consistent with *Ubuntu*.

With Mashau and Kgatle, the TAFES women oppose prosperity theologies of greed, but their solution is to offer *mafanikio* theology instead, itself

---

25. Hadebe, "'Listening to the Elders,'" 27.

26. Manyonganise, "Oppressive and Liberative," 1–7.

27. Manyonganise, "Oppressive and Liberative," 6; Hadebe, "'Listening to the Elders,'" 35; Ras, "Broken Bodies and Present Ghosts," 7.

28. Mashau and Kgatle, "Prosperity Gospel," 1–8.

29. Kubwimana, "An Examination of Contemporary Rwandans"; Ogero, "Reorienting Understanding of Salvation"; Haruna, "Salvation: Prosperity or Poverty"; Moenga, "Salvation: Prosperity or Poverty"; David Ngaruiya, "Seven Dimensions of Salvation."

a prosperity theology. Like the ASET presenters, they were concerned about dualism. Jochebed, Leah, and Damaris criticised theologies that encouraged people only to pray and be in church without working hard.[30] Similarly, Eunice said that God is at work everywhere even in the workplace.[31] The TAFES women saw themselves as opposing the kinds of theologies that divorce the spiritual and the material. While they did not articulate this in terms of missionary legacy or Western dualism, this was because they were telling me the ideas they are responding to, not exploring the history of how they came to be.

Unlike the presenters at the ASET conference, none of the TAFES women spoke about their alternative prosperity theology, *mafanikio* theology, in terms of *Ubuntu*. As we have seen, they understand the source of their *mafanikio* theology to be the Bible. However, as we saw in chapter 7, they do draw on their African cultural background as they develop this theology. While not explicit, then, *Ubuntu* underlies their *mafanikio* theology and is expressed in its holistic orientation.

8.3.2 Other Influences that Overlap with *Mafanikio* Theology's Holism

It is imperative to look first to ascribe *mafanikio* theology's holism to *Ubuntu* before seeking causal links between *mafanikio* theology and foreign influences. Joshua Barron, in his explanation of the Productivity Gospel, describes it as "the empowerment theology of the Prosperity Gospel combined with personal accountability and the Protestant work ethic."[32] Since South Africa's Centre for Development and Enterprise published its "Under the Radar" report arguing that Pentecostalism would spur Africa's economic growth as Calvinism did in Europe during the Industrial Revolution, various scholars have made comparisons between the two movements.[33] However, Barron is not simply speaking of the work ethic in Western terms here; he argues that the Productivity Gospel has "inherited Martin Luther's understanding of

---

30. Interview 19 (Jochebed); Interview 17 (Leah); Interview 3 (Damaris).
31. Interview 1 (Eunice).
32. Barron, "Is the Prosperity Gospel?," 98.
33. "Under the Radar. Pentecostalism in South Africa and Its Potential Social and Economic Role" (South Africa: Centre for Development and Enterprise, 2008); For examples, see Gifford and Nogueira-Godsey, "The Protestant Ethic," 5–22; Hasu, "World Bank & Heavenly Bank," 680.

vocation, the sanctity of work."³⁴ His foundation for doing so is unclear. He references Miller and Yamamori's application of Max Weber's "Protestant work ethic" to support his claim but Miller and Yamamori draw a parallel between Protestant and Pentecostal work ethics rather than suggesting a relationship of source or inheritance: "The Pentecostal ethic is very similar to the Protestant ethic—namely, it produces people who are honest, disciplined, transparent in their business dealings, people who view their vocation, humble or elevated, as a calling by God that warrants commitment."³⁵ They also acknowledge several points at which the Pentecostal ethic differs from Weber's Protestant work ethic.³⁶ Barron thus offers no causal relationship between the Protestant work ethic and the Productivity Gospel. While the work ethic Barron observes may cohere with the Protestant work ethic, it is possible that it has developed independently of it.

Even in cases which draw explicitly on Western theologies, the thought forms and resources may not be Western. In Zimbabwean Kenneth Mtata's examination of Swedish missionary Bishop Sigfrid Strandvik's application of Martin Luther's smaller catechism, he finds that "Strandvik taps into African practices, uses them as the basis for developing an African Lutheran theology of work and radically departs from the predominant modern industrial thinking that dominated work in his colonial context."³⁷ Though Strandvik's goal was Lutheran, that is, to instill Martin Luther's Protestant work ethic, the resources he used were African and he was able to do so because of a coherence between African and biblical values.³⁸ Strandvik thus explained Luther's work ethic in African terms, and even modified the work ethic at times to fit better in an African context. However, the resources for this African Lutheran theology were already present in Africa such that it might be more accurate to speak of Strandvik recognising the overlap between his Lutheran tradition and African values and deploying this for his own Lutheran purposes, rather than of bringing a Lutheran tradition to teach or impart to Africans. In this case, the theology of work has not developed independently from Western

---

34. Barron, "Is the Prosperity Gospel?," 98.
35. Miller and Yamamori, *Global Pentecostalism*, 165.
36. Miller and Yamamori, 179–181.
37. Mtata, "An African Theology," 35–49.
38. Mtata, 49.

theology but neither has it inherited or even combined with it. Instead, as Mtata says, local culture "found new ways of surviving the onslaught" of "aggressive cultural encounters."[39]

Care must be similarly taken in assessing prosperity theologies, especially those that are more palatable to Westerners, to see the agency of local Christians. Even the Lutheran women among the TAFES women at no point referenced their Lutheran identity as they spoke about their *mafanikio* theology. Instead, they referred to the biblical text and how it either cohered with African values or critiqued current practices. However, it ought not be a surprise if what they describe sounds very similar to a Protestant work ethic or, indeed, models of holism from other parts of the world. To the degree that they both rely on the Bible as authoritative, it is reasonable to assume a degree of overlap.

I suggest the language of convergent evolution may clarify the situation. A term from the world of evolutionary biology, it observes the phenomenon of creatures that share remarkably similar complex features without having shared a genetic or evolutionary line. Simon Conway Morris gives the example of the eye: octopi and humans both have complex eyes but our common ancestor goes back at least five hundred million years and, if it had eyes at all, that creature's eyes would have been much simpler.[40] At some point, our evolutionary lines diverged to eventually produce octopi and humans, yet in their divergent, separate, independent lines, we have still both developed complex eyes that are quite similar. Morris's argument is grounded in hypotheses about randomness and convergence that belong to the biological sciences and need not concern us here. However, the phenomenon of two things evolving separately from each other and yet looking remarkably similar provides a parallel when considering theologies of holism in the West and Africa.

Theologically, a degree of convergence in models of holism globally ought not to be a surprise. All Christians draw on the same source material – the Bible – and all are directed by the same Holy Spirit who leads us into truth. Thus, from separate journeys, there can be a convergence. This is not to suppose that the theology that feeds their model of holism will be identical. On the contrary, different Christians' separate pathways result in various unique

---

39. Mtata, 49.
40. Morris, "Life's Solution?," 205–17.

features, and to erase the distinctiveness of each would dishonour the Holy Spirit's creativity in shaping God's people. However, as we observe similarities in models of holism, if we keep in mind this idea of convergent evolution, we can acknowledge what is shared without diminishing the distinctiveness of each.

Mafanikio theology covers many areas of life, lending it an impression of holism. It shares a desire to re-integrate parts of life affected by Greek dualism with integral mission; one way in which it does this is by upholding the sanctity of work, an emphasis it shares with the Protestant work ethic. While all three of these are shaped by the Bible, *mafanikio* theology's holism also draws on and is nourished by the African philosophy of *Ubuntu*.

8.4 Threats to *Mafanikio* Theology's Claim to Holism

In *mafanikio* theology, the prosperity God wants for his people extends over the spiritual, economic, relational, health, inner peace, and intellectual dimensions. It is on the basis of the breadth of these areas that *mafanikio* theology can be thought of as holistic. However, scholars have argued that without political engagement, creation care, and rest, prosperity is threatened. If these three areas are absent in *mafanikio* theology, its claim to holism is threatened, so it is necessary to address these concerns. I shall therefore take each in turn, first political engagement, then creation care, and finally rest. I will argue that, while not prominent, these areas are more present than they first appear, and that *mafanikio* theology contains (currently under-utilised) resources to increase engagement in this area.

8.4.1 Political Engagement

In Martina Prosén's analysis of African Pentecostal soteriology, she notes that the holism on view regards an individual, as "an eternal, spiritual, physical, economic, relational, and psychological being but hardly an active member of society."[41] This list of spiritual, physical economic, etc., is remarkably similar to that of *mafanikio* theology, and she comments that without a sociopolitical element, such a theology can only be potentially holistic. She admits

---

41. Prosén, "Abundant Life – Holistic Soteriology," Ebook edition, Ch.19, 303–19.

that in Africa any act has political implications as, "there is a multi-faceted understanding of people's problems [which includes] both this-worldly and other-worldly explanations."⁴² However, she notes that societal and political structures do not feature in these explanations and Ugandan Nicta Lubaale agrees that, "failure to include socio-political causes of poverty . . . holds back [African Christians] from engaging with the broader issues that keep masses of people in poverty."⁴³

Like the groups Prosén and Lubaale critique, the TAFES women did not reference politics or structural change directly in their *mafanikio* theology. Indeed, Abigail explicitly warned against looking at this level, believing that it would lead to passivity as people would expect the government to do everything instead of taking action themselves. She said:

> Sometimes you find rubbish on the road, and [people say], "Oh dear, government, government, help us to pick up the rubbish outside the gate." Now I as a Christian I want to be a person of initiative, I am able to come out of my gate, bend down and to pick it up myself.⁴⁴

She saw this not only as a way of changing that one situation but also as a way of changing society, by setting an example to others, especially if one is a person of status. She said that others will see your action and copy you.⁴⁵

Amos Yong describes three attitudes towards politics in Pentecostal groups globally: apolitical, political and an indirect political stance, where a group functions as an alternative society, showing a different way.⁴⁶ While Prosén and Lubaale's preference is clearly for the second (political), Abigail advocates the third. For many Tanzanians, structural change sounds like the *Ujamaa* years of socialist government. While these years can be seen as the source of Tanzania's social cohesion, they decimated the economy and therefore did not provide holistically for the nation. They are also seen as having bred a kind of passivity where individual initiative and creative solutions were discouraged.⁴⁷

---

42. Prosén, 308.
43. Lubaale, "The Emerging Church," 79.
44. Interview 2 (Abigail), Swahili quotation 110.
45. Interview 2 (Abigail).
46. Yong, *In the Days of Caesar*, 4–14.
47. Hasu, "World Bank & Heavenly Bank," 686.

The structural argument can sound disempowering because it backgrounds what can be done at the grassroots, as if poverty is solved at the elite level. This does not ring true in the Tanzanian experience, and it also leaves no role for the ordinary person to play in moving themselves or the nation out of poverty. *Mafanikio* theology opposes this kind of hopelessness that leads to passivity, insisting that individuals can make a difference in God's world. Indeed, the TAFES women themselves are examples of this. Several of the TAFES women hold jobs that are at least politically adjacent, even if they have no direct political involvement. For example, Fibi is a human rights lawyer and Eunice's NGO role includes coordinating care for tribal groups who have been displaced by the Tanzanian government.

Political involvement by TAFES members is generally viewed positively in TAFES, even though politics itself is generally considered corrupt. One of the women interviewed is married to a high-level Presidential appointee and several male TAFES Associates have run for political office. At Transformers' Conference, one session was on changing a nation using politics and political power and several of my interviewees attended, though I did not. Meanwhile at TAFES's national missions conference "Go Conference" in 2022, students were encouraged to consider serving God and their nation through political involvement and all students were invited to stand and sing Tanzania's National Anthem *"Mungu Ibariki Tanzania"* ("God Bless Tanzania") as a prayer. However, the TAFES women's preference towards socio-political action, as I have observed it, is towards the counter-cultural avenue of change. Though this an indirect mode of political involvement, it nevertheless models an alternative to the status quo; this in and of itself is a subtle political statement.

While *mafanikio* theology lacks a mandate for structural political advocacy or change, this is not to say that it is apolitical or disinterested in societal change. The TAFES women are motivated by a sense that one must contribute as one is able where God has placed them. Thus, Eunice emphasised that it is not only in church that spiritual things happen and that even small contributions can make a difference:

> Any place is spiritual . . . I am here and I want to live as a born-again person so in these issues of corruption, issues of

underperformance, to be late to work, to not be trustworthy, here at church, at work, just the same.[48]

This emphasis on being involved in God's world at every level could be extended to politics and *mafanikio* theology can thus provide a building block for political involvement. While *mafanikio* theology articulates little political theology, this need not set it at odds with those who desire greater political involvement from Christians; indeed, *mafanikio* theology is a resource which could be used in such an endeavour. Furthermore, if structural change were ever to be implemented in Tanzania, it would be far more effective in a population that valued initiative and industry than in one that was hopeless or passive, and *mafanikio* theology gives people a reason to be active participants in their communities. Such activity may appear insignificant at an elite level but at the grassroots, it is a God-given contribution and shows an alternative way of living. As Simon Chan says, "people need first to experience change within themselves before they can even envisage the possibility of change in the socio-political realm."[49] This is the level at which *mafanikio* theology operates.

8.4.2 Creation Care

Christelle Terreblanche points out that Africa has often been a site for environmental exploitation and wealth transfer to the West, by means of mineral and agricultural extraction.[50] Such treatment of the environment is contrary to *Ubuntu* and she gives several examples of where African communitarian ethics have manifested in opposition to mining operations.[51] Ben-Willie Golo sees theologies that advocate increase and blessing as a threat to such *Ubuntu*-based advocacy. He says, "environmental sustainability requires that, in human beings' quest for their welfare and better life, they are aware of the limits of the capacity of the earth and its resources to sustain meaningful life."[52] He is therefore suspicious of theologies that advocate increase and blessing without cautioning on the importance of caring for the earth in responsible

---

48. Interview 1 (Eunice), Swahili quotation 111.
49. Chan, *Grassroots Asian Theology*, 103.
50. Terreblanche, "*Ubuntu* and the Struggle," 168–89.
51. Terreblanche, 175–177.
52. Golo, "Africa's Poverty," 374.

ways, that it might continue to produce. From a Nigerian context, Chris Manus and Des Obioma express a similar concern about interpretations of the creation mandate in Genesis 1:27–28 which legitimise exploitation of the earth.[53]

The TAFES women frequently referenced Genesis 1:27–28 in their *mafanikio* theology in terms of the responsibility to be at work in God's world. They mentioned neither exploitation of the earth nor environmental advocacy. However, this need not be taken to indicate that they do not view environmental advocacy as important, only that their attention was elsewhere during our discussions. It is relevant that Priscilla founded and is on the board of a climate change NGO, and Zipporah, Susanna and Eunice work for NGOs that include environmental sustainability in their work. Meanwhile Shiphrah and Lois's academic work on development has included attention to sustainable farming practices. Perhaps the fact that they did not connect a theology of prosperity with these professional environmental connections speaks to a deficit or a disconnect in the holism of their prosperity theology, but it can also be taken to indicate what issues they see as pressing. Dorothy Hodgson's warning is pertinent here, that the concerns of the grassroots not be silenced by the agenda of outsiders or other African elites.[54] Climate change is certainly a pressing issue for all, not least poorer nations who will feel its effect more; however combatting it will be achieved by the inclusion and cooperation of the grassroots, not condescension or paternalism.

From the TAFES women's perspective, passivity is the enemy of productivity and Genesis 1:27–28 is a text which teaches that humans are not to be passive in the world. On the contrary, the creation mandate is evidence that God wants his people to be productive by working in his world.[55] Their focus is not on theological ecology, but on theological *anthropology*; they are trying to convince people that humans are made to be workers rather than exploring the ethics of how that work is to take place in God's world. However, there are several threads in their theology which could be developed further and brought to bear for ecological reflection. What I offer here are

---

53. Manus and Obioma, "Preaching the 'green Gospel,'" 1–6.
54. Hodgson, *Gender, Justice, and the Problem of Culture*, 106.
55. Focus Group 1; Focus Group 2.

not deficiencies of *mafanikio* theology but potential ecological implications of *mafanikio* theology.

First, Leah remarked that not all work is decent or God-honouring.[56] Her examples of indecent work were primarily personal (do not be a prostitute, do not steal) not ecological, but she emphasised knowledge of God and his world as a foundation for being able to discern what is good work and what isn't. Ecology could be a part of this and take its place among reflection about what constitutes indecent work.

Second, the women's language regarding creation was one of care, not exploitation. Leah spoke of God preparing everything in the garden for Adam and Eve and giving it to them, but warned against viewing this as something to be taken for their purposes; instead, they were to work it.[57] Similarly, Puah spoke of Adam being sent to look after the garden.[58] Zipporah did use the language of ruling creation but immediately modified this with the reminder that we do not rule in our own right but as God's representatives and that we must reflect his creative capacity.[59] Thus, the women's theology has no place for destructive environmental practices: destruction and prosperity cannot co-exist.

Third, in the scenario of the poor widow in the village, several women alluded to the need for her to learn better farming techniques.[60] Though they did not elaborate on these, I took "better" to refer to more productive and sustainable farming techniques since it is generally the poor who do not have access to these. One example is that cooking with charcoal is ubiquitous in Tanzania even though it requires the destruction of trees, degrading the productiveness of the land. There are more sustainable alternatives, but they all require capital. Similarly, kerosene and other fossil fuels for power are cheaper in the short term than installing solar because of the capital required to set up the latter. There is an awareness here that people's well-being is reliant on the flourishing of the land and so creation care is beneficial for all. However, accessing and using such farming techniques requires a measure of economic

---

56. Interview 17 (Leah).
57. Interview 17 (Leah).
58. Focus Group 1.
59. Interview 16 (Zipporah).
60. Interview 6 (Susanna); Interview 16 (Zipporah); Interview 11 (Lydia); Interview 14 (Bilhah).

prosperity. The ethics of creation care are thus bound up in financial prosperity, a topic about which *mafanikio* theology has a good deal to say.

Finally then, if Tanzanians are to play a role in environmental advocacy, they will do so as their prosperity increases. The first step here must be overcoming an attitude of passivity in God's world or pessimism about what is achievable. *Mafanikio* theology can have a significant role here, with its emphasis on not merely sitting around and praying but being involved in God's world according to how God has set it up. It is no coincidence that some of the TAFES women intersect with environmental advocacy; their theology of *mafanikio* propels them into a variety of arenas. Even if one is to read an ecological aspect as missing from *mafanikio* theology, this does not imply that *mafanikio* theology can have no role in ecological reflection and advocacy. On the contrary, as with political engagement, *mafanikio* theology provides a theological reason to be active in God's world. While theological ecology is not an emphasis of *mafanikio* theology, the paradigm is of creation care, responsibility, and activity, not exploitation or being resigned to the way things are.

8.4.3 Rest and Recreation

Mafanikio theology sees activity in God's world positively and encourages it. The context of passivity and what Jochebed called closed-mindedness provides the impetus for this theology, but the question must be asked whether constant activity is good for human beings. Can a human be considered prosperous if they are constantly working, with no time for recreation? Africans have suffered from double-edged accusations when it comes to work and rest. On one hand, Africans have been perceived as lazy. The *Africa Bible Commentary*'s notes on God's rest in Genesis 2:1–3 provide examples of this, containing strong warnings against laziness.[61] On the other hand, Western scholars have at times claimed that leisure is a concept alien to Africa.[62] *Mafanikio* theology illustrates both of these viewpoints.

Like the *Africa Bible Commentary*, the TAFES women thought it important to combat laziness or passivity and practised this in their own lives. While Priscilla spoke about feeling busy and pressured, to great agreement from

---

61. Assohoto and Ngwena, "Genesis," 13.
62. Mtata, " An African Theology of Work," 39.

the other women, Zipporah, Susanna, and Rhoda felt that resting was inappropriate in the current eschatological age.[63] Meanwhile, at Transformers' Conference in a session called "Rebuilding Our Families," presenter Faith spoke disparagingly of "these *wazungu* [white people] and their games." However, her objection was not to having fun per se. On the contrary, she advocated fun as an important part of family bonding. However, she suggested fun through joking around or telling stories while doing tasks such as pounding maize flour: it was fun alongside productivity or in the service of it. In this, she could be seen to be in agreement with Jürgen Moltmann's criticism of a "fun society" where meaningful joy is replaced by short-term amusement.[64] When work and fun are divorced from each other, as they often are in the West, a week becomes a desert of frantic work punctuated by ever more desperate attempts at rest that fail to satisfy. Weekends must be protected and activities where one serves, such as in community groups or church, come to be seen as an encroachment upon leisure, leading to less participation, or consumerist or incentivised models. *Mafanikio* theology provides a different way into this, viewing work and rest not as opposites, but as an integrated dyad.

This leads to the second issue, that of how to recognise leisure in a particular culture. It would be easy, given the TAFES women's espoused preference for activity and industry, to assume they have no place for rest. However, their behaviour – or their operant theology – suggests differently, when viewed through an African cultural lens. Mtata recounts how, "having worked hard throughout the day with the help of God, traditional African societies spent the evening around the fire, resting and telling stories."[65] This is not rest as retreat from community but rest as participation in community; it was also not rest as pure leisure since African storytelling is often a vehicle for teaching and forming young people. The *Africa Bible Commentary* argues that this is a biblical model: while God rested from his work of creation, he was still doing the work of sustaining the world. Thus, when we rest, "we rest from one activity while we continue with another."[66] In this model, rest need not

---

63. Focus Group 2; Interview 16 (Zipporah); Interview 6 (Susanna); Interview 15 (Rhoda).
64. See discussion in Niemandt, "Rediscovering Joy," 5–6.
65. Mtata, "An African Theology of Work," 45.
66. Assohoto and Ngwena, "Genesis," 13.

mean the cessation of the process of *mafanikio*; it need not even be a pit stop to refresh a person to continue another day. Resting from one thing while picking up another means the continual motion of *mafanikio* is unhindered.

As urban, professional women, many of the TAFES women do not experience the rhythm of days in the fields and evenings around a fire. They work in offices, trail through traffic, and then arrive home to supervise staff. However, they share the other two aspects of rest as mentioned by Mtata and the *Africa Bible Commentary*: the difference between workdays and gathering days, and the change in activity. My observation is that work done in gathered spaces such as Sunday church services or preparing meals at a big event can take on a recreational quality because they are performed while gathered with others. The difference in the work, and the fact that it is done in community, have the potential to make it restful. This illustrates what Mtata argues is a blurring of lines between work and rest in Africa: what appears to be people sitting around having a chat may be building relationships and networking, both essential to work in an African context, and what appears to be work can feel recreational when it is done in community.[67] Nevertheless, the TAFES women did value time spent without domestic duties. Several of them spoke to me of how much fun it was to leave their responsibilities behind and come to focus group, gathering with one another to exchange views and tell stories. However, even in this case, continuing to build *mafanikio* was on view. Deborah confided to me afterwards that the focus group, with its theological discussion, felt like a Bible study, a chance to learn and go deeper with God. This fun activity was therefore not "time out" from *mafanikio*, but "time in" because relationship with God is the source of *mafanikio*.

At first it may appear that *mafanikio* theology advocates unceasing effort without any rest. Certainly, this is a tension that the women acknowledged. Nevertheless, the women's behaviour, when viewed through an African cultural lens, reveals that they do indeed rest, or at least put down some activities in order to take up others. They find it hard to see the point of fun for its own sake, but when it is geared towards productivity, recreation is able to be integrated into the process of *mafanikio*. This is especially evident in gathering with the people of God because their relationship with God is nurtured. Since God is the source of prosperity, such resting work contributes to *mafanikio*.

---

67. Mtata, "An African Theology of Work," 45.

These three issues of political engagement, creation care, and rest are not necessarily a threat to *mafanikio* theology's holism. As with engagement on politics and ecology, *mafanikio* theology's reflection on rest is not as absent as it at first appears. Work and rest are integrated, making rest harder for Westerners to spot, but reflective of *mafanikio* theology's holistic approach. This holism is not necessarily threatened by *mafanikio* theology's apparent lack of engagement with politics and ecology either. A closer look suggests that, propelled by a theology which encourages them to be active in God's world, the TAFES women are involved in both these areas, at least indirectly. While there is more work to be done in these areas, *mafanikio* theology's emphasis on being active in God's world provides an impetus to engage even if it does not outline a charter. *Mafanikio* theology is thus a framework that can be used for engagement on these issues as part of its larger holism.

Zilpah's comment about the cross being relevant to both the spiritual and physical realms is a neat summary of *mafanikio* theology's claim to holism. I have now addressed the issue of threats to *mafanikio* theology's holism on the physical side. However, there have also been questions about whether prosperity theologies neglect the spiritual.[68] *Mafanikio* theology's claim to holism can therefore also be threatened from this direction and so it is to the question of the spiritual dimension of Christ's work on the cross that I now turn my attention.

8.5 *Mafanikio* Theology and the Cross

David Ngong worries that in seeking to avert "situations that diminish human material well-being," prosperity theologies become unbalanced and even end up becoming unchristian.[69] Similarly, Nigerian Baptist theologian Emiola Nihinlola's assessment is that, "It is a plus to the contemporary Pentecostal churches that they have not neglected the need for material prosperity of people in Africa. However, many of them have over-emphasized physical and material welfare at the expense of prosperity of the soul."[70] As we saw in the

---

68. Ma, Ma, and Walls, *Mission in the Spirit*, Kindle edition, 3; Mboya, "Gift Challenges and Transforms," 23; Nihinlola, "Between Prosperity and Spirituality," 29–41.

69. Ngong, "Salvation and Materialism," 3; See also Nkansah-Obrempong, "The Contemporary Theological Situation," 140–50.

70. Nihinlola, "Between Prosperity and Spirituality," 36

scope and limits of *mafanikio* (sections 4.4 and 4.5), the TAFES women held that the source of physical prosperity is God and thus cannot be separated from spiritual prosperity. The accusation of neglect ill-fits the holism with which they approach prosperity. While Zilpah's insistence that Christ's work on the cross is relevant to both spiritual and physical realms is reflected in the holism of *mafanikio* theology, the question remains, how is it relevant or in what way?

Within the International Fellowship of Evangelical Students (IFES) of which TAFES is a part, a story is told of the importance of the centrality of the cross. I heard it as a student in AFES and have heard it used at TAFES fellowships as well. It is the story of the disaffiliation of the Cambridge Inter-Collegiate Christian Union (CICCU) from the national English Student Christian Movement (SCM) in 1910. John Stott wrote that the CICCU was becoming "increasingly disenchanted with the liberal tendencies of the SCM, and especially with its weak doctrines of the Bible, the cross and even the deity of Jesus."[71] At a resolution meeting between Daniel Dick and Norman Grubb (CICCU president and secretary respectively) and the SCM secretary Rollo Pelly, Grubb asked:

> "Does the SCM consider the atoning blood of Jesus Christ as the central point of their message?" And the answer given was, "No, not as central, although it is given a place in our teaching." That answer settled the matter, for we explained to them at once that the atoning blood was so much the heart of our message that we could never join with a movement which gave it a lesser place.[72]

According to IFES historian, Timothée Joset, this story is told and re-told in IFES as "the foundational event legitimating the existence of IFES."[73] This is my experience in both AFES and TAFES as well. Thus, the question of the cross is an important one when considering the theology of a group of women from an IFES group. Zilpah said that the cross is relevant; would

---

71. Stott, *Cross of Christ*, Ebook edition, 14.

72. Stott, 14. Several versions of this story exist. I have chosen to use John Stott's version because that is where I first became familiar with the story. In Stott's book, the cross and the atonement overlap to the point where to speak of the centrality of the cross is to speak of the centrality of the atonement. I have retained this overlap in my discussion.

73. Joset, "The Priesthood of All Students?," 27.

she or the other TAFES women consider it central? While this question of centrality has been a formative one for IFES, assessing it here is complicated for several reasons.

First, I did not ask the women about theology generally or their theology of the cross or what is central. No such direct question was given to them like the one to Pelly. I asked them about prosperity. The cross came up as it pertains to *mafanikio* but the women's comments on the cross cannot be taken as the sum total of their theology of it. That would require another, separate study.

Second, the original story seems to have functioned more as a polemic and identity-former than as an accurate depiction of the concerns of the CICCU leaders at the time. Joset argues that "latest archival research tends to demonstrate that theories of the atonement did not play a significant role in the 1910 split."[74] Rather, this was "later retroactively thought to have been central in 1910, as the result of the 1932 account of the 1919 reunion meeting later described by the in-house historian Oliver Barclay."[75] Such evidence ought to relativize any insistence on centrality: the atonement is included in the IFES doctrinal basis as a "fundamental truth," but there is no mention of centrality.[76]

Third, it must be recognized that the language of centrality is language of disintegration. Making one thing central necessarily distinguishes it from others as peripheral.[77] Proponents of the centrality motif would undoubtedly argue that this is warranted, a biblical emphasis even. Thus, even if the atonement was not as prominent at the 1910 meeting, the centrality of the cross may nevertheless be important to retain. However, if this is the case, it must be recognized that in that version of the formation narrative, the atonement is prioritized over other theological themes, or seen to be primarily relevant to the spiritual realm not the physical. From a holistic perspective this is inadequate because the cross must be viewed as part of a whole if its significance is to be truly appreciated. During our early years in Tanzania, I asked a pastor friend what the centre, core or kernel of the gospel is. He looked at me in astonishment, replying, "Why would you want the smallest version of the

---

74. Joset, 29.
75. Joset, 29.
76. International Fellowship of Evangelical Students, "What We Believe."
77. In section 6.2. I assessed the centrality of Christ in *mafanikio* theology. This was in the context of discipleship and fidelity to Christ and was not about elevating one theological perspective on Christ over others.

gospel instead of the biggest?" For Grubb and others, the issue of centrality was useful in clarifying the extent of a doctrinal disagreement, but it set up a dichotomy where the cross was paramount and social engagement suspect, which plays into the Greek dualism to which models of holism have since been seeking to respond.[78] Furthermore, this dichotomy neglects to reflect on either the importance of social engagement or how the cross may power it.

Thus, here I undertake to examine what *mafanikio* theology has to say about Christ's work at the cross without judging it by the measure of centrality. This is imperative because in *mafanikio* theology, the scope of the cross is broad, connected to both physical and spiritual realms.

8.5.1 *Mafanikio* Theology and the Work of Christ

American theologian Michael J. Gorman notes that there are many images of the atonement in the New Testament, with a standard three major theories: *Christus Victor*, satisfaction, and moral influence.[79] Gorman proposes his own theory of new covenant as more comprehensive than these three which are "atomistic, or non-integrative," in character, pertaining to the mechanics of the atonement.[80] Gorman argues that the effects of these three are penultimate when compared with the ultimate goal which is to create a transformed, Spirit-filled people of God under a new covenant which can be expressed "in more comprehensive and integrative terms like transformation, participation, and re-creation."[81] The sense of being a corporate people coheres with *mafanikio* theology's communal orientation, and the sense of participating "in God's forgiving, reconciling, and covenanting mission to the world" aligns with *mafanikio* theology's emphasis on being active in God's world.[82] However, *mafanikio* theology also offers a perspective on the atonement which is not covered by the standard three theories, and which has the potential to cohere with Gorman's model.

Nigerian-British Anglican Chigor Chike argues that the standard atonement models are overlapping rather than distinct for the African, such that

---

78. See Joset, 30.
79. Gorman, "Effecting the New Covenant," 26–59
80. Gorman, 31.
81. Gorman, 32. More fully, his model refers to the transformation of Christians, their participation in Christ's death, and their re-creation into a covenant people of God.
82. Gorman, 58.

the title "Forgiver" does not contradict titles such as "Victor," "Healer," and "Provider."[83] On the contrary, "it underlines it, because for Africans the forgiveness of sins is what makes the victories, the healing and the provision possible."[84] For Africans, he argues, sin is an affront to God, so God will not answer your prayers. I have depicted this in Figure 8.2. God is distant because of a broken relationship, leaving humans unable to access his power.[85] Instead, they are left with only lesser powers such as witchdoctors.[86]

The problem is not that witchdoctors are too powerful or that evil reigns; after all, God has always been supreme and more powerful.[87] The distance and lack of access are the real problem: prosperity is impossible because people cannot access the one who designed them for it and has the power to live in it. Christ's work as "Forgiver" mends the relationship, giving access to the previously inaccessible power. Once connected to God, the Christian can receive this greater power and pursue God's purposes of *mafanikio*. The move in the atonement is thus not from fear of evil to defeat of evil but from disempowerment (no access to power) to empowerment (having access to power).

The TAFES women did not comment on any models of the atonement, yet Chike's comments have deep resonance with *mafanikio* theology. First, as we have seen, the TAFES women are unequivocal about God's supremacy over other powers; God is not weak or in danger of being defeated. Second, their emphasis on relationship with God as the source of *mafanikio* illustrates that the problem of the human condition has been relational, that humans have been unable to access God's power because of broken relationship. Cut off from the true source of power, a person might resort to lesser powers to pursue prosperity, unless there is a way to effectively access God's power. Such was the concern in the opening story of this thesis, where if God's power is not available, people have little choice but to go to the witchdoctor. Third, when I attended Ruth's weekly seminar as part of my participant observation, she preached on the atonement in terms of access to power. The blood

---

83. Chike, "Proudly African, Proudly Christian," 221–40.
84. Chike, 238.
85. I have depicted only one human here, but this applies at the corporate level as well.
86. Magesa, *African Religion*, 47.
87. This theme is prominent in both African Traditional Religion and the Bible. It is also one of the most popular themes of praise songs in Tanzania. One of Tanzania's most famous worship songs "*Hakuna Mungu kama wewe*" translates, "There is no God like you."

of Christ, she argued, does four things: washes us clean from sin, gives us access to God, breaks the chains and strongholds, and gives us a mark to guard against the devil. The blood of Christ here does not defeat Satan, as in *Christus Victor*; neither is its role to alleviate guilt. This is language of purification and access, which have the effect of gaining power. By Christ's work, the Christian is empowered to wage war against Satan, in the power of God to whom they have access.

As I did not go on to interrogate the theology of the atonement at any depth with the women, the precise nature of how Christ mends the relationship, giving access to God and his power, is unclear. Ruth drew on purity language when she spoke of us being washed clean; Christ may also be a broker or mediator to God who is Patron; a model where he is the sacrifice that appeases God's wrath is a possibility too, since this theme is present in African Traditional Religion. More work would need to be done to determine what models of atonement the women employ. However, what is relevant here, is that key for the TAFES women is the access to God that the work of Christ provides.

Having access to God means being able to avail oneself of his power, so that the Christian then has what they need to prosper, which is God's will for his people. Any act of prosperity, including taking initiative, accepting responsibility, or working diligently, is a deeply spiritual act, because it is done in God's power which is accessed only through Christ's work. Additionally, the person doing it is in fact waging war against Satan.[88] After all, Martha said, Satan does not want people to prosper.[89] The power of God is crucial to these efforts of prosperity. Damaris used the idiom of the blood of Jesus to speak about this: "As Satan fights with the holy ones, they defeat him using the blood of the lamb in the name of Jesus."[90] Such defeat is impossible if God is distant or cut off from human beings. As Rhoda said, "How can God live with us? Through his Son."[91] Relationship with God who is the source of prosperity is vital because through this relationship the Christian gains the crucial power they need for *mafanikio*, that is for prosperity in all areas

---

88. Interview 9 (Shiphrah).
89. Interview 18 (Martha).
90. Interview 3 (Damaris), Swahili quotation 112.
91. Interview 15 (Rhoda).

of life. This explains why spiritual *mafanikio* (relationship with God) is so important for physical *mafanikio*: the relationship must be made right if power for prosperity is to be available.

George Folarin argues that in the theology of Winners' Chapel's David Oyedepo, the atonement restores material blessings, such that a Christian who remains in poverty is sinning against their redemption.[92] The TAFES women's conception of prosperity as a process cuts against the idea that poverty is a sin; for them, the blessings won at the atonement are not automatic. These blessings come naturally as Christians experience the benefits of living God's good way, which they are able to do once they have access to his power. This is far from interacting with God merely for what can be extracted from him; instead, as in Gorman's new covenant, it is part of what it means to be part of God's new covenant people, transformed, and equipped to be active in God's world in a variety of ways.

In *mafanikio* theology, as in Chike's reflection, the atonement not only offers a solution to a spiritual problem of one's relationship with God but is the source of contending with every physical problem as well. Thus, in *mafanikio* theology, Christ's work at the cross deals with both the spiritual and the physical, not as two separate issues, but as related; the solution to them is integrated as well. The cross is thus truly holistic in *mafanikio* theology.

8.5.2 *Mafanikio* Theology and the Way of the Cross

In their theology of the cross, the women position themselves as beneficiaries of it rather than imitators of it. For them, a life modelled on the humiliation or suffering of the cross is inimical to *mafanikio*. Rhoda rejected the idea that, "Jesus lived in poverty and suffered and so we suffer," arguing that Jesus instead suffers in our place "so that we could have eternal life and not so that we would live with problems."[93] It is not that she or other TAFES women have no place for suffering in the Christian life: I addressed this extensively in section 6.2.2. Neither does she have no place for a broken Christ.[94] On the contrary, she sees Jesus's brokenness and suffering as effecting change;

---

92. Folarin, "Contemporary State," 81.

93. Interview 15 (Rhoda), Swahili quotations 113 and 56.

94. Falconer asks this question. Falconer, *Spectacular Atonement: Envisioning the Cross*, 128.

it thus cannot be done away with. In the holism of *mafanikio* theology, the cross must benefit a person both spiritually and physically and there is an integration of these two. Therefore, if the primary paradigm for the Christian life is brokenness or injury, the holism of the cross is threatened.

However, Gorman favours the image in Revelation of the slain lamb, insisting on the priority "of the term cruciform to describe the shape, or structure, of life in union with Christ."[95] In contrast, for the TAFES women, being Christ-shaped does not necessarily mean being cross-shaped, because Christ himself is no longer on the cross. They referred far more frequently to Christ's healing, provision, and miracles than to his death (see Figure 6.4). If a person who is poor or broken comes to Christ, the expectation is not that they will be inducted into a life of continuing to be downtrodden, but that Christ raises them with him, giving them a place in his kingdom bringing about renewal. As Macchia says, "If one listens carefully to prosperity preaching, one can usually detect a very specific target audience, namely, 'defeated' or discouraged Christians who do not yet know personally what Christ or his gospel can mean for their concrete life situation."[96] As we have seen, the problem in Tanzania as the TAFES women see it, is not rampant wealth and greed, but passivity or immoral means of gaining wealth. As we saw in the section about Jesus (6.2.3.), Tanzanian women can be counted among the poor whom Jesus lifts and empowers.

Gorman's cruciformity does not exclude the resurrection. He says, "cruciform participation in Christ is also, paradoxically, participation in Christ's resurrection."[97] He has defended against the charge that he marginalizes the resurrection here, arguing that the two are bound up together and that the language of cruciform over, for example, resurrectiform, is the apostle Paul's.[98] In the course of this argument, Gorman acknowledges that "the ongoing experiential side of salvation (ethics, spirituality) involves participating not only in Christ's death, but also in his resurrection."[99] In support of this, he quotes Paul's language of walking in newness of life (Rom 6:4), being brought from

---

95. Gorman, "Cruciform or Resurrectiform?," 60–83.
96. Macchia, "A Call for Careful Discernment," 228.
97. Gorman, "Cruciform or Resurrectiform?," 62.
98. Gorman, "Cruciform or Resurrectiform?," 62, 64.
99. Gorman, "Cruciform or Resurrectiform?," 67.

death to life (Rom 6:13) and the present resurrection life (Rom 6:23). This experiential angle is vital to understanding how *mafanikio* theology conceives of the Christian life. As we saw in chapter 6, *mafanikio* theology is primarily directed at the *maisha* level, that is, the everyday, rather than the *uzima* level, which is more ideal and future focused. When the women describe their life in Christ then, they are not primarily speaking of a theoretical paradigm for life in Christ but of experience. What does it feel like to live in Christ? It feels like empowerment in the place of passivity and closed-mindedness.

This empowerment may co-exist with suffering. For example, when I asked the TAFES women about Paul and his thorn from 2 Corinthians 12, Eunice, Jochebed and Lydia felt that Paul was both suffering and being sustained by God.[100] Shiphrah and Bilhah spoke of the humbling brought by the thorn as protective of his own faith and ministry, similar to how suffering builds long-lasting *mafanikio*, as we saw in section 6.2.2.4.[101] However, in the case of the widow in the village (section 4.5.3.), they did not see her poverty and vulnerability as a type of Christ. They saw her as bound by forces which held her back. If Christ is to be present here, it will not manifest only in solidarity or empathy but in a change in how she sees herself and her circumstances.

The widow is already suffering, so the question at hand in her situation is how Christ transforms her from death to life. Gorman argues for "participatory simultaneity, [that is] sharing in Christ's death and resurrection at the same time."[102] However, while Paul could be simultaneously suffering and empowered, for the widow, only one part of this participation is manifest. All can see her suffering; what is unclear is how resurrection is manifest, and so it is to this that the TAFES women give their attention. Gorman insists that the two not be separated out, that cruciformity and resurrectiformity exist together, but also that the "downward mobility" of the former leads to the latter.[103] However, this is difficult for many in the majority world to envision. In the case of the widow, how much further down can she go? We also saw in chapter 5 that the women drew a strong causative link between a theology

---

100. Interview 1 (Eunice); Interview 19 (Jochebed); Interview 11 (Lydia).
101. Interview 9 (Shiphrah); Interview 14 (Bilhah).
102. Gorman, "Cruciform or Resurrectiform?," 75.
103. Gorman, 72.

that is congenial to poverty and a lack of prosperity.[104] Meanwhile, they had very real experiences of how prosperity enables ministry (see section 4.6.). Additionally, in Tanzania, words have creative power.[105] For example, Rhoda spoke of calling someone poor as akin to torture, saying what is needed for prosperity is encouragement.[106] This is also part of building the kind of environment in which prosperity is possible (section 5.2.3.). How then can words of death and suffering (cruciformity) produce the experience of life and prosperity (resurrectiformity)? If the TAFES women fail to follow the apostle Paul in this, their contextual reasons are understandable.

The irony is, while the TAFES women eschew the language of following Christ in his death, they live remarkably cruciform lives, if cruciformity is understood in terms of service to others. Indeed, Gorman argues that cruciformity need not manifest as actual suffering but in the form of "self-giving love."[107] Thus, the pursuit of prosperity may not necessarily be un-cruciform if it is married to service of others. By this measure, *mafanikio* theology is indeed cruciform, for the TAFES women place a great emphasis on serving others and using prosperity in the service of others, and their own lives reflect this. While American Lutheran Daniel Peterson worries that a focus on prosperity makes one indifferent to the poor, in *mafanikio* theology, it is the poor whose capacity to care for others is limited.[108] Naomi Haynes notes the Zambian pastor's wife who put her various pots and pans out as a display of wealth. While Haynes initially saw this as ostentatious, she came to understand it as an invitation: advertising wealth sends a message that the person is available to help others.[109] Those who become embroiled in poverty or weakness eschew the opportunity to help others. Thus, the TAFES women invited the widow to see herself as a participant in *mafanikio*, or, as Macchia puts it, "to experience the benefits of Christ as they participate in God's mission in the world."[110]

---

104. Gorman, "Cruciform or Resurrectiform?," 74, 77.
105. Lindhardt, "'If You Are Saved You Cannot Forget Your Parents,'" 244.
106. Interview 15 (Rhoda).
107. Gorman, "Cruciform or Resurrectiform?," 75.
108. Peterson, "We Preach Christ Crucified," 194–201.
109. Haynes, "Pentecostalism and the Morality of Money," 135.
110. Macchia, "A Call for Careful Discernment," 324.

Service and prosperity are thus bound up with one another in *mafanikio* theology. Indeed, prosperity becomes a way of being cruciform because it gives a way to serve others. In *mafanikio* theology, anything that upholds the kind of passivity and deficit which stops people from being active in God's world is not an effective way to serve. As Dorcas said, "God wants us to prosper so we will not be weak or unable to look after ourselves, or unable to serve in other areas God has given us."[111] Christ's sufferings were acceptable because they were productive, achieving the reconciliation of God and his people. As we saw in section 6.2, suffering can also be productive in the Christian's life. However, these sufferings are to be endured not pursued. They are normal parts of the Christian life, but they are not normative. Instead, with *mafanikio* as the paradigm for the Christian life, the Christian is in a constant process of learning, growth and increasing their ability to serve others. Because it is God's power by which the Christian is empowered, it must be wielded in godly ways. As Fibi said, "To serve God there are benefits. To serve is protection. To serve God is peace. To serve God is victory."[112] Thus, service becomes part of the process of *mafanikio*, as the Christian both serves God and benefits from doing so in an increasing *upward* spiral of being conformed to Christ. This is not unbridled prosperity but godly prosperity that serves others. As we saw in section 6.2.4., the TAFES women made little explicit argument for the fruit of the Spirit, but their language is saturated with it. Thus, they cannot advocate selfishness or intemperate pursuit of power. As Allan Anderson says, "The Spirit is not only a Spirit of power, but also a 'holy' Spirit, a gentle dove, a Spirit of humility, patience and meekness, of love, joy and peace. The Spirit is the tender Comforter, the one who comes alongside to help and strengthen people through life's trials and challenges."[113] While Christ's passion does not feature in *mafanikio* theology because this is seen to undercut a person's ability to be of service in God's world, being of service in God's world in godly ways is a major preoccupation of *mafanikio* theology.

For the TAFES women, the cross is the access to power to live life in God's power for God's purposes. It thus touches on every area of life, not only one's relationship with God but also one's material prosperity. This prosperity is

---

111. Focus Group 2. Swahili quotation 114.
112. Interview 4 (Fibi), Swahili quotation 115.
113. Anderson, "African Pentecostalism and Prosperity," 379.

bound up with service such that even when cruciformity is not the explicit paradigm for the Christian life, the Christian life is nevertheless to be one of service since it is here that prosperity is found. Thus, the cross empowers Christians to be of service in God's world.

8.6 Conclusion

Mafanikio theology's claim to holism manifests both in the breadth of areas it covers and in the insistence that there is a greater prosperity that exists when all areas are in concert with each other. Wealth is viewed positively in this holism, as a tool for bringing greater wholeness. Such a communitarian outlook is shared with the African philosophy of *Ubuntu*. Though there is a temptation to see *mafanikio* theology and African prosperity theologies like in Western terms, this must be resisted, and the *Ubuntu* basis recognised and preserved.

Mafanikio theology's claim to holism is based on its insistence that prosperity must be both physical and spiritual. Both these dimensions have been examined to see how adequately *mafanikio* theology deals with them. On the physical side, *mafanikio* theology's holism can seem to be threatened by a lack of reflection on political engagement, creation care, and rest and recreation. However, a closer look complicates this understanding. Rest is present in *mafanikio* theology but in a distinctively African way where the momentum of prosperity is maintained. Meanwhile, *mafanikio* theology has little explicit to say about political engagement or creation care, but the women's lives show a degree of interaction with both. Moreover, *mafanikio* theology provides a reason to be active in God's world and to believe that a difference can be made. This is a necessary theological precursor to engagement on these issues. *Mafanikio* theology should thus not be viewed in opposition to these activities but as a tool which can be deployed in their service.

On the spiritual side, *mafanikio* theology's holism is powered by its theology of the cross. The cross was found to be a significant factor in empowering Christians for a life of *mafanikio*. This is not because of Christ's defeat of Satan or other powers but because of the unfettered access his death gives to God, such that God's power can be accessed and used in the Christian's life. Thus, the atonement gives the Christian a reason and means to be involved in all parts of God's world, both physical and spiritual. The concept of the atonement as empowerment brings a tension with an emphasis on cruciformity. The idea of sharing in Christ's sufferings appears at odds with being a beneficiary of his victory. Such theology is pastorally and practically driven: in a context where poverty is widespread and people are downtrodden, to elevate cruciformity as a paradigm for the Christian life provides little impetus for change. Nevertheless, despite a resistance to the language of cruciformity, the lives of the TAFES women and the lifestyle they advocate is remarkably geared towards service because prosperity is tied up with service in *mafanikio* theology's holism. Their lives can therefore be understood as cruciform even though this is not the paradigm they use to describe it.

Though perhaps not comprehensive, *mafanikio* theology's interaction with the world is broad, and its emphasis on activity in God's world along with the power to do so because of the cross vindicates its claim to holism.

Figure 8.4 What have we learned about *mafanikio* theology (MT)? (Chapters 4–8)

Chapter 4	Chapter 5	Chapter 6	Chapter 7	Chapter 8
In MT, prosperity is a process of taking steps to move to the next level. This process manifests across all areas of life and when all areas are affected, the result is greater than the sum of the parts. In MT, God is the source of prosperity. In MT, prosperity is characterised by effort, perseverance, righteousness and knowledge.	MT responds to a poverty gospel on one hand and profligate prosperity gospel on the other. MT combats passivity through knowing God rightly, identity change and environmental change. MT locates itself in the Bible, with hermeneutics that emphasise a comprehensive knowledge of Scripture to provide a balanced theology.	MT has a strong family resemblance to other prosperity theologies from Zambia, South Africa, Malawi, Cameroon and Kenya. These are different to how "prosperity gospel" is often described. They are an alternative to it and implicit critique of it. MT promotes perseverance, sympathy, and lament in suffering. MT calls people to Christ himself not just his things. MT embodies the fruit of the Spirit.	MT offers an alternative to a materialistic spirit by drawing on African communal values and Christian ideas of stewarding God's world well. MT draws on holism and communalism as aspects of African worldviews. It modifies pragmatism and dynamism to locate power in God and advocate fidelity to him. Because MT operates in African terms, it can be considered to have decolonising potential. MT operates in African patronage terms, including mutual obligation of God and humans.	MT's holism is built on the African ideal of *Ubuntu*. On the physical side of holism, MT has potential for growth in rest, creation care and political engagement and is a resource that can be used in these areas. On the spiritual side, MT's theology of the cross is holistic as the atonement gives access to God and his power, equipping the Christian for participation in every arena of life. MT advocates a life of service while avoiding the language of cruciformity for cultural and historical reasons.

CHAPTER 9

Conclusion

9.1 "What Is the TAFES Women's Theology of Prosperity?"

While there is a burgeoning understanding among some scholars that prosperity theology in Africa is more diverse and complex than what the "big men" preach, little is known about the nature of prosperity theology in Tanzania, in interdenominational contexts or among women. This study has provided data on these demographics by answering the question, "What is the TAFES women's theology of prosperity?" Using ethnographic methods of semi-structured interviews, focus groups and participant observation, a theological data set was formed from which *mafanikio* theology emerged. This theology was then explored further in a set of concentric circles, starting from Tanzania and moving out into broader conversations.

In chapter 4, *mafanikio* theology's prosperity was not a level a person attains but a process of taking steps to move to the next level economically, spiritually, relationally, physically, intellectually, and in terms of inner peace. While this prosperity can be applied to each area individually, there is a greater prosperity that comes when all of these are integrated and work together. God is the source of this prosperity, such that any prosperity which is to last must flow from relationship with him; meanwhile the prosperous Christian life will be characterized by effort, perseverance, righteousness, and knowledge.

Mafanikio theology was seen in chapter 5 to be shaped by its historical and cultural context in Tanzania, and by the Bible. It charts a third way between an historical poverty gospel and current profligate versions of the prosperity gospel, both of which promote passivity and misunderstand who God is. *Mafanikio* theology, in contrast, offers a reliable path to prosperity through a positive outlook which comes from knowing God and oneself rightly, and enables a person to follow the Bible's teaching for wealth creation. The women's extensive knowledge of the Bible prevents any one passage from becoming a controlling lens. They saw this as essential to avoiding the extremes of assuming relationship with God to be irrelevant to material prosperity or seeking material prosperity in ways that are not God-honouring.

The nature of the TAFES women's *mafanikio* theology was further explored in chapter 6 by examining where it fits among Africa's other prosperity theologies. It was found that it operates as a critique of profligate prosperity gospels and is strongly focused on discipleship. This capacity for discipleship was then examined using the framework of the Parable of the Sower, with particular attention given to *mafanikio* theology's capacity to engender perseverance in suffering and fidelity to Christ. *Mafanikio* theology was found to be a model in which prosperity theology and discipleship are wed.

From African prosperity theologies to African theology more generally, I undertook to further understand the nature of *mafanikio* theology's Africanness in chapter 7. Prosperity theologies have been accused of being both not African enough and too African (syncretistic). The first accusation stems from concern about the extreme materialism of some prosperity theologies, which threaten communal African values. However, in *mafanikio* theology, prosperity is set in the service of others, expressing a coherence between communal African values and Christian teachings. On the issue of being too syncretistic, *mafanikio* theology's holism, communalism, pragmatism, and dynamism were investigated and it was found that these are both maintained and modified to varying degrees, such that *mafanikio* theology can be thought of as both authentically African and properly Christian. *Mafanikio* theology's decolonising potential was briefly noted before examining a dimension of African culture in which *mafanikio* theology operates, that is, patronage. Patronage's reciprocity was found to be an African way of incorporating prosperity into relationship with God while also maintaining God's people's relational obligations to him, such as fidelity and gratitude.

While at this point, *mafanikio* theology had been found to be an African theology of discipleship, one dimension needed still further exploration in chapter 8: *mafanikio* theology's claim to holism. The TAFES women claimed a breadth in their *mafanikio* theology, yet in both physical and spiritual areas, there appeared to be deficiencies. On the physical side, these deficiencies were found to be less neglected than at first supposed, and *mafanikio* theology was also found to hold potential for further engagement on them, because of its emphasis on initiative and activity in God's world. Meanwhile, on the spiritual side, it was unclear how a tendency towards holism could cohere with the kind of emphasis on the centrality of the cross which has been widespread in IFES. However, the cross was found to be foundational for *mafanikio* theology, providing access to God and his power, opening up the whole of creation for the Christian's involvement in the world, which is to be service-oriented. *Mafanikio* theology was thus vindicated in its claim to holism, not because it is an exhaustive theology of every area of life but because it encourages the Christian to seek prosperity in every part of life.

Mafanikio theology can therefore be understood as a holistic African theology of prosperity. In this theology, prosperity is God's will for his people and relationship with him is the source of it. Meanwhile, the Bible guides and provides the parameters for prosperity and prosperity is expressed in modes which are consistent with African cultural values. In *mafanikio* theology, prosperity is something all God's people are equipped to pursue, and they extend it to all of creation.

9.2 Original Contributions of this Research

The primary original contribution of this research has been to profile *mafanikio* theology from a number of different angles, examining it in detail (chapter 4), setting it in its context (chapter 5), assessing its goals (chapter 6), discussing its Africanness (chapter 7), and considering its holism (chapter 8). It is, to my knowledge, the first study of the prosperity theology of any group of Tanzanian women and one of very few of Tanzanians at all. It thus offers one part of an unfinished jigsaw.

Additionally, this study has used ethnographic methods in order to contribute an emic perspective on a prosperity theology. While I am an outsider, my grounded theory approach has been to let the data speak even as I take on the task of interpreting it. This research thus gives unprecedented insight into the convictions of TAFES women.

Third, this study takes an explicitly theological approach in contrast to the tendency towards sociological explanations of women's involvement in prosperity movements. This study has thus not only described theological convictions but introduced a new theological player in African Christianity.

Fourth, in addition to introducing *mafanikio* theology, this research has engaged and assessed it theologically, interrogating the seriousness with which it takes the Bible, its capacity to grow disciples of Jesus who are holy, able to persevere and exhibit the fruits of the Spirit, and the sophistication of its holism. This research has found *mafanikio* theology to be a thoroughly Christian theology.

Fifth, in grounding *mafanikio* theology in its African context, this research has moved away from the tendency to speak of African prosperity theologies in Western terms, highlighting the importance of contextual (not merely contextualized) theologies.

9.3 The Significance of *Mafanikio* Theology

Mafanikio theology offers a way to pursue prosperity that is thoroughly African. Though it departs in key ways from prior African theology, it engages and speaks to deep-seated African values of holism, communalism, pragmatism and dynamism. It also offers a way of relating to God as Patron which is deeply familiar in the African context and its holism is grounded in the African value of *Ubuntu*. In this sense, it is a far more consistent and contextualized prosperity theology than the prosperity theologies it critiques. Its implications are far-reaching and here I offer some of them.

First, *mafanikio* theology charts a course between two historical positions in Tanzania, which I have classified as profligate prosperity gospel and a poverty gospel. *Mafanikio* theology offers a real third way, one where Christians are taught to endure suffering but not valorize it, where prosperity is sought and celebrated but in the context of discipleship and community.

Second, *mafanikio* theology adds to the growing evidence that prosperity theology in Africa is diverse. Generalisations about prosperity theology are no longer appropriate, and obscure rather than clarify the situation on the continent. Additionally, such generalizations miss that theologies like *mafanikio* theology are an ally in the fight against profligate prosperity gospels.

Third, *mafanikio* theology illustrates the liveliness and sophistication of grassroots theology and women's theology in Africa. None of the women in this study were church pastors and yet they all have strong theological opinions and teaching ministries to varying degrees of formality.[1] African theology is not only what is written at an elite level or taught in Bible colleges or church services; it is also what is enacted at a sympathy visit or offered in the midst of giving business advice, or taught at a women's seminar. Neither is this theology merely received from pastors to be parroted by the grassroots. The women did not quote their pastors; they quoted the Bible and they were critical of some pastors and teachers. They also applied their *mafanikio* theology to their own lives and responded thoughtfully to various scenarios I gave them. *Mafanikio* theology is highly nuanced, seeking to equip the Christian to persevere in following Christ in a complex world.

Fourth, *mafanikio* theology demonstrates the importance of Bible reading and Bible study as the engine room of theology. The women in this study have been shaped by TAFES's emphasis on Bible reading and Bible study and they all identified this as a major influence in their lives and theology. This is one of TAFES's great contributions to Tanzanian Christianity. Theological education is a gift to be valued and several of the women were keen to pursue it in the future, a natural result of their love for the Bible. It is this same love that has powered the development of their *mafanikio* theology.

Fifth, *mafanikio* theology's foundation in African philosophical constructs and approaches to the Bible can give confidence in and appreciation of the adequacy of non-Western building blocks for theological reflection, including globally. *Mafanikio* theology is not only highly relevant to its own context; it is also sound theological reflection that other cultures may benefit from. Though the context is different, there are lessons Westerners can glean. For example, as a student in campus ministry in Australia, I was presented with vocational ministry as not only a superior option for following Christ but almost the only truly legitimate option. As campuses in Australia and elsewhere recognise the need to form Christians in all professions, theologies

---

1. After the research period, Ruth became a lay pastor in addition to her professional and other ministry roles. Her denomination does not ordain women but allows them to take the title of pastor.

like *mafanikio* theology which have been reflecting deeply on prosperity in God's world can be a tremendous resource.

9.4 Recommendations for Further Research

This research has been necessarily narrow, exploring the theology of one group of Tanzanian women. It would be worthwhile to ascertain how far-reaching their ideas are across different demographics. For example, these women are all wealthy and educated; how much currency do such views have among poorer or rural women? These women are all Christian. Is there a similar theology among Muslim women or is it unique to Christianity? I have also explored these women's theology on its own terms without making much comparison with theologies held by men. In terms of a gender dimension, I have thus been able to comment on gender only where the women link their theology to it, but I have not sought to show how similar or different it might be from theologies held by men or in mixed groups. Such a comparison is worth further study.

This study of *mafanikio* theology raises new directions for theological research as well. This study has given a glimpse into TAFES women's theology of the atonement but the treatment of it has been necessarily brief. I did not ask any questions about the atonement in my fieldwork so the women's mention of it was incidental rather than giving a full treatment of the topic. How does their construction of the atonement sit alongside other theories? How does it cohere with African Christologies such as Christ as Ancestor or Mediator? The access-function of the atonement present in *mafanikio* theology also needs to be further explored and assessed from a biblical perspective.

Several other dimensions of *mafanikio* theology deserve more attention than I have given them here. In particular, a fuller treatment of the role of patronage in prosperity theology in Africa could be fruitful. While I have briefly referred to a fear-power lens for understanding African Christianity, this also remains underdeveloped in missiological research, especially compared to the burgeoning interest around the world in honour-shame paradigms.

Another implication of *mafanikio* theology that is worthy of further research is how it could be deployed in development contexts. Religion is too often shunted off to the side in NGOs and development studies such that development cannot be truly holistic because it excludes the spiritual.[2] In *mafanikio* theology terms, it is cut off from the source of prosperity. There is already some recognition among some scholars that Pentecostal churches are succeeding where NGOs fail. This is not only because of the missing religion factor; churches also offer existing local networks that NGOs struggle with. However, theology certainly has a part to play here. *Mafanikio* theology offers a local, contextual model of prosperity that is theologically integrated and could be useful to NGOs in understanding one missing element and how they might better understand and cater to the needs of those they are seeking to serve.

Finally, *mafanikio* theology offers several lessons that would be of benefit to any Christian. These include: that prosperity is for sharing not hoarding; that spiritual and physical must be integrated; that wealth must be obtained in good, godly ways; that closeness with Jesus powers life; that God (not myself) is the source of prosperity; that activity in God's world is necessitated by Christian discipleship; and that the pursuit of prosperity can be good and holy. It would be worth Christians from other cultures engaging *mafanikio* theology as a conversation partner on these topics.

This study has found that *mafanikio* theology is a holistic African theology of prosperity. *Mafanikio* theology grows people in the kind of faith, hope and love that can persevere, as they are active in God's world for his purposes. The spheres of *mafanikio* theology mirror those of personified wisdom in Proverbs 31:10–31. The woman in Proverbs 31 is involved in God's world economically (v.14–18, 24), spiritually (v.30), relationally (v.11, 12, 15, 20, 23, 28), physically (v.13, 17), intellectually (v.26) and in terms of inner peace (v.25). Like Proverbs 31:10–31, *mafanikio* theology teaches how to live well in God's world. To paraphrase Proverbs 31:31, an appropriate response to each of the women who have developed *mafanikio* theology is to:

> Honour her for the work she has done,
> And let her works bring her praise.

---

2. Freeman, "The Pentecostal Ethic," 1.

CHAPTER 10

Afterword: Advancing the Mission Conversation in Australia

In 2024, a lecturer at an Australian Bible college commented to me that while my research about TAFES women and their *mafanikio* theology was "interesting," it was for "over there," because "here we teach in the western theological tradition." This attitude saddened me, not because he dismissed my research, but because it assumed that Australian Christians have little to learn from African Christians. As Dutch missiologist Benno van den Toren traces, such an outlook is common and widespread:

> In sub-Saharan Africa, all theological disciplines constantly engage with the flood of theological perspectives coming from the North Atlantic world, whereas in the North, intercultural engagement with theological voices from elsewhere is mainly limited to departments of Missiology, Intercultural Theology, and World Christianity.[1]

The late British missiologist Andrew Walls described missiologists as the "intellectual brokers" who "create and maintain cross-cultural Christian contact and understanding."[2] Missiology exists because Christians of different backgrounds need each other. The letter to the Ephesians makes a passionate case that by the blood of the Lord Jesus Christ, two distinct socio-cultural groups – Jews and Gentiles – have been made one, indeed are one new

---

1. van den Toren, "Integral Salvation and Integrated Theology," 12–23.
2. Walls, *Crossing Cultural Frontiers*, Kindle loc Loc 5848.

humanity, both reconciled to God. We cannot stand apart from each other and worship the same Jesus, because he builds us together into his body; we are one and we only fully realise that reality when we are part of each other (Eph 2:20–22). Thus, systematic theology that remains within one tradition will always have diminishing returns. Yet, missiologists bring new perspectives and data and explore new dimensions for topics already discussed by our theological colleagues. Missiology is therefore not the niche interest area for those who will go elsewhere; it is the frontier of theology whether you will go elsewhere or not.

When I was asked to give the Alf Stanway Lecture in Mission, I took it as an opportunity to demonstrate how the Australian church might stand to learn and benefit from an African theology, specifically, *mafanikio* theology. This Afterword is a lightly edited version of that lecture, which was entitled, "Pleasure Pain . . . and Prosperity: Advancing the Mission Conversation in Australia."[3]

10.1 Pleasure, Pain . . . and Prosperity

Thank you for having me here at the Alf Stanway lecture in Mission. I am delighted to be here and humbled to be bringing it to you. Tonight, I am going to attempt to bring to us a majority world theology and argue not only that it is interesting, not only that it is fit for purpose for its context, but to make a case that it is relevant for us in the Australian context and might even be the very thing we have been waiting for!

So, what are we waiting for? I am going to argue that we are looking for an idiom and a message that is intelligible in a pleasure-pain worldview. Some of us would be familiar with the idea of the pleasure-pain worldview, but to get us thinking about that, let me start with the cultural moment of the year: Taylor Swift's Eras Tour.

---

3. The Alf Stanway lecture in Mission is an annual public lecture, a joint venture between Ridley College and CMS Victoria. Bishop Alfred Stanway was an Australian missionary bishop in Tanzania in the 1950s and 60s and later deputy principal of Ridley College in Melbourne.

10.1.1 Swift and Emotional Cosmology

Whether you are a fan or not is, in one sense, irrelevant. Ninety-six thousand fans piled into the MCG (Melbourne Cricket Ground) to see Swift perform on just one night and an estimated 1.2 billion dollars was injected into the city's economy.[4] Alongside the Eras Tour, Melbourne University held a "Swiftposium" where scholars came together to reflect on the cultural impact of Taylor Swift, with many arguing that it is unparalleled in Australia since the Beatles' 1964 tour.[5] Swift is not only an American phenomenon but a global one, in an era when Gen Z have more in common culturally with others their age in different countries than they do with their own parents, according to Gen Z researchers Jolene Erlacher and Katy White.[6]

Part of Swift's appeal is her authenticity; there's a vulnerability to her lyrics as she sings of both falling in love and heartbreak, and she is almost confessional as she gives voice to anger, revenge, and betrayal. Yet, she is also only telling a story that suits her. When she was profiled in Time Magazine, Swift related the story of her falling out with Kim Kardashian and Kanye West. She spoke of it being a low point, of being cancelled, of having her career wrenched from her. At one level, this story does not ring true for the journalist, Sam Lansky. After all, during this same period, Swift's album reached no.1 on the US Billboard charts and went triple platinum. Objectively, there is another story to tell; the truth of the matter is not contained by Swift's version of it. She might be being authentic or telling us how she sees it, but how truthful is that? Sam Lansky considers pointing this out to her. But then, he refrains. Instead, he thinks, "Who am I to challenge it, if that's how she felt? The point is: she felt cancelled. She felt as if her career had been taken from her. Something in her had been lost, and she was grieving it."[7]

In other words, what matters is how Taylor Swift feels about what happened, and it is on that basis that Lansky (and presumably we) are to relate to her. Swift is a good example of a world where cosmology is emotional: the

---

4. Quinn, "She Came, We Saw."

5. "Swiftposium 2024: An Academic Conference on Taylor Swift," 11–14 Feb 2024, University of Melbourne.

6. Erlacher and White, *Mobilizing Gen Z*, ix. Gen Z are people born between 1996 and 2010.

7. Lansky, "Taylor Swift: 2023 Person of the Year," *Time* December 6, 2023.

universe is primarily one of feelings and it is feelings that determine how we see ourselves in the world. This is a feature of the pleasure-pain worldview.

10.1.2 Worldview Paradigms

Worldview paradigms have been a feature of missiology since the mid twentieth century. Christian anthropologist Eugene Nida first identified guilt-innocence, shame-honour, and fear-power in 1954 in his anthropological textbook Customs and Cultures, though he was probably drawing on work from a decade earlier by sociologist Ruth Benedict.[8] These dyads are based on pursuit/avoidance pairs, so, for example, you pursue innocence and avoid guilt. More recently, Jayson Georges's work on honour and shame has brought to light the need to speak to people in cultural idioms which they understand.[9]

If you come from a culture where guilt-innocence is prominent, your great preoccupation will be with dealing with what Martin Luther called "an extremely troubled conscience." God punishes sinners, and you know you are one, so how can you possibly be counted innocent? Here the good news is that in Christ, we are declared righteous. On the great day of judgement, the great judge will find you innocent, on account of Christ. This version of the gospel will be very familiar to us in Australia. Relating to one another on the basis of guilt or innocence has been prominent in Australia for generations.

Yet, Daniel Kasomo, writing about guilt in African thought, argues that Africans often do not confess sin unless it is discovered, because doing so would draw attention to their sin, which would shame their family. Far more important than dealing with my personal sense of guilt or innocence is maintaining the honour of the family, so confession is to be avoided at all costs, and forgiveness is offered, not for the offense that was committed but for the shame that resulted. It's about restoration of the "harmony in the community, more than it is about addressing the guilt caused by the offense."[10] A call to "repent or believe" or "confess your sins and receive forgiveness" may struggle to gain traction in such a culture. A different message is needed, one which is good news for those in an honour-shame context.[11]

---

8. See: Nida, *Customs and Cultures*,; See also: Merz, "The Culture Problem," 129, 131.
9. See: Georges, *The 3D Gospel*.
10. Cited in Freeman and Calenberg, "Understanding Honor-Shame Dynamics," 431.
11. See list in Hayes, "The Gospel: More Than We Thought,".

Worldview paradigms alert us to the fact that people in other cultures see the world differently, and they ask us to think outside of our normal way of seeing the world, that we might communicate who Jesus is in a way that makes sense to them. This is not about marketing or selling Jesus; it's about knowing him even from within your own culture. After all, Jesus incarnated himself as a human, into a particular culture. Following him means doing the same.

The use of worldview paradigms can encapsulate several pitfalls, because cultures are far more complex than these paradigms indicate. First, we are more than our desires. For example, you might desire to be declared innocent, but your beliefs about whether you are an individual or part of a collective will determine what you do with that desire. Other cultural dimensions come into play and interact with desire. Second, even if we are only looking at this one dimension of culture, they are not completely distinct. The lines blur between them, and human beings have the capacity to hold more than one desire at a time. Having a preference for a guilt-innocence mode of relating does not make you immune to shame for example. Third, as Australian missiologist Darrell Whiteman says, "there can be as much variation among people within a worldview as there is between people with different worldviews."[12]

Worldview paradigms are dangerous when they essentialise, seeking to fit people and cultures into categories rather than seeing and knowing them in their particularity and complexity. However, they can be a useful tool in helping us to identify when we might need to re-think our message.[13] To come back to the Taylor Swift story, Sam Lansky identified that interrogating whether Taylor Swift's career was actually ruined would be fruitless. The point was, that she felt it was. Those of us for whom guilt and innocence are of primary interest will find this difficult to comprehend. We will believe that Swift is only entitled to feelings if they are reflected in the facts – these will determine whether she is guilty or innocent. However, in a pleasure-pain framework, feelings are paramount.

10.1.3 Pleasure-pain

Pleasure-pain is a newcomer when it comes to worldview paradigms. It has been proposed by my colleague at CMS-Australia, David Williams as a fourth

---

12. Whiteman and Adeney, *Crossing Cultures with the Gospel*.
13. Whiteman, "Shame/Honor, Guilt/Innocence, Fear/Power," 348–56.

option, to add to guilt-innocence, shame-honour and fear-power.[14] In this paradigm, morality is defined by the pursuit of pleasure and the avoidance of pain, and because this world is constructed in feelings, the pursuit of pleasure is happy, affirming feelings and the avoidance of pain is emotions that do not feel good, for example, guilt. Williams says, "Perhaps the voice of the pain / pleasure culture is an inner therapist, who says: 'Go for it, you're worth it, be true to yourself.'"[15] Williams has yet to subject his theory to academic peer review but at a popular level, it has resonated for many pastors and missiologists, including here in Melbourne. While an academic discussion over the validity of worldview paradigms generally and the pleasure-pain worldview specifically is yet to be fully realized, the use of these paradigms as a grassroots level necessitates engagement with them.

Williams draws on the work of Charles V. Taylor and James K. A. Smith to wrestle with a world that is secular, that is, that has no place for God or anything spiritual. In this world, an objective standard of morality is meaningless and the world is constructed in the mind. Williams gives an example where if you don't feel married to your partner, sexual engagement with others is not unfaithfulness, because the legal status is not the primary factor in constructing reality.[16] In the case of Swift then, she is not lying about her career being ruined; she is authentically sharing her truth. In fact, to measure oneself by an external standard without attention to one's own feelings would be lying; it would be pretending, covering up, holding back. Like you had something to hide, like there was something shameful, like you were fearful.

I encourage you to look up Williams's argument and engage with it if you have not already, but I am going to turn now to looking at the difficulties we might encounter when engaging with people of a pleasure-pain worldview. The first problem is simply that we live in different worlds. Observe the following Venn diagram.

On the left we have the pleasure-pain worldview. In this world, the preoccupation is pleasure now, and reality is found in feelings. Meanwhile, in Aussie evangelical circles, we primarily conceive of salvation in spiritual terms. (When I say Aussie evangelical, I am using a broad brush, but whether

---

14. Williams, "Introducing the Pleasure-Pain Worldview."
15. Williams "Introducing the Pleasure-Pain Worldview."
16. Williams, "Pleasure, Pain and the Secular Worldview."

you prefer Alpha or Christianity Explored, you are trying to turn people's attention to a reality outside of themselves, to consider God and his standards, and their ultimate destiny.) In contrast, in the pleasure-pain worldview, everything is about the internal. It is easy here to end up speaking past each other. It is like if someone says, "Tell me about the moon," and you reply, "It is inhabited by Ewoks." The question is about Earth's moon; the reply is from an entirely different universe – the Ewoks live on the forest moon of Endor in the Star Wars universe! The circles in this Venn diagram are purposely not overlapping, because we have little in common.

Let me interrogate this issue further by highlighting two points of tension we may feel as we seek to communicate the good news of Jesus in a pleasure-pain context.

First, because objective reality is rejected in favour of feelings, it makes it very difficult to talk about sin or judgement. After all, these concepts are predicated on there being a standard – God's standard – of which humans fall short. In a pleasure-pain worldview, the objective reality of judgement is marked at best irrelevant and at worst, harmful. It is irrelevant because it seeks to establish an outward measure of morality, like trying to establish the facts behind whether or not Swift's career was ruined, or whether or not the person was legally married. Such objectivity is mistrusted, in part because facts are seen to be too easily doctored, in a world where the powerful have time and again relied on their status and networks to cover up the truth. Or, at worst, talk of sin can be seen as harmful, because it asks a person to face and assume a negative identity – "I am a sinner" – which does not feel good, and is therefore perceived as doing violence to the soul. So, how do you communicate the gospel when you cannot talk about sin?

Many of us would have felt this conundrum in our experiences of evangelism. Jesus says, "Repent and believe the good news" (Mark 1:15) and, in order to repent, you first have to know that you're a sinner. Therefore, we set about convincing people that they are sinners. However, we often find that they do not care about this, because you are talking about an objective reality, not their subjective feeling. However, they very much care about you telling them they are a sinner, and they shy away from that negative label. In the end, we find that trying to convince people of sin often does not get us anywhere. They either do not care, or they see us as being judgy, even mean! As much as we try to say that it is God's standard, not our standard, and we do not measure up either, the experience of the person listening is that you – the person trying to tell them about sin – are the problem. You are the one making them hear these uncomfortable things. You are painful. In a pleasure-pain worldview then, you are the thing they need saving from.

The second problem for us with the pleasure-pain worldview is that the path to discipleship is not immediately clear. Williams argues that a person with a pleasure-pain worldview would expect an interaction with the divine to feel "good and powerful and mystical and nice."[17] Yet, Jesus is not the therapist telling you to be true to yourself. He said, "If anyone would follow me, they must deny themself, take up their cross and follow me," (Matt 16:24). The way of Jesus is not avoiding pain and pursuing pleasure, but of suffering and glory. There is very little here with which a person from a pleasure-pain context can resonate. Williams stresses, it's not suffering now and glory later. In John's gospel, suffering and glory are part of the one continuum. Jesus's suffering is not fruitless; it's glorious, because it has other-person-centred love at its core. Suffering and love are united in the person of Jesus, and this is the pattern we are to follow.

The question must be asked, where is pleasure here? Worldview paradigms exist to show us when we need to speak in different idioms, to make ourselves understood. It is unfruitful to tell pleasure-pain people of a suffering-glory gospel, no matter how you nuance it, if you are not speaking the language of pleasure and pain. Williams's argument is biblically rich, but it is also deeply foreign to a pleasure-pain worldview. It is possible this approach is appropriate; the gospel is foolishness to those who are perishing; it is counter-cultural. However, the foreignness ought to give us a little jolt, because it is every tribe and tongue and nation who will bow before the Lamb, not every tribe and tongue and nation except those with a pleasure-pain worldview. Speaking in ways that make sense in a pleasure-pain worldview is part of faithful witness, so that the good news might be heard even in a pleasure-pain context. How can they hear without someone preaching to them? (Rom 10:13) I suggest that we do not yet have a message like this in Australia, and yet the Holy Spirit has not abandoned us. He has been developing a biblically rich theology which can help us, though the place he's been doing it might surprise us. This theology is an African prosperity theology.

---

17. Williams, "Pleasure, Pain and the Secular Worldview Part 6," 6.

10.1.4 Prosperity Theology

If your heartbeat increased a little bit when you heard me talk about prosperity theology, if your mind went straight to the prosperity gospel, you're in good company. I suspect that's where most of us would go with it. You may have read Kate Bowler's book *Blessed: A History of the American Prosperity Gospel*, or seen the documentary *American Gospel*, profiling preachers such as Benny Hinn, Joel Osteen, Kenneth Copeland.[18] In those you would have heard of a theology which says that God's plan for his people is abundance, that he wants to heal them from every malady, but that you need to have the right method of bringing this about, whether it be speaking truth into existence, or having more faith, or giving more money to God, and all of this is wrapped up in a manipulative bundle that preys on vulnerable people and is often little more than a sham invented to increase the wealth of already mega-rich pastors. In such theologies, there is no space for suffering, and discipleship is overshadowed by the desire for wealth. To pick up on Jesus's words in the Parable of the Sower, these theologies are the rocky soil where the seed cannot take root because the ground is too shallow, and the thorny soil where growth is choked by the cares of this world. This, I think, is the version of the prosperity gospel that most of us would know; it is what comes to mind when we think of prosperity theology. It will continue to be if we allow our understanding of prosperity theology to be shaped by what is happening in North America. To be sure, the North American church is a very loud voice in World Christianity. However, there is far more to the story. In recent years, missiologists, missionaries, and anthropologists working in Africa have observed something quite different.

In South Africa, Maria Frahm-Arp observed three "clusters" of prosperity theology.[19] She surveyed ninety-seven pastors in and around Johannesburg. They ranged from small congregations of fifty with a pastor who had another job to support himself, to megachurches of forty thousand people. And she found that the prosperity theology among them was not uniform. The smallest group, about 28 percent was called miracles prosperity, and it's probably more like what we think of when we typically think of prosperity gospel – achieving prosperity through miraculous wealth by applying God's laws of faith

---

18. Williams, "Suffering and Glory."
19. Frahm-Arp, "Pentecostalism, Politics, and Prosperity," 1–16.

or vanquishing the devil. The next biggest group, abilities, also believes in applying God's laws of faith in order to see prosperity but sees this happening in rather ordinary ways, basically living according to biblical principles. In this theology, if you are not seeing prosperity, there is probably some kind of blocker in your life, likely an unrepentant sin. Finally, the largest group, is progress prosperity. This type is much more communally oriented. Here, all of us are seeking prosperity together, whether we have a little or a lot, and prosperity is found, not in how much one has, but in making progress. In this model, a bike for one who walks is prosperity. It is a much more modest version compared to what we might stereotypically think of, and it is the largest group.

Frahm-Arp is not alone in making these observations. British anthropologist Naomi Haynes did her fieldwork on the Zambian Copperbelt and she has identified what she calls a limited prosperity gospel, which is similar to Frahm-Arp's progress prosperity.[20] Meanwhile Tomas Drønen, working in Cameroon, argued that the flashy prophets have been seen to define the prosperity gospel but that didn't reflect what he was seeing at a local level where people were still teaching about prosperity, but without those same excesses.[21] Then, in Kenya, Joshua Barron has written about what he calls the productivity gospel.[22] His work is more observational than ethnographic but he argues that among the middle class in Kenya there is a marriage of a desire for prosperity with the Protestant work ethic, so what at first sounds like prosperity gospel may have something different going on beneath the surface. All of these theologies are using the language of prosperity; they all have the conviction that God wants good things for his people and that those good things are not merely spiritual, not merely in the new creation. In that sense, they are all prosperity theologies. Some of them are prosperity theologies with a place for suffering; some are prosperity theologies which emphasise working hard; some are aimed at growing deeper roots, not shallower ones. Therefore, when you hear the words "prosperity theology" rather than jumping straight to thinking of Benny Hinn, let me encourage you to first ask, "what kind of prosperity theology?" because it might not be the American one.

---

20. Haynes, "Pentecostalism and the Morality of Money," 127.
21. Drønen, "Material Development and Spiritual Empowerment?" 209.
22. Barron, "Is the Prosperity Gospel, Gospel?," 88–103.

To this array of prosperity theologies, I add another alternate prosperity theology, *mafanikio* theology.

10.1.5 *Mafanikio* Theology

Mafanikio is the Swahili word for success; it is the word people use when speaking about prosperity, and it was the name that I gave to the prosperity theology held by the women in my PhD research. Rather than choosing an English word, I've retained the Swahili because I want us to remember where this theology came from – the Holy Spirit has grown this beautiful, deep, sophisticated theology in East Africa.

Let me give you a bit of context as to where this theology has come from. First, the women this research is based on were graduate women of the Tanzania Fellowship of Evangelical Students – TAFES – which is the IFES group in Tanzania, part of the same family of campus movements as CU (Christian Union) here in Victoria. I chose:

- Graduate women because they are older and in positions of influence.
- TAFES women because that is who we were working with, and it gave me a breadth of demographics while retaining a commonality. The women in the research came from ten different Christian denominations, sixteen tribes, and lived in eight urban centres, but they are all middle-class professional women.
- Women because most research about the prosperity gospel is with pastors who are mostly men. However, the greatest influence in a person's spiritual formation is often a woman, but little is known about what women teach or think.

The second thing to know about *mafanikio* theology is that it is an oral theology – there is no "Collected Works of TAFES Women." I created my data set from a combination of attending TAFES events, conducting semi-structured in-depth interviews and focus groups.

Third, it was very clear from the data that the theology the women held – what I've called *mafanikio* theology – is a prosperity theology. In focus groups, I asked the women to reflect on the following statement, given at a church in Dar Es Salaam:

> God wants us to prosper in all areas of our lives here on Earth! It is not God's desire to see his children suffering spiritually, intellectually and physically on earth where they are supposed to be ambassadors of the Almighty God.

There was a spirited discussion about the ambassadors part, but the rest of it was uncontroversial. There was unanimity on God wanting to prosper his people. In that sense, it is a prosperity theology. The question that arises then is, how do they understand this prosperity, and how do they believe it comes?

In *mafanikio* theology, prosperity is:

> a process of taking steps to move to the next level, which can be applied in the economic, spiritual, relational, physical, and intellectual spheres as well as to the experience of inner peace.

There are two things to note here. First, prosperity is not a destination or a point that you reach. It is a process, much like Frahm-Arp's progress prosperity. The definition contains many movement words including process, taking steps, moving, and going to the next level. These are important because this sense of process rather than destination is rooted in the creation mandate in Genesis 1.[23] God tells humankind to be fruitful and multiply; here the creative process is part of what it means to be human, and equally, if you stop being fruitful or stop multiplying – if the process of prosperity halts – then your humanity is tarnished and you are not in the will of God. Therefore, a person cannot rest on their laurels or say, "I have succeeded, I am prosperous." God will always have something more for you to do or learn or move towards. This constant striving is part of what it means to be human in God's world, to be at work, undertaking the process of prosperity.

This sense of process allows all of us, whether rich or poor, to take part in prosperity. If we are all are on that journey, it does not matter whether you have a lot or a little, you are on the same trajectory, part of the same process of being fruitful in God's world. It is highly dignifying for the poor because it is not their poverty which defines them but their orientation. Poverty is not the thing that shows you are not prosperous; inertia is what shows you are not prosperous. It is inertia that is the opposite of prosperity. I wondered what that meant for contentment, and the women told me, godliness with

---

23. See also: Davis, "The Contribution of Luphurise Mawere's."

contentment is great gain (1 Timothy 6:6). However, contentment is not about stopping in the pursuit of prosperity; it is about working within the means that God has given you as you pursue prosperity, which is what God calls human beings to do. The process is where prosperity is found.

The second key thing to note about *mafanikio* theology is that it is holistic. The definition contains a long list of spheres – economic, spiritual, relational, physical, and so on. All these different prosperities rely on each other. For example, you do not expect a business to flourish if you are not attending to relationships, or education to flourish if you are neglecting your health. Likewise, a flourishing business opens up new relational opportunities, and good education is likely to lead to better health outcomes. This is why selfishly storing up wealth for yourself is at odds with true prosperity, because it does not lead to good relationships and it is predicated on another's deprivation. All parts of life are interconnected.

This holistic sense of prosperity was how the women understood "Seek first the kingdom of God and all these things will be added unto you" (Matt 6:33). It is a nonsense to think of looking for prosperity without God. After all, he is the giver of prosperity – in all areas. Those who look like they have prosperity but are not right with God are building on sandy ground and it will not last. Similarly, if you come to God only for the sake of gaining wealth, you are simply using God and have not attended adequately to your spiritual prosperity. The TAFES women were unequivocal about this: seek God first, then the other things will be added, but you cannot seek God as a means to things because that is not really seeking God.

There is much more to be said about *mafanikio* theology, but at this point, we have a sufficient understanding to attempt the task of applying it to the pleasure-pain worldview. At first this may seem like an odd match. After all, the pleasure-pain worldview has come to prominence in a wealthy society, and *mafanikio* theology has emerged out of deep reflection on poverty. Similarly, the pleasure-pain worldview assumes a secular framework, in which the supernatural is irrelevant, whereas *mafanikio* theology places knowing God at its centre. Indeed, in a Venn diagram, there are still great areas that do not overlap.

Nevertheless, there are resonances. For pleasure-seeking people, a theology that offers prosperity is naturally closer. Similarly, when it comes to where reality takes place, both the world of feelings and the holism of *mafanikio* theology are deeply existential. For both, experience matters and the subjective is part of the picture. In the end, *mafanikio* theology was developed for a different context, so it won't be a perfect fit for the pleasure-pain worldview. The task of communicating Christ to pleasure/pain people is ours, those who live among people for whom pleasure-pain is prominent. However, *mafanikio* theology can be a resource for us as we do that.

Mafanikio theology can be applied to the areas we identified earlier in which there is a mismatch between how we understand the gospel and the pleasure/pain worldview. These areas are:

1. We have an issue of communicating the gospel, because we struggle to work out how to talk about sin to a pleasure/pain culture, and forgiveness of sins is largely irrelevant;
2. If we're thinking about discipleship, we struggle to see how a worldview that has no place for pain can account for suffering or hear Jesus's call to take up your cross and follow him.

How can *mafanikio* theology help us with these two areas?

10.1.6 *Mafanikio* Theology, Pleasure-pain, and Sin

On the first issue, there is a commonality to pleasure-pain and *mafanikio* theology in that neither are particularly preoccupied with sin or judgement. Instead, their questions are about how to experience the good life. At one level, we may object to *mafanikio* theology's neglect of sin as a theme, but it's also true that this opens up a point of connection with a pleasure-pain way of thinking.

Indeed, *mafanikio* theology does have a theology of sin, but it is not the presenting issue. *Mafanikio* theology leads with something other than sin. An examination of the women's treatment of Matthew 19:23–24 will help us here. In this verse Jesus says that it is harder for a camel to go through the eye of a needle than for a rich man to go to heaven. This verse is often used to pit wealth and salvation against each other, to say that we ought to pursue the spiritual not the physical. Yet the way the TAFES women saw it was that it says it is hard, but not impossible. In fact, when the disciples question Jesus about it, Jesus says, "With God all things are possible" (Matt 19:26). Their conclusion was: it is very hard, but not impossible, so we need to give great attention to righteous living. This is not a theology that is soft on sin or righteousness.

In fact, because of the preoccupation with wealth, dealing with sin in your life is seen as something which is important to do. Nevertheless, sin and the resulting guilt is not the great weight on a person's heart. The most pressing question for them is, "Is it possible to prosper?" The holism of *mafanikio* theology suggests that you need to have your relationship with God right – you need to be forgiven of your sins – if you are to experience prosperity in other areas. It's not that *mafanikio* theology has no place for sin, but dealing with sin is the means to an end, not the presenting issue.

Likewise for people for whom pleasure-pain is prominent, the question "Will this feel good to me?" is far more relevant than, "Can God forgive me, a sinner?" Perhaps we want to say, salvation is not about feeling good, it's about an objective reality of God's judgement. However, if we say that, it is like we are talking about Ewoks on the forest moon of Endor when we were asked about the moon orbiting Earth. We have failed to move with the grain of what people are already feeling, and instead have offered them something unintelligible.

We must ask ourselves then: does the Christian life feel good? Do we have language for that? Some of us may have felt good when we had our sins forgiven, because we were suddenly relieved of the burden of guilt, but our idioms are of innocence, not pleasure, and not prosperity. Do we have anything to say about how the Christian life affects prosperity in the economic, the relational, the intellectual, or the physical? Does a good God give these? Are they a gift from him? People with a pleasure-pain worldview need to hear a holistic gospel, one where, in the words of Psalm 34, they can taste and see that the Lord is good, where they can experience and feel that the Lord is good.

Though people in pleasure-pain contexts grasp for pleasure, they rarely possess it in any meaningful sense: the pursuit of pleasure in a pleasure-pain landscape produces and is a response to crippling loneliness and deep anxieties. We Christians in the West often fear that if we lean too much into the more material spheres, we will lose the spiritual dimension: we will end up just like any other community group, and in the end, they can offer emotional healing or help people with their businesses, but only we can offer them the gospel of forgiveness of sins. In a pleasure/pain context, however, the far bigger danger is that in neglecting these other dimensions, we affirm to hurting people the belief that God only offers prosperity in one area (spiritually), and that other kinds of prosperity are gifts from our society, rather than gifts from God. Yet, we serve a God who is making a people for himself, who calls us into community, a community where God's goodness is experienced in his people. The need for community is greater than ever before. I saw recently a course developed by an Anglican pastor here in Melbourne on friendship, and I thought, "What a wonderful gift from God!" It is easy to think of pleasure-pain people as indulgent, to characterize them as sinful. Certainly, they are looking for fulfillment in the wrong places, but they are doing so out of very real needs and deficits, and Psalm 34 is a Psalm for people such as these, for the afflicted. Tasting and seeing that the Lord is good happens in the context of real adversity; it is about finding life and the goodness of God as you face the nitty-gritty of life, not escaping from it. We need to learn from the holism of *mafanikio* theology: start with experiencing that the Lord is good, build on that foundation. Let that reality saturate our language.

10.1.7 *Mafanikio* Theology, Pleasure-pain, and Suffering

This does lead us to the question of suffering. The Christian life is not only one of victory. The message that victory is the only experience of the Christian life is part of that inauthentic prosperity gospel which is unable to deal with reality. Yet, Tanzanian women live day to day with the reality of poverty. So, how do they wrestle with the issues of suffering, and how might this help us as we seek to engage the pleasure/pain worldview?

In order to answer this question, I asked the women about suffering, and especially about the life of Paul, how he counted worldly things as loss compared to knowing Jesus, or how when he cries out to God to take away his thorn, he is told, "my grace is sufficient for you" (2 Cor 12:9). When I did, they bristled at the notion that these experiences of Paul were normative for the Christian life. They saw these experiences of Paul as something of a special case, not because they were an aberration but because of the testimony of Paul himself. They reminded me, he was also a tentmaker and a traveller, and he did not see these aspects of his life as somehow at odds with following Christ. On the contrary, he saw them as worthy of imitation in 2 Thessalonians, of what it means to live as a disciple of Christ now rather than simply waiting in idleness for Christ's return. The norm, they told me, is not passivity or submission, but activity, a process of prosperity.

Again, this perspective can benefit us as we seek to engage those for whom pleasure-pain is prominent. When it comes to suffering, we remember Jesus's words, "Anyone who would follow me must pick up their cross," (Matt 16:24) and we remember the cross took Jesus even to death. Even so, do we forget those other words of Jesus, "Come to me you who are weak and heavy laden and I will give you rest? . . . For my yoke is easy and my burden is light," (Matt 11:28, 30). I am not suggesting we pit these two teaching of Jesus against each other; I am suggesting we find a way to integrate them. This is what the TAFES women do with their *mafanikio* theology.

In *mafanikio* theology, suffering is both part of the process of prosperity, and a reason to pursue further prosperity. Because prosperity is a process, obstacles and setbacks are a natural part of that. Furthermore, they are a necessity. Each new phase of the process of prosperity requires more of a person – greater character, new knowledge, and skills – if they are to bear the burden of prosperity and carry it without faltering. One woman described suffering as growing the muscles you need to bear your prosperity. Suffering is not at odds with prosperity here, but the means by which you are able to participate in it. God is a kind of personal trainer, present and gradually increasing your prosperity in manageable chunks. Here, suffering is not a sign of God's abandonment, but of his presence and his desire to bless you. Suffering is not a threat to your success; it is how God ensures it. Because the goal is prosperity, resignation to suffering does not make sense. Suffering is not accepted as simply part of life with nothing to be done about it, at least not a Christian life, in which one is called to fruitfulness, not passivity.

Let me round of this discussion by suggesting how this understanding of suffering engages a pleasure-pain worldview. It must be said that this understanding of suffering integrates what the pleasure-pain worldview has separated. Here, pleasure and pain are not opposites any more than prosperity and suffering are opposites. This is a challenge for the pleasure-pain worldview, but if we are going to bring a challenge to it, I contend that this is a good one to start with, because it is still largely speaking in the same idiom. As in the pleasure-pain worldview, the process of prosperity drives one's focus away from the big esoteric questions of attempting to reconcile prosperity and suffering and towards the present moment, and what the next step is. Therefore, a person can ask, where is prosperity in this moment, at this time? This is where *mafanikio* theology is instructive for a pleasure-pain worldview. As

I've just noted, those holding a pleasure-pain worldview are highly anxious, lonely, and easily overwhelmed. *Mafanikio* theology relieves this burden, by narrowing the focus away from the big questions. *Mafanikio* theology asks, "What next step in front of you?" and it offers a God who is here with you, with wisdom for this moment, this time, this place.

Mafanikio theology is the theological equivalent of a grounding exercise. Grounding techniques are exercises that help you to refocus on the present moment, taking you away from anxious or overwhelming feelings. For example, you might ask, "What can you hear right now?"; "What can you smell?"; "Can you see something that is green?"; "What can you touch?" These exercises take a person out of their panic and back into their body and their environment. For an anxious generation, *mafanikio* theology acts similarly. In the face of the inquiry that feels difficult or painful – the kind of questions pleasure-pain people are likely to shy away from – *mafanikio* theology asks, "How is God here, in this moment?" Being a disciple of Jesus is something you can grasp onto here. It is not necessary to start with the ultimate destination, the cosmic or eternity. The starting point is instead, on the next step and the presence of God with you in it. Of course, those bigger spiritual issues must be addressed as their muscles grow – to fail to do that would be to fail to be holistic. And yet, there is a trust here in a good God who is present in our lives, and that knowing him in the small things is part of how we know him in the big. There is a sense in which *mafanikio* theology relieves suffering, not by magically making it disappear but in helping us to ground our theology and to know God with us.

10.1.8 Conclusion

To sum up then, what does *mafanikio* theology offer a pleasure/pain context?

- *Mafanikio* theology offers to us an idiom which is more conversant with pleasure and pain with questions like "Does God want my good?" and a response to that in the affirmative;
- *Mafanikio* theology's holism affirms the dignity of the material, of experience and feeling, and connects these to discipleship;
- For the anxious and the overwhelmed, *mafanikio* theology makes space for faith to be in this world; and by doing so, it makes space

for suffering, because as you yoke yourself to Jesus, you find his plan for you is for your flourishing.

Let me conclude by saying that one of the objections to this approach to the pleasure-pain worldview could well be that it sounds like a superficial Christianity, because it tiptoes around cultural sensitivities and diminishes the importance of things like sin and judgement. I hope that is not what you have heard tonight, because I do not think that is what I am doing. However, if I were going to straw woman myself, that is the argument that I would make.[24] It might go something along the lines of: if you do not talk about picking up your cross and following Jesus, Christians will not lead sacrificial lives in which they are serving others and Christ. This is certainly a concern. In my role with CMS SANT (Church Missionary Society South Australia and Northern Territory), I work nurturing and encouraging people into mission, which obviously requires sacrifice! The last thing Australia, or indeed the world needs, is Christians whose faith is baptized by individualism and consumerism. However, something that surprised me observing the TAFES women was how these women, who eschew the language of cruciformity lead remarkably cruciform lives. They pour themselves out like drink offerings in the service of God and his people, whether it be fostering children, pastoring people in addition to their many other responsibilities, or advocating for the most vulnerable in society sometimes at considerable cost or danger to themselves. That is what happens when someone meets Jesus in their own language and idiom. It transforms them and they become like him. However, that only happens as they hear about Jesus in a way that makes sense to them. That is what we have been exploring tonight.

In light of all this, let me leave you with some questions from tonight's lecture:

- Have you allowed your rightful aversion to American prosperity gospel to push you away from believing in a good God who gives good gifts to his people? Pleasure-pain people need to hear of God and his good gifts.

---

24. A straw man argument distorts or exaggerates a person's argument and then attacks the distorted version.

- Have you taken to heart Jesus's words about taking up your cross and following him, yet failed to reflect on his words about his burden being easy and his yoke being light? Pleasure-pain people need to experience a God who is gentle with them in their brittleness.
- Can you learn from Tanzanian women that Paul's teaching on suffering is not the sum of his life or teaching or his gospel? Pleasure-pain people need to be shown how to live well, not simply hear about how to die well.

This is not about being selective with the Bible. This is not about pandering to an indulgent generation. This is about the conviction that the gospel is indeed good news, transforming news, including to a pleasure-pain people.

APPENDIX 1

Map of Tanzania's Regions

Map of Tanzania's Regions[1]

---

1. Adaped from https://en.wikipedia.org/wiki/Tanzania#/media/File:Tanzania,_administrative_divisions_-_de_-_colored_(+details).svg. Accessed 13 June 2025. Creative Commons Attribution-ShareAlike 3.0 Licence.

APPENDIX 2

List of Interviews

Interview 1 (Eunice), 13 February 2021, Arusha.
Interview 2 (Abigail), 14 February 2021, Arusha.
Interview 3 (Damaris), 24 February 2021, Dar Es Salaam.
Interview 4 (Fibi), 6 March 2021, Dar Es Salaam.
Interview 5 (Junia), 17 April 2021, Mwanza.
Interview 6 (Susanna), 17 April 2021, Mwanza.
Interview 7 (Puah), 18 April 2021, Mwanza.
Interview 8 (Salome), 13 May 2021, Morogoro.
Interview 9 (Shiphrah), 13 May 2021, Morogoro.
Interview 10 (Lois), 14 May 2021, Dodoma.
Interview 11 (Lydia), 14 May 2021, Dodoma.
Interview 12 (Mariamu), 14 May 2021, Dodoma.
Interview 13 (Anna), 2 August 2021, Dodoma.
Interview 14 (Bilhah), 3 August 2021, Dodoma.
Interview 15 (Rhoda), 4 August 2021, Dodoma.
Interview 16 (Zipporah), 4 August 2021, Dodoma.
Interview 17 (Leah), 9 October 2021, Moshi.
Interview 18 (Martha), 9 October 2021, Moshi.
Interview 19 (Jochebed), 29 October 2021, Dar Es Salaam.
Interview 20 (Ruth), 3 November 2021, Dar Es Salaam.

APPENDIX 3

List of Focus Groups

Focus Group 1, 17 April 2021, Mwanza.
Participants: Susanna, Chloe, Puah, Naomi, Junia, Joanna, Eve
Focus Group 2, 6 November 2021, Dar Es Salaam.
Participants: Deborah, Jael, Zilpah, Dorcas, Sarai, Priscilla, Huldah

APPENDIX 4

List of Participant Observations

2 February 2021 Jerusalem Zone Associates meeting, Dar Es Salaam
Speaker: Mercy

27 April 2021 *Pole* visit to the home of Family KJ, Dar Es Salaam
Speaker: Various, including Deborah, Priscilla

3 September 2021 Seminar at Transformers' Conference: Coping with Modern Parenting, Dodoma
Speaker: Peace

4 September 2021 Seminar at Transformers' Conference: Rebuilding Our Families, Dodoma
Speaker: Faith

11 September 2021 Session at TAFES Staff Orientation and Training: Change Management, Dar Es Salaam
Speaker: Joy

27 October 2021 Women's Bible Study Seminar, Dar Es Salaam
Speaker: Loveness

30 October 2021 *Pole* visit to the home of Family KY, Dar Es Salaam
Speaker: Various, including Deborah, Priscilla

APPENDIX 5

Semi-structured Interview Questions

1. *Niambie maana ya mafanikio.*
Tell me the meaning of prosperity.

2. *Niambie tofauti na ustawi.*
Tell me the difference with well-being.

3. *Niambie mahusiano kati ya mafanikio na utajiri.*
Tell me the relationship between prosperity and wealth/riches.

4. *Mtu anafanikishwa vipi?*
How is a person prospered?

5. *Biblia inatufundisha nini kuhusu mafanikio?*
What does the Bible tell us about prosperity?

6. *Kama mwanafunzi wa TAFES akija kwako kwa ushauri kuhusu asome kitabu gani katika Biblia kuhusu mafanikio utasemaje?*
If a TAFES student came to you for advice about what book of the Bible to read about prosperity what would you say?

7. *Mwanafunzi huyu akienda kanisani kumuomba Mungu mafanikio na akakuomba mifano mizuri ya maombi kuhusu mafanikio, utasemaje?*
If this student was going to church to pray to God for prosperity and asked you for good examples of prayers about prosperity, what would you say?

8. *Mtu akifikia mafanikio, maisha yake yanaonekanaje?*
If a person attains prosperity, what will their life look like?

9. *Biblia inatuambia kuhusu watu walioteseka, kwa mfano Paulo na mwiba wake. Akaomba sana Mungu aondoe mwiba wake lakini Mungu akasema "Neema yangu yakutosha; maana uwezo wangu hutimilika katika udhaifu." Mstari huu unatufundisha nini kuhusu mafanikio?*
The Bible tells us about people who were troubled, like Paul and his thorn. Paul prayed a lot for God to remove the thorn but God said, "My grace is sufficient for you, for my power is made perfect in weakness." What does this passage teach us about prosperity?

10. *Dhani kuna Bibi mjane kijijini. Yeye ni Mkristo mwaminifu kabisa. Anaenda kanisani kila siku kwa maombi, anajitahidi shambani, anawatunza wajukuu wake lakini baado yeye ni maskini. Je, anapata mafanikio?*
Suppose there is a widowed grandmother in a village. She is very faithful Christian. She goes to church every day for prayers, she works hard in the fields, she looks after the grandchildren but still she is poor. Does she have prosperity?

11. *Je, unaweza kuniambia kinyume cha mafanikio?*
Can you tell the opposite of prosperity?

12. *Je, mtu anaweza kusimamisha mafanikio yake na kupumzika?*
Can a person stop pursuing prosperity and rest?

13. *Niambie kuhusu kuridhika.*
Can you tell me about contentment?

14. *Je, njia ya kutafuta mafanikio ni sawasawa kwa wanaume na wanawake?*
Is the the road to prosperity the same for men and women?

15. *Kuna kitu chochote zaidi ungependa kusema kuhusu mafanikio?*
Is there anything else you want to say about prosperity?

APPENDIX 6

Focus Group Questions

1. God wants us to prosper in all areas of our lives here on Earth! It is not God's desire to see his children suffering spiritually, intellectually, and physically on earth where they are supposed to be ambassadors of the Almighty God.

2. Good health demonstrates the power of your faith. A person who is prayed for but not healed either lacks faith or has not followed well the spiritual law of sowing abundantly.

3. *Ungependa kufanya nini katika maisha yako? Hata Jehovah anafanya kitu katika maisha yako. Simama na useme, "More money, more supply. I'm going to have billions. Mine mine mine mine."*
What do you want to do in your life? Surely Jehovah is active in your life. Stand and say, "More money, more supply. I'm going to have billions. Mine mine mine mine."

4. *Watu wote ambao wanasikiliza na kuamini wahubiri wanaowaahadi watapata nyumba, gari, milioni, bilioni, na mafanikio katika biashara, wote pamoja – wale wahubiri na wasikilizaji – wamefarakana na imani na hawamfuati Yesu Kristo.*
All people who listen to and believe preachers who promise that they will have a house, a car, millions, billions, and success in business, all of them together – the preachers and the listeners – have departed from faith and do not follow Jesus Christ.

APPENDIX 7

Mind-map of Codes

Below is a mind-map I used to organize my codes. Three levels of coding are included in this mind-map. Some codes, such as Bible verses and Bible figures, were broken down further. A larger version of this image is available at: https://photos.app.goo.gl/HhPo7mPExLLU7ih17.

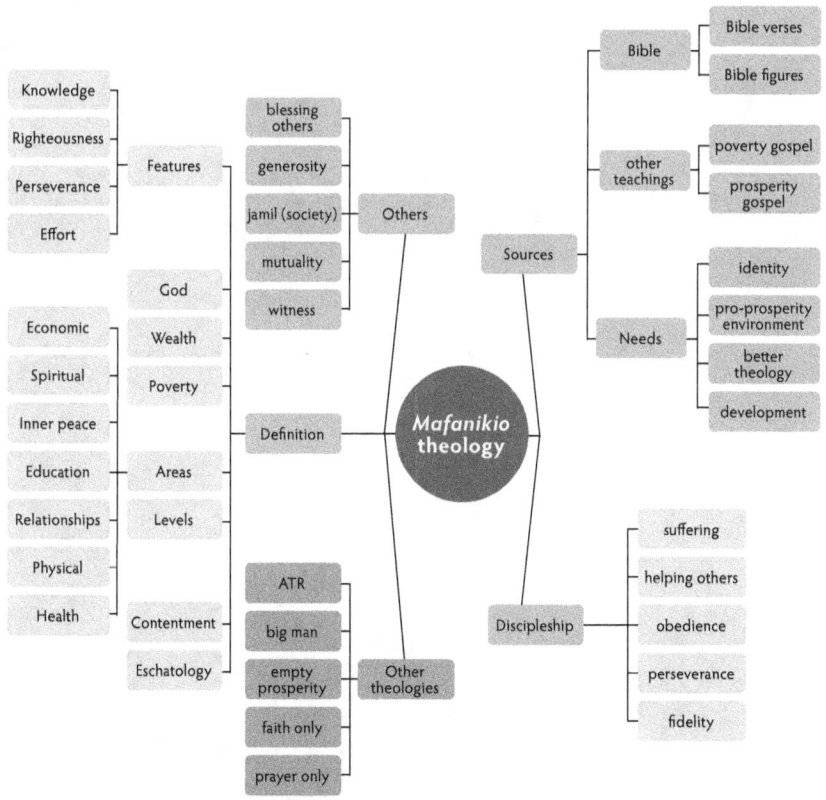

APPENDIX 8

Swahili Quotations

All quotations from the ethnographic data are given in English in the main body of the thesis. Below are the quotations used in the thesis in their original Swahili form.

1. Na hata kufanikiwa ukiwa na maana ya kutafsiri Kiswahili prosperity, prosperity Kiswahili, nadhani haina tafsiri nyingi zaidi ya kufanikiwa. (Priscilla)
2. Hali ambayo mimi au mtu yeyote anaweza kuiona ambayo ni ya tofauti kutoka kwenye hali ya chini kwenda hali ya juu au kutoka kwenye kutokuwa nacho kuwa hali ya kuwa nacho au hali ya kutokuweza kwa hali ya kuweza. (Leah)
3. Mafanikio ni ile hali ya mtu kuongezeka katika mtazamo chanya ... Mtu ametoka mahali fulani ambapo hali imekuwa chini kidogo halafu amepanda. OK naweza nikasema mabadiliko—mafanikio ni hali ya mabadiliko chanya ni kwenye maisha ya mtu. (Puah)
4. Mafanikio ni kitu endelevu. Huwezi kusema nimefikia and that is it. (Bilhah)
5. Hatua moja inazaalisha nyingine. (Rhoda)
6. Huwezi kusema, "Nimemaliza, nimefika," kwa sababu sisi kama Wakristo, always kuna kitu Mungu anakuita kufanya zaidi. (Zipporah)
7. Kila anachokitegemea ikiporomoka. Anarudi sifuri chini... Lakini suala la mafanikio ni suala la endelevu and inahitaji bidii. (Damaris)

8. Umemaliza maskini umekaa hapa, umekufa, hujafanya kitu chochote katika dunia, hamna tofauti na wewe kuwepo au usingekuwepo. (Dorcas)
9. Mafanikio yanategemea na kufanikiwa kwa maeneo yote ... ni kama hujala chakula na kama kuna changamoto unayopitia unakosa kupata chakula unaweza kukosa na amani. (Eunice)
10. Utakutana na giza ambazo itakuwa utakutana na barabara mbovu gari lako litaharibika, utakuwa na watu ambao wana furaha na wewe kwa sababu umefanikiwa mwenyewe. Umeweka wanakutenga wanapoisolate kwa hiyo kuisolate siyo mafanikio. Kwa sababu ... utapata na shida unapohitaji watu. Hawatakuja mwenyewe ghorofa. Atakupa peke yako. Kwa sababu una maeneo ambao hela huwezi kusaidia. Unahitaji watu. Kule mali na hela hayasaidii. (Fibi)
11. Mafanikio yanatoka Mungu mwenyewe kwa sababu Mungu ameshakusudia kila mtu kwamba anafikia wapi. Aliponiumba mimi alijua kwamba, Shiphrah nataka afike hapa. Kwa hiyo inatufundisha kwamba tukiishi sawasawa na mpango wa Mungu tutafikia yale mafanikio kwamba Mungu aliyakusudia kwa ajili yetu. (Shiphrah)
12. Mafanikio yetu sisi yaanza kwanza rohoni. (Lydia)
13. Kama roho inafanikiwa hapo mafanikio yatafuata huko juu. Kwa hiyo Biblia inataka kwanza roho zetu zifanikiwe tuwe na mahusiano na Mungu. (Damaris)
14. Mara nyingi sisi hatumtaki Mungu, tunataka mambo yake yaani vitu vyake vile ndio tunavitaka. Ambao sasa ni shida kubwa katika Ukristo. Kwa hiyo mimi nikiongea na huyu mtu nitamwambia ... sheria ya Mungu inasema umjue kwanza yeye halafu mema yote yatakuja. (Susanna)
15. Akaae aombe akiomba vitu vitakuja au wataenda vitashuka. (Chloe)
16. Maana ya kumpenda Mungu ni ndio sisi tukaishi kwa msingi yote na kanuni, sio kwa sheria, lakini tuna ile relationship na Mungu. (Priscilla)

17. Biblia inatufundisha kwamba Mungu ndiye chanzo cha mafanikio. Mungu anampa mtu akili. Mungu anampa mtu uelewa, maarifa. (Lois)
18. Hakuna mafanikio nje ya Kristo. (Huldah)
19. Shetani anapinga sana mafanikio. (Martha)
20. Amefariki, pesa haziwezi kumsaidia. (Fibi)
21. Ikamfaidia nini mtu akiupata ulimwengu wote na kupoteza nafsi yake, itamfaidia nini. That means kwa Biblia haikufanikiwi chochote ukipata pesa, mali, watoto, nini na kupoteza nafsi yako ... I think mafanikio ni ile nafsi yako iwe salama kwa Mungu wako utakapomaliza yote duniani umelala ufike na Mungu. (Bilhah)
22. Labda ninapindisha pindisha mafaai ofisini kwa kujenga ghorofa langu ... Siwe na mafanikio ... uko nje ya mpango na kusudi la Mungu. (Abigail)
23. Kwa sababu unaposema utajiri na maskini, utajiri sio tu kwamba eti mimi nina nyumba tano ama sita. Ninaona utajiri kama una mahali pa kulala, unakula, huo ni utajiri. (Martha)
24. Watu wengi wanatafsiri mafanikio kama utajiri. Mafanikio sio utajiri kwa hiyo mafundisho haya yasiwe sahihi. (Anna)
25. Haina shida kama inakuwa in the right perspective ya kimungu. (Ruth)
26. Unaweza ukawa na fedha na ukawa mtu wa hofu ya Mungu. (Ruth)
27. Biblia inakubali kabisa anaweza akawa mtajiri. (Bilhah)
28. Mara nyingi tunafikiri kijijini watu wanapata shida lakini unaweza kwa kutampo kijijini yaani ana amani na anaishi na ana furaha ingawa ... maisha anayoishi ni magumu. Hizo tunafikiri, "Mbona hana hiki au hiki, mbona anaishi kwenye nyumba mbaya?" Lakini kumbe yeye yaani mazingira kwake yanaona ni ndiyo sawa. (Eunice)
29. Huwezi kusema hana mafanikio kwa sababu anaye Kristo ambaye Kristo ndiye mwenye vyote. (Ruth)
30. Mungu anaweza kumtokezea na kumfanyia namna yeyote. (Leah)
31. Mafanikio yapo kwa sababu ana afya nzuri, Mungu anampa ulinzi, anampa chakula, anakula, hata kama analala chini ...

Mungu anampa uhai. Ipo siku Mungu atamwonekea katika yale anayoomba. (Lois)

32. I have been in that situation and God feeded [sic] me. Kwa hiyo issue ni kwamba ninaamini katika Mungu kumtunza. Kitu cha thamani ni kwamba yeye kuendelea kukaa na Mungu. (Puah)
33. Hajapata mafanikio ya mali. Lakini amepata mafanikio ya wajukuu. (Martha)
34. Hatuwezi kusema amefanikiwa kwa sababu baado kuna vitu anavistruggle especially yaani chakula kwa siku. (Rhoda)
35. Naona kuna udhaifu hapo moja. Kwamba huyu mtu sawa kumjua Mungu lakini hawa wajukuu wale ambao anaowazaa wanakuja kumwelekea hapa. Kwa nini wasiwatulize? Hiyo ni njia moja kuendelea kumfanya huyo Bibi aendelee kuwa maskini. (Susanna)
36. Maadili mazuri, hofu ya Mungu, kufanya kazi kwa bidii basi mtu anafanikishwa. (Zipporah)
37. Kwa hiyo unaweza kuona mtu anayeishi mazingira magumu kama hayo lakini moyoni ana amani kubwa kushinda hata mtu aliyeko mjini anafanya kazi anapata mshahara lakini haitoshi kutimiza mahitaji yake. (Eunice)
38. Kinyume cha mafanikio. Nikiongea kutofanikiwa lakini kinyume cha mafanikio ni kushindwa, kutofanikiwa kutoendelea. Kinyume cha mafanikio ni, siwezi kusema ni umaskini, lakini ni kushindwa kufikia malengo yako. Kwa sababu siwezi – nikasema kinyume cha mafanikio ni umaskini – Kiswahili kigumu kukieleza vizuri – lakini kuna umaskini wa roho na kuna umaskini wa mwili na kuna umaskini mengi mengi. Kwa kinyume cha mafanikio ni kufeli ni kushindwa kufikia mambo ambao unatarajia. Ni kuwa nyuma ya maendeleo. Unapokuwa na malengo na watakwi kufikia unapokuwa kutamani kufanya vitu mbalimbali unashindwa kuvifikia. (Fibi)
39. Kuridhika sio sawa na kusema nitasimama . . . Kuridhika watu wanaconfuse na kuridhika na kukaa kwenye comfort zone. (Ruth)
40. Kuridhika ina maana kwamba, yale mafanikio umepata kwa njia halali. (Martha)
41. Sina hiki nataka . . . hata kama sio nitafanya kwa njia zozote. (Zipporah)

42. Moja kwa moja na furaha. (Leah)
43. Lakini kwa upande wa kiroho huwezi kusema, "Nimeshafanikiwa ninamfahamu Mungu sitaacha kuomba na kusoma Biblia." Tunasema ni mchakato ukiwa ni kila wakati yaani ni endelevu. Kwa hiyo kwa upande wangu mimi mafanikio, huwezi kusema, "Nimefika tayari," ila pia Mungu ametupa kitu ndani yetu hautosheki unatamani kuwa bora zaidi. (Salome)
44. Aliwapa kazi ya kuzaa na kuongezeka. (Leah)
45. Biblia inatuambia kama tukifika mbinguni ndio tutastarehe, hakuna tatizo. (Susanna)
46. Tunaishi kwenye community, hatuisolate ... Demand ipo kila siku, kuna wahitaji, kuna yatima, kuna wagonjwa. (Lois)
47. Kwamba mimi naona maisha yanaendelea vizuri lakini jamii inayonizunguka baado ina matatizo. Kwa hiyo nikikaa hivi ina maana sipendi jamii. (Salome)
48. Kwa ajili yake sio kwa ajili yetu sisi wenyewe. (Shiphrah)
49. Ili tuweze kujenga ufalme tunatakiwa kielimu kiwe vizuri kiroho kiwe vizuri hata physically unaweza kumconvince mtu kama anaona pia wewe uko kwenye hali nzuri kuliko ya kwake. (Susanna)
50. Yesu alivyosulubiwa msalaba alikaa namna hii [stretches out arms] maana yake upande moja kugusa kiroho na mwingine maisha kawaida, meaning social services, huduma ya kijamii, elimu, afya, na mahitaji yote yanaohusiana na mahitaji yote ya maisha ya binadamu ya hapa duniani. (Zilpah)
51. Kinaharibisha jina la Mungu. Yaani tuwe vile vinavyo kushare yaani tunavyofanya tu jina la Mungu lisaidiwe. (Abigail)
52. Unakuta mtu wa eneo la poor poor, maskini hapati mahitaji ya kutosha mwisho wa siku mtu anakuja anakata tamaa hata katika imani yake na Mungu. Lakini kama umfundishe kwa habari ya kufanya kazi Biblia inasema asiyefanya kazi asile. (Zilpah)
53. Alikuwa anaweza kuruka kwenda kufanya injili lakini alitembea alitenda boat, alifanya na he is our role model. (Rhoda)
54. Nilinyosha hela yangu juu ile shilingi elfu moja nikafumba macho nikaamini kwamba Mungu anaweza kuibadilisha ile shilingi elfu moja ikawa elfu kumi. Naomba kuwauliza Mungu anaweza

au hawezi? Mungu anaweza. . . . Nilinyosha juu, nikamwomba Mungu, nikafungua macho, ilikuwa elfu moja. (Huldah)
55. Mungu amesema tumebarikiwa kwenye kazi za mikono yetu. (Mariamu)
56. Yesu aliteseka ili sisi tupate uzima wa milele na sio kuishi na shida. (Rhoda)
57. Asichoke wala kukoma. (Lois)
58. Kuwa na Mungu haimaanishi kwamba hutapita kwenye ugumu ila having God inasaidia kuona ulivyoenda kwa nyepesi lakini kuwa na Mungu inakusaidia kubeba lile ngumu bila kurudisha na dhambi. (Puah)
59. Haina maana kwamba mafanikio yameondoka. (Eunice)
60. Si kwamba imani zetu zimefanya nini – ziko chini, hapana. (Naomi)
61. Watu wanaweza kuwa hali nzuri baado imani zao sio nzuri sana. (Joanna)
62. Mapenzi ya adui. (Shiphrah)
63. Amejitukuza hata kwa mtu ambaye ni kuwa down. (Abigail)
64. Fanya kitu sahihi kwa watu sahihi na kwa majira sahihi na muda sahihi. (Fibi)
65. Kitu cha kwanza, 'Mungu anifinyange anitengeneze kumpendeza yeye. Niwe mtu anayeweza kumpendeza Mungu.' (Puah)
66. Mungu, bless me where you want me to be, enyi wewe unaponitaka. No matter mazingira no matter mshahara, no matter what, bless me ambao nipo katika kusudi lako. (Puah)
67. Mafanikio ambayo hayataharibu mahusiano na watu, mafanikio ambayo hayataharibu watoto . . . [au] kanisa. Kwa hiyo tunahitaji hekima na mwongozo wa Mungu zaidi kufikiapo mafanikio. (Lydia)
68. Tunashindwa kuprosper kwa sababu hatukufanya vitu Mungu originally alivyotuumba. We have less time with our kids, we have less time to make our homes . . . Wanawake, tuko overused. (Priscilla)
69. Mtu anafanikishwa kwa maarifa, skills, kufundishwa, kuelekezwa. (Rhoda)
70. Aombe Mungu ampe hekima, maarifa, busara. (Lydia)

71. Closemindedness inamwathiri mafanikio ... If you are closed-minded, you will not reach your goal because you will be just staying with one perspective [like] this is what I did and I got it, or this is how the pastor says. (Jochebed)
72. Shika elimu. Soma bidii. (Fibi)
73. Kama ataniuliza [kuhusu mafanikio], "Mimi napenda kulima," eeh ndiyo nitampeleka kwenye Biblia asome vizuri aelewa principles za kawaida za kimungu za kufanya biashara na kufanya hivi. Aapply the principle pamoja na kufanya kazi kwa bidii pamoja na kumtafta Mungu. (Bilhah)
74. Mungu akaniachilia maarifa na nikaweza kufanya kila kitu kwa kutumia maarifa niliyopewa nikaweza kufanikiwa. (Leah)
75. Lakini nyuma kulikuwa watu walikuwa na wanasema hutakiwi kuwa na fedha nyingi hutakiwi ... mafanikio ya kufanana na asiyempenda Mungu. (Martha)
76. 'Eh Biblia labda inapingana na mafanikio.' (Leah)
77. Kwamba it's all about myself, wanakuja wanaamini, myself, mafanikio is all about me and me. (Ruth)
78. Kitakusababisha kufanikiwa kazini unapata gari kitaongeza mshahara. (Eunice)
79. Moto wa maombi. (Eunice)
80. Ni vigumu kwa watajiri kuingia kwa ufalme wa mbinguni. Haikusema haiwezekani. Kwa hiyo akisema ni vigumu kwa watajiri kuingia katika ufalme wa mbinguni anamaanisha inawezekana kuingia hupo lakini vigumu. (Bilhah)
81. Vijana wengi wanaambiwa waanze chini wanakataa ... Ukimwambia nilianzia chini wanasema, 'No haiwezikani,' lakini kumbe inawezekana! Even I nilianza chini nilikuwa na hela napata changamoto niliibiwa lakini tusikate tamaa, naenda na mwisho wa siku inawezekana. (Rhoda)
82. Nina nguvu zisizoleki. I'm unlimited. Nina nguvu. Ninaamini ... naweza kufanya jambo lolote as long as Mungu yupo pamoja na mimi. (Fibi)
83. Kwa sababu ni mwanamke wa TAFES nimebeba Mungu ndani yangu lakini nimebeba umama ndani yangu. Mwanamke wa TAFES kwa sababu anajua Mungu ana neema la Mungu, Biblia,

ndani yake, anabeba Mungu ndani yake. Kwa kila mambo anayoongeza unabeba uwanawake. (Fibi)

84. Kuna wengine hutofanikiwa. Ni kwa sababu amesema, "Mimi ni maskini sijafanikiwa, sina pesa," yeye anasema umaskini.... umaskini wa roho. (Fibi)

85. Kubless wengine kama Mungu aliambia Abraham, I bless you to be a blessing. (Ruth)

86. Nilikuwa mwaminifu katika kazi yangu. (Eunice)

87. Mimi ni mwamini ninaamini katika Biblia ninaposoma neno la Mungu. (Ruth)

88. Bible inatushape. (Fibi)

89. Na ignorance haina excuse ... pazia lile lilipasuka, wote tunaface Mungu direct.... Ukweli na uzima upo kwenye neno la Mungu. So mhubiri alichosema naamini ninatambua asimame na kutumia akili zake. (Priscilla)

90. Biblia inatuelekeza mafanikio. (Jochebed)

91. Timotheo wa pili sura ya tatu mstari wa kumi na sita Biblia inasema kila andiko linafaa kwa mafundisho ya kutuonya, kutuadhibisha, na kutufundisha. Kwa hiyo kila neno kwenye Biblia lina fundisho ambayo inatufanya tufanikiwe. (Lois)

92. Mungu anazungumza sana katika kitabu cha Deuteronomy kwamba ukimfuata Mungu, be sure hizi baraka zitaambatana na wewe. (Zipporah)

93. Kila kitu kina taratibu, kina principle, na utaratibu wa namna gani ya kupata hizo hela. (Zilpah)

94. Alivyoambia wana wa Israeli, ataangalia mashamba yako ... lakini haitupi excuse kuwa wavivu kwa sababu kuna changamoto hapo watu kutofanikiwa chochote kwa sababu wanasema, "Bwana, sisi kama unaweza ndege wa angani wanakula," kwa hiyo huyu anakaa tu. Sasa, that's wrong. Kwa sababu Mungu anasema asiyekula, "asiyefanya kazi na asile." Kwa hiyo lazima tuishi a balanced life. (Ruth)

95. Mistari mistari inategemeana. (Bilhah)

96. Kuna mambo mengi mengi mengi [katika] Agano ya Kale. Hatuwezi kusema "Haya ni ya iliyopita" lakini – not true. They also apply to us. (Damaris)

97. Baado [Ayubu] hakumwacha Mungu. (Salome)
98. Ayubu alikuwa mtu wa imani sana na hata alipata ugonjwa. (Susanna)
99. [Biblia] ni roadmap ya kila kitu, inamwongoza kila kitu. (Anna)
100. Mungu anaviruhusu ili sisi tutambue nafasi yake ya Baba kwetu. (Puah)
101. Anataka aone kwamba unamtumaini yeye kuliko kila kitu. (Lois)
102. Misuli ya kuendure ya kuvumilia taabu na shida. (Fibi)
103. Anaonyeka au ana imani zaidi kwamba yule ana kitu kile lakini baado anamwamini Mungu anamtumikia Mungu. (Anna)
104. Mungu anaweza kuamua ukapata vitu mara moja. Lakini mara nyingi anatoa kwa hatua akiendelea kukufundisha ili uweze kusimama kwake. (Susanna)
105. Nikiwa bilionea, je, roho yangu iko tayari kubeba haya mafanikio na kuendelea kukaa na Mungu? (Puah)
106. Nilifungua biashara, nilianza kufanya biashara ya duka nikafanya biashara nikafanya biashara. Then wakaja wezi usiku wakavunja wakavunja wakachukua baadhi ya vitu wakachukua vingine wakaacha vingine wakaacha. Moyo wangu iliinama, Oh God, what is this? Ilikuwa wakati ngumu. Nifanyeje? Mungu akasema tufanye kazi kwa idi, nikafanya kweli, nipate pesa nilitoa sadaka nihelp others help my family lakini wamekuja wezi wamevunja . . . Lakini katika changamoto pia kuna vitu unavijifunza. Kwa hiyo nikajifunza pia niweke hii, maybe milango hivi, niweke hii, niweke more security pale, na nini lakini nisiweke vitu vyote dukani niweke vichache na wale wanaokuja kuchuka vingine nisiweke vyote kwa mfano inawezekana kutokea kama hivyo kwa hiyo from there nikaendelea nikaendelea wakaja next time. Kuna siku tena walikuja walifanya uvamizi kuja na kwangu walikuta nimeboresha milango ile kwa hiyo hawakuweza na naendelea kumwomba Mungu anisaidie. Najua naweza nikaweza ulinzi wangu lakini Mungu ndio ni mlinzi. (Rhoda)
107. Kwa hiyo Biblia inatuambia kwamba Mungu ndio kila kitu yaani ndio yeye ni provider wa kila kitu. Na tunaambiwa kabisa kwamba ukiwa wewe ni medical doctor, sio kwa akili yako. Ni Mungu. (Lois)

108. Umeokoka, Mungu anakubariki sana kwa hiyo uendelee kukaa ndani ya wokovu, endelea kufuatilia na kujifunza Mungu anasema nini katika neno lake kuhusiana na yale ambao yanakuhusu kufanya kama wajibu. (Zipporah)
109. Moyoni utamshukuru Mungu. Lakini kusema kwa watu, "Ndiyo nimefanikiwa!" ni kama nikijidai—ni pride. (Eunice)
110. Sometimes unakuta labda kwa barabarani oh taka taka zipo maeneo, [watu wanasema] "Jamani serikali serikali tusaidie kuziokota takataka nje ya geti." Sasa mimi kama Mkristo natakia yaani naweza kuinitiate vitu, vitu vingine unaweza kutoka na kushuka kwa kufanyia mwenyewe. (Abigail)
111. Kila mahali sisi ni kiroho . . . Niko hapa na natakia kuishi kama mtu aliyeokoka kwa hiyo kwenye issues kama za corruption, issues za kuunderperformance, kuchelewa kazini, kutokuwa mwaminifu, hapa kanisani, za kazini ukiwa na kanisani ndiyo wa fikiri ndiyo hapa. (Eunice)
112. Shetani alivyopigana na watakatifu walimshinda kutumia damu ya mwandakondoo kwa jina la Yesu. (Damaris)
113. Yesu aliishi kimaskini aliteseka na sisi tuteseke? Hapana. (Rhoda)
114. Mungu anataka tufanikiwe kwamba tusiwe watu ambao tuko wanyonye, watu ambao hatuwezi kujihudumia wenyewe, hatuwezi kuhumudia pengine Mungu ametupatia. (Dorcas)
115. Kumtumikia Mungu kuna faida. Kumtumikia Mungu ni ulinzi. Kumtumikia Mungu ni amani. Kumtumikia Mungu ni ushindi. (Fibi)

Bibliography

Adeleye, Femi B. *The Preachers of a Different Gospel: A Pilgrim's Reflections on Contemporary Trends in Christianity*. Grand Rapids/Carlisle: Zondervan Academic/HippoBooks, 2011.

Adogame, Afeosemime U. "African Christianities and the Politics of Development from Below." *Hervormde Teologiese Studies* 72, no. 4 (2016): 1–11. doi:10.4102/hts.v72i4.4065.

Agadjanian, Victor. "Women's Religious Authority in a Sub-Saharan Setting: Dialectics of Empowerment and Dependency." *Gender and Society* 29, no. 6 (2015): 982–1008.

Ageboyin, Deji. "A Rethinking of Prosperity Teaching in the New Pentecostal Churches in Nigeria." *Black Theology* 4, no. 1 (January 2006): 70–86.

Aguwuom, Innocent Ogueri. "'Everything Is Permissible, but Not Everything Is Beneficial' (1 Cor. 10:23): Pneumatological Christology of the Parousian Church of Christ and (Ab)Uses of Spiritual Power in Nigerian Pentecostalism." In *Pentecostal Mission and Global Christianity*, edited by Wonsuk Ma, Veli-Matti Karkkainen, and J. Kwabena Asamoah-Gyadu, 67–86. Regnum Studies in Mission. Oxford: Regnum, 2014.

Akiri, Mwita. "The Prosperity Gospel: Its Concise Theology, Challenges and Opportunities." Presented at the Gafcon Jerusalem Conference 2018, Jerusalem, June 22, 2008. https://www.gafcon.org/resources/the-prosperity-gospel-its-concise-theology-challenges-and-opportunities.

Anderson, Allan. "The Gospel and African Religion." *International Review of Mission* 89 (2000): 373–83.

Anderson, Allan H. "African Pentecostalism and Prosperity: Continuity and Discontinuity." In *African Pentecostalism and World Christianity: Essays in Honor of J. Kwabena Asamoah-Gyadu*, edited by Nimi Wariboko and Adeshina Afolayan, 249–61. African Christian Studies. Eugene: Pickwick Publications, 2020. Kindle edition.

———. "The Newer Pentecostal and Charismatic Churches: The Shape of Future Christianity in Africa?" *Pneuma* 24, no. 2 (2002): 167–84.

Angrosino, Michael. *Doing Ethnographic and Observational Research*. The SAGE Qualitative Research Kit. London: SAGE, 2007. Kindle edition.

Archer, Margaret, Claire Decoteau, Philip Gorski, Daniel Little, Doug Porpora, Timothy Rutzou, Christian Smith, George Steinmetz, and Frederic Vandenverghe. "What Is Critical Realism?" Perspectives: A Newsletter of the ASA Theory Section (blog), December 23, 2016. http://www.asatheory.org/current-newsletter-online/what-is-critical-realism.

Arthur, Justice Anquandah. "Prosperity Theology(Ies): The Case of Mensa Otabil and the ICGC." *Interkulturelle Theologie* 43, no. 4 (2017): 401–19.

Asamoah-Gyadu, J. Kwabena. *African Charismatics: Current Developments within Independent Indigenous Pentecostalism in Ghana*. Leiden; Boston: Brill, 2005.

———. "'Get up . . . Take the Child . . . and Escape to Egypt': Transforming Christianity into a Non-Western Religion in Africa." *International Review of Mission* 100, no. 2 (November 2011): 337–54.

———. "Learning to Prosper by Wrestling and by Negotiation: Jacob and Esau in Contemporary African Pentecostal Hermeneutics." *Journal of Pentecostal Theology* 21, no. 1 (2012): 64–86.

———. "Pentecostalism in Africa and the Changing Face of Christian Mission: Pentecostal/Charismatic Renewal Movements in Ghana." *Mission Studies* 19, no. 2 (2002): 14–39.

———. "'To the Ends of the Earth': Mission, Migration and the Impact of African-Led Pentecostal Churches in the European Diaspora." *Mission Studies* 29, no. 1 (2012): 23–44.

Assohoto, Barnabé, and Samuel Ngwena. "Genesis." In *Africa Bible Commentary*, edited by Tukunboh Adeyemo, 2nd ed. 9–84. Grand Rapids: Zondervan, 2010.

Attanasi, K. "Introduction: The Plurality of Prosperity Theologies and Pentecostalisms." In *Pentecostalism and Prosperity: The Socio-Economics of the Global Charismatic Movement*, edited by Amos Yong and Katherine Attanasi, 1–12. London: Palgrave Macmillan, 2012. Kindle edition.

Balcomb, A. O. "Disenchanting Pentecostalism: A Response to Paul Gifford's 'Christianity, Development and Modernity in Africa.'" *Journal of Theology for Southern Africa* 159 (November 2017): 22–38.

Balcomb, Anthony Oswald. "Primal or Indigenous?" *Religion and Theology* 28, no. 1–2 (2021): 64.

Barron, Joshua Robert. "Is the Prosperity Gospel, Gospel? An Examination of the Prosperity and Productivity Gospels in African Christianity." *Conspectus: The Journal of the South African Theological Seminary* 33, no. 1 (2022): 88–103.

Bebbington, David W. *The Evangelical Quadrilateral: Characterizing the British Gospel Movement*. Waco: Baylor University Press, 2021.

Becker, Amy Julia. "Worshiping at the Church of Taylor: The Goodness of a Taylor Swift Show Points to Our Need for a Deeper Goodness." *The Christian Century* 141, no. 1 (January 2024): 72–74.

Bell, Judith, and Stephen Waters. *Doing Your Research Project: A Guide for First-Time Researchers*. 7th ed. Maidenhead: Open University Press, 2018. Ebook edition.

Bennett, Zoe. *Your MA in Theology: A Study Skills Handbook*. London: SCM, 2014.

Bernard, Russell H. *Research Methods in Anthropology: Qualitative and Quantitative Approaches*. 5th ed. Plymouth: AltaMira, 2011. Kindle edition.

Biwul, Joel K. T. "Preaching Biblically in the Nigerian Prosperity Gospel Context." *Africa Journal of Evangelical Theology* 32, no. 2 (2013): 121–34.

Blaikie, Norman, and Jan Priest. *Designing Social Research: The Logic of Anticipation*. 3rd edition. Cambridge: Polity, 2019. Kindle edition.

Boamah, Kwaku. *The Cross or Prosperity Gospel: Persecution and Martyrdom in the Early Church*. Carlisle: Langham Academic, 2022. Kindle edition.

Bongmba, Elias K. "Reflections on Thabo Mbekis African Renaissance." *Journal of Southern African Studies* 30, no. 2 (2004): 291–316.

Boniface-Malle, Anastasia. "Interpreting the Lament Psalms from the Tanzanian Context: Problems and Prospects." PhD thesis, Luther Seminary, 2000.

Bowler, Kate. *Blessed: A History of the American Prosperity Gospel*. Oxford: Oxford University Press, 2013. Kindle edition.

Brooks, Abigail, and Sharlene Nagy Hesse-Biber. "An Invitation to Feminist Research." In *Feminist Research Practice*, edited by Sharlene Nagy Hesse-Biber, 2–24. Thousand Oaks: SAGE, 2007.

Broyles, C. C. "Lament, Psalms Of." In *Dictionary of the Old Testament: Wisdom, Poetry and Writings*, edited by Tremper III Longman and Peter Enns, 384–99. Downers Grove: IVP Academic, 2008.

Burgess, Richard. "Megachurches and 'Reverse Mission.'" In *Handbook of Megachurches*, edited by Stephen Hunt, 243–68. Leiden: Brill, 2020, doi:10.1163/9789004412927.

Cameron, Helen, and Catherine Duce. *Researching Practice in Ministry and Mission: A Companion*. London: SCM, 2013. Kindle edition.

Carter, Jason A. *Inside the Whirlwind: The Book of Job through African Eyes*. Eugene: Pickwick Publications, 2017. Kindle edition.

Cezula, Ntozakhe Simon. "Reading the Bible in the African Context: Assessing Africa's Love Affair with Prosperity Gospel." *Stellenbosch Theological Journal* 1, no. 2 (2015): 131–53, doi:10.17570/stj.2015.v1n2.a06.

Chan, Simon. *Grassroots Asian Theology: Thinking the Faith from the Ground Up*. Downers Grove: IVP Academic, 2014. Kindle edition.

Chesnut, R. Andrew. "Prosperous Prosperity: Why the Health and Wealth Gospel Is Booming across the Globe." In *Pentecostalism and Prosperity:*

The Socio-Economics of the Global Charismatic Movement, edited by Amos Yong and Katherine Attanasi, 215–24. London: Palgrave Macmillan, 2012. Kindle edition.

Chike, Chigor. "Proudly African, Proudly Christian: The Roots of Christologies in the African Worldview." *Black Theology* 6, no. 2 (2008): 221–40, doi:10.1558/blth2008v6i2.221.

Clarke, Clifton. *Pentecostal Theology in Africa.* African Christian Studies Series. Eugene: Pickwick Publications, 2014. Kindle edition.

Comaroff, Jean. "Pentecostalism, Populism and the New Politics of Affects." In *Pentecostalism and Development: Churches, NGOs and Social Change in Africa*, edited by Dena Freeman, 41–66. London: Palgrave Macmillan UK, 2012. Ebook edition. Accessed at: https://ebookcentral.proquest.com/lib/smbc/detail.action?docID=1058303.

Comaroff, Jean, and John Comaroff. "Ethnography on an Awkward Scale: Postcolonial Anthropology and the Violence of Abstraction." *Ethnography* 4, no. 2 (June 1, 2003): 147–79.

Cox, Roland Paul. "Culturological Analysis of 'The Culture Test' and The 3D Gospel." *Missiology* 52, no. 1 (January 2024): 56–73. https://doi.org/10.1177/00918296231206593.

Cozens, Simon. "Shame Cultures, Fear Cultures, and Guilt Cultures: Reviewing the Evidence." *International Bulletin of Mission Research* 42, no. 4 (2018): 326–36. https://doi.org/10.1177/2396939318764087.

Creswell, John W. *Educational Research: Planning, Conducting, and Evaluating Quantitative and Qualitative Research.* 4th edition. Boston: Pearson, 2011.

Darkwa Amanor, Kwabena J. "Pentecostal and Charismatic Churches in Ghana and the African Culture: Confrontation or Compromise?" *Journal of Pentecostal Theology* 18, no. 1 (2009): 123–40.

Dale, Moyra. *Islam and Women: Hagar's Heritage.* Oxford: Regnum Books International, 2022. Kindle edition.

Deacon, Gregory, and Damaris Seleina Parsitau. "Empowered to Submit: Pentecostal Women in Nairobi." *Journal of Religion & Society* 19 (2017): 1–17.

Dilger, Hansjörg. "Healing the Wounds of Modernity: Salvation, Community and Care in a Neo-Pentecostal Church in Dar Es Salaam, Tanzania." *Journal of Religion in Africa* 37, no. 1 (2007): 59–83.

Donovan, Vincent. *Christianity Rediscovered.* London: SCM Press, 2012. Kindle edition.

Doss, Gorden R. "A Malawian Christian Theology of Wealth and Poverty." *International Bulletin of Missionary Research* 35, no. 3 (2011): 148–52.

Drønen, Tomas Sundnes. "Material Development and Spiritual Empowerment?: Pentecostalism in Northern Cameroon." *PentecoStudies* 14, no. 2 (2015): 205–18, doi:10.1558/ptcs.v14i2.26100.

———. "Weber, Prosperity and the Protestant Ethic: Some Reflections on Pentecostalism and Economic Development." *Svensk Missionstidskrift* 100, no. 3 (2012): 321–35.

Dube, Musa W. "Between the Spirit and the Word: Reading the Gendered African Pentecostal Bible." *Hervormde Teologiese Studies* 70, no. 1 (2014): 1–7, doi:10.4102/hts.v70i1.2651.

Edwards, Vincent. "Proverbs Entrepreneurial Lessons for Today: Proverbs 31:10–31." *Journal of Biblical Theology* 4, no. 1 (January 2021): 203–12.

Ehioghae, Efe M. "Prosperity Gospel and the Burden of Poverty: The Nigerian Conundrum." *Valley View University Journal of Theology* 2 (2012): 31–46.

Ehioghae, Efe M., and Joseph A. Olanrewaju. "A Theological Evaluation of the Utopian Image of Prosperity Gospel and the African Dilemma." *IOSR Journal of Humanities and Social Science* 20, no. 8 (2015): 69–75.

Eriksen, Annelin, Ruy Llera Blanes, and Michelle MacCarthy. *Going to Pentecost: An Experimental Approach to Studies in Pentecostalism* Oxford; New York: Berghahn Books, 2019. www.jstor.org/stable/j.ctv9hj8pw.12.

Erlacher, Jolene, and Katy White. *Mobilizing Gen Z: Challenges and Opportunities for the Global Age of Missions*. Littleton, CO: William Carey Publishing, 2022.

Estes, D.J. "Wisdom and Biblical Theology." In *Dictionary of the Old Testament: Wisdom, Poetry and Writings*, edited by Tremper Longman III and Peter Enns, 853–58. Downers Grove: IVP Academic, 2008.

Falconer, Robert. *Spectacular Atonement: Envisioning the Cross of Christ in an African Perspective*. Bryanston: South African Theological Seminary Press, 2015.

Fatokun, Samson. "Women and Leadership in Nigerian Pentecostal Churches." *Studia Historiae Ecclesiasticae* 32, no. 3 (December 2006): 193–205.

Folarin, George O. "Contemporary State of the Prosperity Gospel in Nigeria." *The Asia Journal of Theology* 21, no. 1 (April 2007): 69–95.

Frahm-Arp, Maria. "Pentecostalism, Politics, and Prosperity in South Africa." *Religions* 9, no. 10 (October 2018): 1–16, doi:10.3390/rel9100298.

Freeman, Dena. "The Pentecostal Ethic and the Spirit of Development." In *Pentecostalism and Development: Churches, NGOs and Social Change in Africa*, edited by Dena Freeman, 1–38. London: Palgrave Macmillan UK, 2012. Ebook edition. Accessed at: https://ebookcentral.proquest.com/lib/smbc/detail.action?docID=1058303.

Freeman, S. E., and Richard D Calenberg. "Understanding Honor-Shame Dynamics for Ministry in Sub-Saharan Africa." *Bibliotheca Sacra* 175, no. 700 (October 2018): 425–38.

Gabaitse, Rosinah. "Pentecostal Hermeneutics and the Marginalisation of Women." *Scriptura* 114 (2015): 1–12.

Gabrielson, Timothy A. "Along the Grain of Salvation History: A Suggestion for Evangelical Hermeneutics." *Trinity Journal* 36, no. 1 (2015): 71–90.

Galgalo, Joseph D. "Syncretism in African Christianity: A Boon or a Bane?" In *African Contextual Realities*, edited by Rodney L. Reed, kindle loc. 1712–2107. Africa Society of Evangelical Theology Series. Carlisle: Langham Global Library, 2018. Kindle edition.

Gallagher, Sarita D. "The Elephant in the Room: Towards a Paradigm Shift in Missiological Education." In *Papers*, 91:108–25. Wilmore, Kentucky: First Fruits Press, 2017. https://place.asburyseminary.edu/firstfruitspapers/92.

Gbote, Eric Z. M., and Selaelo Thias Kgatla. "Prosperity Gospel: A Missiological Assessment." *Hervormde Teologiese Studies* 70, no. 1 (2014): 1–10, doi:10.4102/hts.v70i1.2105.

Georges, Jayson. *Ministering in Patronage Cultures: Biblical Models and Missional Implications*. Downers Grove: IVP Academic, 2019. Kindle edition.

———. *The 3D Gospel: Ministry in Guilt, Shame, and Fear Cultures*. Timē Press, 2014.

Gifford, Paul. "'Africa Shall Be Saved'. An Appraisal of Reinhard Bonnke's Pan-African Crusade." *Journal of Religion in Africa* 17, no. 1 (1987): 63–92. https://doi.org/10.2307/1581076.

———. "Christian Fundamentalism and Development." *Review of African Political Economy*, no. 52 (1991): 9–20.

———. "Ghana's Charismatic Churches." *Journal of Religion in Africa* 24, no. 3 (1994): 241–65. https://doi.org/10.2307/1581301.

———. "The Development and Political Role of Africa's Pentecostal Churches." "Small" States in International Politics. Konrad Adenauer Stiftung, 2015.

Gifford, Paul J. "Expecting Miracles: The Prosperity Gospel in Africa." *The Christian Century* 124, no. 14 (July 10, 2007): 20–24.

Gifford, Paul, and Trad Nogueira-Godsey. "The Protestant Ethic and African Pentecostalism: A Case Study." *Journal for the Study of Religion* 24, no. 1 (2011): 5–22.

Gitau, Wanjiru M. "SATS Symposium: meet the African scholar." YouTube, November 12, 2021. https://www.youtube.com/watch?v=dVtlNIRpklI.

———. *Megachurch Christianity Reconsidered: Millennials and Social Change in African Perspective*. Downers Grove: IVP Academic, 2018. Kindle edition.

Golo, Ben-Willie K. "Africa's Poverty and Its Neo-Pentecostal 'Liberators': An Ecotheological Assessment of Africa's Prosperity Gospellers." *Pneuma* 35, no. 3 (2013): 366–84. https://doi.org/10.1163/15700747-12341366.

Gorman, Michael J. "Cruciform or Resurrectiform?: Paul's Paradoxical Practice of Participation in Christ." *Ex Auditu* 33 (2017): 60–83.

———. "Effecting the New Covenant: A (Not so) New, New Testament Model for the Atonement." *Ex Auditu* 26 (2010): 26–59.

Habtu, Tewoldemedhin. "Proverbs." In *Africa Bible Commentary*, edited by Tukunboh Adeyemo, 2nd ed., 773–812. Grand Rapids: Zondervan, 2010.

Hackett, Rosalind I. J. "Women, Rights Talk, and African Pentecostalism." *Religious Studies and Theology* 36, no. 2 (2017): 245–59. https://doi.org/10.1558/rsth.35161.

Hadebe, Nontando Margaret. "'Listening to the Elders of African Theology': Ubuntu and Trinitarian Theology as a Response to the Call for the Integration of Inculturation and Liberation Theologies." *Grace & Truth* 33, no. 3 (November 2016): 26–38.

Harries, Jim. "Overcoming Invented Ogres: African Traditional Religions and World Religions in African Christian Perspective." *Evangelical Review of Theology* 42, no. 2 (April 2018): 171–84.

———. "Re-Strategising Mission (and Development) Intervention into Africa to Avoid Corruption, the Prosperity Gospel and Missionary Ignorance." *Transformation* 38, no. 4 (October 1, 2021): 359–72. https://doi.org/10.1177/0265378821994595.

Haruna, Ugah. "Salvation: Prosperity or Poverty." Presented at the Africa Society for Evangelical Theology Conference, Nairobi, March 4, 2022.

Hasu, Paivi. "Prosperity Gospels and Enchanted Worldviews: Two Responses to Socio-Economic Transformation in Tanzanian Pentecostal Christianity." In *Pentecostalism and Development: Churches, NGOs and Social Change in Africa*, edited by Dena Freeman, 67–87. London: Palgrave Macmillan UK, 2012. Ebook edition. Accessed at: https://ebookcentral.proquest.com/lib/smbc/detail.action?docID=1058303.

———. "World Bank & Heavenly Bank in Poverty & Prosperity: The Case of Tanzanian Faith Gospel." *Review of African Political Economy* 33 (September 1, 2006): 679–92. https://doi.org/10.1080/03056240601119257.

Hayes, Katherine Murphey. *Proverbs*. Vol. 18 of *New Collegeville Bible Commentary*. Collegeville: Liturgical Press, 2013.

Haynes, Naomi. "Pentecostalism and the Morality of Money: Prosperity, Inequality, and Religious Sociality on the Zambian Copperbelt." *The Journal of the Royal Anthropological Institute* 18, no. 1 (2012): 123–39.

———. "'Zambia Shall Be Saved!': Prosperity Gospel Politics in a Self-Proclaimed Christian Nation." *Nova Religio* 19, no. 1 (August 2015): 5–24, oi:10.1525/nr.2015.19.1.5.

Hennink, Monique, and Bonnie N. Kaiser. "Sample Sizes for Saturation in Qualitative Research: A Systematic Review of Empirical Tests." *Social Science & Medicine* 292 (January 1, 2022): 1–10. https://doi.org/10.1016/j.socscimed.2021.114523.

Heuser, Andreas. "Charting African Prosperity Gospel Economies." *Hervormde Teologiese Studies* 72, no. 4 (2016): 1–9, doi:10.4102/hts.v72i4.3823.

———, "Religio-Scapes of Prosperity Gospel: an Introduction." In *Pastures of Plenty*, edited by Andreas Heuser Peter Lang GmbH, Internationaler Verlag der Wissenschaften: Frankfurt am Main, 2015) 15–30.

Hicks, Douglas A. "Prosperity, Theology and Economy." In *Pentecostalism and Prosperity: The Socio-Economics of the Global Charismatic Movement*, edited by Amos Yong and Katherine Attanasi, 224–38. London: Palgrave Macmillan, 2012. Kindle edition.

Hiebert, Paul G. *Anthropological Insights for Missionaries*. 17th edition. Grand Rapids: Baker Academic, 1986.

"Higher Education Students Admission, Enrolment and Graduation Statistics 2012/13-2017/18." Tanzania Commission for Universities, 2018. https://tcu.go.tz/?q=content/higher-education-statistics

Hodgson, Dorothy L. *Gender, Justice, and the Problem of Culture: From Customary Law to Human Rights in Tanzania*. Bloomington: Indiana University Press, 2017.

Ilo, Stan Chu, and Joseph O. Ogbonnaya. "Introduction." In *The Church as Salt and Light : Path to an African Ecclesiology of Abundant Life*, edited by Stan Chu Ilo, Joseph O. Ogbonnaya, and Alex Ojacor, xiii–xxi. Eugene: Pickwick, 2011.

International Fellowship of Evangelical Students. "What We Believe." IFES (blog), 2019 2014. https://ifesworld.org/en/beliefs/?switch_language=en.

Ireland, Jerry M. "African Traditional Religion and Pentecostal Churches in Lusaka, Zambia: An Assessment." *Journal of Pentecostal Theology* 21, no. 2 (2012): 260–77, doi:10.1163/17455251-02102006.

James, Deborah. "New Subjectivities: Aspiration, Prosperity and the New Middle Class." *African Studies* 78, no. 1 (January 2, 2019): 33–50, doi:10.1080/00020184.2018.1540516.

Je'adayibe, Gwamna Dogara. "'Where Your Treasure Is': A Consideration of Jesus' Teaching on Possessions." *Africa Journal of Evangelical Theology* 20, no. 1 (2001): 29–45.

Jennings, Willie James. *After Whiteness: An Education in Belonging*. Grand Rapids: Eerdmans, 2020. Kindle edition.

Jervis, L. Ann. *Galatians*. Understanding the Bible Commentary Series. Grand Rapids: Baker Books, 2012.

Joset, Timothée. "The Priesthood of All Students? Historical, Theological and Missiological Foundations of a University Ministry: The International Fellowship of Evangelical Students (IFES)." PhD thesis, Durham, 2021.

Kalu, Ogbu. *African Pentecostalism: An Introduction*. Oxford: Oxford University Press, 2008.

Kalu, Ogbu Uke. "Preserving a Worldview: Pentecostalism in the African Maps of the Universe." *Pneuma* 24, no. 2 (2002): 110–37.

Kategile, Mary L. "The Bible and Gender Equality in Church Leadership in Tanzania." *Stellenbosch Theological Journal* 6, no. 1 (2020): 41–54.

Katongole, Emmanuel. *Born from Lament: The Theology and Politics of Hope in Africa*. Grand Rapids: Eerdmans, 2017. Kindle edition.

Kigame, Reuben, Anne Njoroge, and Eunice Kamaara. "From Knowledge to Wisdom: An African Perspective to Life." *Theologies and Cultures* 12, no. 2 (December 2015): 85–109.

Kipacha, Ahmad, Justina Dugbazah, and Simeon Mesaki. "Religious Teachings and Development Concepts in Tanzania: Insights from Tanga and Arumeru." In *Religion and State in Tanzania Revisited: Reflections from 50 Years of Independence*, edited by Thomas Ndaluka and Frans Wijsen, 107–28. Münster: Lit Verlag, 2014.

Kirkpatrick, David C. "C. René Padilla and the Origins of Integral Mission in Post-War Latin America." *The Journal of Ecclesiastical History* 67, no. 2 (April 2016): 351–71, doi:10.1017/S0022046915001670.

Kraft, Charles H. *Anthropology for Christian Witness*. Maryknoll: Orbis, 2013. Kindle edition.

Kubwimana, Joel. "An Examination of Contemporary Rwandans Understanding of Salvation and a Holistic African Response." Presented at the Africa Society for Evangelical Theology Conference, Nairobi, March 5, 2022.

Landman, Christina. "Mercy Amba Ewudziwa Oduyoye: Mother of Our Stories." *Studia Historiae Ecclesiasticae* 33, no. 1 (May 2007): 187–204.

Lansky, Sam. "Taylor Swift: 2023 Person of the Year." Time Magazine, December 6, 2023. https://time.com/6342806/person-of-the-year-2023-taylor-swift/.

Larbi, Emmanuel Kingsley. "The Nature of Continuity and Discontinuity of Ghanaian Pentecostal Concept of Salvation in African Cosmology." *Asian Journal of Pentecostal Studies* 5, no. 1 (January 2002): 87–106.

Lassiter, Kate. "Seeking Wisdom, Naming Puzzles: Pastoral Hopes for Theological Ethnography." *Practical Matters Journal* Spring 2010, no. 3 (March 1, 2010): 1–5. http://practicalmattersjournal.org/2010/03/01/seeking-wisdom/.

Laurent, Pierre-Joseph. "Transnationalisation and Local Transformations: The Example of the Church of Assemblies of God of Burkina Faso." In *Between Babel and Pentecost: Transnational Pentecostalism in Africa and Latin America*, edited by Andre Corten and Ruth R. Marshall-Fratani, 256–73. Bloomington: Indiana University Press, 2001.

Lauterbach, Karen. "Fakery and Wealth in African Charismatic Christianity: Moving beyond the Prosperity Gospel as Script." In *Faith in African Lived Christianity: Bridging Anthropological and Theological Perspectives*, edited by Karen Lauterbach and Mika Vähäkangas, 111–32. Brill, 2020, doi:10.1163/j.ctvrxk46s.10.

Lewison, Elsie. "Pentecostal Power and the Holy Spirit of Capitalism: Re-Territorialization in the Charismatic Cosmology." *Symposia* 3, no. 1 (2011): 31–54.

Liamputtong, Pranee. *Researching the Vulnerable: A Guide to Sensitive Research Methods*. 1st edition. London: SAGE, 2006.

Liesen, Frank. "Contextualizing the Prosperity Gospel in Germany: A Theological Assessment." *Contemporary Issues in Evangelical Missiology* 2, no. 1 (2021): 52–73.

Lindhardt, Martin. "'If You Are Saved You Cannot Forget Your Parents': Agency, Power, and Social Respositioning in Tanzanian Born-Again Christianity." *Journal of Religion in Africa* 40, no. 3 (2010): 240–72, doi:10.1163/157006610X530330.

———. "Mediating Money:: Materiality and Spiritual Warfare in Tanzanian Charismatic Christianity." In *The Anthropology of Global Pentecostalism and Evangelicalism*, edited by Joel Robbins, Simon Coleman, and Rosalind I. J. Hackett, 147–60. New York: NYU Press, 2015.

———. "More than Just Money: The Faith Gospel and Occult Economies in Contemporary Tanzania." *Nova Religio* 13, no. 1 (August 2009): 41–67, doi:10.1525/nr.2009.13.1.41.

———. "The Ambivalence of Power: Charismatic Christianity and Occult Forces in Urban Tanzania." *Nordic Journal of Religion and Society* 22, no. 1 (2009).

Longman, Tremper, and Raymond B. Dillard. *An Introduction to the Old Testament*. 2nd ed. Grand Rapids: Zondervan Academic, 2006.

Lubaale, Nicta. "The Emerging Church in Africa and Holistic Mission: Challenges and Opportunities." In *Holistic Mission: God's Plan for God's People*, edited by Brian Woolnough and Wonsuk Ma, 76–85. Oxford: Regnum Studies in Mission, 2010. Kindle edition.

Lucas, E.C. "Wisdom Theology." In *Dictionary of the Old Testament: Wisdom, Poetry and Writings*, edited by Tremper III Longman and Peter Enns, 901–12. Downers Grove: IVP Academic, 2008.

Lugazia, Faith. "Towards an African Inculturation Biblical Pneumatology: A Response to the Rise of Neo-Pentecostalism in Tanzanian Christianity." PhD thesis, Luther Seminary, 2010.

Lyimo, Godrick Efraim, and Aud V. Tonnessen. *Empowerment and Autonomy of Women*. Eugene: Wipf and Stock, 2016. Kindle edition.

Ma, Julie C., Wonsuk Ma, and Andrew F. Walls. *Mission in the Spirit*. Eugene: Wipf and Stock, 2011. Kindle edition.

Ma, Wonsuk. "Blessing in Pentecostal Theology and Mission." In *Pentecostal Mission and Global Christianity*, edited by Wonsuk Ma, Veli-Matti Karkkainen, and J. Kwabena Asamoah-Gyadu, 272–91. Oxford: Regnum Studies in Mission, 2014. Kindle edition.

Macchia, Frank D. "A Call for Careful Discernment: A Theological Response to Prosperity Teaching." In *Pentecostalism and Prosperity: The Socio-Economics of the Global Charismatic Movement,* edited by Amos Yong and Katherine Attanasi, 224–38. London: Palgrave Macmillan, 2012. Kindle edition.

Magesa, Laurenti. *African Religion: The Moral Traditions of Abundant Life.* New York: Orbis, 2014.

———. "Christian Discipleship In Africa In The 21st Century." *AFER* 36, no. 5 (1994): 283–99.

Manus, Chris U., and Des Obioma. "Preaching the 'green Gospel' in Our Environment: A Re-Reading of Genesis 1:27–28 in the Nigerian Context." *HTS Theological Studies* 72, no. 4 (2016): 1–6, doi:10.4102/hts.v72i4.3054.

Manyonganise, Molly. "Oppressive and Liberative: A Zimbabwean Woman's Reflections on Ubuntu." *Verbum et Ecclesia* 36, no. 2 (2015): 1–7, doi:10.4102/ve.v36i2.1438.

Marshall, Ruth. "Power in the Name of Jesus." *Review of African Political Economy*, no. 52 (1991): 21–37.

Marshall-Fratani, Ruth. "Mediating the Global and the Local in Nigerian Pentecostalism." *Journal of Religion in Africa* 28, no. 3 (1998): 278–315.

Masango, M. J. S. "African Spirituality That Shapes the Concept of Ubuntu." *Verbum et Ecclesia* 27, no. 3 (2006): 930–43.

Mashau, Thinandavha D., and Mookgo S. Kgatle. "Prosperity Gospel and the Culture of Greed in Post-Colonial Africa: Constructing an Alternative African Christian Theology of Ubuntu." *Verbum et Ecclesia* 40, no. 1 (2019): 1–8, doi:10.4102/ve.v40i1.1901.

Maura, Michael Otieno. "The Blessings of the True Gospel." In *Prosperity? Seeking the True Gospel*, 91–106. Nairobi: African Christian Textbooks, 2015.

Maxwell, David J. "'Delivered from the Spirit of Poverty?': Pentecostalism, Prosperity and Modernity in Zimbabwe." *Journal of Religion in Africa* 28, no. 3 (1998): 350–73.

Mbamalu, Abiola. "'Prosperity a Part of the Atonement': An Interpretation of 2 Corinthians 8:9." *Verbum et Ecclesia* 36, no. 1 (November 3, 2015): 8, doi:10.4102/ve.v36i1.1418.

Mbe, Akoko Robert. "From Asceticism to a Gospel of Prosperity: The Case of Full Gospel Mission Cameroon." *Journal for the Study of Religion* 17, no. 2 (2004): 47–66.

Mboya, Thomas J. B. "Gift Challenges and Transforms Prosperity Gospel." *AFER* 58, no. 1–2 (March 2016): 16–42.

Mbugua, Ken. "A False Gospel." In *Prosperity? Seeking the True Gospel*, 1–14. Nairobi: African Christian Textbooks, 2015.

———. "The Gospel Life." In *Prosperity? Seeking the True Gospel*, 49–64. Nairobi: African Christian Textbooks, 2015.

Mburu, Elizabeth. *African Hermeneutics*. Carlisle: HippoBooks, 2019. Kindle edition.

McKinnon, Allan Smith. "On Being Charismatic Brethren: Roots and Shoots of Pentecostal Evangelicalism in Tanzania." PhD thesis, University of Birmingham, 2017.

Meek, Esther Lightcap. *A Little Manual for Knowing*. Eugene: Cascade, 2014. Kindle edition.

Merz, Johannes. "The Culture Problem: How the Honor/Shame Issue Got the Wrong End of the Anthropological Stick." *Missiology* 48, no. 2 (April 2020): 127–41. https://doi.org/10.1177/0091829619887179.

Messi-Metogo, Eloi. "Religious Indifference and Critique in Traditional Africa." In *Is Africa Incurably Religious?: Secularization and Discipleship in Africa*, edited by Benno van den Toren, Joseph Bosco Bangura, and Richard E. Seed, 30–49. Oxford: Regnum Books International, 2020. Kindle edition.

Methula, Dumisane W. "Decolonising the Commercialisation and Commodification of the University and Theological Education in South Africa." *HTS Teologiese Studies / Theological Studies* 73, no. 3 (November 15, 2017): 1–7, doi:10.4102/hts.v73i3.4585.

Meyer, Birgit. "Christianity in Africa: From African Independent to Pentecostal-Charismatic Churches." *Annual Review of Anthropology* 33 (2004): 447–74.

———. "Commodities and the Power of Prayer: Pentecostalist Attitudes Towards Consumption in Contemporary Ghana." *Development and Change* 29 (December 16, 2002): 751–76, doi:10.1111/1467-7660.00098.

———. "'Delivered from the Powers of Darkness': Confessions of Satanic Riches in Christian Ghana." *Africa* 65, no. 2 (1995): 236–55.

———. "Pentecostalism and Neo-Liberal Capitalism: Faith, Prosperity and Vision in African Pentecostal-Charismatic Churches." *Journal for the Study of Religion* 20, no. 2 (2007): 5–28.

Mhando, Nandera Ernest, Loreen Maseno, Kupakwashe Mtata, and Mathew Senga. "Modes of Legitimation by Female Pentecostal-Charismatic Preachers in East Africa: A Comparative Study in Kenya and Tanzania." *Journal of Contemporary African Studies* 36, no. 3 (July 3, 2018): 319–33, doi:10.1080/02589001.2018.1504162.

Miller, Donald E., and Tetsunao Yamamori. *Global Pentecostalism: The New Face of Christian Social Engagement*. Berkeley: University of California Press, 2007. Kindle edition.

Moenga, Micah. "Salvation: Prosperity or Poverty. An Assessment of African Pentecostal Christianity." Presented at the Africa Society for Evangelical Theology Conference, Nairobi, March 4, 2022.

Morris, Simon Conway. "Life's Solution: What Happens When We Re-Run the Tape of Life?" *Studies: An Irish Quarterly Review* 97, no. 386 (2008): 205–17.

Moschella, Mary Clark. *Ethnography as Pastoral Practice: An Introduction*. Cleveland: Pilgrim Press, 2008.

Mtata, Kenneth. "An African Theology of Work: A Lutheran Perspective." *LWF Documentation* 56 (December 2011): 35–49.

Mugambi, Kyama M. *A Spirit of Revitalization: Urban Pentecostalism in Kenya*. Waco: Baylor University Press, 2020. Kindle edition.

Murphy, Roland. *Proverbs*. Vol. 22 of *Word Biblical Commentary*. Nashville: Thomas Nelson, 1998.

Musau, Patrick Mwania. *The African Woman as an Agent of Evangelization : Her Role and Function in the Mission Activity of the Church in Africa*. Aachen: Shaker Verlag GmbH, 2009.

Mwaura, Philomena N. "Gender and Power in African Christianity: African Instituted Churches and Pentecostal Churches." In *African Christianity: An African Story*, edited by Ogbu Kalu, 410–45. Pretoria: University of Pretoria, 2005.

Mwaura, Philomena N., and Damaris Seleina Parsitau. "Gendered Charisma: Women in the Mission in the Neo-Pentecostal Churches and Charismatic Movements in Kenya." In *Putting Names with Faces*, edited by Christine Lienemann-Perrin, Atola Long Kumer, and Afrie Songco Joye, 123–46. Nashville: Abingdon Press, 2012.

Nel, Marius. *The Prosperity Gospel in Africa: An African Pentecostal Hermeneutical Consideration*. Eugene: Wipf & Stock, 2020. Kindle edition.

Ngaruiya, David. "Seven Dimensions of Salvation in African Christianity." Presented at the Africa Society for Evangelical Theology Conference, Nairobi, March 5, 2022.

Ngong, David Tonghou. "Salvation and Materialism in African Theology." *Studies in World Christianity* 15, no. 1 (2009): 1–21, doi:10.3366/E135499010900032X.

Ngowi, Honest Prosper. "Economic Development and Change in Tanzania since Independence: The Political Leadership Factor." *African Journal of Political Science and International Relations* 3, no. 4 (2009): 259–67.

Ngwobia, Ukoha, Jean Bosco Kambale, and Mathias Ngomo. "Misleading Theologies of Wealth and Poverty in the Context of Faith." In *Addressing Contextual Misleading Theologies in Africa Today*, edited by Bosela E. Eale and Njoroge J. Ngige, 204–304. Regnum Studies in Mission. Oxford: Regnum International, 2020.

Nida, Eugene A. *Customs and Cultures: The Communication of the Christian Faith*. 2nd ed. Pasadena: William Carey Library, 2000.

Niemandt, Nelus. "Rediscovering Joy in Costly and Radical Discipleship in Mission." *Hervormde Teologiese Studies* 72, no. 4 (2016): 1–7, doi:10.4102/hts.v72i4.3831.

———. "The Prosperity Gospel, the Decolonisation of Theology, and the Abduction of Missionary Imagination." *Missionalia* 45, no. 3 (2017): 203–19, doi:10.7832/45-3-199.

Nihinlola, Emiola. "Between Prosperity and Spirituality: A Theological Examination of the Perspective of the Church in the 21st Century African Society." *Ogbomoso Journal of Theology* 11 (2006): 29–41.

———. "'By His Wounds We Are Healed': A Theological Examination of the Nature of Healing in the Atonement." *Ogbomoso Journal of Theology* 18, no. 1 (2013): 19–26.

Njoroge, Nyambura J. "Let's Celebrate the Power of Naming." In *African Women, Religion and Health: Essays in Honour of Mercy Amba Ewudziwa Oduyoye*, edited by Isabel Apawo Phiri and Sarojini Nadar, 59–74. Eugene: Wipf & Stock, 2012.

Nkansah-Obrempong, James. "The Contemporary Theological Situation in Africa: An Overview." *Evangelical Review of Theology* 31, no. 2 (April 2007): 140–50.

Nnamunga, Gerard Majella. "Decolonising African Theology: Challenges from within and Trajectories." *Interreligious Studies and Intercultural Theology* 5, no. 1–2 (July 22, 2021): 121–28, doi:10.1558/isit.20561.

Obadare, Ebenezer. "'Raising Righteous Billionaires': The Prosperity Gospel Reconsidered." *Hervormde Teologiese Studies* 72, no. 4 (2016): 1–8, doi:10.4102/hts.v72i4.3571.

Ogero, Okelloh. "Reorienting Understanding of Salvation in the Light of Ubuntu." Presented at the Africa Society for Evangelical Theology Conference, Nairobi, March 5, 2022.

Ogungbile, David. "African Pentecostalism and the Prosperity Gospel." In *Pentecostal Theology in Africa*. African Christian Studies Series, edited by Clifton R. Clarke, kindle loc.3434-3884. Eugene: Pickwick, 2014. Kindle edition.

Ojo, Matthews A. "Pentecostalism, Public Accountability and Governance in Nigeria." *Ogbomoso Journal of Theology* 13, no. 1 (2008): 110–33.

Okorocha, Cyril C. "Religious Conversion in Africa: Its Missiological Implications." *Mission Studies* 9, no. 2 (1992): 168–81.

Olademo, Oyeronke. "New Dimensions in Nigerian Women's Pentecostal Experience: The Case of DODIM, Nigeria." *Journal of World Christianity* 5, no. 1 (2012): 62–74, doi:10.5325/jworlchri.5.1.0062.

Omenyo, Cephas. "Charismatic Churches in Ghana and Contextualization." *Exchange* 31, no. 3 (2002): 252–77.

Orobator, Agbonkhianmeghe E. *Religion and Faith in Africa: Confessions of an Animist*. Maryknoll: Orbis Books, 2018.

Oyugi, Peter Mdebe. "Why Prosperity Gospel Preachers Are Prospering While Most of Their Members Are Suffering." In *Christianity and Suffering: African*

Perspectives, edited by Rodney L. Reed. Africa Society of Evangelical Theology Series. Carlisle: Langham Global Library, 2017. Kindle Edition.

Padilla, C. René. *What Is Integral Mission?* Global Voices, edited by Rebecca Breekveldt. Oxford: Regnum Books International, 2021. Kindle edition.

Parsitau, Damaris S. "Agents of Gendered Change: NGOs and Pentecostal Movements as Agents of Social Transformation in Urban Kenya." In *The Pentecostal Ethic and the Spirit of Development: Churches, NGO and Social Change in Neo-Liberal Africa*, edited by Dena Freeman, 203–20. London: Palgrave Macmillan, 2012. Ebook edition. Accessed at: https://ebookcentral.proquest.com/lib/smbc/detail.action?docID=1058303.

Pattison, Stephen. "Some Straw for the Bricks: A Basic Introduction to Theological Reflection." In *The Blackwell Reader in Pastoral and Practical Theology*, edited by James Woodward and Stephen Pattison, 135–45. Oxford: Blackwell, 2000.

Peterson, Daniel J. "We Preach Christ Crucified: Rejecting the Prosperity Gospel and Responding to Feminist Criticism Using Luther's Second Theology of the Cross." *Dialog* 48, no. 2 (2009): 194–201.

"Pew-Templeton Global Religious Futures Project: Tanzania." Accessed September 26, 2022. www.globalreligiousfutures.org.

Prosén, Martina. "Abundant Life—Holistic Soteriology as Motivation for Socio-Political Engagement: A Pentecostal and Missional Perspective." In *The Routledge Handbook of African Theology*, edited by Elias Kifon Bongmba, 303–19. London; New York: Routledge, 2020. Ebook edition. https://www.perlego.com/book/1580237/the-routledge-handbook-of-african-theology-pdf

Quayesi-Amakye, Joseph. "A Yeast in the Flour: Pentecostalism as the African Realisation of the Gospel." *Studia Historiae Ecclesiasticae* 42, no. 3 (2016): 71–84.

———. "Prosperity and Prophecy in African Pentecostalism." *Journal of Pentecostal Theology* 20, no. 2: 291–305. Accessed February 5, 2020.

Quinn, Karl. "She Came, We Saw, She Conquered: What Taylor Swift Taught Us about Ourselves." The Sydney Morning Herald, February 14, 2024.

Randles, Jennifer, Lynne Gerber, and Orit Avishai. "The Feminist Ethnographer's Dilemma: Reconciling Progressive Research Agendas with Fieldwork Realities." *Journal of Contemporary Ethnography* 42, no. 2 (2013): 1–33.

Ras, Isabella F. "Broken Bodies and Present Ghosts: Ubuntu and African Women's Theology." *HTS Teologiese Studies / Theological Studies* 73, no. 3 (October 31, 2017): 7, doi:10.4102/hts.v73i3.4651.

Richards, E. Randolph, and Brandon J. O'Brien. *Misreading Scripture with Western Eyes: Removing Cultural Blinders to Better Understand the Bible*. Downers Grove: IVP, 2012.

Robbins, Joel. "World Christianity and the Reorganization of Disciplines: On the Emerging Dialogue Between Anthropology and Theology." In *Faith* in *African Lived Christianity: Bridging Anthropological and Theological Perspectives*, edited by Karen Lauterbach and Mika Vahakangas, 15–37. Brill, 2020, doi:10.1163/j.ctvrxk46s.10.

Robert, Dana L. "World Christianity as a Women's Movement." *International Bulletin of Missionary Research* 30, no. 4 (October 2006): 180–88.

Roberts, Vaughan. *God's Big Picture: Tracing the Storyline of the Bible*. Nottingham: IVP Books, 2003.

Sakupapa, Teddy Chalwe. "The Decolonising Content of African Theology and the Decolonisation of African Theology: A Decolonial Analysis." *Missionalia: Southern African Journal of Missiology* 46, no. 3 (2018): 406–24, doi:10.7832/46-3-277.

Schliesser, Christine. "On a Long Neglected Player: The Religious Factor in Poverty Alleviation." *Exchange* 43 (December 22, 2014): 339–59, doi:10.1163/1572543X-12341336.

Schnabel, Eckhard J. *Mark: An Introduction and Commentary*. Vol. 2 of *Tyndale New Testament Commentaries*. Downers Grove: IVP Academic, 2017.

Shaw, Karen L. H. "Wisdom Incarnate: Preaching Proverbs 31." *The Journal of the Evangelical Homiletics Society* 14, no. 2 (September 2014): 44–53.

Slee, Nicola. "Feminist Qualitative Research as Spiritual Practice: Reflections on the Process of Doing Qualitative Research." In *Faith Lives of Women and Girls*, edited by Nicola Slee, Fran Porter, and Anne Phillips, 13–24. Abingdon: Routledge, 2013.

Snape, Dawn, and Liz Spencer. "The Foundations of Qualitative Research." In *Qualitative Research Practice: A Guide for Social Science Students and Researchers*, edited by Jane Ritchie, Carol McNaughton Nicholls, Jane Lewis, and Rachel Ormston, 2nd edition: 2–23. Los Angeles: SAGE, 2013.

Snodgrass, Klyne R. *Stories with Intent: A Comprehensive Guide to the Parables of Jesus*. Grand Rapids: Eerdmans, 2008.

Soards, Marion L., and Darrell J. Pursiful. *Galatians*. Macon: Smyth & Helwys Publishing, 2015.

Soothill, Jane E. *Gender, Social Change and Spiritual Power*. Leiden: Brill, 2007. Kindle edition.

———. "The Problem with 'Women's Empowerment': Female Religiosity in Ghana's Charismatic Churches." *Studies in World Christianity* 16, no. 1 (2010): 82–99, doi:10.3366/E1354990110000766.

Spinks, Charlotte. "Panacea or Painkiller? The Impact of Pentecostal Christianity on Women in Africa." *Critical Half* 1, no. 1 (2016): 21–25.

"State of University Education in Tanzania 2018." Tanzania Commission for Universities, 2018. https://tcu.go.tz/sites/default/files/The%20State%20of%20Higher%20Education.%202019.pdf.

Stott, John. *Cross of Christ*. Ebook. Downers Grove: InterVarsity Press, 2006. Accessed at: https://ebookcentral.proquest.com/lib/smbc/reader.action?docID=2009881&ppg=1

Strauss, Mark L., and Walter S. Wessell. *Mark*. The Expositor's Bible Commentary. Zondervan Academic, 2017.

"Swiftposium 2024: An Academic Conference on Taylor Swift." University of Melbourne, Parkville, 2024. https://swiftposium2024.com/.

Taasisi ya Taaluma za Kiswahili. Kamusi Ya Kiswahili-Kiingereza Swahili-English Dictionary. 2nd ed. Dar Es Salaam: University of Dar Es Salaam, 2014.

Terreblanche, Christelle. "Ubuntu and the Struggle for an African Eco-Socialist Alternative." In *The Climate Crisis: South African and Global Democratic Eco-Socialist Alternatives*, edited by Vishwas Satgar, 168–89. Johannesburg: Wits University Press, 2018, doi:10.18772/22018020541.13.

Thomas, J. C. "Prosperity Preaching: West African Traditional Belief, or a Foreign Import?" *Ogbomoso Journal of Theology* 17, no. 1 (2012): 163–72.

Thomas, Norman E., ed. *Classic Texts in Mission and World Christianity*. Maryknoll: Orbis, 2001.

Togarasei, Lovemore. "The Pentecostal Gospel of Prosperity in African Contexts of Poverty: An Appraisal." *Exchange* 40, no. 4 (October 2011): 336–50, doi:10.1163/157254311X600744.

van den Toren, Benno. "African Neo-Pentecostalism in the Face of Secularization: Problems and Possibilities." *Cairo Journal of Theology* 2 (2015): 103–20.

———. "Integral Salvation and Integrated Theology: African Contributions to Global Theology." *Insights Journal* 10, no. 1 (2024): 12–23. https://insightsjournal.org/integral-salvation-and-integrated-theology-african-contributions-to-global-theology/.

Turaki, Yusufu. *Engaging Religions and Worldviews in Africa: A Christian Theological Method*. Carlisle: HippoBooks, 2020.

———. *Foundations of African Traditional Religion and Worldview*. Otakada.org, 2019.

"Under the Radar. Pentecostalism in South Africa and Its Potential Social and Economic Role." South Africa: Centre for Development and Enterprise, 2008. https://www.cde.org.za/under-the-radar-pentecostalism-in-south-africa-and-its-potential-social-and-economic-role/.

Vähäkangas, Mika. "The Prosperity Gospel in the African Diaspora: Unethical Theology or Gospel in Context." *Exchange* 44, no. 4 (2015): 353–80, doi:10.1163/1572543X12341372.

Walls, Andrew F. *Crossing Cultural Frontiers: Studies in the History of World Christianity*. Edited by Mark R. Gornik. Maryknoll: Orbis Books, 2017.

Wariboko, Nimi. "Pentecostal Paradigms of National Economic Prosperity in Africa." In *Pentecostalism and Prosperity: The Socio-Economics of the Global*

Charismatic Movement, edited by Amos Yong and Katherine Attanasi, 25–60. London: Palgrave Macmillan, 2012. Kindle edition.

Waweru, Humphrey M. *The Bible and African Culture: Mapping Transactional Inroads*. Nairobi: Zapf Chancery, 2011.

Whiteman, Darrell L., and Miriam Adeney. *Crossing Cultures with the Gospel: Anthropological Wisdom for Effective Christian Witness*. Grand Rapids: Baker Academic, 2024.

Wildsmith, Andrew. "The Ideal Life, Jesus, and Prosperity Theology." *Africa Journal of Evangelical Theology* 33, no. 2 (2014): 147–64.

Williams, David. "Pleasure, Pain and the Secular Worldview Part 6: Prayer in a Pain-Pleasure World." CMS (blog), September 1, 2020. https://www.cms.org.au/stories/pleasure-pain-and-the-secular-worldview-part-6-prayer-in-a-pain-pleasure-world/.

———. "Suffering and Glory." CMS (blog), August 3, 2020. https://cms.org.au/stories/suffering-and-glory/.

———. "Pleasure, Pain and the Secular Worldview. Part 3: Shrink-Wrapped Minds." CMS (blog), June 2, 2020. https://cms.org.au/stories/pleasure-pain-and-the-secular-worldview-part-3-shrink-wrapped-minds/.

———. "Pleasure, Pain and the Secular Worldview. Part 3: Shrink-Wrapped Minds." CMS (blog), June 2, 2020. https://cms.org.au/stories/pleasure-pain-and-the-secular-worldview-part-3-shrink-wrapped-minds/.

Wilson, Lindsay. *Proverbs: An Introduction And Commentary*.Vol. 17 of *Tyndale Old Testament Commentaries*. Dowers Grove: IVP, 2017.

Woolnough, Brian. "Good News for the Poor - Setting the Scene." In *Holistic Mission: God's Plan for God's People*, edited by Brian Woolnough and Wonsuk Ma, 3–14. Regnum Studies in Mission. Oxford: Regnum, 2010. Kindle edition.

Yoder, Christine R. *Proverbs*. Abingdon Old Testament Commentaries. Nashville: Abingdon Press, 2009.

Yong, Amos. *In the Days of Caesar: Pentecostalism and Political Theology*. Grand Rapids: Eerdmans, 2010.

Young, Peter R. "Prosperity Teaching in an African Context." *Africa Journal of Evangelical Theology* 15, no. 1 (1996): 3–18.

Zurlo, Gina. *Global Christianity: A Guide to the World's Largest Religion from Afghanistan to Zimbabwe*. Grand Rapids: Zondervan Academic, 2022. Kindle edition.

Langham Literature, with its publishing work, is a ministry of Langham Partnership.

Langham Partnership is a global fellowship working in pursuit of the vision God entrusted to its founder John Stott –

> *to facilitate the growth of the church in maturity and Christ-likeness through raising the standards of biblical preaching and teaching.*

Our vision is to see churches in the Majority World equipped for mission and growing to maturity in Christ through the ministry of pastors and leaders who believe, teach and live by the word of God.

Our mission is to strengthen the ministry of the word of God through:
- nurturing national movements for biblical preaching
- fostering the creation and distribution of evangelical literature
- enhancing evangelical theological education

especially in countries where churches are under-resourced.

Our ministry

Langham Preaching partners with national leaders to nurture indigenous biblical preaching movements for pastors and lay preachers all around the world. With the support of a team of trainers from many countries, a multi-level programme of seminars provides practical training, and is followed by a programme for training local facilitators. Local preachers' groups and national and regional networks ensure continuity and ongoing development, seeking to build vigorous movements committed to Bible exposition.

Langham Literature provides Majority World preachers, scholars and seminary libraries with evangelical books and electronic resources through publishing and distribution, grants and discounts. The programme also fosters the creation of indigenous evangelical books in many languages, through writer's grants, strengthening local evangelical publishing houses, and investment in major regional literature projects, such as one volume Bible commentaries like the *Africa Bible Commentary* and the *South Asia Bible Commentary*.

Langham Scholars provides financial support for evangelical doctoral students from the Majority World so that, when they return home, they may train pastors and other Christian leaders with sound, biblical and theological teaching. This programme equips those who equip others. Langham Scholars also works in partnership with Majority World seminaries in strengthening evangelical theological education. A growing number of Langham Scholars study in high quality doctoral programmes in the Majority World itself. As well as teaching the next generation of pastors, graduated Langham Scholars exercise significant influence through their writing and leadership.

To learn more about Langham Partnership and the work we do visit **langham.org**

www.ingramcontent.com/pod-product-compliance
Lightning Source LLC
Chambersburg PA
CBHW070234240426
43673CB00044B/1782